NATIONAL SECURITY INTERESTS

NATIONAL SECURITY INTERESTS IN THE PACIFIC BASIN

edited by
Claude A. Buss

foreword by
W. Glenn Campbell

HOOVER INSTITUTION PRESS
Stanford University, Stanford, California

The Hoover Institution on War, Revolution and Peace, founded at Stanford University in 1919 by the late President Herbert Hoover, is an interdisciplinary research center for advanced study on domestic and international affairs in the twentieth century. The views expressed in its publications are entirely those of the authors and do not necessarily reflect those of the staff, officers, or Board of Overseers of the Hoover Institution.

Hoover Press Publication 319
Copyright 1985 by the Board of Trustees of the Leland Stanford Junior University
All rights reserved. No part of this publication may be reproduced, stored in a retrieval system, or transmitted in any form or by any means, electronic, mechanical, photocopying, recording, or otherwise, without written permission of the publisher.
First printing, 1985
Manufactured in the United States of America
89 88 87 86 85   9 8 7 6 5 4 3 2 1

Library of Congress Cataloging in Publication Data
Main entry under title:

National security interests in the Pacific Basin.

   Includes bibliographies and index.
   1. Pacific Area—National security—Addresses, essays, lectures. 2. Pacific Area—Strategic aspects—Addresses, essays, lectures. I. Buss, Claude Albert. II. Hoover Institution on War, Revolution, and Peace.
UA830.N38   1985   355'.03301823   85–5642
ISBN 0–8179–8191–8 (alk. paper)

Design by P. Cairns

Contents

Foreword by W. Glenn Campbell ix
Preface xi
Acknowledgments xxi

I. GREAT POWER CONFRONTATION

Introduction
   Claude A. Buss   3

The Pacific Theater: Key to Global Stability
   R. L. J. Long   9

Great Power Confrontation in the Pacific Basin
   B. R. Inman   16

National Defense in the Pacific Basin
   Edward Teller   22

The Interests and Policies of the United States
   Paul Wolfowitz   27

Discussants
   Thomas Hayward   36
   G. J. Price   38

II. NORTHEAST ASIA

Introduction
   Claude A. Buss   45

Security Implications of Siberia
and the Soviet Far East
   Rodger Swearingen   52

Japan's Defense Posture: Toward
Closer Cooperation with the United States
   Yoichi Masuzoe   60

The National Interests of the Republic of Korea
   Koo Youngnok   71

The Republic of Korea and the Major Powers
   Han Sung-Joo   86

Discussants
   Yasuo Takeyama   98
   Tadae Takubo   101
   Naotoshi Sakonjo   103
   Norman Levin   105
   Edward Olsen   107

III. SOUTHWEST PACIFIC AND THE INDIAN OCEAN

Introduction
   Claude A. Buss   111

Australia, New Zealand, and U.S. Security Interests
   Henry S. Albinski   117

Australia and the Security of the Pacific Basin
   T. B. Millar   134

U.S. Installations in Australia: Agenda
for the Future
   Desmond Ball   144

The Interests and Policies of New Zealand
   Richard Kennaway   159

IV. SOUTHEAST ASIA

Introduction
   Claude A. Buss   173

The Security Situation in Indochina
   Douglas Pike   180

The Power Balance as Seen from Jakarta:
A Projection for the 1980s and Beyond
   Lie Tek Tjeng   191

The Interests and Policies of Malaysia:
A Study in Historical Change
   Chandran Jeshurun   197

National Security in the Pacific Basin:
A View from Singapore
   Obaid ul Haq   207

Thailand's Interests and Policies
   Sukhumband Paribatra   214

The Politics of Philippine Security
   Salvador P. Lopez   218

Discussants
   Guy Pauker   231
   Sean Randolph   233
   Chandran Jeshurun   235
   Birabhongse Kasemsri   236
   Stephen Jurika   238
   James Gregor   240
   Salvador P. Lopez   243

V. CHINA

Introduction
   Claude A. Buss   247

China's Role in Pacific Basin Security
   Jonathan D. Pollack   255

The Interests and Policies of the Republic of China
   Tun-Hwa Ko   271

Economic Development and Security:
Perceptions and Policies of the Republic of China
   Shirley W. Y. Kuo   281

The Republic of China and the Pacific Basin:
Policy Perspectives in the 1980s
   Yung Wei   287

Recent Trends in Chinese Foreign Policy
 Ralph H. Clough 293

Chairmen, Contributors, and Discussants 309
Index 313

Foreword

W. Glenn Campbell

Midway through the 1980s seemed to be an appropriate time for the Hoover Institution to bring together the best of scholarship and statesmanship in the United States and friendly countries in the Pacific Basin to exchange personal views on national security and related political, economic, and cultural interests.

As the report on the proceedings of the conference will show, the participants addressed such specific problems as the effects on the Pacific Basin of the global confrontation between the United States and the Soviet Union, the military balance between the superpowers, the stresses and strains within the two alliance systems, the conflicting demands of security and development in the less developed countries, the relationships between foreign policy and domestic politics, the escalating costs of national defense, and efforts to preserve stability and create conditions for progress in East Asia and the Western Pacific.

The absence of hostilities in East Asia and the Western Pacific since the fall of Saigon to North Vietnam on April 30, 1975, is no cause for complacency on the part of the United States, its allies, and its friends. A succession of crises during the decade involving Iran, Lebanon, and the Caribbean could possibly have inflamed the Pacific Basin. Who knows what other crises may be smoldering beyond the horizon?

The linkage between the United States and its highly successful free-market associates in Japan, the Republic of Korea, Taiwan, Hong Kong, and Singapore offers a tempting target for the economically stagnant but heavily armed Soviet Union and its allies in the Pacific Basin. The challenge between the two groups of states and their competing systems varies only in the intensity and nature of the struggle as the leadership changes on either side. The dangers that lurk in continuing confrontation must never be overlooked.

As for the United States, its allies, and its friends, ordinary prudence demands a constant reappraisal of their strengths and vulnerabilities, of their capabilities and challengers. Security is not a one-nation responsibility, resting on the United States alone. Its obligations, including its costs, must be shared by all who would enjoy its benefits.

This conference evidenced the commitment of the Hoover Institution to the security and welfare of the nations and peoples of the Pacific Basin. With no intention of glossing over existing controversies or differences of opinion, its primary purpose was to consider ideas, measures, or policies leading to more effective cooperation on the part of those with similar objectives.

Preface

At the moment of victory in Tokyo Bay in 1945, no American had cause to worry about national security in the Pacific Basin. In spite of the cold war that followed, the United States hastily dismantled its mighty war machine. Soon the Communists gained control of the Chinese mainland, and the Kuomintang regime fled to Taiwan. The subsequent outbreak of hostilities on the Korean peninsula prompted the rebuilding of American military forces and the fashioning of an alliance system to contain further communist expansion. The successful defense of the Chinese offshore islands and the apparently satisfactory course of the war in Vietnam ushered in an era of confidence that was rudely shattered by the retreat from Saigon in 1975.

In the traumatic aftermath of defeat, the administrations of Presidents Ford and Carter seemed content to continue the low-profile prescriptions of the Nixon Doctrine. To friends and allies in Asia, it looked for a time as if the United States might abandon its commitments to Asia.

Meanwhile the breach between China and the Soviet Union became complete. Launching the program of the Four Modernizations, Deng Xiaoping turned toward the capitalist West. The Soviets negotiated a treaty of friendship and mutual cooperation with Vietnam, advanced into Afghanistan, and expanded their military capability to rival, if not to exceed, the power of the United States in East Asia and the Western Pacific.

These events prompted the Hoover Institution to convene this international conference to reappraise the security interests of the United States, its allies, and its friends in the Pacific Basin. The conference would be a meeting place for scholars, businessmen, media personnel, diplomats, and government officials to exchange views on ways to improve the security of their respective countries. Further, it would draw attention to the growing importance of the Pacific Basin and provide another opportunity to re-examine the differences in opinions and perceptions that, if ignored or neglected, could increase the dangers of war.

The conference was based primarily on a set of assumptions regarding national security. Security is not absolute or finite, nor can it be measured solely by military capability or deployment of forces. It includes socioeconomic, political, and cultural as well as military components. It depends upon the skillful management of diplomacy as much as upon the maintenance of a strong political government and a prosperous economy. It is the most vital of the interests of any particular state or government. Regardless of the United Nations, regional associations, or alliance systems, security is the first prerogative and responsibility of any nation, rich or poor.

Security cannot be appraised solely in terms of the status quo as it is perceived at any given time. In an environment of constant flux, the challenge for each nation-state is to respond to every change and to make things happen in a positive way for its own particular benefit. To be solidly based, peace and stability must provide a maximum opportunity for social change with a minimum of violence and use of military force.

With so many variables in the definition of security, no nation can ever be completely satisfied that it is entirely safe from all possible threats. No nation ever thinks it has enough security. Each is the sole judge of its needs and lets its adversaries take care of themselves. What one nation sees as defense, its foe interprets as aggression. In the absence of a rule of law or accepted standards of right and wrong, a balance of power is the arbiter of peace. Perceived parity is the best guarantee of deterrence and successful defense.

The Pacific Basin was assumed to be an identifiable region that is important and will become more so. It embraces the small but important mid-ocean islands and extends in a kind of ellipse from Australia and New Zealand in the southwest, up the coast of East Asia to the island chains of the Kuriles and the Aleutians and down the west coasts of Canada and the United States, thence along the Latin American littoral to Tierra del Fuego.

Covering 63,855,000 square miles, the Pacific Ocean is at once the world's greatest protective moat and one of its busiest commercial highways. Its shores are home to nearly 2 billion people, more than five times the population of Western Europe. Varying widely in ethnic, social, and cultural backgrounds, these people differ vastly in levels of economic achievement. There is a great and growing gap in standards of living between Japan and South Korea on the one hand and North Korea on the other, and between the states in the Association of Southeast Asian Nations (ASEAN) and the Indochinese states of Vietnam, Kampuchea, and Laos. The dynamism of the free-market economies stands in sharp contrast to the stagnation of the socialist-communist societies.

The growing importance of the free nations in the Pacific Basin is of tremendous significance to the United States. In 1982, its trade in the Pacific exceeded its trade in the Atlantic for the first time, and the trend is likely to continue. The American economic stake is matched by the security stake. In spite of apparent peace and stability on its surface, the Pacific Basin strikes as many explosive sparks as Western Europe, the Caribbean, or the Persian Gulf. The Pacific is the western flank of the United States, but it is also the eastern flank of the Soviet Union. It surrounds Japan and washes China. Its adjacent waters include the Bering Sea, the South China Sea, and the Indian Ocean.

Within the Pacific Basin, millions of men are under arms. Many are combat-hardened, well-equipped, and backed by substantial armaments industries. The deadly hostilities in Korea, Vietnam, and Afghanistan were previews of what could conceivably happen again. The balance of power within the Pacific Basin would have to be entirely reconstituted if, for example, China were to resume its alliance with the Soviet Union, if North Korea were to attack South Korea, or if economic conflicts severed the security links between the United States and Japan.

These basic assumptions determined the conceptual framework of the conference, which was structured to probe the two main sources of insecurity in the Pacific Basin—those spillovers from superpower confrontation elsewhere on the globe and those rooted in local and regional conflicts. For convenience in analysis, the Western Pacific, the most dangerous segment of the Pacific Basin, was divided into four subregions or areas: Northeast Asia, comprising eastern Siberia, Japan, and the two Koreas; the ANZUS area of Australia, New Zealand, and the surrounding seas; the ASEAN area, where the five (six with the addition of Brunei) free states of Indonesia, the Philippines, Thailand, Malaysia, and Singapore confront the socialist-communist states of Indochina; and China, on both sides of the Taiwan Strait.

It was decided to invite persons of recognized competence to deliver addresses, prepare papers, or participate in discussions centering around the U.S.-Soviet relationship, the strains and stresses between the United States and its Pacific allies, and the policy dilemmas regarding China. Topics for discussion were suggested to the participants, and direct questions were posed to make the conference as pragmatic and policy-oriented as possible.

With respect to the U.S.-Soviet relationship, it was suggested that attention be directed to threat perceptions, the military balance, and the problems facing both superpowers. Each sees the other as the ultimate threat to its ideology, its political system, and its survival as a nation-state. Each believes that the other is struggling for superiority and therefore worries about the window of vulnerability.

However, the superpowers have lost much of their ability to influence events throughout the world. Other nations, especially Germany and Japan, have grown strong. Nonetheless, because of their networks of global alliances and their global concerns, there is no conflict anywhere that can be solved without reference to their interests. Theirs is the nuclear arsenal, and everyone has a stake in avoiding a nuclear holocaust.

What exactly are the implications of the rapid Soviet military buildup and the demonstrated willingness of the Soviet Union to resort to military action to achieve political objectives? What constitutes an adequate American response? On the positive side, President Reagan has reversed the downhill trend of American power in the Pacific and regained much of the confidence of American allies. Whatever number of ships, planes, and missiles the United States operates, there is no doubt about the quality of its armaments. Its military personnel situation is improving; its ships well-manned. Its forces are well-trained and highly disciplined.

As for nonmilitary considerations, the United States has strong allies who have joined with it of their own free will. The United States has an unmatched economy and a universally envied way of life. Its basic dilemma is how to be strong and solvent at the same time. Will the Congress vote the required funds for national defense in spite of soaring budget deficits? Will the public support military action when the going gets tough? With their commitment to democracy and public opinion, how can Americans formulate and carry out diplomatic policies in line with U.S. security interests?

It is essential to measure accurately the strengths and weaknesses of the Soviet Union. Its strategy differs from that of the United States in many respects. It has had to catch up with the military lead that for so long belonged to the United States. The USSR's global spread is weaker than the United States'. Its allies in Asia—Mongolia, North Korea, and Vietnam—are a constant drain on Soviet resources. The more resources the Soviets employ in Asia, or make available to their allies, the less they have for themselves or for Europe, Cuba, the Middle East, or the Persian Gulf. They are haunted by the specter of a two- or three-front war.

The Soviets are handicapped by massive internal problems. Their territory suffers from disadvantages of geography and climate. Their totalitarian government places titanic strains on their central planners, their handful of national leaders, and their ubiquitous, ham-handed, overburdened bureaucracy. They are plagued by low productivity and chronic shortages.

Because of their poor performance, they are not accepted anywhere as role models. Having lost their ideological appeal, their major resource is military power.

No useful purpose would be served in blinding ourselves to the Soviets' accomplishments. They have erased the American dominance in both the nuclear and the conventional weapons fields. With their Pacific deployments, they can challenge the United States' forward bases and lines of communication west of Guam. In developing Siberia, they have taken initial steps to provide better home bases for their forces in the Far East. With their missiles, new air and sea units, and Camranh Bay at their disposal, they are capable of projecting their power to Southeast Asia and the Southwest Pacific.

Behind all the Soviets' activity in the Pacific Basin is their perception of the U.S. threat. With troops and missiles on the Chinese borders, they can contain Chinese expansion, but they cannot hope to invade China successfully. By strengthening their garrisons on the northern islands off Japan, their objective is not merely preparation for aggression against the Japanese homeland. Is it not more likely that their purpose is to reduce U.S. influence in Asia? They want to deny a closer relationship between China and the United States and, if possible, drive a wedge between the United States and Japan.

As a final topic in U.S.-Soviet relationships, it was suggested that we consider the priority of the Pacific Basin in Soviet interests. It is neither the first of Soviet concerns nor the main arena of U.S.-Soviet confrontation. The problems of the Pacific are among the least troubling considerations in seeking to reduce the existing high global tensions between the superpowers. The Pacific Basin is no obstacle if the United States and the Soviet Union decide to continue their negotiations on such more explosive matters as missile deployment in Western Europe, East-West trade, conflict solution in the Middle East, or arms control.

After U.S.-Soviet relations, conference participants were invited to examine the stresses and strains of the United States' mutual defense agreements with Japan and the Republic of Korea in Northeast Asia, with Australia and New Zealand in the Southwest Pacific, and with the Philippines and Thailand in Southeast Asia. All these agreements commit the United States, in the event of an external attack on any of these nations, to take action in accordance with its constitutional processes.

The United States' defense commitments go far beyond the words of this clause, which admittedly is open to broad or strict construction. Its nuclear umbrella together with its air and naval operations provides a security blanket for the whole region. It has bases in Japan, South Korea, and the Philippines. It uses facilities in Thailand and Australia. It has implemented military assistance programs since World War II. It has supplied arms and transferred dual-use technology to every ally. Civilian bureaucracies in the Philippines and South Korea are sprinkled with ex-military who are graduates of U.S. educational and business institutions.

Among the conference's vital questions was "What common interests do we have that make these alliances worthwhile?" It is not enough to agree that we have a common foe or common ideals. Our perceptions of "democracy," for example, are vastly different. Democracy, U.S.-style, based on Anglo-Saxon experience, stressing popularly elected governments, parliamentary procedures, and individual rights, is alien to Asian traditions. Americans and their allies define "free market" differently. We disagree on how much economic nationalism or social controls can be squeezed into the concept of a "free market." As for "anticommunism," do we mean opposition to ideological concepts, a communist form of government, or communism as practiced by Moscow, Beijing, or some local apparatus? Or do we use "communism" as an imprecise symbol for Soviet or Chinese national power? How can we make the rubric of "communism" cover the widely divergent ideologies of such leaders as Chernenko, Zhao Ziyang, Kim Il-sung, and Le Duan? The United States' allies do not accept simplistic American answers to these deceptively complex questions.

It is elemental that the threat perceptions of the United States and its allies differ. The greatest threat to the United States is the nuclear power of the Soviet Union. It has sufficient faith in its democratic tenets and the strength of its institutions to believe that Soviet propaganda does not endanger it. Its only worry over local or regional conflicts is that they might spark a nuclear war.

The United States' allies view the USSR differently. They see the Soviet Union as a menace, but only as a distant backer of an immediate threat. The United States' primary concern is security; theirs is development. Their domestic institutions are fragile, their economies vulnerable. They think that both Americans and the Soviets are ill-advised to devote so much of their wealth and energy to the arms race, not to the needs of human betterment. If we cannot reconcile these differing views, we can at least understand them and act accordingly.

The chief concern of Americans is the credibility gap. They feel that the U.S. record of costs and casualties in Asia is adequate proof of their commitment to Asia and the Western Pacific. The United States' friends and allies are uncomfortably aware of its vacillations in foreign policy and fear a resurgence of isolationism.

In their view the United States must maintain sufficient strength to balance the power of all enemies and show itself willing to fight for its commitments. They interpret commitments to mean fighting side-by-side with them until victory and thus guarantee their national survival. The United States cannot go that far. Properly, it is committed only to what its national interests dictate. This variation in interpretation calls for skillful diplomatic management.

A further source of stresses and strains between the United States and some of its allies is the gap between the types and amounts of security assistance that the allies would like to receive and those that the United States can provide. If the allies are to build defense establishments to levels that both they and the United States agree are reasonable, they must have outside assistance. The United States is generous with military assistance, a general term for foreign military sales on credit, transfer of military technology, and assistance in military training and education. Its allies warn against hyperactivity in these fields lest it provoke new dangers and create new tensions.

Insisting that a prosperous ally is a strong ally, they would like the United States to be more generous with economic assistance. With recession or high unemployment at home, it is difficult for Washington to satisfy their demands. They expect loans on concessional terms, investments in their infant industries, transfers of high technology, and favorable terms for penetrating the U.S. market. Recognizing that many of their security problems are rooted in the domestic scene and beyond outside help, perhaps the best that the United States can do is to assist them in the development of whatever institutions they envisage would allow progress toward democracy, with proper regard for social control and individual freedom.

Further difficulties are inevitable, given the psychological and cultural differences in the behavior patterns of the United States and its allies. Under the best of circumstances, it is not easy to reconcile Americans' informal, equalitarian tendencies and their allies' ceremonial and hierarchic traditions. Americans must learn how to be firm without being arrogant, how to be considerate without being spineless. How can Americans proffer advice without appearing to interfere in internal affairs? How can they discharge the responsibilities of a great power without taking sides in local and regional quarrels? Above all, how can Americans insist on reasonable protection of the United States' legitimate interests without being accused of neo-imperialism?

Finally, the United States needs to reconsider whether the present arrangements provide the best possible mutual security or whether it should seek an integrated, treaty-based collective defense system, somewhat akin to a Pacific NATO. The U.S. record under the present setup is not bad. In Northeast Asia, relations with Japan and the Republic of Korea are generally cordial, though not without perplexities. In Southeast Asia, relationships since the fall of Saigon range between satisfying and gratifying. In the Southwest Pacific, the common heritage with Australia and New Zealand provides a solid base for coping with arguments and misunderstandings as they appear.

Within the existing system, the United States has provided for constant consultation on security matters, including joint planning, gathering and exchange of intelligence, bilateral or multilateral military exercises, joint training, and cooperative production of weapons and supplies. Links are strong between the United States and each separate ally, but perhaps there is room for improvement in the linkages between those allies in their separate and distant geographic compartments. The issue to be addressed is whether the time has come for a security community to keep pace with the movement toward an economic Pacific community, as witnessed during the past decade.

The last area to be addressed by the conference was China. Without underestimating the importance of the People's Republic, we were primarily concerned with strengthening the security capabilities of the Republic of China, the friendly power on Taiwan.

We noted especially the twists and turns in Beijing's policies since the return of normalcy. The euphoria of the early Nixon years and the temptations to play the China card have disappeared. We are as aware of China's huge problems as we are of its great potential. It seems that the best way to deal with the China of Deng Xiaoping is to treat it exactly as he wants it to be treated—as an independent great power, committed neither to the United States nor to the Soviet Union.

Deng avers repeatedly that the hegemonic superpowers are the greatest sources of trouble, but he regards the Soviet Union as worse than the United States. He looks to the United States for whatever help he can get in loans, investments, military assistance, technology transfers, and access to the U.S. market. He wants U.S. support in every field against the Soviets, but he has no fundamental sympathy for the United States, which he views as the arch-symbol of capitalism and bourgeois degradation. He distrusts the power politics of the Soviet Union and rejects Soviet-style communist ideology. He will not resume the old alliance relationship with the Soviet Union, but, perhaps to counterbalance the influence of the United States, he is willing to enter into diplomatic discussions that could lead toward peaceful coexistence.

The United States' interest in the People's Republic of China (PRC) must be an integral part of its approach to its friends on Taiwan. The United States has been associated with the Republic of China since its establishment in Nanking in 1928. Although it terminated the mutual defense agreement with Taiwan as part of the price for normalization of relations with the mainland, it is committed to the defense and well-being of the Republic of China by the Taiwan Relations Act.

In negotiating with the PRC, the United States must be careful not to lose the remaining good will of the Chinese on Taiwan. It must not further jeopardize their national survival by making military sales to Taipei contingent upon the whims of Beijing. It would damage U.S. security to permit any deterioration in the quality of Taiwan's armed forces. It will take time for Beijing and Taipei to iron out their differences, which they will eventually do without interference or pressure from the United States.

This report of the conference proceedings is divided into five parts, dealing respectively with great power confrontation, Northeast Asia, the Southwest Pacific and Indian Ocean, Southeast Asia, and China. Each part consists of the major addresses or papers, the remarks of discussants, and an introduction by the editor. This report will not only complete the record for the Hoover Institution, but may prove useful for public-minded persons everywhere who, like the conference participants, feel a deep commitment to the security of the United States, its allies, and its friends in the Pacific Basin.

Acknowledgments

It is a pleasure to acknowledge the debt of gratitude owed to all the participants for their generous contributions of talent and good will to the success of the conference. A very special thanks is due to some who were particularly helpful.

Full credit must be given to the staff and fellows of the Hoover Institution. Glenn Campbell, Richard Burress, Dennis Bark, and John Moore provided the necessary support and encouragement. Peter Duignan and Ramon Myers integrated the conference with the long-range Hoover program. John Emmerson, Don Emmerson, Harrison Holland, Paul Ryan, Robert Ward, John Bunzel, Y. L. Wu, and Richard Staar were among those who were always available with valued advice. Albert Wohlstetter, James Stockdale, and Edward Teller gave generously of their wisdom and counsel.

My colleague at the U.S. Naval Postgraduate School, Frank Trager, was my constant companion in planning the conference and conceptualizing the program, and I am profoundly grateful. Sherman Blandin, Pat Parker, Edward Olsen, and Stephen Jurika assisted immeasurably in seeking the right mix of policy orientation and academic research.

Paul Wolfowitz, Sean Randolph, and Everett Bierman took time from their harried Washington schedules to share with us their perspectives on Pacific Basin problems. Clifton Forster and Stanton Jue of the United States Information Service, David Hitchcock in Tokyo, and public affairs officers in American embassies from New Zealand to the Republic of Korea came forward with advice and substantial support of every kind when called upon.

Some very respected veterans of international security conferences gave us the benefit of their experience, especially Charles Wolf, Richard Solomon, Jonathan Pollack, Guy Pauker, and Norman Levin of the Rand Corporation; Robert Scalapino and Harry Kendall of the East Asia Institute at Berkeley; Joe Vasey of the Pacific Forum in Honolulu; John Pustay and John Starron of the National Defense University; and Harold Hinton of the Sino-Soviet Institute at George Washington University.

In addition to the writers of papers, the conference was uniquely enriched by the presence of such distinguished overseas participants as Geoffrey Price and John Melhuish from Australia, Birabhongse Kasemsri from Thailand, and Kim Kyung Won from the Republic of Korea. Equally distinguished Americans Alexis Johnson, Robert Hanks, Thomas Hayward, James Hodgson, and James Gregor graciously served as session chairmen or discussants.

The arrangements for the conference, the essential administrative chores, and the preparation of the proceedings were beautifully attended to by Ellen Montellier, Joyce Frederick, and Theory Burger at the Hoover Institution and by Irene Dixon at the Naval Postgraduate School. To all, a heartfelt "thank you." Steve Jurika deserves more gratitude than I can possibly express for his generous editorial contributions. He spent countless hours in attempting to achieve uniformity and stylistic excellence in our diverse collection of manuscripts.

I
GREAT POWER CONFRONTATION

Introduction

Claude A. Buss

In the Pacific Basin, as the twentieth century nears its end, the ultimate security of all nations depends upon the will and intentions of the United States, the Soviet Union, and their respective allies. The reality of global confrontation is a dominant factor in the decisionmaking processes of the United States, its allies, and its friends as they seek solutions for their bilateral and regional problems. The first task of the conference, therefore, was to examine United States–Soviet relations and to probe deeply into their current effects upon the nations and peoples of the Pacific Basin.

There is no question that the military and economic power of the United States is the linchpin of mutual security in the Pacific Basin. Upon that power depends the maintenance of stability and the opportunity for progress. Hostilities are not likely to occur in the vast Pacific except as a consequence of wars started outside the region. Crises in the Middle East or the Caribbean, or isolated incidents between enemy ships or planes operating eyeball to eyeball in the Mediterranean or the Indian Ocean, make up the stuff of war.

After the Vietnam war, the United States failed to maintain its advantageous military balance of power. While the United States slipped, the Soviet Union worked feverishly to expand and modernize its fighting forces. The Soviet buildup in East Asia and the Pacific, together with events in Iran and Afghanistan toward the end of the Carter administration, awakened the United States to a new sense of danger. It was none too soon, as both friendly and nonaligned Asian states were questioning American capabilities and commitments. With President Reagan, the United States breathed new life into its Pacific security policies.

By the mid-1980s, the United States arrested the long decline of its relative power and achieved an overall balance that provides effective deterrence and defense against a potential aggressor. In some categories of weapons, numbers may favor the Soviet Union, but from the standpoint of overall capability, the fighting forces of the United States have impressive advantages.

It is not necessary to build ship for ship to match the Soviets, if Americans can apply a countervailing strategy involving satellite surveillance and sea-launched cruise missiles. There are no comparable Soviet surface vessels to the U.S. carrier groups in the Pacific. American bombers with cruise missiles enjoy advantages over Soviet Backfire bombers. American submarines are vastly superior to their Soviet counterparts, which are highly vulnerable to sophisticated U.S. antisubmarine warfare techniques.

Above all, the United States is years ahead of the Soviet Union in weapons technology. The Soviets have more tanks, but the Americans have precision-guided missiles to destroy them. The USSR has air defense, but the United States has stealth and effective electronic countermeasures to nullify much of their effectiveness. Against Soviet tactical aircraft, the United States employs superior intelligence and weapons systems. Furthermore, the United States has commercial research and development that the Soviet Union lacks and a corps of highly trained, creative, and innovative engineers. The Soviets lag in computers and microelectronics, with little hope of catching up.

In spite of its comparative advantages, the United States needs more of everything, according to its commanders, and it needs the money to keep its forces modernized and in the highest state of readiness. Manpower requirements are more urgent and costly than added equipment. The United States faces a widening gap between the forces in being and the forces needed to fulfill its global commitments. Threats grow faster than U.S. capabilities. The United States is spread far too thinly, and it cannot rely on such untested experiments as a swing strategy or a rapid deployment force. Ordinarily 40 percent of the United States' armed forces, 5 of its 12 carrier groups, and 14 of its 30 AWACS planes are on continuous overseas assignment.

The United States' military power is magnified by its economic strength. With its wealth of resources, management skills, and labor pool, the productivity of its industry and accomplishments in technology, and its large and growing GNP, the United States has long enjoyed being first among the world's economic giants. In the Pacific Basin, its primacy is challenged by Japan and the so-called second-tier, dynamic, rapidly industrializing countries of South Korea, Taiwan, and Singapore. Together, it is these nations' responsibility to assist the less-favored peoples of ASEAN and the island-states of the Pacific Basin. Their development depends in large measure on access to U.S. resources and markets and on the United States' willingness to help. Their development is the essential underpinning for mutual security.

Throughout the Pacific Basin the image of the United States as the "land of the free and the home of the rich" has a tremendous psychological impact. Prosperity in the United States is essential to its allies as well as to Americans themselves. If the United States is to maintain its economic lead, it must not be by restriction of imports alone but by forging ahead in technology and exploiting its competitive advantages in the international marketplace.

The United States, no matter how strong, cannot go it alone in the Pacific Basin. Adequate national security demands allies, not surrogates or clients, in such specific matters as security of sea-lanes, production of critical mineral resources, and the preservation of stability and peace. Current relations between the United States and its allies are solid, cooperation for security has never been better; yet the United States differs fundamentally from them in its perspectives on the Soviet Union. The United States sees them as aids in its global confrontation with the Soviets, while they see the United States as a vital support in their local or regional conflicts.

Allies and friends seem less concerned than the United States about the seriousness of the Soviet threat. Some see the Soviet Union as more distant and less dangerous than such immediate threats as North Korea, North Vietnam, the PRC, or even a remilitarized Japan. They would prefer more emphasis on détente and less on confrontation. Minority factions in each country tend more to nonalignment than to close association with the United States, whom they see as uncomfortably similar to the USSR in power politics.

In the opinion of those responsible for U.S. security, the Soviet Union is the major source of instability all over the globe. Clashes between Communists and the free world would exist even if there were no arms race. Motivated by innate Russian cultural characteristics and driven by Marxist-Leninist ideology, the Soviets ultimately seek a "consonant international environment." According to Admiral Long, however, the Soviet goal—unchanged since the days of Lenin—is world domination. Their irreversible intention is to expand their empire and their sphere of influence. It is not their tanks, bombers, or submarines that constitute the greatest Soviet threat but the constancy of their political objectives.

The Soviets use military power, political alliances, covert activities, support of insurgencies and wars of liberation, and military assistance to clients in pursuit of their political objectives. In the Pacific Basin, their primary goal is to weaken the United States. This accounts for the expansion and modernization of their strategic and conventional forces and their efforts to drive a wedge between the United States and Japan and to counter the improving relations between the United States and the PRC.

They aim to strengthen their own power base in eastern Siberia, maintain a strong defense against the PRC, and guarantee their own uninterrupted sea communications between the Far East and their home base in Europe. They would like to expand their political influence and the trade and friendship that has so far eluded them in East Asia and the Western Pacific. Brezhnev's goal of a Pacific Collective Defense System was an empty dream.

In the last decade the most dramatic military action has been the Soviet military buildup in the Pacific. One-quarter of the Soviet ground forces—1.1 million men in more than 50 well-equipped divisions—are stationed along the border with China, with perhaps another division in the islands off northern Japan. One-third of the Soviet navy's general purpose forces are in the Pacific, with an impressive array of surface units, supporting aircraft, and missile-launching submarines. From bases at Vladivostok and Camranh Bay, the Soviets can project their power from the Northwest Pacific through the seas of Japan, China, and Southeast Asia to the Indian Ocean and the Persian Gulf. They have added substantial numbers of SS-20s, ICBMs, IRBMs, and Backfire bombers to their strategic forces.

Because of their spectacular new military presence in the Pacific Basin, the Soviets have won a certain respect. They have dispelled the image of U.S. invincibility and raised doubts about the utility and effectiveness of the United States' nuclear umbrella. They may have achieved mutual deterrence, but they have not destroyed the perception of the United States' ability to provide security for those whose very existence depends on the freedom of the seas.

The obvious strength of the Soviet position in East Asia and the Western Pacific is conditioned by its less obvious weaknesses. In the mid-1980s, the Soviet Union is passing through a tense and difficult period. Leadership changes complicate the domestic problems of the bureaucracy. In Europe it faces the challenge of Poland and an arms agreement that would satisfy its anxious neighbors to the west. In Asia it must reckon with the costs of Vietnam and the shock waves produced by its invasion of Afghanistan. It must contend with the PRC for influence in North Korea. It realizes that it cannot conquer the PRC or organize Asia under its own hegemony. It has limitless power to destroy, but it cannot win the hearts and minds of Asians, who may accept Soviet arms but do not appreciate Soviet ideology.

The expansionist policies of the Soviet Union served to deepen the anger and expedite the defense measures of its adversaries. After the Sino-Soviet split, the PRC was vitriolic in its condemnation of Soviet hegemonism. The Republic of Korea became less eager to normalize relations after the Soviets shot down an unarmed Korean airliner. More and more Japanese looked upon the Soviets with distrust and regarded their presence in the northern islands as a blatant violation of their territorial integrity. Under the Reagan administration, the United States gave highest priority to strengthening its defense establishment and set itself squarely against appeasement.

It is no easy task for the United States to formulate and execute effective policies to deal with the Soviet Union in the Pacific Basin. The basic challenge is to prevent the outbreak of nuclear war. Dr. Teller believes the danger of a nuclear war has never been greater. In his view, negotiations make no sense whatsoever. To free the world from the threat of nuclear war, Teller recommends a shift in the United States' strategic aim from retaliation to a space-age defense system that will prevent an effective first strike.

No single formula to deter further Soviet aggression can cover the possible contingencies that might arise in a region as diverse and varied as the Pacific Basin. The United States' policies will be influenced by changes in Soviet and Chinese attitudes toward each other, increasing concerns over security in Japan, the growing assertiveness of the Republic of Korea, and the insistence of less developed countries on their rights and claims in North-South relations. The United States will be constrained in its decisions by factors beyond its control, such as the proliferation of arms and the possible appearance of nuclear capabilities among smaller nations, sharpening conflicts over scarce resources, including offshore oil, disagreements about the relative importance of defense and economics, and divergencies in threat perceptions between the United States and its allies. Too many countries in the Pacific Basin have deep historical traditions and frustrated ambitions that will prevent the application of a single policy.

The United States is also constrained by the handicaps deriving from the inherent nature of the democratic system. With presidential elections every four years, it is difficult to maintain consistency in foreign policy. Continuity is impossible when so many persons or agencies—the State Department, Department of Defense, the White House staff, the intelligence community, the Congress, and the overseas diplomatic establishment—claim responsible roles in the decisionmaking process. A rapidly changing strategic environment or an unexpected crisis demanding immediate response leaves little time to consult precedents or give adequate attention to future consequences.

The United States' Asian allies must be aware that differences in public opinion present difficult problems in the formulation of U.S. foreign policy. Americans simply do not agree on the nature of their national interests or the interpretation of the United States' commitments. Some applaud the increasing polarization between the United States and the Soviet Union; others see it as a new cold war. There is profound disagreement about the limits of military power in the search for security. Some rely heavily on a fighting stance; others argue for dialogue, not confrontation.

It is not easy to raise the money required for national security. Annual defense appropriations are large, therefore unpopular. A substantial number of Americans feel that the United States is paying more than its fair share of mutual security and in the process is damaging its economic and social well-being.

It is generally conceded, however, that the United States must retain a strong military presence in the Pacific Basin and demonstrate willingness to use its forces. A credible force is essential to counter the politico-psychological effects of the growing Soviet display of military might. The American drawdown after Vietnam invited Soviet adventurism and expansionism, culminating in the invasion of Afghanistan.

To have effective policies, the United States must be a credible and dependable ally. It must instill the confidence that under no circumstances will it deny U.S. commitments. While urging Asians to cooperate to the fullest in the quest for security, Americans must avoid interfering in their internal affairs. Considering the sensitivities and cultural differences of Asians, Americans must avoid the patronizing attitudes of which they are sometimes accused.

The record of accomplishments of the Soviets in the Pacific Basin is none too impressive. Seeing themselves generally outmaneuvered by the United States in Japan, the PRC, Korea, and Southeast Asia, they are not likely to reduce agitation in any of these areas. Apart from the ever-present danger of a general crisis or global war, however, the prospects for peace and stability in the Pacific Basin look reasonably good.

THE PACIFIC THEATER: KEY TO GLOBAL STABILITY

R. L. J. Long

I would like to share with you some of my views about the importance of the Asia-Pacific/Indian Ocean region, that area that falls within the United States Pacific Command's area of responsibility.

In my judgment, Asia-Pacific developments have a profound impact on the United States' overall security interests and on the prospects for world peace and stability. I am convinced that no worldwide strategy for peace and stability can be effective if it fails to recognize the importance of the Asia-Pacific theater, not just from a military standpoint, but from economic and political standpoints as well. We recognize that a nation's or region's security and independence derive not only from military might but also from economic and political strength. These three factors, combined with a country's will to act, form the pillars upon which a nation's heritage is based—and upon which a nation's future depends.

One measure of the region's importance centers on its economic relationships. Trade with the Asia-Pacific region accounts for about 30 percent of the United States' foreign trade—more than with any other region. Trade with Japan, its largest partner in the region, exceeds its trade with the United Kingdom, Germany, and France combined. This bilateral relationship, which stands at $60 billion annually, is almost totally dependent on the security of the sea-lanes that bind the two nations. Were this link to be denied, the economic impact on Japan, other Asian countries, and on the United States would be severe. Given the interrelated nature of world economies—and that 16 of the top 30 bilateral trade relationships in the world involve either the United States or Japan—the economic impact of such a disruption would be felt internationally. Unimpeded commerce between Asia and the rest of the globe is vital to worldwide economic stability. The economic growth of the Pacific Basin nations during the past two decades is unparalleled for the past century, worldwide.

Another important aspect of Asia-Pacific trade involves the flow of critical natural resources from the theater to industrialized nations—east and west. The Asia-Pacific nations provide most of the free world's resources and production of strategic commodities, such as rubber, chromium, tin, titanium, and platinum. In addition, most oil produced by the Middle East Gulf states passes through the Indian Ocean sea-lanes to reach European and Asian consumers.

As a major world power, the United States has a unique and critical role in the Pacific. While its defense commitment to NATO is important and has contributed to deterrence of a major war in Europe, I am convinced that the security interests of the United States in the Asia-Pacific theater are equally important.

During my military service the United States has fought three wars in the Pacific. No one wants another. Yet, World War II and Korea showed that hostilities can be prompted, in large part, by an aggressor nation's perception that its opponents lack the resolve to resist adventurism or expansionist efforts. I leave the analysis of the third Pacific war, in Vietnam, to historians. Although some will concede that the United States was "buying time for the nations of Asia," one thing is certain: the result of that war, the drawdown of U.S. Asia-based military forces, was a perceived weakening of U.S. interest and resolve in the Pacific. Such perceptions, I believe, invite adventurism. The invasion of Afghanistan is a case in point.

Experience proves that in dealing with expansionist adversaries, the most effective means of assuring peace is a clear demonstration of strength and resolve—strength and resolve based on political and economic strength and supported by a nation's commitment to the maintenance of strong, *credible* military forces. Military forces are of little value if potential enemies doubt your willingness to ever use them. It is a paradox difficult for many to accept, but nonetheless true: it is the willingness to use force, if necessary, that provides the best guarantee that the use of force will not be necessary. The free world's Peace Through Strength posture was successful in deterring Soviet aggression in Europe and North Korean aggression on the Korean peninsula. In like manner, the maintenance of a strong, survivable nuclear force is the most effective means of assuring that these weapons will never be used. Americans must not permit their abhorrence of war to keep them from the work that their love of peace requires: that work is the maintenance of a strong economy and a strong national defense, to add another dimension to the political and diplomatic search for peace. I know of no American military leader who desires war. The primary measure of success is the ability to deter one. But we must remember that there are some things worse than war—and most of them start with "losing." I believe the current commitment of the United States and other nations of the free world to a stronger defense contributes to national resolve and helps counter more effectively the growing challenges to the free world's security.

This renewed commitment has come none too soon. The Soviet Union has been increasing its presence, power, and influence in every continent. It poses a real and growing threat to all nations that remain outside its immediate area of control. We would do well to reflect upon the fundamental differences between the Soviet government's political values and goals and those of the United States and many other free world nations. The United States and most free world nations respect the sovereignty and the freedom of choice of other nations and peoples. The United States has a great number of friends, and it has many close allies who willingly share a joint commitment to peace and stability. It has no satellites, no puppets, no surrogates—nor does it seek any.

The United States believes in peaceful and legal resolution of problems and the sovereign right of nations to determine and control their destinies. By contrast, the Soviet Union considers conflict and violence as natural regulators of human affairs and reserves for itself the right to control the internal and external policies of those nations that fall into its sphere of influence. The Soviet leadership's goal of world domination has remained unchanged since the days of Lenin. What has changed is the Soviet ability to pursue this objective actively and aggressively. The steady increase in the Soviets' military power in recent years has increased their confidence and credibility as they employ their military muscle to achieve political ends—including an expanded ability to intimidate free world nations and ultimately control their destiny.

Soviet willingness, in December 1979, to use force openly and brutally to add Afghanistan to their empire signaled a new boldness in Soviet behavior: an aggressiveness that I believe derives from their increased military might and a conviction that such actions will not be challenged effectively by the free world.

Acceptance of the very basic premise—that the Soviet Union remains intent on expanding its empire or sphere of influence and is increasingly more capable of doing so—is a prerequisite to understanding the shared need of all free nations to maintain strong, credible defense forces. Recent Soviet actions in Afghanistan, Poland, Southeast Asia, Africa, Latin America, and elsewhere demonstrate that Soviet ambitions have not changed. Of greater concern is that Soviet military capability has increasingly converged with Soviet political ambitions, increasing the USSR's ability to achieve these objectives through intimidation or use of this newly achieved muscle. Nowhere has the Soviet buildup been more ominous than in the Asia-Pacific area. This buildup began in earnest a decade ago. It continues, and the statistics are dramatic. Soviet Far Eastern ground forces have increased from about 20 to over 50 divisions, some half a million troops. The Soviet Pacific Fleet, once a coastal defense force, now operates astride vital sea-lanes through the Pacific and Indian oceans. Threatening these sea-lanes are more than 90 attack submarines and a steadily growing Backfire bomber force. The primary Backfire mission is interdiction of these Pacific sea-lanes. More than 100 Far Eastern–based SS-20 intermediate-range missiles, each equipped with three nuclear warheads, threaten the Asian landmass, Japan, and parts of the United States.

These weapons provide the Soviets with increased leverage to attempt to influence—through intimidation—other nations in the region. Recent veiled threats to employ SS-20s and other weapons against Japan were aimed, in my opinion, at intimidating the Japanese. The presence of Soviet forces in the illegally occupied group of Japanese northern islands serves a similar purpose. The display of Soviet naval power in the Sea of Japan, the East and South China seas, the Gulf of Thailand, the Malaysian and Indonesian straits, and the Indian Ocean and Northern Arabian Sea serves as a constant reminder of growing Soviet ability to project power and political influence in the entire Pacific Basin region. A strong U.S. and free world presence in these areas, in my judgment, is vital to counter the political and psychological effects of this increased Soviet military presence.

The Soviets are a major factor in Asia's current instability. One obvious example is Afghanistan. Their use of force in Afghanistan weighs heavily on the minds of other Soviet neighbors. This invasion highlights an interesting aspect of the Soviets' use of military force. While many nations have employed force against their enemies, the Soviet Union alone employs force consistently against its "friends." Examples are Hungary, Czechoslovakia, and the threats against Poland. Nations seeking to align themselves with the Soviets should be increasingly aware of the potential cost of such "friendship."

In Southeast Asia, Vietnam is paying for Soviet military and economic assistance by providing the Soviets unrestricted access to naval and air facilities at Camranh Bay. In return, they provide aid, mostly military, to Hanoi and occupied Kampuchea. Vietnam's dependence on Moscow appears nearly absolute; it is clearly a Soviet client state. Without this aid, Vietnamese forces could not pursue a policy of regional aggression. And without Vietnam's acquiescence, the Soviets would not threaten free world interests, and sea-lanes, in Southeast Asia.

Throughout the Pacific theater today we see the Soviets attempting to expand their presence and influence. These attempts contribute to instability in the region. The challenge facing the free world is how best to counter this Soviet challenge. This is not solely a U.S. problem. The United States can no longer go it alone in Asia, or in any other portion of the globe—nor should it.

This may raise questions of the need for a Pacific NATO. For several years there have been discussions about a formal Pacific Basin alliance, or community of some type. In my view, we are vaguely pointed in that direction. Admittedly some regional relations were formalized. ASEAN has clearly contributed significantly to economic and political stability in the region. The Asia Development Bank (ADB) has served the region's interests well. Although we may be pointed toward some type of Pacific Basin organization, we still face significant obstacles that may prevent such a comprehensive organization from being formed for at least a decade. I believe this is particularly true of a larger, Pacific-wide security arrangement. A formal security alliance is not on the horizon for what, I believe, are a variety of sound reasons. Meanwhile, the United States and its allies must depend upon their basic bilateral or trilateral security arrangements and strengthen them, within the bounds of political possibilities.

Just prior to my retirement, I met with the top political and military leaders of the United States' strongest regional allies. My visits to New Zealand, Australia, the Philippines, Korea, and Japan renewed my confidence in the strength of U.S. defense relationships and the combined commitment to peace and stability in the region.

In Northeast Asia bilateral ties with Japan have been strengthened considerably. The United States should welcome the Japanese initiative to undertake broader responsibilities for their own self-defense, to include the sea-lanes so vital to their economy as well as the United States'. I believe that Japan should—and will—continue to provide more for its own defense. However, the United States must recognize the important steps taken by Prime Minister Nakasone to support strong defense forces in Japan. And, it should acknowledge Japan's refusal to bow to Soviet threats. In other regional developments, the joint efforts of Prime Minister Nakasone and the Republic of Korea's President Chun to place the important Japanese-Korean relationship on a new and stronger basis is encouraging, but its pace must be determined by those two countries. Meanwhile, defense cooperation between the United States and Korea serves as a model for bilateral relationships based on mutual respect and a combined commitment to peace and stability in Northeast Asia.

In the Southwest Pacific, the important ANZUS agreement with Australia and New Zealand provides a solid foundation for cooperation with two of the United States' most important, long-standing allies. They also play important independent roles in regional stability by providing economic and security assistance to the new Pacific island-states and by maintaining Commonwealth defense ties with Singapore and Malaysia.

The ASEAN grouping, involving Thailand, Singapore, Malaysia, Indonesia, and the Philippines, though not a military alliance, contributes to regional stability through its efforts to resist communist aggression and mobilize international support for a peaceful outcome in Kampuchea. ASEAN served effectively as the free world's conscience and curbed Hanoi's hopes for gradual international acceptance of its aggression. The U.S. relationship with individual ASEAN states is good. The United States' defense relationship with the Philippines is solid, and U.S. forces based on Philippine soil provide a clear demonstration of the United States' intention to remain a strong Pacific power and to honor its treaty commitments. The United States' dealings with Singapore, Malaysia, and Indonesia, all key members of the nonaligned community, are based on mutual respect and a shared belief in benefits accruing from the U.S. presence.

The Kampuchean occupation adds particular importance to the United States' defense relationship with Thailand—a frontline state against further communist aggression in Southeast Asia. The United States played an important role, expediting recent shipments of defensive arms and equipment to Thailand in response to increased Vietnamese provocation along the Thai-Kampuchea border. This effort underscores the long-standing U.S. commitment to promoting regional stability and protecting Thai sovereignty.

I look forward to our discussion this week of U.S./PRC/ROC relations. The United States must guard against an oversimplistic solution to this very complex situation. Although China is not a U.S. ally, the two nations do share some important strategic interests, as well as some important and fundamental differences. Clearly, one parallel interest is the mutual concern over the political objectives of the Soviet Union, supported by its growing military power and influence.

I believe that much of the future is destined to be shaped in Asia. I also believe that stability in this region is necessary to global peace. Free nations in the region are threatened by the Soviet Union or its regional surrogates and sympathizers. Despite national and cultural differences, these Asia-Pacific nations recognize the overriding importance of working together in the interests of peace and economic progress. They are developing mutually beneficial relationships, not only with the United States but with one another. And they are joining with the United States in cooperative efforts that reach beyond the Pacific Basin.

Defense cooperation between the United States and its allies in the region has never been better, and U.S. relations with nonaligned nations who share U.S. beliefs in self-determination and freedom are improving as well.

These improved relations have a direct, positive impact on regional prospects for stability.

In the final analysis, the United States remains the only nation capable of deterring aggression on both a regional and a global basis. When I arrived at Pacific Command Headquarters in 1979, U.S. forces could not guarantee success in a conflict with the Soviets in the Pacific; the Soviet expansion and force buildup of the 1970s made the situation too close to call. I believe also that a failure to reverse the downward trends—in U.S. presence, capability, and perceived commitment—would inevitably tilt the balance in favor of the Soviets.

Now by the increased efforts of the United States and other free world nations—and the growing spirit of cooperation among the United States' friends and allies—their increased willingness to improve their own defenses, and, importantly, the outlook for political and economic stability in the region, I am somewhat more optimistic. I wish I could say that the balance had clearly shifted in the free world's favor. It has not. When I departed the Pacific Command, the situation remained too close for me to call. But it remains too close for the Soviets to call as well.

Although much more remains to be done, I believe the tide is clearly turning. The momentum in the Pacific is now in the free world's favor, and I remain optimistic that the free world shall prevail.

GREAT POWER CONFRONTATION IN THE PACIFIC BASIN

B. R. Inman

The title I was given was "Great Power Confrontation in the Pacific Basin," and I toyed with totally changing it. Who are the great powers and the would-be greats? Looking at the challenges and opportunities in the Pacific Basin over the remaining years of this century, we must acknowledge that great power confrontation takes two essential forms: one military, the other economic. The nature of the struggle is perhaps going to be more exciting than any the United States has faced. If it is to meet it effectively, it must keep together alliances and reduce the possibility that military conflicts will consume U.S. resources.

Viewing the great powers, both military and economic, only the United States holds title to great power in both areas. The Soviet Union is the other great military power, and Japan the other great economic power. Others would aspire to that status, but in my judgment are unlikely to attain it in the remaining years of the century. But one must include the People's Republic of China in any discussion of confrontations over the rest of the century. Finally, other prospective power centers are developing. Other considerations include the evolving patterns of Soviet economic power and Korea, Taiwan, and the ASEAN nations. The military capabilities of North Korea and Vietnam could touch off actions, either in response to the Soviets' desire or their own.

It is unusual for a U.S. intelligence officer to have the opportunity to talk about this country. First, we must examine the military capabilities of the United States as they bear on the shared interests in the Pacific Basin. Over fifteen years the United States drew down its military capabilities in the Basin, particularly the size of the navy. It reduced substantially its potential for maintaining forces throughout the Western Pacific and the Indian

Ocean, accepting a role of maintaining stability there. I agree with Admiral Long's perception that the United States has arrested that long decline and begun the rebuilding process. But it is going to take a very long time for deployable U.S. forces to grow substantially. Meanwhile the threat grows faster than the forces involved. Thus, throughout the early years of the remainder of the century, the United States must substantially stretch its existing military capabilities to play a key role in the Pacific Basin. It is yet to be seen that the United States will sustain the buildup that has begun. Establishing the continuity of that buildup will be much more important than its precise level in any given year. But the priority must be toward usable forces that can discourage the use of military options in the Pacific Basin.

On the economic side, the United States has done better than on the military side. But even there there has been a relative slide. Some of this has been due to economic growth in Western Europe and spectacular economic growth by other countries in the Pacific Basin. There have also been domestic problems that accelerated the relative slide in the great power economic status that the United States once enjoyed. Decline over twenty years in the long-range investment in research and manufacturing quality control have affected the United States' ability to lead the economic confrontation.

What the United States needs most is a consensus on national security policy. It is essential in seeking that consensus that national security be redefined to include diplomacy, foreign aid, arms control, the size of U.S. defense forces, deployment of those forces, and international trade. Unless Americans address national security in that broad framework from the outset, they will not be able to move past the challenges to reach the opportunities in the Basin.

Turning to the other great economic power, Japan, its economic growth has been spectacular. Those of you who visit the markets of Yokohama or Tokyo will recognize instantly that intense competition in the domestic market hones the ability to be competitive abroad. Alertness of both management and government to opportunities for new markets at home and abroad produced quality products in quantity. Aggressiveness in exporting, supported by government-targeted long-term investments in research and development of new technology, helped Japan attain great economic power status. Weighing the Soviet challenge, what contribution can Japan make in the military equation? We must recognize that just as the United States' long slide came from the lack of consensus on national security policy, there cannot be major changes in Japanese military power until the Japanese achieve a national consensus. There is evidence of leadership to accomplish that consensus building. But it will not come easily or quickly, in my opinion. There may well be other measures, such as greater use of economic aid to offset investment needs in other Basin countries, as a less desirable but acceptable alternative to shouldering more of the burden until national consensus can be developed.

I turn briefly to the second tier, with no intent to disparage a remarkable pace of development. The economic roles of Korea and Taiwan offer potentially great advantages in the development of an economic boom in the Pacific Basin, particularly if that boom is accompanied by political stability. That is the critical element in discouraging Soviet opportunism. Alternatively, the United States has to find some role for their national military forces to help with the security of the entire region. I do not prescribe movement toward paper military arrangements. I do not discount the value of such arrangements to demonstrate commitment, but ultimately some of that economic boom must help offset the costs of sustaining military stability throughout the region. Finding the mechanism for consensus would be one of the early challenges to be undertaken.

The regimes of both North Korea and Vietnam will not share in this great Pacific Basin economic boom. Their governments are not prepared for it, and they are not using their manpower effectively to produce economic growth. Frustration will grow in those two countries when they do not share in the great economic boom. So we must contemplate how to discourage their use of force to offset that frustration.

No discussion of prospects for stability, or avoiding confrontation, would be complete without mentioning the People's Republic of China. The PRC is attempting to realign basic commitments from heavy industry to light industry and trying to nail down support of the peasant population, something the Soviets would not try. The effort has several results that affect Beijing's ability to use military force in the Pacific Basin because the economic shift resulted in a substantial cut in investments for the PRC military forces. For the first time the Chinese have pushed their navy out into blue-water operations; yet they slowed investment for new building and replacement of equipment that is getting older. The lack of foreign exchange to import technology is likely to continue the rest of this century unless major finds result from their search for new energy sources in the offshore area. For many years they were not willing to import technology from the West. Now they are very eager, but do not have the hard currency to pay for it. Their support for revolutionary elements on the periphery of the PRC, particularly in Thailand and Malaysia, has been reduced, but I do not think it is realistic to expect that it will ever be ended. The PRC's efforts to portray itself as an emerging leader of the Third World has a positive side. The Chinese cannot have it both ways. They cannot provide substantial support to would-be revolutionaries in the surrounding countries and still portray themselves as neutralist Third World, not involved in great power confrontation. Their concern about long-term Soviet intentions is likely to remain the most dominant factor in PRC considerations about how to deal with the world. I am not prepared to say that the evolving PRC leadership will retain a confrontational attitude toward the Soviet Union. There is a reasonable prospect that they will not return to a military alliance with the USSR, but the United States should not assume that they will be friendly toward its interests.

Let me now turn to the Soviet Union and three elements I believe that one must address. First is the Soviets' evolving military capability. Second is economic stagnation. Third is the evolving thinking process by the Soviets about the use of force. Let me deal first with the evolving military capabilities. From World War II to as late as 1975, there were the clear Soviet objectives that Admiral Long talked about. Their approach to achieving those objectives was well established. If they were dealing with problems on the immediate periphery, the solution was massive use of force to dominate. When it was at a distance from the periphery, there was a mix of options—political action, subversion, subsidies for local communist parties, and provision of low-priced military equipment. From the end of World War II to 1960, the orientation of Soviet military forces was largely defensive. It focused originally on Eastern Europe, but the split with the PRC led to more attention to the Asian region and to the steady buildup that Admiral Long covered in detail. With that came a policy of encircling the PRC. Looking for military forces that would encircle the PRC and confront the United States, I believe, led ultimately to the major buildup in Pacific naval forces. They found it was easier to use their Pacific Fleet for commitment to the Indian Ocean, a move that began in 1967 with the British withdrawal east of Suez. The Soviets have kept a permanent force in the Indian Ocean.

The Soviet economy has always performed poorly by most judgments. Yet it has performed well enough to equip and maintain remarkable military forces in the postwar years. In 1969 when the Soviets assessed the next five-year plan, they saw the remarkable improvement in their overall military capabilities compared with the United States. Their response was to quietly increase that investment and sustain it. While their economy has not permitted them to do many things for consumers, nonetheless there has been a small but steady improvement. They have kept expectations in line with deliverables, and stocks of consumer goods are better than ten years ago, and much better than twenty years ago. Soviet economic progress has been greatly hampered by the pervasive corruption in that society and by the incompetence of the central planning process. The public effort of the new leadership to focus on corruption is not likely to be effective enough to permit the Soviets to enter great economic competition. But it is likely to permit them to sustain their current level of military investment without incentives to decrease such spending. We expect a continued improved updating of their strategic forces and quantum improvements in the capabilities of their conventional forces, particularly in mobility of land, air, and sea components. One of the rare advantages that Soviet society has over that of the free world is the ability to marshal a large and growing merchant marine to provide that mobility.

Finally, consider the evolving Soviet attitudes about growing mobility that have been apparent since 1975. My own assessments relate to their reading the U.S. public debate when the government in Saigon collapsed. But whatever motivated this changed Soviet attitude, the earlier pattern of reluctance to use force at great distances, and the reliance on political action and subversion, changed dramatically with the movement in November 1975 of 15,000 Cuban troops and massive quantities of arms by air and sea into Angola as the Portuguese withdrew. They watched the lack of response, and two years later, when opportunity beckoned, they did the same thing in Ethiopia. In 1978 there were smaller adventures in Yemen and the encouragement, substantial hardware, and financial support for the Vietnamese move into Kampuchea and Laos. The Afghanistan occupation on Christmas Day 1979 followed the earlier pattern of massive use of force on their periphery to salvage a communist government they considered about to slip from their domination. But as one assesses the Soviet performance, while they have begun to evolve new approaches about using that growing mobile force, there has been no direct use of Soviet force where they felt collision with the United States was likely. They have also become much more skillful over these past twenty years in their use of political action. In their framing of the debates and peace campaigns, what has been more visible is their great effectiveness at playing on fears of nuclear conflicts while making major changes in their ability to use conventional forces in conflict.

The Soviet Union will steadily modernize its strategic forces and make major improvements in conventional war-fighting capabilities and conventional force mobility. In command and control of those forces, they are thinking of projecting their forces well beyond the immediate land periphery of the Soviet Union. We will see over the next decade an almost total change in Soviet leadership for reasons of age and health. We may be fortunate that these products of the Khrushchev revolution, who have turned the party into the world's greatest bureaucracy, with great privileged positions, are cautious for fear that they will lose their privileged status. But the decision could go the other way, and they will be even more arrogant about using mobile forces that no Russian ruler has ever had.

As they look for opportunities, if we are fortunate and build strong economies while maintaining alliances in the Pacific Basin, they may decide that it is the region they want to take advantage of by force. It could well be Latin America. If that occurs, then substantial U.S. forces will be diverted to that area. This raises a long-term question about how one sustains an acceptable balance in the Pacific Basin if such diversion occurs. And I might add by way of conclusion that the most important single element for stability and growth in the space of this decade, and for the rest of the twentieth century, in my judgment, will be how the United States manages the economic competition. The United States has to begin not with how it restricts imports but how it leads technology; the United States must renew its commitment to competitiveness within an open international marketplace.

NATIONAL DEFENSE IN THE PACIFIC BASIN

Edward Teller

I hope to be brief for several reasons. Perhaps the most important is that I am not terribly well informed on the subject. Therefore I will limit myself to generalities. I really want to make only two points, one about China and the other about the rest of the Pacific Basin.

China is certainly an unknown. I never have been there, but I have been in Taiwan several times for somewhat extended visits. Taiwan is one of the very few developing countries that is actually developing. Development reflected in the standard of living may not be all important in many cases. But when a very low standard of living exists, as it did in Taiwan in 1950, to develop to a stage where most people do not have to worry about how to stay alive tomorrow is a very essential thing, not only for physical well-being but for the spirit of the people as well.

With the exception of Hong Kong, I have never set foot on mainland China and am not an expert on the subject. I want to tell you less authoritatively that I suspect no expert on China exists outside of China, and I do not know if they exist even inside China. Unfortunately, this probably has had no great effect on the knowledge that we have. One of our most important objectives should be to obtain information. I have no idea how an action of the United States, Japan, Malaysia, Taiwan, Indonesia, or Vietnam will influence Chinese policy. I suspect that we do not have the knowledge to make even reasonable guesses.

A big qualitative change occurred in China in recent years. The average life-style today is very different from that of ten years ago. I suspect that no one can foretell what is coming in the near future. We have little information about how this change was accomplished, much less the details of the change.

The information problem must change, but it cannot until we are fully conscious of the problem and until we get some cooperation from the Chinese government. I believe that questions of commerce and industrial relations, of cultural exchange or sports exchange, or of military preparations are of secondary importance to the overwhelming need to find out as much as we can. Information gathering must be done without prejudice. We should first know and then decide.

Now, let me contradict everything I have said so far. I believe that mainland China is not only an underdeveloped country, but one where the possibilities of rapid development do not exist, either in an economic or in a military sense.

In nuclear weapons, the Chinese did exceedingly well. This area is one about which I do know a little. Developing nuclear weapons requires a small number of people. No one should deny that among any people, and certainly among the mainland Chinese, there are some who are in many respects excellent, absolutely first class. To find a few is not difficult. In the special case of nuclear energy, the Chinese have shown that, in limited areas, they can move as fast as anyone else.

But organizing a billion people and building an industrial base, which needs the expertise of a considerable fraction of the population, requires an educated people. But before people can be taught, teachers to teach the people must be acquired. For this reason, I think that China will not develop like Taiwan and certainly not like Japan.

So here is my recommendation, perhaps impossible to meet, but important to attempt. Find out what happened, who was behind what, what actually changed; what happened, for instance, to the millions of people who disappeared during the Cultural Revolution. This is one-half of the message I want to offer.

The total of all other people in the Pacific area is smaller than the number of people in China. But the other people in the Pacific make up a group larger than one-third of the population of China. So, we are still talking about a large number of varied and remarkable people. In regard to these fantastically diverse and different people, I want to concentrate on only one point. That is the question of military preparedness.

Admiral Long was asked whether, if the Japanese were to take military preparedness more seriously, people in many other parts of the Pacific might not be worried. What I am going to say has particular relevance to this question. Also, what I say should not come as any surprise because I have for the past few years not talked about anything else.

That the danger of nuclear war today is greater than it has ever been cannot be denied. That the nuclear freeze movement is not a realistic answer to that danger, I hardly need to tell you. A bilateral freeze cannot be imagined under conditions where the people in the Kremlin are happy about a demonstration of 700,000 people for the freeze in New York, but when seven demonstrate in Moscow they are so unhappy that they send them to the Gulag Archipelago. I think this alone is sufficient to question the validity of those fantasies in which people like to indulge, peculiarly enough, only when they are free and cannot imagine the conditions of a slave.

Yet the danger of nuclear war is real. Although there is no danger that the human race will come to an end, there is no question that a nuclear war would change the world completely and, in all probability, in a most horrible manner. What has been practiced, if not planned, in the past few decades does not work. We have tried to negotiate with the Soviets. We have done it sincerely for 25 years. I have not heard an argument yet that convinces me that such negotiations make any sense whatsoever in an objective way. When I say objective, I use that word in contrast to political expediency. Once you say "we have to because otherwise," you enter into a field where any argument can be made, and therefore no argument will hold.

Apart from negotiations, we seem to set our hopes on deterrence—deterrence by retaliation. That this is not a pretty idea is obvious. In the balance of terror, the terror is a reality, the balance is much more doubtful. Therefore it is highly desirable that some alternative be found.

One has been found. The remarkable thing is that President Reagan talked about it on March 23, 1983, in very explicit terms. The further marvelous thing is that the U.S. press managed, almost entirely, to disregard this proposal or to discuss it in terms that ensured it would not be taken seriously. The crucial question that Reagan asked was "Is it not better to save lives than to avenge them?"

Is there a real possibility of defense? The president did not claim there is. He said there should be a determined and long-lasting effort made in that direction. This was the first time anyone has attempted to change the unexamined assumption of the great majority of people—the belief that an attack will always win.

Under what conditions can defense win? Only if the efforts for defense become less expensive than the effort either to wipe out that defense or to increase the attacking forces to compensate for the defense. If this situation could be brought about, then the rational military behavior on both sides would give priority to the development of defensive weapons.

Another major consequence would be that if there were a nuclear war, its consequences would be less frightful. But a much more important consequence is that defense is the best deterrent today. That is not an absolute statement. If we were talking about a madman, like Hitler, then defense would not be sufficient for deterrence.

I happen to agree completely with Admiral Long that the ambitions of the Kremlin are not noticeably different from the ambitions of pre-Soviet Russia—ambitions for power, even for unlimited power. But while the Soviet leaders have the ambition to rule the world, they are not inclined to take risks. They have a strong, built-in inclination to take any country they want, but not if that country is strong. If there is defense, the success of an attack is uncertain. Such risks are too great. Therefore, a good defense would be a stabilizing factor.

But how can there be a defense against something as devastating as the atomic bomb? The answer is that modern technology is capable of miracles. Nuclear explosives have immense destructive power, but they also produce an enormous concentration of energy even when they are very tiny explosions. This concentration of energy gives rise to new physical effects. These can be utilized to destroy weapons, weapons that have already been launched, that are already being used.

Accomplishing this requires a great deal more sophistication than the simplist applications of nuclear weapons, but this sophistication has been developed. I would like to tell you about these techniques and put you all to sleep, because the details are a little complex. You are saved only because the United States has an exaggerated system of secrecy that helps the speaker and the listeners when they want to keep the discussion short. Apart from this advantage, the policy of secrecy has only disadvantages. We know that the Soviets know about U.S. defenses. However, we are not allowed to tell the American people nor our allies what the Soviets know. We should tell both the American people and our allies, not the details, but at least the general concepts. I hope that this change will be made.

What factors assist defense? The attacker must cover bigger distances. In a rocket attack, for instance, the attacker must use heavier rockets and send them greater distances. The defender has to construct objects that may have to be more intricate in some respects, but they are smaller, lighter, less expensive, and can be more numerous. Defense has the advantage in every situation with the exceptions that the attacker has the initiative and the element of surprise on his side.

If you want to attack, you need mass, you need money, you need quantity. If you want to defend, you need intelligence and more intelligence. You need infinite intelligence to be prepared for everything. Infinite intelligence does not exist. In the end, the question of whether attack or defense is easier will never be resolved in absolute terms. However, I hope I have indicated that defense does have a chance.

Now I am ready to make a second proposal. The United States should not talk about the defense of the United States. It should not talk exclusively even of the defense of NATO. The United States ought to defend itself, and it ought to defend NATO. But it also should help defend every long-term ally. I would not define the Untied States' allies according to a piece of paper that a president can abrogate. I want to defend those allies whose important interests are identical to those of the United States, those people whose predominant interest is to maintain peace and stability. That should be the single test. I believe that all the noncommunist nations in the Pacific Basin pass that test, either completely or with relative ease.

In the special case of the Japanese, their disinclination to rearm is remarkable and, in a way, very wonderful. But I hope that this disinclination does not extend to purely defensive measures.

Let me also emphasize that the essential lines in policy should not be drawn between nuclear and nonnuclear weapons. The essential lines should be drawn between aggression and defense. If the distinction that instruments serve defense can be made clear, and I think it can, then we should welcome all U.S. allies working on their development because we need the partnership of everyone who wants to make this small globe with the Pacific in its middle a place where there may be problems and disagreements, but where there will be peace.

I believe that the implementation of these two demands is most important. We must find out more about mainland China, and we must find ways to stabilize peace among those people who we know want peace. I believe that this is a difficult program. I also believe that it is a program that we cannot do without.

The Interests and Policies of the United States

Paul Wolfowitz

I would like to stress the awareness in the United States of the great and growing importance of the Pacific Basin. Perhaps the demographic center of the country is shifting westward. Perhaps it is, in part, because there is in Washington an administration that includes many Californians or transplanted Californians. But more fundamentally, it is because of the intrinsic value of the region itself.

I think the region is forcing itself onto the American consciousness. In large measure that is the product of the spectacular economic record of the region, particularly of Japan, Korea, Taiwan, Hong Kong, and the ASEAN countries. That spectacular economic growth is felt in the lives of Americans. For several years, U.S. trade with the East Asia–Pacific region has been larger than that with any other region, including Europe. During the first six months of 1983, a total of $63 billion in two-way trade was conducted between the United States and the countries of this region. That is 29 percent of the United States' total trade. In comparison, the second most important trading region, Western Europe, accounted for $56 billion, or one-quarter of U.S. trade. As important as those facts are, the future seems even more impressive. Given the growth rates of the region, the relative importance seems likely only to increase in the future.

One could take another measure of the region's importance, its demographic statistics. According to one projection, by the year 2000 the population of the East Asia–Pacific region will be over 2 billion people. The growth between now and 2000, roughly 400 million, is about equal to the projected entire population of Western Europe at the end of the century. There will be five times as many people in the Basin as in Western Europe. And where sheer numbers might not matter, large numbers of hardworking and talented people throughout this region are bound to have a major impact on the world.

One could take a third, very different, measure of the importance of this region to the United States, not by looking forward but by looking backwards. In the past 40 years the United States was involved in three East Asian wars. The United States clearly has a major stake in preventing future wars in this region. Fortunately, with the notable exception of Kampuchea, East Asia is at peace. This is not a tranquil peace. It is not a peace due to an absence of historical antagonisms or an absence of tensions and suspicions. And, it is certainly not a peace deriving from an absence of armed force. Indeed, though comparisons are hard to make, one could argue that this is one of the most heavily armed regions in the world. China has more than 4 million men under arms. Vietnam, a nation of only 50 million people, has more than a million men under arms—an extraordinary number for a country of that size. North Korea maintains armed forces of over 700,000 men, and an extraordinary percentage of its GNP is devoted to arming and maintaining these forces. The United States' South Korean ally is not far behind in armed forces, with more than 600,000 men under arms.

But most important, and most threatening of all, is the Soviet Union. It not only poses a threat itself, but it underwrites the aggressive potential of North Korea and Vietnam. One-half to one-third of Soviet armed forces are found in the Far East. The Soviet ground forces in this area number about half a million men on active duty and would number nearly a million if fully mobilized. That is an increase of more than 200 percent in the past eighteen years. The quantitative buildup of Soviet forces during the 1960s and 1970s is being supplemented by qualitative improvements. These improvements have an enormous impact on the region. They caused a dramatic increase in the geographic reach of Soviet offensive and power projection capabilities, far into the Pacific, and even into the Indian Ocean. Most notable, I think, is the increased range of Soviet aircraft, particularly the Backfire bomber, which alters the air balance in the Pacific region. And the power projection capabilities are expanded enormously by Soviet access to the facilities of Camranh Bay.

The favorable security picture in the Pacific, therefore, is not a product of the region's inherent peacefulness, or an absence of force, but rather what seems to be an effective balance of forces. A critical factor in maintaining that balance is the U.S. presence, but equally important—increasingly so—is the cohesion within a tacit community of security interests emerging among the Pacific nations. It is also a product of the broader concept of security that the United States shares with its friends in the region. That concept includes not only military strength, but also recognition of the importance of economic growth and of free institutions.

Despite some potential for violence, I think there are reasons to be cautiously optimistic about the future of Asia, about its ability to maintain the dramatic progress of the past, and about the U.S. role in that region. The fundamental challenge facing the region is to continue its record of progress. The fundamental reason for optimism is not because the region is lacking in problems—it has its fair share—but because of the realism and sophistication with which so many of the countries of the Basin are addressing those problems. Moreover, the United States seems to be regaining its sense of purpose there.

Before a trip I took to Southeast Asia, one of my deputies commented that it would be a good working assumption to assume that the people we were going to be talking to were at least as smart as we. I mentioned that comment when I briefed Secretary Shultz's staff meeting on Southeast Asia after I came back, and one of my colleagues from another regional bureau said, "I wish I had people to deal with like that."

There seems to be a confidence throughout this region—confidence that may perhaps be the product of remarkable progress in the past two decades. There is a belief that the future will be better than the present and therefore it makes sense to make strenuous efforts to make it so. Curiously, fatalism and resignation about the future, qualities once traditionally ascribed to Asia, seem more of a problem in Europe than they are in Asia.

But as much as the countries of the region contribute, I think the United States' role is critically important. If the United States has learned that it cannot solve all the problems of the world, or of this region, by itself, it has also abandoned some of the more extreme versions of the Guam Doctrine's exclusive reliance on the strength of others. It seems to be learning that the best way to advance its interests in a peaceful and stable world is by combining its strength with that of others of like mind. Fortunately, in East Asia it has many such partners, whose strength is growing.

I think that the key to maintaining the relative stability that the region enjoys today, the stability that underpins its remarkable progress, as far as U.S. policy is concerned lies in four related efforts of roughly equal importance: (1) the maintenance of a strong and capable U.S. presence, one backed not only by credible forces but by a demonstrated U.S. will to stand by its commitments; (2) the United States' encouragement of increased efforts by friends and allies in support of those common interests in proportion to their ability to bear those burdens; (3) for lack of a better term, what I call skillful diplomacy, to manage relations and to build ties with the very diverse countries in this region that share fundamental interests with the United States; (4) the effort to encourage continued economic development and, to the extent that the United States can, the political development of countries in the region as well.

One cannot rank these objectives in order of importance; they are perhaps all equally important. If I mention, as the role of the United States, the importance of rebuilding American strength and restoring U.S. credibility, it is perhaps because that is the element of U.S. policy most in question during the past decade.

Indeed, ten years ago the United States suffered the burden of having to answer the question whether it had any security interests in East Asia. The crisis and controversy surrounding Vietnam submerged U.S. awareness of a Soviet military buildup that had been going on for eight years when U.S. participation in that war ended. The exhaustion of the war led to the belief—wishful thinking, clearly—that basic Soviet objectives could be modified by the process called détente. And the guilt feelings that the war produced in some quarters even led to a fashionable view not merely that U.S. strength was unnecessary for preserving peace and protecting freedom, but that it was actually undesirable. The United States paid a high price in the 1970s for those misguided beliefs, and it lost a lot of ground not tending to its defenses that must now be made up. But I think the American people learned from the experience of the 1970s. They approach the world with a new sense of realism and an awareness of the importance of U.S. strength in preserving a peaceful world in which free societies can prosper.

We have seen in the past fifteen years not merely a buildup of Soviet power—bad enough—but a disturbing trend to use that military power. It began in 1976 with Angola, followed in 1977 by Ethiopia, in 1978 in Kampuchea, and in 1979 shockingly with Afghanistan. Year after year we had examples of a growing boldness by the Soviets and their proxies in the use of force. In the past few years we may have seen a respite, but it is only, in my opinion, a temporary one. There are a number of explanations why the Soviets have been a little less active in the use of force. Some of the more comforting ones you might summarize under indigestion, exhaustion, and incompetence. Indigestion in the sense that having swallowed morsels like Afghanistan and Kampuchea, the Soviets are clearly very hard pressed to digest them. Exhaustion in the sense that we see signs of profound crises in the Soviet economy. The Soviet Union clearly suffers from economic failure. But those economic failures so far have not caused a reduction of economic resources devoted to the military.

If there is a pause now, I believe it is due partly to an absence of opportunities and partly to the Soviets' efforts to concentrate on undoing some of their actions of the 1970s that built Western cohesion. It is clear that one of the Soviet priorities in Europe, as in Asia, is to divide the

United States from its allies and to convince influential opinion in the United States, and in allied countries, that these efforts are not necessary. I think they are necessary, and will be necessary far into the future.

The second element of a U.S. policy for this region must be to encourage friends and allies to increase their efforts in support of common interests. This is a valid principle. It applies most importantly to current U.S. efforts to encourage Japan to assume greater responsibilities for its own defense, within the context of the U.S.-Japan mutual security treaty, Japan's constitution, and its political traditions. The Soviet military threat has increased in the past twenty years to where it is increasingly difficult for the United States to meet its responsibilities in all areas, at all times. That, and the presence of new Soviet forces in the Indian Ocean, on the periphery of the Indian Ocean, and in Afghanistan, compels the United States to be flexible in the use and deployment of forces. Japan's assumption of greater responsibility for its own defense will enable the United States more effectively to meet its own responsibilities in the region and in adjacent areas in the event of a crisis.

Moreover, and this point I think needs to be recognized, Japan is not only a rich and prosperous country with enormous industrial potential that would be a prize to the Soviet Union, it is also a strategically located country of tremendous importance. Because of its strategic location, a Japan that can defend its airspace and its territorial seas substantially constrains the Soviet ability to project power in regions that are far beyond Japan itself—without a Japanese soldier, sailor, or airman setting foot outside Japan. The United States is urging Japan to meet in a timely way the targets that it set for itself in its five-year defense plan. Washington is trying to emphasize not just arbitrary percentage increases, but rather important roles and missions to be performed by each nation.

Even with the recent increases, Washington does not believe the Japanese defense budget is adequate to meet those targets. The growth of Soviet military power in the region makes continued efforts along these lines imperative. The United States understands the concerns of Asian countries stemming from the possibility of unlimited Japanese rearmament. The Japanese people have their own reasons not to want that to happen. But I think the concerns we hear from some of the Asian countries are not so much concerns about Japan as about the United States. Their concern is that the United States will use the strength of Japan as an excuse for retreating from its responsibilities, and indeed, we frequently hear the comment that "as long as you are here, we are not concerned about what the Japanese do." If some of the United States' friends in the region knew the difficulties that Washington, and the Japanese government, faces in trying to achieve what is really a rather modest increase in Japan's defense capabilities, they would be reassured that a resurgence of Japanese militarism is not in sight.

The United States is interested not only in Japan's military efforts. Indeed, for the reasons already mentioned, those efforts are necessarily confined to Japan's defense and its territory. In other respects, however, Japan can contribute in areas far beyond its homeland. Increasingly, Japan's enormous economic strength contributes to global stability. One particularly striking example, in view of the enormous stake the European allies share with the United States and Japan in the Persian Gulf, has to do with three countries—Turkey, Egypt, and Pakistan. These countries, although keys to stability in Southwest Asia, unfortunately are not endowed with huge resources of oil to handle the formidable economic problems they face. People on my own Japan desk are surprised to learn that Japan contributes more economic assistance to Pakistan than any other country, more economic assistance to Egypt than any country in Europe, and more economic assistance even to Turkey, a NATO ally, than any European country other than Germany. It is a remarkable measure of what Japan has begun to do, and all this has happened in the past five years. Five years ago Japan's role in those countries, and certainly in Turkey and Egypt, was minimal.

Japan is not the United States' only strong and important ally in the Pacific Basin. Australia and New Zealand are the oldest U.S. allies. As an Indian Ocean nation, Australia plays a major role, and an important role, and sees a role beyond the region in contributing, as New Zealand does, to the multinational peacekeeping force in Sinai. Increasingly we find Australia playing a role in the ASEAN region, training large armed forces from neighboring countries. As we discussed very productively during the recent meeting of the ANZUS Council in Washington, Australia and New Zealand together assume important responsibilities in the effort to help the weak economies of the small Pacific island-countries. This weakness has rightly been compared to the weakness we see in the Caribbean.

The ASEAN countries also increased their efforts in recent years not merely in development, but in better equipping their forces. Their priority must remain in the economic area, investment for development. But they have recently begun to cooperate with one another. Given the historical antagonisms between them, the cooperation we see among them, and with the United States, is remarkable.

The third element of U.S. policy I mentioned is the use of skillful diplomacy to manage relations and build strong ties with the many diverse countries in the region the share the United States' fundamental interests. I have used the word "skillful," inadequate as it is. Perhaps "flexible" is the word that comes to mind. I do not mean the policy of a weak middle power playing one country off against another, leaving the rest of the world guessing where it stands. That is not a role appropriate for the United States, and it is not a role on which countries in this region can count. However, given the diversity of the countries in the region—some nonaligned, some traditional U.S. allies, China not only a communist state but a former bitter enemy—flexibility in the way the United States approaches them, approaches appropriately tailored to the circumstances, is one of our highest priorities.

The region's concern with growing Soviet power is increasingly tying together nations of diverse systems and ideologies, and it is creating a growing community of interests in the Pacific—interest in stability and in economic growth—interests of which Americans are a part. While respecting the existing very real interests, the United States has to build on those shared interests. This will require leadership and diplomatic skill.

ASEAN, though a nonaligned grouping, showed remarkable leadership on the issue of Kampuchea. The United States has a very active dialogue with ASEAN and with its members individually. It supports their approach to that extremely difficult problem. The two sides must work out irritants on such issues as one that you may have never heard of but which occupied my time in the last few weeks—the disposal of the United States' tin stockpile, 150,000 tons of it. The United States acquired it in the 1950s and now considers it excess. Unfortunately, to the economies of three of those countries it represents a potential major disrupting force.

But China represents the sort of challenge to U.S. diplomacy about which I am talking. A peaceful and stable China is of enormous importance to the Pacific Basin. This is not only in the United States' interests, but also in those of China's neighbors. Successful U.S. relations with China therefore remain high on the Reagan administration's agenda. That was one of the important factors behind the recent decision to liberalize the transfer of technology to China. At the same time, because of differing histories, cultures, and political values, the United States and China will not always see eye to eye. As the volume of interaction has grown, so too have opportunities for disagreement. Ten years ago there would never have been a dispute with China over textile imports to the United States. What is required is continued balance on the United States' part, adroit diplomacy in both countries building on common interests, and management of the problems that exist. I believe that both countries recognize the great importance of good relations.

Taiwan will remain a sensitive issue. A good relationship with China is important both to the United States and to wider regional stability. But this relationship must be based on mutual interest in good relations. It cannot be purchased at the cost of Taiwan's basic interests.

Last, and perhaps most important, continued economic development of the region and the evolution of representative governmental institutions are essential to long-term security in the region. True security depends not only on military power, but on internal strength. We recognize that the long-term challenge in the region is to continue successful economic development and the evolution, even modest evolution, of representative institutions. The remarkable economic progress of the past decade has been built on adherence to principles of economic freedom and self-reliance. More than 90 percent of the investment resources for development of the Asian countries derive from internal sources, internally generated capital. Beyond that, direct private foreign investment plays a major role, more important even than official development assistance. The markets the United States provides for products of the developing countries in 1982 returned to the developing countries 17 times as much as they received from official development assistance. The Southeast Asian nations earned $65 million from their exports, 30 times what they received from foreign assistance. Nevertheless, official development assistance continues to be important because it reinforces other efforts and is a significant symbol of the United States' commitment.

The United States must also encourage the development of democratic institutions wherever appropriate. Different countries in the region are at different stages on the road to democracy. We see encouraging signs of progress. Not long ago Malaysia ended a remarkable political feat that very few countries have accomplished—a peaceful, democratic transition of power from one leader to another. The United States should encourage that kind of development, not just because of its preference for democracy but also because mechanisms for the orderly succession of power are extremely important to the long-term stability of this region. Yet, Washington should resist the temptations to interject itself too deeply in the internal processes of other states.

I conclude with a general observation about the difficulties of maintaining a consistent long-term U.S. policy for this region. It is difficult not merely because many Americans still live on the East Coast, but because it is very hard to conceive of a policy for the region as a whole. In part, it is difficult because distances are so great and the countries so different. Further, the multilateral institutions that exist in Europe, particularly NATO, to focus the United States' efforts and to coordinate the efforts of its friends do not exist in the Pacific. Such institutions, if they are to come into being at all, are a long way in the future. In many cases the United States is the only country with which other countries that have deep historical tensions and rivalries can cooperate. By cooperating with the United States, they tacitly coordinate their relations with one another. To me, signs of a revival of U.S. confidence and strength in this region are important and heartening. Those signs of restored health began even in the last years of the Carter administration. For whatever reasons, that administration's disastrous decision to withdraw troops from Korea was reversed not by an election, but by a decision of the Democratic administration. The flirtation with the so-called swing strategy, which could have denuded the U.S. naval presence in the Pacific, ended before the Reagan administration took office. I think the Reagan administration has made substantial progress, most notably through the president's funding of the needed military programs to make the U.S. naval and military presence in the Pacific Basin sustainable. In many other ways, the United States has been working to rebuild relationships, bilaterally and collectively, with the nations of this region. As a Pacific nation with global responsibilities, the United States has unique and important roles to play. It is a sign of Asia's new maturity that the United States plays its role on a basis of full partnership with a community of increasingly dynamic and self-confident nations.

I would like to quote James Mitchener, who wrote in 1952,

> There is only one sensible way to think of the Pacific Ocean today. It is the highway between Asia and America and whether we wish it or not, from now on there will be immense traffic along that highway. If we know what we want, if we have patience and determination, but if above all we have understanding, we may ensure that the traffic will be peaceful, consisting of tractors and students and medical missionaries, and bolts of cloth. But if we are not intelligent or if we cannot cultivate understanding in Asia, then the traffic will be armed planes, battleships, submarines, and death. In either alternative we may be absolutely certain that from now on, the Pacific traffic will be a two-way affair. I can foresee the day, and indeed that day has already come, when the passage of goods and people and ideas across the Pacific will be of greater importance to America than a similar exchange across the Atlantic.

His vision was remarkably clear. In the 1980s, as regional and global events propel us into a new era of immense promise and continuing peril, our own vision of the future must be no less clear.

DISCUSSANTS

Thomas Hayward

I want to focus on the word "stability," which is often interpreted differently by different nations. In the military we tend to view the stability issue in terms of confrontation of forces. I am very pleased that Admiral Inman took the occasion to fill us in on other aspects, including the political and the economic. However, my own background suggests that I had better focus on the potential use of military force.

To me, stability does not mean *status quo,* nor does it mean a relative balance of power *as it is,* or the development of national interest or regional interest *as they are presently conceived.* Stability implies maximum progress in economic, political, and educational matters throughout the region. The quest for stability and progress must somehow be kept within bounds without resorting to military force.

In the past 40 years, three wars attest to the United States' failure. One wonders just how successful the United States will be in preventing the next great war from breaking out in the Pacific Basin. This must surely be the principal U.S. objective.

Admiral Inman focused on the major powers in the Pacific Basin—the United States, the Soviet Union, Japan, and the People's Republic of China. Admiral Long, former commander in chief of the Pacific Command (CINCPAC), called attention to Washington's annual lack of perception that the world is round and that the Pacific is important. Washington's continual emphasis on Europe frustrates every commander of the Pacific Fleet. Every member of the U.S. Joint Chiefs of Staff wants the United States more involved in Pacific issues. They know that the four global powers are Pacific powers, which is not true of any other region in the world. They know that the Pacific Basin plays a significant role in world affairs and will play a much more significant role in the future.

Let me divert for a moment to speak of potential military conflicts in the Pacific Basin. It is true that many nations in the region are not greatly concerned about the Soviet Union, or U.S.-USSR confrontation, or strategic nuclear umbrellas that protect them, or even about the deployment of SS-20 missiles in the eastern part of the Soviet Union. Rather, their focus is on internal subversion, or infiltration, or succession issues that are all very key and very important.

We must remember that all the states in the Pacific Basin are more involved than they would like in great power global confrontation. The Pacific Basin is deeply affected by events that occur elsewhere than in the Pacific. This has been highlighted over the past four years by events in the Middle East starting with the overthrow of the Shah, moving through the hostage situation in Iran, the outbreak of war between Iran and Iraq, to the invasion of Afghanistan. The continuous conflicts involving Arabs has made the Indian Ocean and its littoral nations matters of deep concern to leaders of the great powers.

The United States' involvement in the Middle East has greatly increased CINCPAC's responsibilities. Other scenarios may place still heavier burdens on the shoulders of naval officers of the U.S. Seventh Fleet and the Pacific Fleet. Such eventualities are often overlooked by U.S. military officers, as well as by political leaders in the variety of nations that rim the Pacific Basin.

The war between Iran and Iraq threatens the world with military action, including the Pacific Basin. With each passing week, we see taking place one of the great oil spills of all time. One wonders whether the next misuse of missiles (or some other capability available to either side) might close the Persian Gulf. That is not outside the realm of possibility. If that does occur, it could place on the United States, specifically on the forces in the Pacific Basin, an obligation to respond in a hard military way.

Eventualities such as these would have immediate effects on Japan and other U.S. allies in the Pacific Basin, although I agree with Admiral Inman that the Soviets have shied away from situations that threaten a direct U.S.-USSR collision. If something like Afghanistan evidenced further Soviet adventurism, the Carter Doctrine—which has not been refuted by the Reagan administration—puts the world on notice that a U.S. military response is a real possibility. The flow of oil to all the world, communist or noncommunist, is so critical that naval forces might find themselves engaged to prevent its interruption.

I have been dismayed by those who always say that then we have a limited regional war at sea. It is in this context that I approach the subject of a major military confrontation in the Pacific Basin. It is not easy to imagine either the United States or the Soviet Union limiting its actions to units in the Indian Ocean. What would be the effects in the Mediterranean, for example, which is a confined body of water in which the two navies look at each other eyeball to eyeball on a daily basis? What would happen in the South China Sea, near the opposing bases of Camranh and Subic bays. With Soviet submarines roaming the China Sea and the Southwest Pacific, what would the Seventh Fleet commander do when he sights an enemy periscope?

In times of stress, such things as these make up the stuff of war. It is the miscalculated and the unplanned for which we can never be adequately prepared. While it may be of more interest to some Pacific Basin countries to focus on internal issues or immediate cross-border issues, they must recognize that they might become engulfed in great power confrontation, whether that confrontation arose inadvertently or resulted from causes initiated elsewhere.

The last major point I want to make deals with the responsibilities of other nations in the region for a higher degree of military capability to help prevent the Soviets from taking aggressive action. I believe the responsibility is highest today upon Japan.

I am encouraged by some words of Prime Minister Nakasone, but gravely discouraged by Japan's recent actions. I think particularly of its defense policy declarations, its reaffirmation of the three nonnuclear principles, and its actions with respect to the national budget and further investments in defense. Apparently, "comprehensive security" in Japanese terms means very little progress towards bearing a greater share of Japan's own defense requirements.

Japan is not implementing its own established White Paper policy on adequate national defense capability. The objectives of the White Paper, reaffirmed annually for the past four or five years, call for truly effective control of lines of communication several hundred, or even a thousand, miles out and a real air defense capability, which means much better surveillance and a stronger intercept capability. Were Japan to achieve these objectives, the United States would have more flexibility in using its forces to confront the Soviets.

G. J. Price

As an Australian, I inevitably bring a slightly different perspective on security interests in the Pacific Basin. A point of view from Australia is rather important.

Admiral Hayward whipped us off to the Indian Ocean. Not content with that, he moved us on to the Mediterranean, but we did not quite reach the Atlantic, the North Sea, or the Baltic. His remarks highlighted the fact that the security of what we call the Western world (misnomer as that term may be) is one and indivisible. "Global defense" may determine how one's own country may become involved in hostilities.

It is interesting to note that this was one of the matters discussed during the recent meeting of ASEAN's Council of Ministers in Washington. It was recognized that global happenings have an impact on the ANZUS alliance—on the United States, but more so on Australia and New Zealand. The far-ranging communiqué recognizes this, which is so often ignored.

In Australia, we find that security is a complicated business. We can no longer look only one way, either to Europe or to Asia. Increasingly we must look two ways, facing the Pacific and the threat, with possibility of confrontation, that exists in the Indian Ocean.

In the Indian Ocean itself, the threat of force is localized specifically in the core of the northwestern Indian Ocean or Southwest Asia. From Australia, geographic orientations are rather confusing. In Washington or on the Pacific Coast, you talk about the Far East in describing China, Japan, and the rest of Asia when you should be talking about the Far West. North, east, south, and west are vastly different from an Australian viewpoint.

As an Australian diplomat looking at these things for some time, I recognize that regional threats and menaces really do have global aspects. One thing remains constant for Australians: the alliances with the United States and the alliances and other kinds of friendly understandings with other countries who find themselves oriented in the same direction politically and philosophically as Australia and New Zealand.

Looking at the subject of great power confrontation in the Pacific, it occurred to me that one does not have to consider the problems and issues of maintaining military force, nor even see confrontation in terms of confrontations between military forces. As important as a pact is the question of great power deterrents in the Pacific-Asian concept, not the more narrow term, the Pacific Basin.

In the Pacific Basin, looking at the need for and importance of great power deterrents, the ability to deter is infinitely more preferable than the possibility of having to confront. This line of thought should be pursued more than it is. Successful deterrence, of course, lies behind the existence of major military powers. And I realize that to have the ability to deter, we must have the military strength to back the diplomatic, political, and economic activities, which include questions about trade and aid that would make that deterrent something that is meaningful and effective.

What we have to do is to provide time and opportunities for growth in the countries that have not yet gone to the communist side. Providing opportunities to grow will discourage temptations to use political activities or thoughts of revolution to solve difficulties and to achieve the aims that they, the communist countries, see before them.

While we talk about confrontation and the need to deter and how we can find a balance, we must try to open up a better dialogue, a better discussion, with "the other side." Looking at the polarization that has taken place in Asia, all of East Asia from Siberia to the Camau peninsula, including the People's Republic of China but excluding the Republic of Korea, is communist. We must develop better means of improving our dialogue with them in search of a balance of all the forces—military, diplomatic, and economic—that make for peace.

I do not know whether it is inevitable that polarization implies confrontation, which in turn implies a maintenance of tension. If polarization and confrontation are natural facts that will exist forever, where will these things lead us in the long run? Will they lead to explosion or finally to a point where tensions must relax, helping us to find a better means of pursuing our own aims and our own development without the continuing need to be concerned about the possible application of force by either side to achieve its aims.

These are the sorts of things that must come into any discussion of the possibility of great power confrontation in the Pacific Basin. How do we in Australia see the world, going into the twenty-first century. These are our constants: primarily our strategic, political, and general understanding and alliance with the United States. Accepting U.S. concern for confrontation, we want to take any step toward trying to find a balance that may lead to the relaxation of tensions with which we live.

With regard to China, as an Australian I think that the most important factor in China's situation is that in spite of issues and disputes, it maintains a pragmatic strategic understanding with the United States. China, of course, belongs to neither camp. Its relations with the Soviet Union, however, are more troublesome and threatening than those with the United States, Japan, and Western Europe. This is of great significance to Australia and New Zealand, particularly in their relationships with the ASEAN group of countries.

Looking at the rather anomalous position in which the PRC now finds itself following the collapse of the Cultural Revolution, we can see a perfect challenge for confidence-building measures. We can seek to provide the mainland Chinese with some kind of shield, a breathing space, to carry on their modernization programs and solve their problems with Taiwan. If we can do that successfully, we will receive part of the answer to Admiral Inman's question, "Where will China go in the future?"

We cannot be sure China's future leaders will be of the same mind as its leaders today. The more we can provide confidence for the present leadership, the less we have to be concerned about the possibility of a regression in their thinking and about their place in the international community.

Finally, I wish to refer to economic competitiveness and economic development. This is the key idea in the Pacific Basin that will reduce the tensions created by the need to commit ourselves to the security demands of confrontation. A very important illustration is found in the emergence in the South Pacific of a number of small island-states, island-republics that themselves could prove fertile ground. Without assistance, they could cause the same concerns to Australia, New Zealand, the ASEAN members, and possibly Japan as the concerns caused the United States by some nations in Central America.

We need to do some long-range thinking about these island-states in the South Pacific. Although some have fewer people than live in a small town in the United States, they have needs that must be met. They are entitled to some satisfaction in their daily lives. They are too important to be simply brushed aside. Australia and New Zealand do much to assist them, but by themselves they cannot do everything that is needed. The future of the Pacific islands merits considered attention in looking at the problems of the Pacific Basin.

II
NORTHEAST ASIA

INTRODUCTION

Claude A. Buss

Within the Pacific Basin, national security issues are most sensitive in the Northeast Asia subregion comprising the Northwest Pacific Ocean area, Siberia and the Soviet Far East, Japan, and the Korean peninsula.

The Soviet Union is an important Asia-Pacific power. The greater part of the Soviet homeland stretches from east of the Ural mountains to the Pacific Ocean. Its boundary with China is the longest in the world, nearly three times as long as that between Canada and the United States. Sentimentally, Moscow is as deeply attached to Vladivostok as to Murmansk.

The eastern territories of the Soviet Union constitute a vast but underdeveloped treasure house of such strategic and economic resources as petroleum, natural gas, coal, timber, hydroelectric power, metals and minerals, and chemical raw materials. The potential wealth of Siberia goes far in explaining Soviet interests and policies in Northeast Asia.

The commercial development of these resources could produce hard currency to pay for the industrial equipment and high technology needed to lift the Soviet Union out of its economic morass. The enormous scale of Siberian development activity is illustrated by the BAM railway, scheduled to open in 1985, which will be two and a half times the length of the Alaska pipeline. It will cross seven mountain ranges, sixteen large rivers, and 300 miles of permafrost. The new railway, together with pipelines, industrial plants, and the commercial ports of Wrangel and Sovietskaya Gavan, will have immense security implications for the entire Pacific Basin.

The construction of this imposing strategic-military complex in Siberia and the Soviet Far East, including Sakhalin and the Kurile Islands, is convincing evidence of the Soviet Union's metamorphosis from a European to a global power. Naturally it heightens Chinese, Korean, and Japanese fears of expansive Soviet power and influence in East Asia, but it also shows that the Soviets have far more at stake in the Pacific Basin than the negative interests of deterring the United States, containing China, threatening Japan, and interdicting the sea-lanes.

To counter Soviet expansion in Northeast Asia and the Pacific Basin, a solid, cooperative relationship between the United States, Japan, and the Republic of Korea is the key to mutual security.

The Japanese are by no means monolithic in their security attitudes and policies. Following the devastation of their country in World War II, they have been slow to overcome the ghastly memories of the atom bomb and their ruined cities. They oppose any return of ultra-militarism that might lead to war. They do not want their business leaders to become "merchants of death," and they do not like their prime ministers to refer to Japan either as an "ally" of the United States or as an "unsinkable aircraft carrier" in the Western Pacific.

Japanese policies relating to East Asia are likewise inhibited by the echoes of World War II. They are aware that the "Co-Prosperity Sphere" and the Japanese occupation cannot be forgotten in Korea, China, and Southeast Asia. The people of those countries too are "once burned, twice shy," and Japan must use utmost caution in adopting any initiatives in dealing with its neighbors.

Japan looks with a certain fear and misgiving at the Soviet development of Siberia and the Soviet Far East. The Soviets have every right to maximize their assets in the Pacific Basin. Japan flirts with the idea of providing economic assistance for the development of these Soviet territories but will not commit itself substantially without the assured cooperation of some private American firms, which has not been forthcoming.

Japan will not turn its back on either half of the Korean peninsula. Although more evenhanded than the United States in dealing with North Korea, Japan has been generous in the assistance it has offered to South Korea since the 1965 reconciliation treaty. Japan recognizes that stability in South Korea is essential for the peace of Japan, but neither country is prepared to have Japan play a more intimate role with South Korea in regional defense.

Recognizing that security in Northeast Asia is strengthened by satisfactory relations with Australia and Southeast Asia, Japan pays careful attention to those areas. Japan enjoys a cordial and mutually profitable economic relationship with Australia. Neither side wants to add a "J" to "ANZUS," thus extending their formal engagements. Both are content working to expand their trade and limit their political contacts to ordinary diplomatic intercourse.

Japan has done remarkably well in removing the scars from Southeast

Asia, which successive prime ministers have visited in the past decade. Fukuda traveled throughout the area, bearing gifts and promising to cooperate with ASEAN members to strengthen solidarity and resilience. Nakasone followed, with soft words to allay fears of a renewed Japanese armed drive to the south. He was told by Suharto in Indonesia, "We have no objection to Japan's defense efforts;" by Prem in Thailand, "We welcome Japan's sea-lane defense policies;" by Marcos in the Philippines, "To defend its own country is the inherent right of the Japanese people;" and by Mahathir in Malaysia, "There is no longer any problem in connection with Japan's sea-lane defense plan." Japan's great contribution is stimulating economic development in the ASEAN region.

Tokyo enjoys peace with both Beijing and Taipei. The Beijing-Tokyo Peace and Friendship Treaty of 1978 preserved a climate of understanding in which Japan extended substantial loans to China. This is a reasonable price to pay for keeping the PRC at a comfortable distance from the USSR. Japan hopes that whoever succeeds Deng Xiaoping will follow the same course with the capitalist West.

Far from having abandoned Taiwan, Japanese are perhaps more welcome now than they were in the colonial era. Japanese trade and investments in Taiwan are healthy and growing. All three parties in the Tokyo-Beijing-Taipei triangle seem to have found an acceptable formula for coexistence.

Japanese diplomats have become more prominent on the world scene. Whether at the United Nations or in summit meetings, Japanese spokesmen have abandoned their reticence to address such multinational topics as arms control, the welfare of the less developed countries, human rights, NATO, or the European Economic Community. They are interested in the Law of the Sea, the Lebanon war, or any topic relating to their lifeline to Middle East oil. The time is approaching when Japan, like the USSR, can say that no situation in the world can be solved without its participation.

United States–Japan problems are easy to discern but difficult to solve. As this conference brought out, perhaps the most baffling is the gap in perceptions of superpower confrontation, especially in the Pacific Basin. Many Japanese are none too sympathetic to the "neo–cold war" policies of President Reagan, whom some accuse of being a "trigger-happy warmonger." They think that Americans and Russians are responsible for the Pacific Basin's dangerous tensions and argue that neither the communist nor the anticommunist camps would be viable without its adversary relationships.

Many Japanese believe that, deliberately or otherwise, the Americans underplay their own strengths and exaggerate the capabilities and intentions of the Soviets. The Japanese do not accept the American perception of a worldwide communist bloc or its crusade for world domination. To some Japanese, communists are as diverse and fragmented as capitalists.

Most Japanese sense that communism has lost its appeal as an ideology, and the Soviet Union has no influence or prestige in East Asia apart from its inclination to use military power.

Japanese vary widely in their perceptions of the Soviet threat; at one extreme is a minority that feels the U.S. connection is the sole source of Japan's national danger. Were it not for linkage with the Americans, the Japanese merchant marine could sail the seven seas without concern for enemy submarines, and the Japanese could live in peace and prosperity without fear of attack or invasion. To this minority, the Japanese and the Russians have no problems worth a war, but it is the sad Japanese fate to be hitched to the American star.

Such opinions are fading, especially since the Afghanistan invasion, and more Japanese are alert to the grave menace inherent in Soviet power. They realize that their nation could be the number-one target of Soviet aggression. They see President Reagan as a valued ally who has restored confidence in U.S. commitments to East Asia and the Western Pacific.

The inevitable effect of this dichotomy in Japanese attitudes is that many Japanese appear unconcerned about their national security. It is comfortable for them to rely on the mutual defense agreement, the presence of U.S. forces in Japan, and the U.S. nuclear umbrella. Consequently there is little public pressure to alter any of the U.S.-Japan security understandings or to increase the Japanese share of the costs of mutual defense.

Simply stated, many Americans pressure the Japanese to spend more, four or five times more, for mutual defense. They accuse the Japanese of taking a free ride at the expense of American taxpayers. They argue that Japan should assume greater responsibilities in military research and development, ocean surveillance, defense of their own nation, and protection of maritime lines of communication up to 1,000 miles from its coasts. Short of advocating a nuclear role for Japan, many Americans want the Japanese to play a role in regional and global security affairs commensurate with their economic power.

In reply, the Japanese point out that the huge amounts they spend on their own defense compare favorably with either West Germany or the United Kingdom. They are buying sophisticated weapons and supplies. Neither the public, the Diet, nor the media will allow them to do more. They insist that they cannot wreck their economy to increase their military potential. In their view, a prosperous Japan is far more vital than a rearmed Japan to the peace and prosperity of the Pacific Basin.

The third major factor in Northeast Asian security is the Republic of Korea, or South Korea. South Koreans are fiercely proud of their country and its achievements since independence. They want to be recognized not merely as a flank to protect Japan, but as an important adjunct. They see their contributions to regional defense as equally vital as those of Japan.

The heart of South Koreans' concerns is their survival as a nation-state, not their place in any grand U.S. design for mutual security. Their national interests are to avoid another war on the Korean peninsula, preserve the U.S. alliance, develop their economic and political systems in accordance with their own values, protect their nationals wherever they may be, and enhance the stature of the Republic of Korea (ROK).

The need for security against the threat from the north amounts to a national obsession, outweighing the secondary interests of economic growth and political development. In the name of security, the ROK devotes 6 percent of its GNP and 37 percent of its national budget to defense and maintains a more authoritarian system of government than many of its citizens would like.

Much of South Koreans' sense of insecurity is their uncertainty about the reliability of the U.S. commitment. The current interests and policies of the allies may be congruent, but they can never be identical. The ROK wants U.S. troops on its soil for their psychological support. The presence of American ground forces is the most effective deterrent of the North and guarantees that Americans will jointly resist should their forces come under attack by North Korea. The South Koreans want U.S. troops to remain for another five or ten years, perhaps indefinitely. On the other hand, the Americans want to feel free to consider withdrawal or redeployment of at least some of those ground forces should they be needed elsewhere.

South Koreans' faith in the U.S. commitment was badly shaken by the vacillating Carter administration. The basis of their doubt still remains. They fear that American sentiment for withdrawal might reappear, especially if the American economic situation should tighten. President Chun is pleased with President Reagan's cordiality and generosity, but another administration with different foreign policies might succeed to office in Washington. Some basic differences complicate U.S.-ROK relations. Americans are not pleased with some economic policies of the ROK or its authoritarianism. The United States wants South Korea to be strong militarily, but not too strong. The United States does not want South Korea to develop a nuclear capability and is unwilling to put nuclear weapons under South Korean command.

South Koreans realize that their country might be too close to the United States. Their pride is hurt by the asymmetry of the bilateral U.S.-ROK relationship. It is difficult for them to follow an independent policy when they have disagreements with the United States. Successive oil crises convinced them that it was not beneficial to be identified with the pro-Israel policies of the United States. They could not afford to boycott Arabian oil, and they desperately needed their lucrative construction contracts in Middle Eastern countries, including Libya and Iraq. They cannot be accepted in the nonaligned movement as long as they are so closely tied to the United States.

In dealing with Japan, either directly or in tandem with the United States, it is impossible for South Korea to erase the scars of the colonial period. It hopes that Japan will appreciate South Korea's strategic importance and be ready to provide more economic assistance for development. It wants Japan to take a more active part in regional defense, but fears the possible re-creation of the Japanese military juggernaut.

South Korea is willing to have Japan assume a larger role in strategic planning and military exercises, but is unwilling to share with Japan command of Korean soldiers. It will accept limited growth of Japanese military power only within the parameters of the U.S.-Japan defense relationship and strongly opposes the development of a Japanese nuclear capability. Above all, it does not want Japan to assume any responsibilities now borne by the United States in regional defense.

In dealing with the nonhostile communist countries, including the USSR and the PRC, the Republic of Korea is not going to depart too far from American leadership. It accepts that the high degree of tension between the United States and the USSR tends to tighten the U.S. commitment to South Korea, but it dislikes the corresponding closeness of the USSR to North Korea. It is also skeptical of the apparent rapprochement between the People's Republic of China and the United States and Japan. Because of sentimental bonds, the ROK wants no further abandonment of Taiwan's interests. Furthermore, it opposes transfer of technology, information, equipment, or weapons to the PRC because of the direct pipeline connecting Beijing and Pyongyang.

Certain that a reduction of tension between the superpowers in the Pacific Basin would better serve its national interests, the Republic of Korea endeavors to create better relations with the Soviet Union as well as with the People's Republic of China. It is South Korea's hope that a closer understanding with the two communist giants would discourage North Korea from any rash military attack on the South. It is not likely, however, to enjoy success in its cautious efforts at détente with either power as long as both are locked in a conflict for primacy in Pyongyang.

The Republic of Korea, Japan, and the United States must consider possible alternative scenarios. The close relationship between President Chun, President Reagan, and Prime Minister Nakasone is not necessarily permanent. Perceptions of interests would change, as would policies, if minority groups in any one of the three countries were to gain in influence or succeed to power.

In Korea, the aspiration for national identity, embracing both South and North, could assume greater importance in the hierarchy of national interests. In pursuing an intelligent unification policy, President Chun has been able to curb the rise of a more assertive nationalism.

Many courageous South Koreans oppose the authoritarian regime of President Chun, its intimacy with the United States, and, to a lesser degree, with Japan. They resist what they call foreign meddling in South Korea's internal affairs. They are unhappy about excessive military aspects of foreign assistance.

A substantial minority feels that current perceptions of national interests are out of balance, that it makes no sense to be preoccupied with security to the exclusion of economic and political development. Although willing to die to preserve a government that would enshrine their sacred values of freedom and justice, they do not wish to be called upon to sacrifice their lives for another repressive regime. Single-minded dedication to security could lead to exhaustion or limitation of popular tolerance. It is up to President Chun to combine the pursuit of effective security policies with the type of government he is sworn to preserve.

SECURITY IMPLICATIONS OF SIBERIA AND THE SOVIET FAR EAST

Rodger Swearingen

I will condense the essence of Siberia's place in the security scheme in terms of three interrelated strategic roles: (1) Siberia as an economic/strategic "treasure house," key to the Soviet GNP; (2) Siberia as a commercial center—the economic and political implications for Western Europe and Eastern Asia; and (3) Siberia as a strategic military complex—impact on Northeast Asia, the Western Pacific, and the United States.

Siberia as an Economic/Strategic Treasure House

Siberia clearly holds the key to the economic and strategic future of the Soviet Union. A. G. Aganbegyan, of the Soviet Academy of Sciences, writes: "Siberia is richly endowed with natural resources... unique in scale and quality: oil, natural gas, coal, hydro-electric power, as well as rich deposits of ores, nonferrous and ferrous metals, chemical raw materials, vast reserves of fresh water and ample space, including cities for industrial production."[1]

Siberia's significance in overall strategic development planning was more recently elaborated in a pertinent passage from a roundtable discussion entitled "The 'Sibir' Programme of Action," carried on Moscow Radio on March 25, 1982:

> Siberia plays a leading role in the All-Union balance. This is shown by the following facts: Siberia now produces 25 percent of the output of the country's entire mining industry. Through its resources, virtually the entire increase

in the production of fuel, commercial timber, and sawn timber was obtained in the last Five-Year Plan period. Today, every third cubic metre of gas which is extracted comes from Siberia. The share of Siberian machine-building products is growing constantly. A growing role for Siberia is envisaged in the further development of the country's economy. All these "global" problems are encompassed by the 'Sibir' programme. It incorporates 40 inter-related target programmes within the framework of which questions of the comprehensive utilization of the mineral resources of the western and eastern regions, problems of the socio-economic development of the West Siberian, the Angara-Yenisey, the Kuzbass and the Kansk-Achinsk fuel and energy complexes, the opening up of the BAM zone and of the Lake Baikal area, and many others are decided. Taking part in drawing up the programme were scientists from 50 institutes and over 350 scientific research and planning and design organizations, which represent 60 ministries and departments under Union and republican jurisdiction.[2]

The urgency of the Sibir program reflects the deterioration of the Soviet economy. The development of Siberian strategic resources is vital for the progress and welfare of the Soviet state. The primary resources involved are petroleum, natural gas, coal, electric power, and strategic minerals and metals.

With regard to petroleum, the world's largest producer in recent years has been the Soviet Union, which also boasts of the world's largest reserves. Perhaps less well known is that petroleum plays a critical role in Soviet foreign trade. It has over the years accounted for up to 50 percent of vitally needed hard currency. In the last quarter of 1982, the Soviet oil industry appears to have sustained a rate of production of 12.5 million barrels per day, of which a substantial proportion came from the wells of Siberia.

As for natural gas, the Soviet Union boasts that one-third of all proven natural gas reserves in the world are in Siberia. The Eleventh Five-Year Plan calls for a 50 percent increase in current levels of production. Soviet gas projects rely heavily on Western turbines, compressors, and pipe, plus Western finance and loans—providing ammunition for Western critics of high-technology transfer. The Soviet government appears totally committed to its ambitious program for Siberian natural gas. It is the most feasible and promising of the strategic economic projects.

Siberia's vast coal reserves are essential for the steel industry, which is in deep trouble. Under the Tenth Five-Year Plan, work began on the coalfields situated along the Trans-Siberian railroad in Kemerovo oblast, where an annual output of 40–50 million tons is projected. An increasing amount of coal has been scheduled for export to Japan for years to come. Moscow, in its quest for hard currency, expects to match its mounting exports of natural gas to Western Europe with comparable increases in bituminous coal to Japan.

In the development of electric power, during the past decade and a half the Soviets have built a great number of electric power stations, producing considerably more energy than can be used locally.

By the mid-1970s, Siberia was generating nearly 19 percent of the Soviet Union's electric power production and close to 40 percent of its hydroelectricity. With the completion of large Siberian power stations during the 1980s and the construction of long-distance transmission lines to the European part of the USSR, Siberia is expected to supply electricity to the nation's European grid—with the prospect of ultimately selling power to Western Europe.

Electric power, natural gas, and, to a lesser extent, petroleum and coal represent the priority items in the manageable and relatively successful Siberian resource development. None of these areas, however, is without the problems and pitfalls characteristic of the Soviet economic system.

To round out this brief inventory of the key elements in the Siberian strategic treasure house, a word about strategic minerals and metals may be very helpful. The Soviets are determined to become self-sufficient. Thanks to Siberia's rich resources, they have virtually succeeded. With respect to copper, nickel, lead, zinc, cobalt, iron ore, manganese, and chromium, the Soviets are essentially self-sufficient. They lack only tin and bauxite. This vital role of Siberian resources is essential in understanding the importance that the Soviets ascribe to their interests and policies in the entire Pacific Basin.

Siberia as a Commercial Complex

Moscow looks to the commercialization of some of these strategic resources to produce hard currency. Natural gas, oil, and electric power have been targeted for Europe. Siberia's vast timber resources, along with coal and natural gas, provide the complementary economic core for the Soviet acquisition of industrial equipment and high technology from Japan.

Western Europe's concern with Siberia is not of recent origin. A 1974 NATO study of Siberia's natural resources examined both the commercial and strategic dimensions, expressing guarded optimism and appropriate apprehension.[3] By 1980 Western Europe received about 8 percent of its oil and 10 percent of its natural gas from the Soviet Union. The transmission of Siberian electric power to Western Europe, as suggested, is a considerably more difficult and distant proposition.

Washington's recent strategic and political concerns about Soviet–West

European commercial connections centered on a projected Soviet gas pipeline designed to transport some 40 billion cubic meters of natural gas over 3,000 miles. Both the Carter and Reagan administrations expressed concern over the magnitude of the Soviet military threat and the degree to which Western technology transfers served to increase that threat. Imposition by the Reagan administration of extraterritorial and retroactive controls on oil and gas technology provoked intense controversy at home and outrage in Western Europe. The different United States–European priorities and perceptions were underscored dramatically when foreign governments and firms in France, the United Kingdom, West Germany, and Italy simply defied U.S. orders. The controls were lifted after Allied agreement to study the problem.[4]

Looking eastward to East Asia and the Pacific, trade and commercial relations with China, while still limited, show signs of improvement as talks between Moscow and Beijing continue. Political considerations still cloud commercial contacts with a divided Korea. But Japan attracts substantial Soviet commercial attention, and the attraction is mutual.

For a variety of economic and political reasons, the successful joint Japanese-Siberian development projects are those with maximum *mutual* economic benefit and minimum perceived Western security implications. This means that timber, coal, natural gas, and offshore deep-well oil drilling dominate current Soviet-Japanese economic intercourse and are viewed by both Moscow and Tokyo as sensible and significant.

In a recent article on Soviet-Japanese trade relations, Soviet economist V. Spandaryan pointed to the "geographic proximity" and "mutually supplementary structure of trade," noting that starting in 1966, trade between the two countries doubled every five years.[5] The nature of this trade should be noted: Siberian fish, coal, gas, minerals, and timber for Japanese ships, port facilities, development loans, engineering expertise, industrial equipment, and high technology.[6]

A brief word is essential on the new Baikal-Amur-Mainline Railway (BAM), a second Siberian transcontinental link. When completed, BAM will stretch some 3,145 kilometers (2,000 miles) from Ust-Kut on the Lena River north of Lake Baikal to Komsomolsk on the Amur, where it will connect with a line to Vladivostok via Khabarovsk. From Komsomolsk on the Amur, BAM will terminate 200 miles farther along at the new Soviet port, Sovetskaya Gavan, on the Gulf of Tartary. Overall, the new railway will be roughly two and a half times the length of the Alaska pipeline and will challenge difficult terrain and impossible climatic conditions like those encountered in the formidable Alaskan pipeline venture. BAM, we are told, "will cross 7 mountain ranges, 16 large rivers, and transverse 500 kilometers (more than 300 miles) of permafrost." Completion of BAM was originally scheduled for 1982, but for reasons suggested and bureaucratic conditions characteristic of the Soviet system, the plan appears to be about three years behind schedule.[7]

Assisted by Japanese loans, equipment, and engineering skills, the two new major Pacific ports of Wrangel and Sovetskaya Gavan are, in 1983, largely operational. With BAM in near-full operation, probably in 1985, the economic and strategic implications for Siberian economic exploitation and for further Soviet military development in the region and in the Pacific Basin are immense.

Siberia as a Strategic Military Complex

Most ominous for the West is the expanding role of Siberia and the Soviet Far East in the Soviet Union's massive strategic military buildup. This military buildup has been going on for decades.[8] The process generates and sustains its own momentum. Moscow has shown no inclination to negotiate seriously or to reduce either military spending or forces in being.

While it is fashionable to view the dramatic increase in Soviet military strength in the Far East as a reaction to the 1969 border skirmishes with China and the 1972 Sino-American rapprochement, a closer look suggests a larger rationale. The strategic military development of Siberia and the Soviet Far East may be seen as the logical extension of communications, ground force, naval, air, and missile capabilities to the Asian region as part of the Soviet Union's metamorphosis from a European to a global power.

Events and trends in East Asia and the Western Pacific during the past decade dramatically reflect heightened Soviet attention to that region of the world. The Soviets have recently established a new High Command in the Far East to coordinate policy planning and strategic and tactical operations for the region. There has been a marked quantitative and qualitative improvement in Soviet ground forces—to 51 divisions with high-technology weapons and first-line equipment.

One-quarter of the Soviet air force, or about 2,120 aircraft, is now employed in the Far East. More than half of these aircraft are high-performance, third-generation types. Additional supersonic Backfire bombers have recently been delivered to both naval and air units.

About one-quarter of the Soviet's naval strength, which comprises some 2,740 ships of all types, is now assigned to the Pacific Fleet. These include some 135 submarines, about 65 of them nuclear-powered, and one Kiev-class aircraft carrier. These forces are augmented by the largest merchant marine in the world, which is in effect an adjunct of the Soviet navy. The expansion and improvement of commercial port facilities at Wrangel and Sovetskaya Gavan has already been noted.

Some 30 percent of the Soviet Union's entire strategic missile force, both ICBMs and SLBMs, are reported to be deployed in Eastern Siberia and the Far East. There has also been an upgrading of theater nuclear forces; between one-quarter and one-third of the SS-20 missiles in the Soviet arsenal and about the same number of Backfire bombers are now thought to be deployed east of the Urals. Substantial upgrading of naval facilities at Vladivostok also appears under way. Petropavlosk is far north, lacks rail communication, and is closed by ice during the winter months.[9]

A separate comment may be reserved for Japan's Northern Territories, the Kurile Islands, claimed by Japan but increasingly occupied and militarized by the Soviet Union.

Substantial evidence of the development of Soviet naval, air, and radar installations on these islands goes back a decade or more and has mounted year by year since 1978. The addition of up to a division of Soviet ground forces with tanks, surface-to-air missiles, and helicopter gunships casts further gloom over the future of these territories.[10] Nor is the Soviets' record of retreat from other areas under their control and occupation encouraging. Soviet expansionism, directly or by proxy, is a way of life. That it should be necessary to make this point after all these years is part of the problem.

How is the Soviet military buildup in Siberia and the Soviet Far East viewed by the powers most concerned? One of the major planks of China's foreign policy is "defense against the Soviet Union." A recent article in the *Beijing Review* focused on the question. Entitled "Building Up the Siberian Base," the article concluded: "Obviously a major goal in the drive to open up Siberia is to strengthen the Soviet Union's military posture in Asia and facilitate its expansion farther east and south."[11] Korean foreign policy and defense specialists, who have already met the challenge from the north once in their lifetime, are no less apprehensive.[12]

Japanese public opinion, government pronouncements, and defense policy all suggest their concern with the increasing capabilities and unclear intentions of the great neighbor to the north.

U.S. ambassador to Japan Mike Mansfield clearly shares these misgivings about the Soviet military buildup in the region. He speaks repeatedly about the danger to the United States of putting too many of its security eggs in the European basket to the detriment of its defense needs and commitments in the Western Pacific.[13] For all Americans, their allies, and friends, an awareness of the Soviet threat throughout the Pacific Basin is cause at this critical time to tighten their bonds of mutual security.

Notes

1. A useful Soviet overview is contained in A. G. Aganbegyan, ed., *Regional Studies for Planning and Projecting: The Siberian Experience* (The Hague: Mouton Publishers, 1981), 312 p. The editor and twenty other specialists at the Academy of Sciences Institute of Economics and Organizations of Industrial Production in Novosibirsk take an unusually professional and candid look at the problems and prospects of Siberia's economic development and related issues.

2. Moscow Radio, March 25, 1982.

3. NATO Directorate of Economic Affairs, *Exploitation of Siberia's Natural Resources;* main findings of a roundtable held January 30–February 2, 1974, in Brussels.

4. U.S. Congress, Office of Technology Assessment, *Technology and East-West Trade: An Update* (Washington, D.C.: Government Printing Office, May 1983).

5. V. Spandaryan, "Soviet-Japanese Trade Relations," *Far Eastern Affairs* (Moscow), no. 4 (1980): 88–89.

6. Cf. V. Aleksandrov, "Siberia and the Soviet Far East in Soviet-Japanese Economic Relations," *Far Eastern Affairs*, April–June 1982, pp. 21–32.

7. See chapter on Siberia in Rodger Swearingen, *The Soviet Union and Postwar Japan: Escalating Challenge and Response* (Stanford: Hoover Institution Press, 1979); and Allen S. Whiting, *Siberian Development and East Asia: Threat or Promise?* (Stanford: Stanford University Press, 1981). Most recent status report on the situation is Victor Mote's "Reflections on the BAM: Nine Years and Still Counting," in *Soviet Geography: Review and Translation*, April 1983, pp. 280–88.

8. Detailed in successive Japan Defense Agency White Papers published annually, which characterize the Soviet Union as a "threat to Japan."

9. Meetings with Japanese Defense Agency specialist in Tokyo, July 1982. Information and data from Japan Defense Agency, *Defense of Japan,* White Paper (August 1982) and *Asian Security* (Tokyo: Research Institute for Peace and Security, 1982).

10. The question is examined in some detail by Yutaka Hashimoto, a councilor in the Northern Territories Affairs Headquarters, Prime Minister's Office, in an article entitled "The History of Japan's Northern Territories," *Look Japan,* May 12, 1982.

11. "Building Up the Siberian Base," *Beijing Review,* no. 19 (May 11, 1982).

12. Conferences with Korean Foreign and Defense ministries specialists, Seoul, summers 1979 and 1981. Discussed by Takuya Kubo, "Soviet Russian Aims in East Asia," *Korea and World Affairs,* Winter 1979, pp. 485–94.

A recent view of the issue within the context of relations with the United States is Yu-Nam Kim's "U.S.-Korean Security Interdependence: With Special Reference to Northeast Asia," in *Journal of East and West Studies*, Spring–Summer 1983, pp. 47–64.

13. Conversations with Ambassador Mike Mansfield in Tokyo in the summers of 1979, 1981, and 1982.

Japan's Defense Posture: Toward Closer Cooperation with the United States

Yoichi Masuzoe

Japan is repeatedly accused of hitching a "free ride" on defense costs through its alliance with the United States. In fact, Japan is spending only 1 percent of its GNP for defense compared with 6 percent for the United States. Most Americans consider the time has come for Japan, now the second largest economic power, to accept a "fair share" of the defense burden. This view is widely shared also by European countries, whose defense budgets average 3–4 percent of GNP. The greater the U.S. trade deficit with Japan, the louder American business and political leaders complain that Japan is fattening its prosperity by leaving its defense to the American taxpayer. Two entirely different issues, trade and defense, are thus linked to complicate Japanese-American disputes.

The following analysis illustrates the reasons for the reluctance of the Japanese government to take a larger responsibility for defending Japan and then examines whether Japan will do more than it is at present.

Japan's Reluctance to Expand Its Defense Role

Those who discourage a Japanese military buildup refer, first of all, to the constitution promulgated under the U.S. occupation. According to the official interpretation of Article 9, the no-war clause, Japan may not send troops overseas or join in a collective security system. The Japanese government is permitted only defensive weapons.

A recent opinion poll reveals that only 24 percent of the Japanese wish for a revision of the no-war clause, and 41 percent see no need to amend it.[1] Although Article 9 might constitute an obstacle to more positive cooperation with its allies in the long run, Japan can enhance its military capabilities within its constitutional limitations.

Another important constraint is the antidefense and the anti-U.S. bias of the Japanese mass media. Most newspapers vigorously support any action against a greater Japanese defense effort. The press covers largely, for instance, antinuclear movements, but it does not even hint at possible Soviet involvement in peace rallies in the West. Japanese journalists describe President Reagan as a warmonger, but they seldom analyze the social changes that led to his overwhelming victory over Carter. It is, therefore, difficult for Japanese political leaders to favor overtly an increase in military strength without provoking fierce attacks by the press.

The third domestic constraint is the budget deficit. The Ministry of Finance has suffered from a lack of revenue since the first oil shock of 1973–1974. The Japanese government can no longer expect an increase in revenue, particularly from a corporation tax, because of the lasting recession. In fiscal year 1982, as much as 21 percent of the total revenue was covered by issuing public bonds. This is very high compared with other industrial countries (6.1 percent in the United States, 9.8 percent in the United Kingdom, 11.2 percent in West Germany, and 10.7 percent in France). The late Premier Masayoshi Ohira tried in vain to introduce a new type of indirect tax that might remedy financial difficulties. In March 1981 his successor, Zenko Suzuki, organized a study group on "administrative reform" that proposed tight measures to reduce government expenditures. Suzuki declared that he would "stake his political life" upon this reform. Yasuhiro Nakasone, head of the Agency for Administrative Reform before succeeding Suzuki as prime minister in November 1982, also placed high priority on this reform. Under such circumstances, it is difficult to increase defense spending while cutting back most domestic programs.

The Japanese people are keenly aware of the recent Soviet military buildup. They are concerned about Soviet forces deployed in the Far East. According to the White Paper published by the Defense Agency in 1981, 360,000 troops, some 2,210 planes, and about 800 ships are deployed in this region. These figures are the same as the U.S. estimates. The assessment of Soviet military capabilities shows no difference between Tokyo and Washington. The Japanese government is aware of the stationing of Backfire bombers and SS-20 missiles in the Far East and of the division of Soviet troops stationed in the Northern Territories.

Why, then, does Japan hesitate to increase its military strength? Don't the Japanese feel themselves threatened by the Soviet Union? There are two main factors involved in a threat: capability and intention. Many Japanese think that the Soviet Union has no intention of invading Japan.

Most Japanese do not like to think seriously about an "improbable" war. The "prepare for war if you want peace" argument is not popular in Japan.

Another reason Japan is reluctant to share the defense burden is its self-perception of vulnerability. Most Japanese do not think their country is as strong as internationally acclaimed. They are aware that Japan has become the second largest economic power in terms of GNP and that its economic performance is excellent. But they still believe that Japan is extremely vulnerable because it depends on other nations for its energy resources and raw materials. It is difficult for Japan to understand why such a dependent country should play an active role in international politics. This Japanese view often frustrates the United States. If the security of oil supplies is so vital for Japan, many Americans ask, why is it not doing more to contribute toward stability in the Persian Gulf?

In partial answer to this question, the Japanese government proposes the concept of "comprehensive security." This concept is explicit: that a nation's security should be sought by comprehensively combining diplomatic, economic, military, and other means. Some Japanese even think that economic assistance can replace military forces. The role of military strength is downplayed in Japan.

The fourth reason for Japan's unwillingness to upgrade its military capabilities can be found in its attitudes toward the United States. Any request of the U.S. government to Tokyo, either in the field of defense or with regard to trade, is considered in Japan as *gaiatsu* (foreign pressure), as if Japan were assaulted by a natural disaster such as a typhoon or earthquake. Most Japanese try to escape from gaiatsu instead of making efforts to meet U.S. demands. Caspar W. Weinberger, U.S. secretary of defense, says that he is "concerned that Japan's capability for self-defense at this point remains short of what is clearly required."[2] But his opinion is not widely shared by many Japanese. Some argue that American jealousy of Japan's economic success leads Washington to ask Japan to undertake actions that might diminish its economic potential.

The Japanese press's emotional reaction to the recent IBM industrial spy case shows the prevailing Japanese mistrust of American motivations. The Japanese enterprises that committed the crime were considered victims of an aggressive U.S. attack on Japan. Hitachi and Mitsubishi therefore gathered sympathy from the Japanese public.

American requests for Japan to share the defense burden are often described as part of a U.S. policy to weaken Japan. Some antidefense groups believe that Americans are seeking to sell sophisticated military equipment to Japan to help balance the U.S. trade deficit.

Changing Japanese Attitudes

These Japanese characteristics might be too big an obstacle to overcome. However, some changes in defense policy and public opinion are detectable. Even if these changes are insufficient from the United States' point of view, they are a good sign for those who advocate a greater international role for Japan.

Notwithstanding the no-war clause of the constitution, Japanese attitudes toward defense have been changing quietly but drastically, especially since the Soviet invasion of Afghanistan. An average of only 23 percent favored the Self-Defense Forces (SDF) in the 1950s, but in 1980, 78 percent wished to maintain the SDF compared with only 5 percent who did not.[3]

The second encouraging factor is a marked increase in the number of Japanese who appreciate the alliance with the United States. When asked by *Asahi Shimbun* public opinion surveys "Do you think the U.S.-Japan Security Treaty is beneficial to Japan?" 55 percent of the respondents answered in the affirmative in 1981 compared with 49 percent in 1978 and 34 percent in 1974.[4]

Even if the Japanese government undertakes a military buildup within constitutional limits, however, the readiness of the public to contribute more to the security of the free world is debatable. First, the majority of Japanese want to maintain the current size of the SDF, although the proportion of those in favor of strengthening the forces has increased slightly since the Afghanistan crisis.[5] Second, most Japanese still wish to abide by the "three nonnuclear principles."[6]

The majority of the Japanese mass media remains antidefense and anti-American. Changing the orientation of the leading newspapers into a more pragmatic, less parochial one will not be easy. Sooner or later, however, the healthy attitude of Japan's new middle class will be reflected in the editorial pages of the public press.

Another evidence of progress is the Japanese government's efforts to allocate more money to defense in spite of severe budgetary pressures. The annual growth rate of the defense budget amounts to almost 7 percent even though the "zero ceiling" principle applies to other programs.

Japanese perceptions of the Soviet threat are changing. My study of the Soviets illustrates the following fundamental characteristics of their foreign policy:

1. The Soviet Union has not abandoned the concept of the need for a continuing struggle between socialism and capitalism. The Soviets

consider their politics of "peaceful coexistence" to be a just, ideological struggle against imperialism, but regard the ideological offensive led by noncommunists against communism as a return to the cold war and interference in the internal affairs of other states. Moscow, in its turn, claims the right to meddle in the internal affairs of other nations in the name of "loyalty to the socialist international." Such was the case in Czechoslovakia in 1968 and in Afghanistan in 1979.

2. The Soviet Union perceives a growing threat that it may be confronted with a new containment policy pursued by an alliance of the United States, Western Europe, Japan, and China. It is not surprising, therefore, that the USSR, seeing itself encircled by enemies in the Northern Hemisphere, should be tempted to break through this encircling ring to gain influence in the south—in Africa, the Middle East, Indochina, and Latin America—where Japanese, American, and European sources of energy and raw materials are also located.

3. The Soviet Union always tries to use military power to impose its will on other sovereign states if Moscow regards them as not strong enough to resist intimidation.[7]

These three points should be considered when a nation formulates its policy toward the Soviet Union. From a Japanese viewpoint, the Reagan administration's approach has been one-sided, emphasizing the first and third points—the expansionist character of the Soviet Union. In common with Western Europe, Japan does not always follow the United States when the latter attempts to curb trade with the Russians. Many Japanese, as well as Europeans, pay enough attention to the Soviet fear of being encircled by hostile nations to try to seduce communist rulers away from aggressive military and political policies through growing economic interchanges. In January 1982 despite U.S. pressure, France signed a 25-year contract to purchase 282.5 billion cubic feet of natural gas a year from the Soviet Union. West Germany pursued its pipeline deal with Moscow. The Americans were irritated by the gas-for-pipeline deal, which they thought would make Western Europe excessively dependent on the Russians for energy supplies and thus vulnerable to Soviet political pressure. But as West German Chancellor Helmut Schmidt replied to an American reporter: "You [the Americans] have not given us a single gallon of oil, and you can't do it, or of gas. You cannot do it. So we have to diversify. In the first instance they [the Soviets] will use it [a great profit on delivering gas] to pay for your grain. And if you sell grain by the millions of tons to the Soviet Union, they'll have to pay for it. And they will have to earn some money."[8]

Paris and Bonn believe that the economic difficulties of the Soviet Union will not allow Moscow to jeopardize the commitment to supply gas to Western Europe.

The U.S. government has also failed to convince Japan not to join in bilateral projects for gas and oil development in Sakhalin and Siberia. Many Japanese argue that economic cooperation with the Soviet Union will create a favorable atmosphere for détente, and they regard the U.S. approach as too militaristic. What most Japanese political leaders easily forget, however, is the international reality that the ultimate power in world politics is military power. It is vital for Japan to pay more attention to the Soviet military buildup. Japan also should enhance its military capabilities substantially if Tokyo wants to ask Washington to take a multifaceted approach toward the Soviet Union.

Nevertheless, Japan has been more cooperative than any other ally when asked by the United States to join in sanctions against the Soviet Union, such as boycotting the Olympic games in 1980 and banning the transfer of high technology to the communist bloc. Although the gaiatsu feeling is likely to play an important role each time Japan receives U.S. requests, the Japanese government should be encouraged to join hands with the U.S. government against Soviet expansionism.

Steady Increase in Economic Aid and Military Capabilities

Those who accuse Japan of getting a free ride often overlook the security aspects of the economic factor in national defense. Japan has devoted itself to economic achievement, but no one can deny that Japan's strong economy in itself helps undermine the expansion of Soviet influence, thus contributing to peace and security. Japan's excellent economic performance leads others to expect it to play a "locomotive" role, along with the United States and West Germany, in helping the world out of any recession. Japan should continue to be a world-leading economic power, and it should be a good example of the superiority of industrialized democracy to communism. The Ministry of International Trade and Industry has proposed "high technology–oriented nation-building," emphasizing the importance of technological innovation to solve problems such as energy and Third World development.[9]

In 1981 Japan spent $3,170 million on overseas economic assistance, one of the three elements composing Japan's "comprehensive security" policy. This figure is not small compared with the aid expenditures of other major developed countries: $5,760 million by the United States, $4,022 by France, $3,182 million by West Germany, and $2,194 million by the United Kingdom. Nevertheless, in terms of GNP percentage, Japan's figure of 0.28 is relatively small. France, West Germany, and the United Kingdom score 0.71, 0.46, and 0.43 percent respectively, whereas the U.S. figure equals 0.20 percent of GNP. Japan is committed to doubling its overseas aid level between 1979 and 1984. The efforts of the Japanese government should be encouraged, although economic assistance cannot totally replace military forces.

With regard to economic aid, significant progress has been made. Japan is now expanding foreign aid programs, particularly to countries of such strategic importance as Thailand, Pakistan, Turkey, Greece, Jamaica, the Sudan, Egypt, and the Gulf states.

Despite historical, geographic, and political conditions, most Japanese now recognize the need for closer cooperation with the West, and the Japanese government is upgrading the Self-Defense Forces. In March 1980, Japan sent two destroyers and eight antisubmarine patrol aircraft with some 700 seamen to a RIMPAC exercise with naval forces of the United States, Canada, Australia, and New Zealand. Some Japanese raised the collective security issue related to the no-war clause of the constitution, but public opposition to this multinational exercise was not as strong as expected. Japan also participated in the second RIMPAC exercise, held in 1982. Joint exercises between the SDF and U.S. forces have grown in frequency and scope each year.

Growing military cooperation between Japan and the United States has been observed in the field of joint planning. Under the "U.S.-Japan Guidelines for Defense Cooperation" adopted in 1978, U.S. and Japanese military staffs have worked together formulating specific plans not only for the defense of Japan but also for Japanese facilitative assistance to U.S. forces in meeting emergencies elsewhere in East Asia.

Japan has also increased its financial contribution to the maintenance and improvement of U.S. bases in Japan. In fiscal year 1982, Japan paid $1 billion, or half the total cost, of maintaining these facilities. In recent years, this financial support has embraced new areas such as partial assumption of local labor costs and the construction of new operational facilities. Japan should continue to increase its share of the costs for the maintenance of U.S. military facilities in Japan and the Japanese government should revise the Status of Forces Agreement[10] if it proves to be an obstacle to greater financial contributions.

The improvements mentioned have helped establish more favorable security relations with the United States, and Japan has been upgrading its military capabilities steadily and substantially, if not as rapidly as Washington expects. In July 1982, then–Prime Minister Suzuki endorsed the Defense Agency's plan to spend a total of $64 billion, including $18 billion on military hardware and equipment, under the new defense buildup program (1983–1987 Mid-Term Operations Estimate [MTOE]) being prepared for fiscal 1983–1987. The SDF will buy 75 F-15 fighters, 50 P-3 antisubmarine patrol aircraft, 373 Type-74 tanks, 43 AHIS antitank helicopters, and fourteen destroyers among other equipment. It is anticipated that the percentage of defense expenditures to GNP will certainly exceed the current ceiling of 1 percent during the 1983–1987 period, in view of slow economic growth. The 1983–1987 MTOE has the goal of reaching military force levels contained in Japan's 1976 National Defense Program Outline (NDPO). If this plan is carried out, the SDF capabilities will increase substantially. Achievement of the 1983–1987 MTOE goals will show that the free rider theory is not well founded.

Conclusions

The NDPO, approved by the Japanese government on October 19, 1976, should be revised to fit the current international situation. The 1976 NDPO was designed on the assumption that (1) détente between the United States and the Soviet Union would continue, (2) credibility of the U.S.-Japan Security Treaty would not be jeopardized, (3) Soviet expansionism would be curbed by such factors as NATO's military buildup, revolts in Eastern Europe, and a poor Soviet economic performance, (4) there would be no Sino-Soviet rapprochement, and (5) the status quo in the Korean peninsula would be maintained. Under the general atmosphere of détente, the targets set in the NDPO were to be modest. According to the 1976 NDPO, Japan is supposed to repel by itself only a "limited and small-scale aggression."

However, the international situation has changed greatly since 1976. The Soviet Union invaded Afghanistan in December 1979, and Soviet troops are still stationed there. The Polish crisis has damaged East-West relations. Washington continues sanctions against Moscow. The Soviet Union has started making friendly overtures to China. The time has come to rewrite the NDPO because some of its assumptions are no longer valid. Any defense buildup should be prepared in accordance with external environment.

The SDF should enhance their capabilities, particularly in the field of air defense and antisubmarine warfare. That would mean an increase beyond the force level set in the 1976 NDPO. According to my calculations,[11] the air force should have, for instance, 18 E-2C airborne early warning aircraft, 220 F-15 fighters, and 70 surface-to-air missiles (SAMs), and the navy should be equipped with 87 destroyers, 24 submarines, and 259 antisubmarine patrol aircraft, including 100 P-3Cs.

Japan should drastically increase its own war reserve stockpiles. The SDF cannot effectively resist even a "limited and small-scale" aggression with the ammunition and fuel they have stocked. An increase in stockpiles would contribute to the enhancement of SDF sustainability.

The geographical area included for self-defense should be greatly expanded. Even if the Japanese military posture remains strictly defensive, Japan may have to break loose from its present geographic restraints to protect its sea-lanes to overseas resources. My plan mentioned earlier for upgrading air defense and antisubmarine capabilities is based on this assumption. In May 1981, Prime Minister Suzuki promised President Reagan to defend Japan's surrounding sea space as far as west of Guam and north of Luzon. Prime Minister Nakasone repeated this promise when he met President Reagan in January 1983. These decisions may be regarded as the first step to expanding Japan's defense area.

A Potomac Associates poll shows the steady growth in American public support for the proposition that the United States should come to the defense of Japan if attacked by the Soviet Union or China—from a low of 37 percent in 1974 to 68 percent in 1980.[12] Also, Americans regard the Japanese in predominantly favorable and essentially accurate stereotypes, such as well-educated, industrialized, modern, hardworking, creative, peaceful, loyal, straightforward, competitive, disciplined. The American public seems capable of making the sometimes difficult distinction between strategic allies and economic rivals.

However, most Japanese lack confidence in Americans. An *Asahi Shimbun* public opinion survey conducted in spring 1981 reveals that only 22 percent of Japanese believe in American good will to help defend Japan, whereas as much as 59 percent have no confidence in the United States at all.[13] According to yet another recent *Asahi Shimbun* poll,[14] 61 percent of the American respondents regard U.S.-Japanese relations as good, while only 32 percent of Japanese respondents believe so. Nearly half the Japanese are afraid of deteriorating bilateral relations compared with 37 percent of Americans.

Despite growing appreciation and public support in the United States for closer alliance relations with Japan, the Japanese do not have much confidence in Americans. This accounts for the somewhat obsessive "American demands as pressure" reaction. The gaiatsu presentation by the Japanese press amplifies in its turn the public mistrust in American motivations, thus forming a vicious circle.

It is absolutely necessary to end this credibility gap between the Japanese and Americans. The Japanese press should be less emotional and use less out-of-context reporting of matters affecting U.S.-Japanese relations. The Japanese government has to resolve disputes with Washington and forge more positive, resilient ties between the two nations. On the other hand, the United States could learn and use more sophisticated ways to ask its allies to join in efforts to defend mutual interests. The Japanese (and the Europeans) cannot always follow U.S. policies, which sometimes prove inconsistent, selfish, and shortsighted.

Nevertheless the United States, Europe, and Japan share common security interests, and good relationships with one another are vital to each member of the alliance. As for U.S.-Japanese relations, which have evolved into the most important bilateral relationship in the world, the fundamental problem is a disparity between American expectations of Japan in the economic and defense areas and Japan's ability and/or willingness to meet these expectations. Both Washington and Tokyo should make every possible effort to minimize this disparity. This problem is manageable and can be worked out without disrupting basic ties uniting the two nations. Japan is now moving forward in its alliance with the United States, and a growing number of Japanese recognize the need for assuming greater international responsibilities.

Notes

1. *Asahi Shimbun*, March 25, 1981.

2. Address before a joint meeting of the Commonwealth Club and the World Affairs Council in San Francisco on April 28, 1981.

3. *Jiji Tsushin*, October 11, 1980.

4. Those who answered in the negative were 18 percent in 1974 and 13 percent in 1978 and 1981.

5. The results of *Asahi Shimbun* public opinion polls are as follows:

Attitudes Toward the SDF
(percentages)

In favor of	January 1978	January 1980	March 1981
—strengthening	19	25	22
—the current level	57	58	61
—diminishing	11	7	7
—abolishing	5	4	4
—no opinion	8	6	6

6. Japan will not manufacture nuclear weapons, will not maintain such weapons on its territory, and will not permit them to be introduced into its territory.

7. Yoichi Masuzoe, "The Soviet Perception of Security: Some Changes in Foreign Policy?" *Proceedings of the Department of Social Sciences, University of Tokyo* 30 (1980).

8. *New York Times*, February 19, 1982.

9. Japan, MITI, *The Vision of MITI Policies in the 1980s* (1980).

10. This agreement, based on Article 6 of the United States–Japan Security Treaty, prescribes the stationing of U.S. troops in Japan.

11. Policy paper by the working group on Japan's defense posture, in Japanese (Tokyo: Research Institute for Peace and Security, 1981).

12. William Watts, *Americans Look at Asia: A Need for Understanding* (Washington, D.C.: Potomac Associates, 1980).

13. *Asahi Shimbun*, March 25, 1981.

14. Ibid., April 13, 1982.

THE NATIONAL INTERESTS OF THE REPUBLIC OF KOREA

Koo Youngnok

Just like any other nation's foreign policy, the Republic of Korea's foreign policy is guided in part by fuzzy concepts known as national interests. If interests or national interests are necessary elements of a nation's foreign policy, one must assume that they are collective interests that all, or a majority of, members within a given society share. Those who argue that nations act in terms of self-interest, or interest defined in terms of power, are likely to conclude that "a wise self-interest is usually the limit of their moral achievement. The demands of self-interest and national self-protection inspire actions that appear to override all accepted moral impulses."[1]

Whether such a solid doctrine of self-interest exists and motivates Korea's foreign policy is open to question. Arnold Wolfers has aptly pointed out:

> When political formulas such as national interest gain popularity, they need to be scrutinized with particular care. They may not mean the same thing to different people. They may not have any precise meaning at all. Thus, while appearing to offer guidance and a basis for broad consensus, they may be permitting everyone to label whatever policy he favors with an attractive and possibly deceptive name.[2]

A Korean American scholar has maintained that the Korean public's main function in foreign affairs is largely "mobilizational, supportive, and demonstrative," for the public's demands and aspirations have never been an important element in foreign policy input.[3] Such characterization of the Korean foreign policy–making mechanism is perhaps only a part of the whole picture. Nonetheless, such characteristics tend to make the concept of national interests more difficult to define in Korea.

However, some of Korea's national interests are not immensely difficult either to define or classify in order to understand the direction of its policies. Most Koreans living in the South will agree that avoidance of war on the Korean peninsula, maintenance and preservation of the Korea-U.S. alliance system, preservation and enhancement of Korean values and institutions (even though they may be quasi-democratic by American standards), generation of economic prosperity, and protection of Korean nationals are the broadly based national interests of the Republic of Korea.

There are myriad problems in defining these concepts and prioritizing the interests of the ROK. Another dimension of the difficulties is in conflicting interests, exemplified in the clash of national security interests with the preservation of national institutions and values, particularly during the Yushin period.[4]

I have defined Korea's national interest as the political outcome from a struggle among various subjective views and preferences. Nevertheless, there seems a broad consensus regarding the short-term goals of the ROK. President Chun Doo Hwan has defined "the interlocking goals of the Korean people" as "national security, economic well-being, and political development [which] have to be pursued simultaneously and vigorously."[5] As a medium- or long-range goal, national unification is one of the most important interests of South Korea, for this goal has been the long-standing desire of all Koreans.[6] While South Korea's long-term regional and global interests have never been clearly defined or articulated for foreign policy purposes, the cumulative contacts, experiences, and transactions with nations in the region and abroad tend to define South Korea's far-reaching regional and global interests (explained later in this paper).

In terms of policy priorities, the interests of the ROK may be formulated and classified in a hierarchy of national security, economic development, political development, national unification, regional interests, and global interests. Let us examine South Korea's six major short- and long-term interests and policies.

National Security

Unlike most other countries since World War II, the Republic of Korea has had a rather difficult and precarious existence. Divided Korea, with two diametrically opposed political ideologies on the peninsula, each vying for control of the other, has had a profound effect on both sides. The war exacted a very heavy toll on the Korean people as well as on the United States and other allies. The quasi-state of war on the peninsula is symbolic of the bitter competition for survival between the divided halves of Korea. There is no disputing the importance of South Korea's national security to the nation's survival; it has always headed the list of national priorities. Every other goal or interest depends on achieving this objective.

The Republic of Korea's security is aggravated by North Korea's armed provocations, espionage infiltrations and activities, and attempts at guerrilla subversive activity. Much of South Korea's sense of insecurity is also due to the vacillations in U.S. policies toward Korea.

Among events that tended to reinforce South Korea's insecurity was the collapse of South Vietnam in 1975. To most South Koreans, rightly or wrongly, the Vietnam debacle meant that once U.S. forces left, the American people would be reluctant to support South Korea in case of war, regardless of the consequences.[7] In some respects, this reasoning was a natural outcome of the United States' Vietnam experience.[8]

Carter's reversal of the U.S. troop withdrawal, confirmed during his official visit to Seoul in June 1979, and President Reagan's revitalization of the containment of the Soviet Union and his declaration of U.S. defense capabilities against communist nations was, for Koreans, a welcome relief from fears of a total troop withdrawal. Nonetheless, South Korean confidence in the U.S. protector was badly shaken, as manifested in the last days of President Park Chunghee in its resolve to build a self-reliant defense, foreign policy, and defense industry infrastructure.

The diminished credibility of the United States was partly responsible for the tightening and regimentation of the Korean political system. The Yushin system was mainly based on the rationalization that in a life-or-death struggle with North Korea, the South would be ill-prepared to survive were it not regimented and highly mobilized. Ultimately, South Korea realized that it must be completely self-dependent. Thus, augmentation of power at the sacrifice of all other values became a dominant theme for Korea during the Park regime. Perhaps a similar sentiment was expressed by President Chun Doo Hwan when he said that "only powerful nations have been able to take the initiative in shaping the course of history and thus have enjoyed prosperity. Conversely, weak nations have been swept onto the backstage of history, or have disappeared altogether like bubbles on a stream."[9] To South Koreans, the issue of security became not just an important goal of national policy, but an obsession.

Economic Development

In spite of many deserved criticisms, it is difficult to deny President Park's accomplishments in the field of economic development. He was acutely aware of the backwardness of the Korean economy and its effect on South Korea's national security. To Park, the only way for an independent Korea to survive was to industrialize rapidly so as to build a strong foundation for national defense, disregarding at times other important values such as human rights and peaceful transfer of power. His preoccupation with economic development strategy was more a matter of faith than a rational goal.

Prior to Park, the South Korean economy was characterized as underdeveloped: a stagnant economy and a high inflation rate. Per capita income of South Koreans was less than $100, and the government was dependent on foreign aid. The determined Park government laid the basis for industrial development during the critical years 1962–1978, as evidenced by the annual growth rate of 9.4 percent. South Korea's exports registered an annual increase of 40.2 percent, and industrial production increased by approximately 20 percent per year. Trade and international economic cooperation played a major role in South Korea's economic development.[10]

A large share of the credit for Korea's phenomenal economic development belongs to the United States. The aggregate amount of $4.4 billion in U.S. economic aid to the ROK laid the basic foundation of Korea's early period of industrial development. A survey of South Korea's economic growth shows how high a priority Koreans place on economic development. South Korea's gross national product jumped from $2.4 billion in 1966[11] to $65.9 billion in 1982, and per capita income rose from a mere $95 per year to $1,678 during the same period.[12]

To sustain economic growth, the Republic of Korea's fifth economic and social development plan was unveiled in August 1981. President Chun termed it Korea's "second take-off." By 1988 South Korean per capita income is to exceed $2,000, and the GNP will rise to $90 billion.[13] As South Korea's national defense and political stability hinge largely on economic development and stability, the government's emphasis on economic development is understandable. Presently, the ROK allocates 6 percent of the nation's GNP and 37 percent of the national budget to the defense establishment.[14] National survival is clearly linked to political stability and is regarded as essential to achieving other goals.

Political Development

Fostering a noncommunist nation and laying the foundation for a democratic government in Korea was one of the most important interests and goals of the U.S. government following World War II.[15] The creation of a separate government in South Korea under United Nations' auspices and the subsequent election of Syngman Rhee as the first president of the Republic of Korea in 1948 laid the foundation for a democratic nation. The new nation, however, faced insurmountable domestic problems as a democratic political process attempted to take root. Faint hope and expectation were shattered rudely by the Korean War. Wartime mobilization, the use of extraconstitutional power by the chief executive, and the consequent domestic political turmoil provided the regime with ample opportunity to consolidate its power. Rhee's abuse of power to subdue his opposition brought about a rigid polarization of Korean politics that is akin to the zero-sum game model.

Since the founding of the republic, establishment of a stable and democratic government has been one of the most desired goals of the Korean people. The attainment of security and economic development were so clearly interrelated to the achievement of domestic political stability that one without the other could hardly provide for the well-being of Korea. Nonetheless, a vicious cycle of political instability became a dominant characteristic of Korean politics. Rhee's constitutional amendments of 1952 and 1954 were designed to ensure his re-election. Park's constitutional amendments of 1969 allowed him to seek a third term in 1971. The Yushin Constitution of 1972, among other things, allowed the incumbent president an indefinite term of office and almost unlimited executive decisionmaking powers and made the election process indirect. In all cases the rationale for amending the constitution has been similar: either the pretext of national security or economic development or both. The regimes have resorted to threats and intimidation in attempts to keep dissenters in line. Whether the polarizing tendency of the South Korean political process is responsible for such constitutional revisions or the coercive constitutional amendments are responsible for the faction-ridden political process is not easy to answer. It is sufficient to say that both factors contributed immensely to political instability and became major obstacles to Korea's goal for political development—a stable, democratic form of government.

In a message upon the promulgation of the new constitution on October 27, 1980, President Chun stated:

> We have failed to achieve a peaceful change of government by a free choice of the people, even though this should be the touchstone of a democratic constitution. Instead, we have witnessed repeated arbitrary revisions of the constitution designed to permit the chief executive to hold on to power for a prolonged period, thereby virtually precluding a peaceful change of government.[16]

To prevent the recurrence of another constitutional revision to prolong the tenure of the incumbent president, an important innovation was incorporated in the new constitution: one seven-year term for the president and the prohibition of any constitutional amendment altering the term of the president while in office. The positive contribution of such a crucial variable in the Korean political process cannot be underestimated, though appraising the contribution such a factor will make toward Korea's political stability will require many years of critical monitoring. In the Republic of Korea, maintenance of a stable democratic political order is as important as issues of national defense and economic development. Neither national defense nor economic development can be achieved without a sound, workable system of government.

National Unification

Major surveys conducted by both private and governmental sources reported that a large majority of the population in the South identified the goal of unification as being "the supreme national goal."[17] As important as the issue of unification may be, it cannot be placed above interests that address the question of national survival, for there can be no unification of a divided political entity unless the South wishes to be absorbed by the communist North. Certainly most people in the South do not wish to be unified under communism. Therefore the goal of unification, as one of the ROK's national interests, cannot precede the security of the nation.

The Korean dialogues began and stalemated in the early 1970s. They were an interesting yet sad reflection of a divided nation unable to reach meaningful agreement. The Red Cross and the South-North Coordinating Committee talks proved that the diametrically opposed regimes on the Korean peninsula are miles apart in their thought patterns and motives for contacts and transactions. Under no circumstances can peaceful unification of divided Korea come about without mutual confidence gained through the reorientation of motives and methods of resolution of the Korean states.

To revive the discontinued dialogues, President Chun proposed in his 1981 New Year's Policy Statement that President Kim Il-sung, of North Korea, come "to visit Seoul without any condition attached and free of any obligation on his part."[18] Chun also stated that he is prepared to visit North Korea or any other place designated by President Kim. Many other attempts to revive the deadlocked talks have failed to solicit a positive response from the North Korean regime. Such efforts are not likely to pave the way for the resumption of dialogues in the immediate future.

The Republic of Korea has pursued two different but not necessarily opposed policies for the future of Korea: pursuing internally a policy of strengthening national defense capabilities, rapid economic development, and political stability while externally pursuing a policy of regional and global recognition and cooperation. The government of the ROK will continue to initiate proposals to resume dialogue, hoping that North Korea may respond to such initiatives. The assumption underlying this unification policy is that when the ROK is strong militarily, economically, and politically and is able alone to withstand any North Korean aggression, the North Koreans will realize that it is not in their interests to be aggressive or pursue a confrontational strategy. Then and only then are they likely to talk about the mutual problems of a divided Korea. Although this assumption may be wrong, there is no other option, for South Korea cannot afford the illusion of an easy approach to national unification, neglecting other priorities and values.

Regional Interests

Because of the ROK's limited resources and power, little attention was paid to regional cooperation in the 1950s. Perhaps much of South Korea's indifference to regional cooperation was due to the reconstruction of the war-torn country following the Korean War. The first visible interest in regionalism was its sponsorship of the First Ministerial Meeting for Asian and Pacific Cooperation (ASPAC) in Seoul in 1966.[19] The genesis of ASPAC and the main motives for such a cooperative enterprise were military, economic, and cultural cooperation among the member-nations. South Korea's original interest was to form a regional collective defense system against communist powers in the region, even though such cooperation was difficult to achieve from the beginning.

The internal diversity of views on the purpose of regional cooperation made it difficult to develop a viable regional organization. Japan, Malaysia, and other members were not interested in, and indeed were opposed to, any regional alliance system.[20] The ROK's readjusted position and subsequent regional developments made it difficult for ASPAC to function as a regional organization. ASPAC was practically defunct from the early 1970s. Regardless of ASPAC's fate as a regional organization, the Republic of Korea was interested in regionalism, though the idea was not timely.

President Chun's interest in regional cooperation was highlighted in June 1981 when he made official visits to Indonesia, Thailand, Singapore, Malaysia, and the Philippines. He visited Australia in November. Moreover, his proposal for a Pacific summit, to discuss important matters of mutual concern and mutual cooperation in the region, reinforces South Korea's long-established interest in regionalism. President Chun's proposal is clearly oriented toward economic development of the region.[21]

The Republic of Korea's motives for promoting regional cooperation may be complex. South Korea's past interest in regionalism and its growing economic and diplomatic interdependence make it inevitable that its national interest can best be served through active regional cooperation. The web of regional interdependence can offer a sense of security in the area, enhancing Korea's image abroad. Perhaps equally important, through pooling of resources, technology, and capital, all member-nations are likely to benefit. The ROK's interest is congruent with the interest of all nations in the Pacific Basin—an active promoter of regional cooperation.

Global Interests

The Republic of Korea's interests have become global as the nation expanded its diplomatic networks and economic relations. Over a hundred nations maintain diplomatic, consular, or other relations with the ROK. Over a million South Korean technicians, construction workers, fishermen, doctors, and others have worked abroad in the past twenty years. At its peak, construction alone was significant in creating an image of South Koreans as global workers: 98 construction companies operated in 34 countries. Much of the foreign currency earnings from Korea's global commitments support the nation's foreign exchange and domestic industrial infrastructure. Without such earnings, Korea's internal economic development and its defense establishment would suffer severely.

In addition, Korea's foreign trade constitutes almost 70 percent of its GNP. The rise in oil prices in the Middle East affected Korea in two ways: while the situation seemed likely to benefit Korea's exports and construction projects in that region, the impact on the domestic economy was largely negative, and exports to other regions suffered.

Even in national defense, the "swing strategy of American military doctrine would have had a significant impact and consequences had such a policy been implemented in a crises situation in Western South Asia or in the Middle East, for it would have meant a sudden removal of some U.S. troops in Korea to the crisis area. The change of policy by the United States was hailed as a major contribution to the stability of Korea and Northeast Asia."[22] Obviously, a stable and prosperous world is essential to the Republic of Korea.

Dilemma of Conflicting Interests

One of Korea's interests, not specifically outlined in this paper, is perhaps political and economic independence. The issue of political independence relates to the achievement of other important goals. Independence in a world of interdependence seems to cause conflict among important national interests, though South Korea's pursuit of independence is essential to the stability of its political system. South Korea's need for independence is highlighted and aggravated by North Korea's political philosophy of *juche*: "an independent stand, discarding dependence on others, displaying the spirit of self-reliance and solving one's own affairs and one's own responsibility under all circumstances."[23] In essence, juche is an ideology of independence and self-reliance in the pursuit of important national interests such as politics, national defense, and the economy. Preservation of national integrity is important in itself if it does not lead to autarky and political isolation in a world of interdependence. North Korean performance in economic and diplomatic endeavors has not been successful, as manifested in its inability to pay its foreign debts and its unsuccessful attempts to prevent the 1983 Interparliamentary Union Conference meeting in Seoul. North Korea's foreign borrowings signifies that the idea of juche is a goal that cannot be realized. This applies also to its national defense, as North Korea has a treaty with the People's Republic of China and depends heavily on China and the Soviet Union for weapons.

The Republic of Korea's heavy dependence on the United States seemed to have resolved many problems, even though such a relationship creates difficulties both at home and abroad. The emergence of nationalist sentiments in the ROK has complicated its dependence on the United States. Although the U.S. forces in South Korea are a vital part of its national defense, they can also be a cause for domestic political agitation. Psychological dependence can be a hindrance to the mental growth of citizens of a sovereign nation. Loans and investments from the United States and Japan can stimulate the South Korean economy as well as be causes of political instability. The ROK is the world's fourth largest debtor, with foreign loans of $40 billion. Only Brazil, Mexico, and Argentina have greater indebtedness. This a record of which no Korean is proud. Foreign investment amounts to slightly over $1.2 billion. Japan's share is over $640 million; the United States' less than half that.[24] Regardless of its dependency, the nation has little choice but to pursue this pattern, for no combination of political independence and autarky is likely to resolve South Korea's defense and economic problems.

Political independence is a long-sought goal of the ROK. Heavy security and economic dependence inevitably invited U.S. interference in the internal affairs of the ROK, especially during the regimes of Syngman Rhee (1948–1960) and Park Chunghee (1963–1980). The forced constitutional amendments and repressive measures practiced by those regimes while in power can hardly be defended under any ground rules of democratic politics. Well-deserved condemnations, protests, and sanctions came from allies and friends abroad. Meddling in the internal affairs of the republic has often been counterproductive and has inflicted enormous damage to Korean pride. There are good reasons for South Korean demands on the United States that mutual relations be based upon symmetrical relations rather than the asymmetrical relationship of the past. However, no nation's relations are equal in a world of power politics, and as long as dependent relations continue, such desires are not easily fulfilled. Mindful of this dilemma, the United States must make a sincere effort to correct any such imbalances in Korean-American relations. The achievement of major political, defensive, and economic independence is a national interest of the ROK, a high-priority item in the hierarchy of interests. South Koreans should also recall that no nation can truly be independent in the age of interdependency; the reality of international politics is not always in harmony with the ideal of independence.

Another area of conflicting national goals may be in national defense and political development. South Korea's preoccupation with national defense has clearly undermined the building of democratic institutions. Two opposing views co-opted the realm of national defense and political development. The government has always assumed that national defense and political stability take priority over democratic institutions and practices. Both the Rhee and Park regimes seemingly operated under that assumption. Internal political stability is clearly related to national power and defense, as it is an essential ingredient of national power. The political opposition viewed the situation differently—that is, defense against the communist North should begin with the practice of democracy at home. The purpose for which the Republic of Korea stands against North Korea is negated if the South is just another repressive regime. These two views were rationales for fierce power struggles in Korea during the past three decades. When such a power struggle resembles a zero-sum game, it is difficult to strike a delicate balance between the two extremes. The present regime's major task is to institute innovative systems and procedures to moderate the two extremes. Such an undertaking, if it is to be successful, will probably take a long time.

Another conflict of interest among national goals may be national defense and economic development. The ROK devotes a large portion of its

GNP to support the national defense establishment. Such a large investment channeled into national defense can be burdensome, for these resources could be diverted to the accelerated economic development of the nation. To Korea's economic development, a little added investment in the industrial sector would probably make a very crucial difference over the long term, and the rising living standard will undoubtedly contribute to the stability of the political system. Fortunately, South Koreans support national defense expenditures with equanimity. There is virtually no dissent on this point.

Evolving Policies

One important disadvantage of being a close ally of the United States has been in dealing with communist or with nonaligned nations. South Korea's growing economic power and its aggressive but faithful working relationship with nations in the Middle East and Africa have, in some instances, helped in dealing with the problem of identification with the United States. In Libya, South Korean–run construction projects and sales of merchandise probably contributed to the opening of diplomatic relations with that country in 1980. In Iraq, South Korea maintains a consulate general. Even with only limited diplomatic representation, the Republic of Korea has substantial business transactions with Iraq. Regarding "nonhostile communist countries," the ROK's efforts to develop quasi-diplomatic relations as well as full diplomatic relations will probably pay off. The Soviet Union has already responded cautiously by allowing a limited number of South Koreans, including one cabinet member, to attend various international conferences on Soviet soil. North Korea's pressure and protests seemed to constrain Soviet behavior, however. Vying for influence over North Korea has been a competitive game between the Soviet Union and China. Such wooing of North Korea by both powers has adversely affected South Korea's efforts to deal with either of the communist superpowers.

The ROK has undertaken the expansion of its world horizons by sponsoring major international events: the planned meeting of the Interparliamentary Union, the Asian Games in 1986, and the Olympics in 1988, for example. It is expected that these meetings will bring official representatives from many nonaligned and communist countries. Hosting these important international events may be considered symbolic of the Republic of Korea's efforts to elevate its international standing. Lee Bum Suk, minister of foreign affairs, stated in a speech entitled "Foreign Policy Objectives in Advanced Korea" that developing and maintaining friendly relations with North Korea's allies—China and the Soviet Union—is one of the most important elements in maintaining a durable peace on the Korean peninsula. He contended that "the progress of our northward policy may provide a turning point for the normalization of relations between South and North Korea."[25] South Korea's deep desire to live in peace with its communist neighbor was clearly demonstrated in its VIP reception of passengers aboard a hijacked Chinese airplane in early May 1983. The emotional reception and attendant hospitality shown by the Korean government were criticized even by some well-meaning Koreans. That the Chinese agreed to use the country's official name, the Republic of Korea, in the agreement for the release of passengers also excited many South Koreans.[26] Some Korean and foreign observers speculated that the meticulous handling of the incident by the South Korean government would pave the way for unofficial contact with China. Such a hope was cruelly shattered when the Chinese government refused to issue visas allowing South Korean representatives to attend the meetings of United Nations–sponsored specialized organizations on Chinese soil.[27]

Although the ROK considers cross-recognition of both North and South Korea by major Western powers and communist countries a means of easing tension and restraining North Korea's behavior toward the South, North Korea and its allies have resisted such a policy.[28] The Republic of Korea, in principle, accepts cross-recognition, but chances for realizing such a policy are remote. South Korea's *Nordpolitik* reflects its determination to seek and realize such a goal. That does not mean that it will pursue such a policy at the risk of sacrificing its primary national interests.

The ROK has expressed reservations about the U.S. policy encouraging American diplomats abroad to engage in conversation with North Koreans whenever contact is initiated by the other side. The "smile strategy" of the U.S. State Department is based upon the logic that natural and frequent contact between the two countries' diplomats will contribute to improved relations between them and ease tensions on the Korean peninsula, perhaps leading to eventual cross-recognition of the two Koreas. The ROK's reservations to the strategy are based on the assumption that such gestures might be misunderstood by North Korea and make it more recalcitrant in dealing with the South.

In any case, the ROK is opposed to this policy and that of the blanket issuance of visas to North Korean scholars attending professional conferences.[29] Similar concerns were also expressed over Japan's alleged moves to expand contacts and trade transactions with North Korea, particularly the Japanese government's affirmative reaction to a private group's attempt to set up a North Korean trade office in Tokyo.[30] In line with the hardening of policy toward North Korea, the ROK successfully opposed North Korea's admission to the IMO in May 1983 and is reviewing the June 23, 1973, Declaration of Peace and Unification, which contains seven principles of foreign policy. Noteworthy is a report that the fourth principle, outlining South Korea's willingness to tolerate North Korea's participation in international organizations "if it is conducive to the easing of tension and the furtherance of international cooperation," is being revised or changed. The record of the past ten years is negative on this point as far as the relations between the two Koreas are concerned.[31] The policy should not be construed as South Korea's long-term policy, for the republic has been reasonably flexible in its policy vis-à-vis other nations if persuaded to change its stand for reasons beneficial to national interests. This policy is not necessarily a retrogression but a reflection of the state of tension on the Korean peninsula.

The Republic of Korea's national interests, in order of priority, are national security, economic well-being, political stability, reunification, regional interests, and global interests. Political and economic independence may also be included. Basically, the issues of independence are in the realm of political decisionmaking and will. In an interdependent world, the Republic of Korea is constrained by many factors of national security and economic development that preclude a narrow concept of political and economic dependence. The structure of South Korea's security system and economic development is so deeply ingrained in its relations with others that any abrupt move toward an ethnocentric goal may jeopardize the patterns of development and disrupt the nation's security system. However, at some stage in Korea's political and economic development, such a goal is likely to emerge as a dominant political and diplomatic issue and will command the highest priority.

A major task of political decisionmakers in Korea is to balance different national goals that, by necessity, are long-term without sacrificing urgent issues such as national security and political and economic development. Balancing these goals is difficult, but very important. Pursuing lopsided goals, at the risk of neglecting other equally important goals, might distort the personality and characteristics of the political community and the structure of government. No single goal, no matter how just, can be pursued over a long period to the exclusion of others. Pursuit of any one goal is associated with emergency thinking, which can lead to exhaustion or the limits of the people's toleration. I do not imply that the Republic of Korea fits the above category. If at all, the latter part of the Yushin period was a case in point. Concurrently, there is a visible effort to correct such imbalances in goal seeking, though progress has been slow. Recognition of a linkage between the different interests of the Republic of Korea is an important assignment for Korea's leaders.

Notes

1. Kenneth W. Thompson, *Understanding World Politics* (South Bend, Ind.: University of Notre Dame Press, 1975), p. 143.

2. Arnold Wolfers, "National Security as an Ambiguous Symbol," *Political Science Quarterly*, December 1952, p. 481.

3. Chae-Jin Lee, "The Direction of South Korea's Foreign Policy," *Korean Studies* 2 (1978): 103.

4. Charles B. Marshall, "The National Interest," in Robert A. Goldwin et al., eds., *Readings in American Foreign Policy* (New York: Oxford University Press, 1959), pp. 665–66.

5. *Selected Speeches of President Chun Doo Hwan* (Seoul: Korea Textbook Co., 1981), p. 115.

6. Ibid.

7. Koo Youngnok, "Reflections on the Future of Korean-American Relations," *Korean Journal of International Studies*, Spring 1983, p. 137; and "Future Perspectives on South Korea's Foreign Relations," *Asian Survey*, November 1980, p. 1157.

8. Ralph N. Clough, *Deterrence and Defense in Korea* (Washington, D.C.: Brookings Institution, 1976), pp. 23–24.

9. *Selected Speeches of President Chun Doo Hwan*, p. 164.

10. Sang-Chul Suh, "South Korea's International Economic Relations," *Asian Survey*, November 1980, p. 1140. See also Jungsae Kim, "Recent Trends in the Government's Management of the Economy," in Edward Reynolds Wright, ed., *Korean Politics in Transition* (Seattle: University of Washington Press, 1975), pp. 225–79.

11. Bank of Korea, *Economic Progress in Korea* (Seoul, 1972), p. 2.

12. *Yonhap Annual, 1982* (Seoul: Yonhap News Agency, 1981), p. 280.

13. *Selected Speeches of President Chun Doo Hwan*, p. 280.

14. Ibid., p. 113. The original projections have been adjusted downward to less ambitious goals. It has been announced that a complete revision of the original plan will be unveiled in November 1983 (*Dong-A Ilbo*, July 13, 1983).

15. Nathan N. White, *U.S. Policy Toward Korea* (Boulder, Colo.: Westview Press, 1979), p. 29.

16. *Selected Speeches of President Chun Doo Hwan*, p. 42.

17. *Dong-A Ilbo*, April 20, 1970.

18. *Selected Speeches of President Chun Doo Hwan*, p. 20. For North Korea's reaction, see Claude A. Buss, *The United States and the Republic of Korea: Background for Policy* (Stanford: Hoover Institution Press, 1982), p. 161.

19. Member-nations were Australia, China, Japan, Korea, Malaysia, New Zealand, the Philippines, Thailand, Vietnam, and an observer from Laos (cf. Tong-

Won Lee, "ASPAC: A Dynamic for Regional Cooperation," *Korean Quarterly*, Winter 1968–69, pp. 359–67).

20. Koo Youngnok, "The Conduct of Foreign Affairs," in Wright, *Korean Politics in Transition*, p. 231.

21. Soo Yong Auh, "Toward Pan-Pacific Cooperation: A Korean View" (Paper presented at the Thirteenth International Conference of the Korean Institute of International Studies on "Regional Cooperation Among the Asian Pacific Nations: Joint Prosperity in the Year 2000," Seoul, Korea, July 5–9, 1983), p. 6.

22. *Dong-A Ilbo*, June 15, 1983.

23. Kim Il-sung, *Revolution and Socialist Construction in Korea* (New York, 1971), p. 87, as quoted in Edward A. Olsen, "The Implications of Resource Scarcity on the Korean Peninsula," *Korea Observer*, Winter 1981, p. 401.

24. Cf. Koo Youngnok, "Reflections on the Future of Korean-American Relations," p. 142.

25. *Korean Times*, June 30, 1983.

26. *Chosen Ilbo*, May 6–11, 1983.

27. Ibid., July 13, 1983.

28. *Dong-A Ilbo*, April 13, 1983.

29. Ibid., February 26, 1983.

30. *Hankook Ilbo*, July 12, 1983.

31. *Dong-A Ilbo*, June 30, 1983.

THE REPUBLIC OF KOREA AND THE MAJOR POWERS

Han Sung-Joo

The Republic of Korea perceives an ever-present danger of a military provocation by North Korea. The South Korean sense of threat to its security is the result of North Korea's heavy military buildup, offensive strategic dispositions, militarization of the society, militant and aggressive rhetoric, and adamant refusal to accept accommodation with South Korea.

The degree and nature of North Korea's threat to the South, in turn, are affected by the relations among the major powers and between those powers and the two Koreas. This paper will examine South Korean security interests in light of the policies and roles of the major powers in East Asia.[1]

The United States

From the South Korean view, U.S.-ROK relations have been satisfactory since President Reagan took office in 1981. Korean officials particularly appreciate the cordial relationship after many years of considerable difficulty and strain. They feel that on most important issues, particularly those concerning security, the two countries are in agreement.

There are many signs of the new cordiality. High-level security consultations are held frequently. At every opportunity, U.S. officials express strong support for the ROK government on issues involving South Korean security and inter-Korea relations. Early in February 1983, Secretary of State George Shultz made a well-publicized visit to Korea that seemed to satisfy both sides. In February and March, Korean and U.S. forces conducted Team Spirit '83, a 45-day joint military exercise in which 118,000

Korean and 73,000 American soldiers and more than 30 naval vessels, including the aircraft carriers *Enterprise* and *Midway,* participated. For fiscal year 1984, the Reagan administration earmarked more funds ($323 million) for the Korean military aid program than in previous years. Finally, President Reagan's visit to Korea in November 1983 reaffirmed U.S. support and commitment to the ROK.

Relations between the United States and South Korea passed through three different phases during the Carter administration. Its initial two years, the relationship between the two countries sank to a nadir. President Carter announced his troop withdrawal plan, the U.S. investigation of the Korean lobbying scandal was conducted in full view, and the administration was openly critical of South Korea on the human rights issue.[2]

During the second phase, which lasted until the death of President Park Chunghee in October 1979, the Koreagate investigation ended, and President Carter reversed his troop withdrawal decision. Relations improved as the United States moved closer to the South Korean views of the North Korean military threat and the strategic importance to the United States of the Korean peninsula. Washington seemed to conclude that it was better to work with the South Korean government (which may be imperfect by U.S. political standards) than to jeopardize its solvency and effectiveness and seriously risk the country's political, economic, and social stability as well as its security. President Carter's eventual, if reluctant, acceptance of the Park government was demonstrated by his visit to Korea in summer 1979.

The third phase of the Carter administration's Korean policy began with the death of President Park in October 1979. In the immediate post-Park stretch, the United States was intent on facilitating a smooth transition to stable and competitive politics. However, the inflated expectations of a full-fledged democracy gave way to massive student demonstrations, social instability, and subsequent tightening of controls with the declaration of martial law in May 1980. The Carter administration initially disapproved what it considered to be retrogression in and postponement of democratization, then reconciled itself to accept what appeared to be an inevitable development. By the end of the Carter presidency, the South Korean government felt comfortable enough with the U.S. administration that its leaders were not excessively worried about a possible Carter victory in the November 1980 presidential elections.

However, the main strain between the two countries, which persisted to the end of the Carter administration, was what the South Korean government considered unwarranted interference in Korea's internal affairs. The Carter administration tried to promote human rights and democracy, but did not consider the limited U.S. leverage in the Korean domestic political process. Thus its human rights policy applied to Korea had mixed consequences, at best. It achieved little more than consciousness raising, but succeeded in offending the Park government.[3]

President Reagan took full advantage of his predecessor's difficulties in dealing with the Korean question. By inviting President Chun to Washington, President Reagan accomplished what Carter could not secure with protests and warnings. Reagan gave the Korean government assurance of support and thus a greater degree of self-confidence and sense of autonomy. He succeeded in making the South Korean government more flexible and accommodating. Further, in one bold stroke Reagan put the world on notice that his administration intended to practice what he had been preaching— placing security and loyalty ahead of other considerations.

President Reagan's basic strategic objective in Asia was to end what he considered a decade of retreat and vacillation by the United States. To "check Soviet expansionism in the region and restore American leadership," he hoped to build a loose grouping of friendly powers, with Korea an important element in the scheme. He made no secret that the U.S. military posture in Asia in general, and in Korea in particular, would be strengthened rather than weakened and that the United States would not be niggardly in supporting a Korean force improvement program. President Reagan and his aides showed great concern about the Soviet military buildup and the security threat it presented in the area. They appeared to recognize the Korean peninsula as an area of intrinsic strategic value rather than as an outpost for the defense of Japan—an impression often conveyed by previous U.S. administrations.

The Reagan-Chun meeting produced a joint communiqué in which President Reagan unequivocally averred that "the United States has no plans to withdraw U.S. ground combat forces from the Korean peninsula" and confirmed that it would "make available for sale to Korea appropriate weapons systems and defense industry technology necessary for enhancing Korea's capabilities to deter aggression."[4] The Reagan policy concerning arms sales to Korea was obviously intended to inform North Korea and the Soviet Union of the firm U.S. commitment to South Korean security and to demonstrate its faith and support for the government. It was also intended to pressure Japan to do more for regional defense. Needless to say, South Korea is satisfied with the Reagan security policy. Korea is persuaded that the United States no longer judges its security interests in Korea through the "Japanese prism," as sometimes seemed to be the case.

Strengthened ties with the United States have also had a significant bearing on Korean relationships with other countries. They have enabled Korea to take a firmer stance vis-à-vis Japan concerning economic cooperation and security issues. South Korea has also paid greater diplomatic attention to countries other than the United States. President Chun's trips to Southeast Asia in 1981 and to Africa and Canada in 1982 can be understood in this light.

Although the Reagan administration has shown an unequivocal attitude toward North Korea and on inter-Korea relations, the South Korean government is sensitive to the possibility that the United States might establish a direct and official relationship with North Korea, against South Korean wishes. Soon after taking office, the Reagan administration disassociated itself from the Carter proposal of June 1979 (reluctantly approved by President Park) for a tripartite conference involving the United States and the two Koreas. The Reagan administration insisted that any relationship with North Korea must be based on symmetrical actions taken by the communist powers (PRC and/or the Soviet Union) toward the South.

The United States has also supported President Chun's proposal for a personal meeting between the South and North Korean leaders and other proposals advanced by South Korea. Furthermore, top U.S. officials (in many cases military officers) have called attention to the heavy North Korean military buildup in recent years and emphasized the seriousness of the North Korean military threat to South Korea.

Nevertheless the South Korean government is uneasy when the number of U.S. visitors to North Korea increases or when North Koreans are allowed to visit the United States. Recently South Korea has shown concern over the reported possibility that North Korean scholars might visit the United States to attend academic meetings. It was also sensitive to a new report that American diplomats had been instructed to seek contacts with their North Korean counterparts. While South Korean diplomats themselves probably had similar instructions, the ROK government was concerned that it might mean a new concession to North Korea by the United States.

Clearly, South Korea is mainly interested in preventing the erosion of a bargaining position that the United States and the South Korean government have maintained so far against North Korea and its principal allies, the PRC and the Soviet Union. South Korea insists on reciprocity and symmetry in major power relations with the two Koreas. Thus, it supports a "cross-recognition" formula under which the United States and Japan would establish an official relationship with North Korea while the Soviet Union and the PRC would do the same with South Korea. Such a policy is designed to give notice to the communist powers that Seoul would welcome the opportunity to establish official relations. At the same time, South Korea hopes to discourage the United States and Japan from unilaterally making official contact with North Korea without reciprocal actions taken by its communist allies.[5]

Japan

South Korea is sensitive to any indication that Japan does not appreciate the importance of the Korean peninsula to its security or that Japanese leaders are unwilling to admit its importance. The following statement, found in the 1982 Japanese *Defense White Paper,* is as far as Japan would go in recognizing Korea's strategic importance to Japan: "The maintenance of peace and security on the Korean Peninsula is very important for peace and stability of the entire region of East Asia, including Japan."[6] The ROK was also disappointed with Japan's failure to oppose publicly President Carter's plan to withdraw U.S. ground troops from Korea in early 1977.

The South Korean government is also dissatisfied with the occasional statements made by top Japanese officials discounting what South Korea considers the serious security threat presented by North Korea. It contends that in view of Japan's security linkage with South Korea, Japan should expand its economic cooperation with Korea and facilitate consultations on security and other issues among the United States, Japan, and Korea. The South Korean government finds the Nakasone cabinet much more agreeable than the previous ones.

Of potential concern to South Korea is U.S. pressure on Japan to increase its defense spending and assume a greater regional security role. The Reagan administration, unlike its predecessor, is unequivocal about its desire to see Japan expand its military capabilities within existing political and economic constraints. There is a widely held perception, probably justified, that close security cooperation between the United States and Japan cannot be maintained unless Japan engages in a rather large-scale military buildup.

There is no guarantee that it would be easier for a rearmed (or rearming) Japan to maintain its alliance with the United States. Increasing Japan's military capability and confidence, particularly if accompanied by a sense of diminishing U.S. power and credibility, may result in greater assertiveness by the Japanese and increased tension between them and their American allies. Moreover, there are many—both in and outside Japan—who are concerned that once the current lid on military spending is lifted, Japan may become a military power.

A Japanese military buildup will almost certainly cause a Soviet reaction that would accelerate the arms race and increase tension in the area. The Soviet Union may be tempted to create a local crisis to test Japanese will and strength, creating an opportunity to weaken, destroy, or otherwise pre-empt Japan's military capabilities. But the most serious security threat to other Asian countries from an accelerated Japanese military buildup is the possibility that, either from confidence in Japanese military capability or from friction with a rearmed Japan, the United States may choose to reduce or end its military presence in the region.

Should the United States withdraw its security umbrella from Japan because of growing dissension between the two countries, a rearmed Japan would be extremely vulnerable to a pre-emptive Soviet attack or nuclear blackmail. In such circumstances, countries near Japan, particularly South Korea, would be subjected to multiple threats.

South Korea is not in a position to express these concerns, at least officially. The ROK considers the Soviet military threat to be real, and it cannot oppose an arms buildup aimed at counterbalancing Soviet military capabilities. The United States, South Korea's principal ally and defender, is insistent upon Japan's military buildup and its assuming a greater regional security role. Greater Japanese security consciousness of the Soviet Union and its allies (including North Korea) would be helpful in promoting South Korea's security against a North Korean military threat.

In any event, the Republic of Korea can only insist that the Japanese arms buildup program be carried out within the context of the U.S.-Japan alliance and mutual coordination; that the United States should not reduce its military presence or security commitment even when Japan strengthens its military capabilities and expands its regional security role; that the Republic of Korea should be included in the consultation, planning, and implementation of a stronger regional security posture in Northeast Asia; and that Japan should expand its economic cooperation with other Asian countries to strengthen regional security capabilities.

The Soviet Union and the PRC

Since the early 1970s, South Korea has sought security through both military readiness and diplomatic efforts. It assumed that cultivating communications and understanding with the USSR and the PRC would ultimately contribute to the country's security by making them less willing or likely to provide military support for North Korea and perhaps even discourage North Korea from engaging in military adventures. To the South Koreans, it is particularly important to seek accommodation with the Soviet Union, the only country capable of providing North Korea with the advanced equipment and matériel needed for modern warfare. When North Korea enjoyed a close relationship with the Soviet Union, the period was characterized by greater North Korean militancy. In its relations with the Soviet Union and the PRC, Pyongyang moved from neutrality (1958–

1962) to a pro-PRC period (1963–1964), back to "equidistance" (1965), and to a pro-Soviet period (1966–1970) before turning closer to the PRC in the 1970s. Observing this fluctuation, a pro-Soviet tilt seemed to coincide with more militant rhetoric and greater aggressiveness toward the South.[7] South Korea could reason that an ROK-USSR rapprochement would contribute to reducing Soviet willingness to support the North Korean military buildup and perhaps to a peaceful settlement and stabilization of the Korean situation.

Since the late 1970s, however, tension has increased between the United States and the Soviet Union, mainly as a result of the formidable military buildup by the Soviet Union. South Korea recognizes both the positive and negative consequences of that development for its foreign relations and security. Increased tension between the two superpowers is likely to increase the sensitivities and alertness of the United States and Japan concerning security problems in Northeast Asia, leading to their reaffirmation of the strategic value of Korea. Recognition of the increased Soviet threat may foster stronger security ties not only between the United States and Japan, but also between each of those two countries and the PRC. It might also cause a deterioration in the relationship between North Korea and the Soviet Union if the latter were to pursue an expansionist ("hegemonistic") policy, which the former would resent.

The consequences could be negative for South Korean security. Increased tension between the United States and the Soviet Union may result in stepped-up military aid and support for North Korea by the latter and even encouragement of military action against the South. It might lead to an all-out arms competition in the region and Soviet superiority in the regional military balance. Deteriorating relations between the two superpowers may have more negative than positive impact on security in the Korean peninsula. The reasons are (1) it may contribute to a continued or accelerated arms race between the two Koreas, increasing the chances of intended or inadvertent armed conflict between the two sides; (2) Japan may decide to rearm, further heightening tension in the region and security threats to both Koreas; (3) it will be more difficult for South Korea to improve its relationship with either the Soviet Union or the PRC; and (4) the United States may not be able to play a balancing role between the USSR and the PRC.

To South Korea, the Soviet Union is allied to North Korea, and Soviet military might represents both a direct and indirect threat to its security. Hence it has adopted a seemingly contradictory policy of showing concern over a deteriorating relationship between the two superpowers while approving and perhaps even encouraging a stronger U.S. military posture against the USSR.

It is possible to expect that the People's Republic of China, as it cooperates more closely with the United States and Japan, may increase its pressure on North Korea to adopt a less militant and more accommodating policy. Yet one cannot foreclose the possibility that North Korea may decide to emulate China in its emphasis on economic development and thus seek expanded relationships with the United States by accepting a "cross-contact" process of the two Koreas with the major powers.

On the negative side, however, the Soviet Union may feel threatened by an "encirclement" by a three-power coalition of the United States, the PRC, and Japan and decide to increase tension in Northeast Asia by encouraging an aggressive policy by North Korea. Pyongyang may resent and thus react negatively to the PRC's accommodating attitude and pragmatic policy, leaning toward the Soviet Union and adopting a more militant policy. Furthermore, the United States may overestimate the PRC's potential contribution (both military and political) to the security and stability of the area and relax its security posture and reduce its military presence. Finally, growing military cooperation between the United States and the PRC may give North Korea access to U.S. military technology, information, and equipment.

Recent developments show that Beijing feels the need to balance its leaning toward the United States with a supportive gesture toward Pyongyang and an accommodating attitude toward Moscow. Thus the euphoric expectation that a U.S.-PRC rapprochement would help bring about a new ROK-PRC, or even South–North Korean, relationship has proven unrealistic. South Korea still hopes that the United States and/or Japan can enlist the PRC's cooperation to reduce tension in the Korean peninsula. The South Korean government has made it clear that it wants to be on friendly terms with the PRC, hoping that when and if the opportunity comes, the PRC may expand its relationship with South Korea and take more positive steps to improve the security of the Korean peninsula.

In its policy toward the USSR and the PRC, South Korea must consider several important questions: (1) how far it should go in seeking rapprochement with them; (2) whether it is in its interest for North Korea to remain tilted toward the PRC, to move closer to the Soviet Union, or to adopt a more "equidistant" policy; and (4) whether rapprochement with the two communist allies of North Korea should be considered a requisite step toward South–North Korean rapprochement, or vice versa. These questions defy easy or simple answers, lending themselves only to tentative speculation.

South Korea has gone far in signaling its willingness to establish official contacts with the Soviet Union and the PRC. They are well aware of South Korean readiness to communicate with them, and given their basic decision to stay at arm's length, there are no concessions or promises that can radically improve the existing relationships. Yet South Korea might well avoid taking actions or stands that could be considered hostile to the Soviet Union. South Korea does not really have either a "Soviet card" or a "China card" to play, but there is no need to forfeit beforehand the possibility of a future relationship.[8]

Although the ROK government has little influence over Pyongyang's position in the Sino-Soviet rivalry, it should carefully evaluate the consequences for South Korea of each of the North Korean alternatives (pro-Soviet, pro-Chinese, or equidistance) as a necessary step in formulating its policy toward the USSR and the PRC. Many observers feel that because of Sino-Japanese and Sino-American cooperation, the PRC is now less inclined to support or tolerate a militarily aggressive act or policy by North Korea. However, reality seems much more complicated than this reasoning suggests. There are severe limits to how far North Korea can change its political, economic, and military policies, even with a substantial tilt toward China. The reason can be found in the tightly closed nature of the regime and its need for regimentation to maintain autocratic rule. The regime and its militant southern strategic orientations are bound to change, but it will be a slow process.

Experts observe that North Korea has maintained its rigid policy toward South Korea because it has exploited the Sino-Soviet conflict to its advantage. As each communist power is seriously concerned about pushing Pyongyang closer to the other side, neither would wish to invite a dialogue or rapprochement with South Korea. Thus, once Pyongyang falls within the orbit of either of the two powers, it is more susceptible to the restraining influence of the power on which it becomes dependent. According to this reasoning, the power that presumably "lost" North Korea would feel freer to pursue an official relationship with the Republic of Korea.

However, Pyongyang's departure from its relatively equidistant policy may bring undesirable consequences for South Korean security. If Pyongyang opts for a pro-Soviet position, it would mean increased opportunities and temptations for the Soviet Union to wage a proxy war in Korea, particularly if there is a serious deterioration of relations with the United States and/or the PRC. The Soviet Union may also use North Korean ports for military purposes. The domination of North Korea by either the Soviet Union or China is likely to result in greater tension and possibly an armed clash over Korea among some combination of the communist countries, which may further upset the stability of the peninsula. Even if an armed clash can be avoided, a more solid alliance between North Korea and one of its two neighboring communist powers would present a greater security threat to South Korea.

Whether South Korea should make a greater effort to cultivate relations with the Soviet Union or the PRC may be regarded as academic inasmuch as neither of them has responded positively to ROK initiatives for official contacts. Even in the absence of greater receptivity, however, South Korea may have to decide where its diplomatic efforts should be concentrated and whether a choice has to be made. Explicitly friendly gestures to the PRC by the ROK government would invite hostile reactions from the Soviet Union, which has shown great sensitivity to the possibility of an anti-Soviet front in East Asia consisting of the United States, the PRC, Japan, and, possibly, South Korea. The Soviet Union may become more supportive of Pyongyang to counterbalance such a coalition should it come about. It would be hostile toward the ROK to show its displeasure. Still, an effort at rapprochement with the Soviet Union by South Korea may cause apprehensions in the United States and Japan concerning South Korean motives and would seriously upset the Chinese. Furthermore, such an effort is not likely to bring a more positive response from the Soviet Union than can be expected under the present circumstances. A logical conclusion then, at least for the time being, is that South Korea should not stray too far from its present policy of discreet openness and basically equal distance toward the Soviet Union and the PRC.

It is difficult to expect either the USSR or the PRC to take a more accommodating and flexible attitude toward South Korea without some major change in the South-North relationship. Only when Pyongyang accepts the status quo on the peninsula, and when the relationship between the two Koreas improves considerably, can the Soviet Union and the PRC feel free to establish an official relationship with South Korea. With the acute Sino-Soviet rivalry, it is difficult to expect that either of the two powers can exercise a significant influence over Pyongyang on matters of unification policy and strategy toward South Korea. A closer ROK-USSR or ROK-PRC relationship is therefore likely to be preceded by some improvement in the relationship between the two Koreas.

Conclusion

Several conclusions may be drawn from this review of South Korean security interests and options concerning the major powers. For South Korean security it is essential that the United States maintain its military presence in Northeast Asia, particularly in the Korean peninsula. Increased tension between the United States and the Soviet Union resulting from the latter's military buildup in the area has contributed to the greater security commitment by the United States. However, Korea's long-term security interests would be better served should the two superpowers reach an accommodation in their relationship, particularly in the area of conventional and strategic arms.

South Korea tends to feel that its security will improve with time inasmuch as the gap in economic and technological capabilities of the two Koreas will widen and the military balance between them move in its favor. Moreover, North Korea may eventually emerge from its dogmatism and militancy, although it is not likely to happen soon. Hence, short-term security interests take priority over longer-term interests.

Second, for its own security South Korea recognizes the importance of a strong U.S.-Japan security relationship. Although South Korea does not favor the idea that the United States is interested in Korean security primarily as a means of defending Japan, it is considered essential for South Korean security that the United States maintain a strong military presence in and security commitment to Japan.

However, the ROK is ambivalent about U.S. encouragement of a military buildup by Japan. Its attitude is that although it is desirable from the viewpoint of regional security that Japan assume a greater share of the defense burden, it portends certain risks, one of which is the possibility of a major reduction in the U.S. military presence in the area. Therefore, South Korea regards a limited expansion of the Japanese security role acceptable as long as it strengthens the U.S. security role in the area and is pursued within the context of the U.S.-Japanese alliance framework.

Third, South Korea recognizes that its relationships with the Soviet Union and the PRC have an important bearing on its security, but that they cannot be improved drastically even by a more active solicitation of friendship by South Korea.[9] Given the Sino-Soviet rivalry and the absence of a South–North Korean reconciliation, the two communist powers would be reluctant to undertake a major policy shift and risk contributing to the consolidation of Beijing-Pyongyang or Moscow-Pyongyang ties. Meanwhile, they seem confident that as long as they do not foreclose the possibility of an eventual diplomatic relationship with South Korea, the ROK government will not opt for an overtly hostile attitude or behavior against either.

South Korea has little choice but to continue with the course it followed in the 1970s: (1) seeking an accommodation with the Soviet Union and the PRC without going so far as to make overtures or concessions that would cause a strong negative reaction from the other major powers; (2) preparing itself diplomatically and militarily for a possible Soviet or Chinese policy shift in support of a militarily adventuristic policy by North Korea; and (3) supporting and facilitating a cross-contact process between the major powers and the two Koreas, based on the principle of reciprocity, and making efforts to reopen dialogue and seek an eventual accommodation with North Korea.

Notes

1. The military and strategic aspects of South Korean security are discussed in greater detail in Choi Chang-yoon, "Korea: Security and Strategic Issues," *Asian Survey*, November 1980, pp. 1123–139.

2. See Han Sung-Joo, "South Korea and the United States: The Alliance Survives," *Asian Survey*, November 1980, pp. 1077–179.

3. See Stanley Hoffmann, "Requiem," *Foreign Policy*, Spring 1981, p. 6.

4. *Korea Herald*, February 3, 1981.

5. *Korea Times*, February 9, 1983.

6. *Defense of Japan, 1982* (Tokyo: Japan Times, 1982), p. 102.

7. Han Sung-Joo, "Political and Military Interests of North Korea," *Journal of Asian Studies* 23, no. 1 (January 1980).

8. "South Korean Policy Toward the Soviet Union," in Han Sung-Joo, ed., *Soviet Policy in Asia: Expansion or Accommodation?* (Seoul: Panmun Press, 1980), p. 333.

9. In May 1983 the ROK foreign minister publicly stated that the government put a priority on establishing normal relations with both Beijing and Moscow.

DISCUSSANTS

Yasuo Takeyama

Japan needs the United States and the United States needs Japan as dependable allies in this precarious world.

Since the shock to the Japanese when Nixon unexpectedly announced his forthcoming visit to China and the oil crisis of 1973, rivalry between shortsighted nationalist protectionism and enlightened globalism has made it difficult for Japan to chart a course in world affairs. If Japan could correctly assess potential dangers and possibilities, it would know how to mobilize all its resources, human and material, to fulfill its chosen mission.

In the long run, to the threshold of the twenty-first century, the destiny of Japan will be profoundly affected by the deployment of sophisticated weaponry (including nuclear missiles and nuclear submarines); the recovery of the world economy, particularly as it affects the Third World; the utilization of offshore oil and gas deposits in East and South Asia; the course of U.S.-USSR relations; the extent to which China implements its modernization program; and the potential rivalry between the overseas Chinese and Islamic populations in Southeast Asia.

In the short run, great importance must be attached to the succession problem in China, the possibility of healing the breach between China and the Soviet Union, the spillover politico-strategic effects of the succession to Kim Il-sung on the Korean peninsula, the explosive dangers inherent in such insurgency situations as exist in Thailand and the Republic of the Philippines, and the instabilities caused by the expansive policies of the Socialist Republic of Vietnam.

In a global context, the entire Pacific Basin will experience fallout from conflicts in such critical places as the Middle East and Central America. Soviet policies throughout the world may be aggravated by personal power struggles within the Kremlin, choppy Soviet relations with the Warsaw Pact satellite countries, costly involvements in Afghanistan and Vietnam, and its own deficiencies in the three M's: money, management, and manpower.

In spite of political and economic suffering, the Soviets will do their best to separate the Western allies. Using whips or carrots, smiles or threats, they will use every means—propaganda, economic, diplomatic, and military—to confuse and weaken their adversaries.

As for the People's Republic of China, it needs a peaceful international environment to implement its grandiose modernization plans successfully. Its leaders believe that the fundamental strategic and economic interests of the United States and the PRC are complementary and that the PRC needs to buy U.S. high technology and military equipment. They are disillusioned over the United States' military sales to Taiwan and straitjacketed by the successive "provocative" statements of the Reagan administration. Some PRC officials are suspicious that the United States looks upon the PRC as a "potential adversary" rather than as a "strategic friend."

The Chinese emphasize their desire for continuing close cooperation with Japan. They are interested in a "Pan-Pacific community." They are determined to pursue an "open door policy" in dealing with the capitalist world and to carry out their ambitious projects for special economic zones. They want to know how the PRC and Japan can work together more closely for peace and prosperity in the Pacific Basin.

Now let me turn to the United States. The 1970s taught Japan that in its relations with the Western alliance, its security policies must be closely linked with its economic policies—that it should play a more positive strategic and political role to secure national survival and that its place in the world would depend more on economic than military accomplishments.

Since Japan is a country with a rapidly aging population and a rapidly maturing economy (that is, economic growth is slowing and the economy is becoming more service oriented), the key issue for Japan in the coming twenty years will be how to maintain vitality and dynamism in its economy. The immediate problem is to adopt financial policies to bolster the economy (revaluing the yen, for example, say up to 180–90 to the U.S. dollar) under prevailing stringent budgetary conditions.

Serious perception gaps complicate the defense factor and U.S.-Japan relations. The Japanese still think of their country as "small" compared with the United States, which is "big" and whose affections are extremely capricious. They resent the allegation that Japan is getting a free ride in security affairs. They remind Americans that a prosperous Japan contributes more to stability in East Asia than a rearmed Japan and that Japan spends great amounts on defense both in absolute terms and in comparison with others.

While Americans blame Japan for much of their unemployment, the Japanese reply that Americans themselves are responsible for their inability to compete. The Japanese contend that they sell more cars, cameras, and televisions simply because their products are cheaper and better.

Japan has difficulty with the argument that it should spend more for mutual defense. The crucial problem in strengthening Japan's defensive capability is not whether it will increase its defense budget to such and such a percentage from the current 1.5 percent of GNP. Rather it is to redefine—in close collaboration with the United States under the Japan-U.S. security pact—the assumed threat, the expected mission, and the role that should be played by land, sea, and air defense forces, and the preparedness of the respective forces.

Many well-informed Japanese are skeptical whether they genuinely have comprehensive security in accordance with the National Defense White Papers, which have been adopted annually since 1976. They have the uneasy feeling that they are lagging far behind when compared with other nations' defense plans, such as Switzerland's detailed Concept of General Defense adopted in 1973.

Further rearmament is supported by increasing numbers of Japanese, and it is of course welcomed in Washington—that is, a greater Japanese defense buildup is welcomed, but independence is not. But the two go hand in hand. If the United States wants Japan to share the burdens of mutual defense, it must share the power. Prime Minister Nakasone has said that "a nation without defense is without policy." In the long run, Japan must have its own self-defense capability because, like it or not, the ultimate power in world politics is military power. It is important that Japan be treated as a full and equal ally, not as a U.S. protectorate. If Japan is to build its air and naval capability to the extent required to protect the sea-lanes 1,000 miles from its coast, it must be to meet its own defense needs and not merely to accommodate the United States.

It never has been clear exactly what the United States wants Japan to do to maintain the central balance with the USSR. A common program needs to be worked out in such activities as information gathering through electronic means or reconnaissance satellites, more extensive antisubmarine patrols, and a significant increase in air defense capability. Japan has much to offer the United States in military technology, for example, in electronic miniaturization, portable missile development, fiber optics for long-distance communication, and radar wave absorbers (which allow aircraft to escape detection).

Elections and changes in administrations have an inevitable effect on U.S.-Japan relations. The Japanese are as concerned as Americans about the United States after 1984. They wonder how defense and economic issues will be handled between the two allies. Will the United States continue on the path to recovery and revitalize the world economy? Will it contribute to international financial stability by aiding the South in North-South relations? Above all, will it exacerbate the U.S.-USSR confrontation, or will it find acceptable ways and means to reduce international tensions?

In Japan, election after election confirms the Liberal Democratic Party (LDP) in office, and no alternative looms anywhere on the horizon. Whether it is Prime Minister Nakasone or some other leader, the security plank in the party's platform remains constant: "Japan needs the United States as a dependable ally in this precarious world."

Tadae Takubo

Nakasone's diplomatic activities, ranging from his visit to Seoul in January 1983 to his participation in the Williamsburg Summit in late May, have left a rather clear-cut "geometric line" behind. The line is not necessarily beautiful, but it has indicated fairly distinct direction as compared with his predecessor's inconsistent foreign policy.

Nakasone launched his diplomatic activities in January when he visited South Korea. It was the first tête-à-tête between the leaders of both countries. The late Premier Eisaku Sato went to Seoul to attend the inauguration ceremony of the then-president Park Chunghee, and former Premier Kakuei Tanaka also went to South Korea to participate in the funeral of Mrs. Park, but the visits were merely ceremonial.

The timing of Nakasone's visit was remarkably well chosen. First, the so-called textbook problem, stemming from a clumsy description of the history of relations between Japan and Korea, had been resolved. Second, Kim Dae Jung, who was kidnapped from Tokyo and imprisoned in Seoul, left for the United States before Nakasone's visit. Kim Dae Jung posed a knotty problem between Japan and Korea; his departure settled one of the difficult problems between the two countries. Nakasone enjoyed a big success in Seoul. All newspapers in South Korea welcomed the meeting. A joint statement stressed "Japan-Korean friendly relationship of a new dimension." An agreement was finally reached on the crucial issue of economic cooperation, as Japan offered a $4 billion loan.

Immediately after he returned from Seoul, Nakasone went to Washington. President Reagan once hoped Japan would increase its economic assistance to South Korea. Accordingly, Nakasone's visit to Seoul was very helpful in paving the way for his call in Washington. Nakasone was the most crisp of all Japanese premiers who have ever visited Washington. Some of his utterances—"common destiny community," "blockade of three straits," and "unsinkable aircraft carrier"—caused a heated debate in the Japanese Diet after his return.

President Reagan, however, welcomed Nakasone's clear-cut remarks. Nakasone was invited to a breakfast meeting in the White House. Nakasone and Reagan call each other by first names, Ron and Yasu. Nakasone's visit to the United States deserves a rather high grade in the sense that it patched up Japan-U.S. relations, which had been strained by his predecessor, Suzuki.

After returning from Washington, Nakasone sent the secretary general of the LDP, Susumu Nikaido, and later former foreign minister Yoshio Sakurauchi as his special envoys to Beijing in order to explain what he had done in Washington. Sakurauchi is a senior leader in the Nakasone faction in the LDP.

China apparently hoped to have Nakasone come to Beijing himself, but there were diplomatic and protocol problems to be cleared, as well as considerations involving the ASEAN countries. Nakasone sought to satisfy Chinese leaders' pride by dispatching high-ranking LDP members such as Nikaido and Sakurauchi.

Then came Nakasone's visit to the ASEAN countries. There was no doubt that Nakasone was gravely concerned about ASEAN's continued criticisms of Japan's plan relating to defense of the sea-lanes 1,000 miles from Japanese shores, announced by former prime minister Suzuki in Washington. Nakasone assured all ASEAN leaders that Japan would concentrate on "exclusively defensive defense" within the framework of its war-renouncing constitution, would not become a major military power, and would maintain the so-called three nonnuclear principles.

In reply, ASEAN leaders said the following:

1. Indonesian president Suharto: "No one should criticize a nation's defense effort to secure freedom, and I naturally have no objection to such efforts."
2. Thai prime minister Prem: "We welcome Japan's sea-lane defense plan as a step that contributes to the peace and stability of the region."
3. Singapore's prime minister Lee Kuan-Yew: "We fully understand and support Japan's defense policy, and no one thinks that Japan will take a road to militarism in the future."
4. Philippine president Marcos: "To defend their own country is the inherent right of the Japanese people."
5. Malaysian prime minister Mahathir: "There no longer exists any problem in connection with Japan's sea-lane defense plan."

I think it is worthy of praise that Nakasone drew those remarks from the ASEAN leaders.

If Nakasone's visit to Seoul was the start of his diplomatic activities, his participation in the Williamsburg Summit marked his arrival. I do not mean to say this is the end of Nakasone's diplomacy, but I can safely say that the first leg of his foreign policy journey was accomplished at the Williamsburg Summit.

Before Nakasone left for Williamsburg, I wrote an article in the Japanese weekly magazine *Sekai Shuho* to the effect that Nakasone was facing a critical point. He would either reveal himself as a mere "Japanese statesman" or demonstrate that he was a "worldwide statesman." For a Japanese statesman to succeed in his own country, he must act and speak in accordance with the Japanese yardstick. Nakasone chose the latter alternative; his predecessor the former.

In my judgment, the most important theme at Williamsburg was the intermediate-range nuclear forces (INF) problem, which concerns the SS-20s threatening Europe from the eastern side of the Soviet Union. If Nakasone had wanted to be a Japanese statesman, he would not have said anything about INF, but he participated in the discussion as a member of the Western alliance. No Japanese prime minister has ever engaged in a discussion of nuclear security problems. After he came back, he did not lose the upper house election.

Nakasone is playing a very important role in the whole context of Reagan's strategy toward the Soviet Union. Nakasone's diplomacy has only been launched. Greater challenges and tests are bound to come in the near future. Whether he reverts to an old-style Japanese statesman or advances to a worldwide statesman remains to be seen.

Naotoshi Sakonjo

I wish to give my opinion about matters of concern to the Self-Defense Forces of Japan, especially my former service, the Maritime Force (MF).

The Ground Force (GF) is the major service and has been since the early days of General MacArthur. In those days the United States was the predominant maritime and air power in this region. In 1982 the MF's budget amounted to 64 percent and the Air Force's (AF) to 68 percent of the GF's budget.

It is politically very difficult to reduce the size of the GF, which has 155,000 personnel. In contrast, the MF has 42,000, and the AF 44,200. The United States is making greater demands on Japan for improvements in air defense and antisubmarine warfare capabilities. Past history shows Japan's difficulty in meeting these demands. Many Japanese believe that maritime defense should be given first priority because of the danger of the Soviet challenge to Japan's sea-lanes. But the GF has many supporters in the Diet as well as in the public at large, and it may be safe to say that Japan will not be able to make more than steady and gradual progress toward assuming more maritime responsibilities.

The Japanese people generally do not support a substantial military buildup. A public opinion survey in 1983 showed that 18.6 percent supported the amendment of Article 9 of the Japanese constitution, and 38.4 percent opposed it. Since the mid-1970s, however, the Japanese public has deepened its understanding of defense and recognizes the increasing Soviet military threat. The great majority in Japan now admits the necessity of the Japan-U.S. security treaty and the Self-Defense Forces.

According to a public opinion survey in 1982, 39 percent thought the present level of defense spending was appropriate, 10.4 percent found it insufficient, and 22.5 percent believed it was too high. The annual increase in the defense budget was 7.6 percent in 1981, 7.8 percent in 1982, and 6.5 percent in 1983. The ceiling on the 1984 defense budget request was set at 6.88 percent, showing that even Prime Minister Nakasone cannot increase the defense budget significantly. In recent years the budget deficit has been about one-third of total national spending, and the total deficit amounts to about two years' total spending. It must be borne in mind that although the increase in the defense budget has been very modest, expenditures on other projects have remained virtually stationary. Therefore, to my regret, it is expected that drastic defense increases will not be possible in spite of the demands of many U.S. congressmen.

Japan supports and will ratify the new Law of the Sea. Japan extended its territorial waters from three to twelve miles in 1977 except at four straits, namely Soya (La Perouse), Tsugaru, Tsushima, and Osumi, where three-mile territorial waters are still maintained, chiefly because of the three nonnuclear principles. The AF will have nine E2Cs by 1987. We would like to introduce the AWACS, which have much more capability than the E2C, but the AWACS are three times as costly. Nevertheless, I think Japan must have AWACS in order to protect the sea-lanes 1,000 miles offshore against Soviet bombers, combined with F15s to be based at Iwo Jima. The MF will introduce 72 P3Cs by 1987. I support this increase because the P3C is the world's best patrol aircraft and the most effective platform for antisubmarine warfare sensors and weapons. I rather doubt the effectiveness of escort-type surface combatants and their submarine detection capability in view of their vulnerability to stand-off missiles fired by Soviet Badger and Backfire bombers.

Control of the straits is a very controversial issue. Many Japanese fear that if U.S.-Soviet conflict starts anywhere in the world, for instance in the Middle East, the United States will inevitably invite Soviet attack. The Japanese government has repeatedly stated that Japan will not lay mines in the straits unless directly attacked by the Soviet Union, but many are still skeptical. In March 1983 I wrote an article in which I proposed that the Defense Agency should ask the U.S. Defense Department to make clear that the United States will never demand or request Japan to block the straits unless Japan is attacked by the Soviet Union, thus supporting the position of the Japanese government. I believe that the MF should give higher priority to this mission. It goes without saying that it is hard to detect and destroy Soviet submarines once they are out in the Pacific.

At a U.S.-Japan security conference held in Honolulu in fall 1982, the United States reportedly told Japan that it will protect sea-lanes beyond 1,000 miles. I would like to know how, though I know that the U.S. Navy has P3Cs in the Western Pacific and Indian oceans.

With regard to regional cooperation in Northeast Asia, none of a military type can be expected with Korea or Japan in the foreseeable future except exchange of information, students, and port calls of warships. We Japanese are not ready to assume any regional responsibilities in military fields. Our neighbors believe that Japan is obligated to the United States by the security treaty merely to defend Japan, not to play a regional role, and that an alliance with any country other than the United States breaches the spirit of the Japanese constitution. I would like to add that the Korean people would also strongly oppose an alliance with Japan if this issue arose.

Norman Levin

The interests of the United States and South Korea are remarkably congruent in their bilateral, regional, and global relations. The United States shares a major interest in South Korea's national security, both in its own right and as a link to the security of the entire region. The United States has made clear repeatedly its commitment to defense. It sustains a military presence in Korea and has given ample evidence of the capacity and the will to reinforce and back up that presence. The United States has worked consciously to keep South Korean defense expenditures roughly to a level of 6 percent of the GNP. Similarly, the United States shares an interest in South Korea's economic development, both for its own sake and as a deterrent to North Korean aggression.

Americans are also interested in the political development of South Korea, believing that the growth of democratic institutions is essential to genuine security. The United States seems to talk more of stability than of unification, but it supports South Korea's unification policies. The United States will not participate in negotiations with North Korea unless South Koreans are also involved.

The United States sees the political and economic growth of South Korea as beneficial for the entire region. The hosting of the International Parliamentary Union, the Asian Games, and the 1988 Olympics seems to be a vote of confidence in South Korea's long-term stability.

Sometimes there appears to be uncertainty and suspicion in South Korea regarding U.S. intentions. During the Carter administration, U.S. policies were tentative and vacillating, thus creating doubts about the certainty of the United States' commitment. But doubts were lightened by the last year or two of President Carter's term and by President Reagan. Candor compels us to admit that a basis for doubt still remains.

South Korea cannot be confident how long the American military will remain or how broadly American commitments will be interpreted. As the South Korean economy grows, there is mounting displeasure in key circles in both South Korea and the United States concerning South Korean economic policies, resulting in attitudes that could have sobering effects in the security area. The controversies over human rights and the authoritarian government could also become disruptive forces in United States–South Korean relations.

The prevention of further strategic arms competition may be worthwhile to highlight. We must be careful of the effects of superpower confrontation on regional interests. There is ambivalence in South Korea concerning the wisdom of U.S. pressure on Japan to rearm. South Korea worries that the effects of such pressure would reduce the American sense of responsibility and possibly pave the way for the United States to withdraw from the region. The question is not how to transfer U.S. defense responsibilities to Japan, however, but how to encourage Japan to share more of the burdens of mutual defense.

On the question of deterrence vis-à-vis North Korea, the United States will probably decrease its proportional participation over time as South Korean economic, technological, and military capabilities expand. American and Korean planners will have to grapple continuously over the relative role to be played by each.

With regard to the appropriate military strategy to deal with the North Korean threat, which is based on forward defense, it is a question whether emphasis should not be shifted to coping with actions caused by commando infiltration.

Finally, the problem of U.S. and Korean forces will have to be reconsidered in the larger framework of East Asian security. The positioning of U.S. forces, while central to the defense of South Korea, must be constantly reviewed with regard to the security of Japan and the broader Asian region. With the buildup of Soviet forces, the American forces in Korea and the U.S. bases in Korea and Japan take on a larger deterrent and strategic role. As the United States confronts a growing Soviet military challenge, the position of Korea and the U.S. forces in Korea must be constantly reassessed from a worldwide point of view.

Edward Olsen

For containment in Northeast Asia, more than the bilateral U.S.-Japan and U.S.–South Korean agreements are necessary. A Japan–South Korea understanding must be added if there is to be satisfactory regional security. Although less significant than those in Japan, the United States has strategic stakes in South Korea and in the rest of Asia. The United States needs to pressure Japan to do more to protect those stakes. Unless Washington prods, the more the United States relieves the Japanese from burden sharing, the fewer incentives there are for them to do, for themselves and for the region, what needs to be done. What the United States does in the Asia-Pacific region serves Japan's interests at least as much as those of the United States, and probably more.

Comparatively speaking, Japan is getting a free ride for national defense despite the approximately $1 billion it spends annually on the U.S. forces in Japan. All of the Asian countries spend proportionately more than Japan on their share of mutual defense burdens. Even if the United States is willing to continue as the major provider of defense in the Pacific-Asian region, it should call upon Japan to do more economically to make up for its shortcomings in the strategic area.

Americans might ask themselves why they should be more ready than the Japanese to defend Japan bilaterally or regionally. Americans should work at facilitating the Japanese ability to arrive at a domestic consensus on spending for defense. Many Japanese question the United States' right to order them to do anything more than they choose. To compensate for this perception, Americans should use their own decline in comparative strength as a lever to induce the Japanese to fill the gaps left by their weakness.

The United States should adopt a negotiating stance like that of the Japanese, saying, "So sorry, we really do have a problem." Let them take more responsibility in trying to find the solution. The United States should work out a careful proposal to renegotiate a security treaty on the basis of real reciprocity. Washington should make it clear that the United States will do for Tokyo only what Tokyo is willing to do for it. Of course, this means that the United States will have to make the Japanese full partners in matters of planning and strategy.

The United States and Japan should talk about what needs to be done, not about expenditure of a certain percentage of GNP. Under complete reciprocity, Tokyo should be prepared to provide as much for the United States as Washington will make available to Japan. Japan should be responsible for its own defense, the United States likewise, and each should share equally in regional defense programs. Japan's capabilities should be measured not only in terms of forces in the field, but also in terms of its ability to pay for regional defense. If the United States can spend approximately $45 billion of its defense budget for the Pacific Basin, Japan should quadruple its budget commitments for the same security purposes.

Japan could and should contribute to more effective defense of South Korea, even if many South Koreans are still suspicious of the Japanese. Japan could help South Korea militarily in joint strategy, air and naval cooperation, and technological transfer. If a three-way understanding involving the United States, Japan, and South Korea could be agreed upon, it would strengthen the U.S. commitment to the region and would also stimulate the Japanese to do more for regional defense.

I also think it would be advantageous for South Korea to have Japan help alleviate the threat from the North. This would, in turn, lessen the strains in the South and make more money available for national development.

III
SOUTHWEST PACIFIC
AND
THE INDIAN OCEAN

Introduction

Claude A. Buss

The range of national security problems in the Pacific Basin is shown most clearly in the contrast between the Northwest Pacific and Northeast Asia at one extreme and the Southwest Pacific and Southeast Asia at the other.

The North Pacific washes the eastern gateway to the Soviet empire. The South Pacific, extending to the Southern Ocean off Antarctica, is geographically most immune from any perceived enemy threat. To the United States, Australia and New Zealand, though far away in the Southern Hemisphere, are essential allies in strengthening the fabric of peace in the Pacific area. From their own points of view, Australia and New Zealand are fortunate in their location. Surrounded by great expanses of water, their prime responsibility is to provide for their own defense. As members of the Australia–New Zealand–United States (ANZUS) alliance, they are called upon to carry a share of the burdens of mutual security.

The conference session on the Southwest Pacific and the Indian Ocean addressed a series of questions designed to examine the effectiveness of mutual security policies, extant or under consideration. How do the United States, Australia, and New Zealand differ in perceptions of the balance of power in the Pacific Basin? To what extent are national interests congruent and can divergences be reconciled? What is the optimum role for ANZUS members in such security matters as monitoring Soviet activities, exchanging intelligence, conducting joint exercises, and coordinating production of weapons and supplies? How can the three countries make certain that economic conflicts will not undermine their collective defense structure? Has the time arrived to consider more formal economic cooperation or to create some new institution specifically dedicated to collective security in the Pacific Basin? How can all three nations preserve a consistent relationship despite the periodic changes of government resulting from their democratic processes? These questions provided a focus for the papers and the discussions.

Australia and New Zealand share with the United States a common cultural background and a common heritage of a market economy and parliamentary democracy. The ANZUS alliance, born in the afterglow of World War II, is more than a treaty. It reflects a deep-seated and very strong association that goes beyond security.

In global terms, Australia and New Zealand see eye to eye with the United States in opposing Soviet expansionism, communist ideology, and a totalitarian way of life. Both are confident that the United States has a preponderance of power in the Pacific Basin, but they recognize the mounting Soviet threat. They, too, believe that peace depends upon the maintenance of a balance of power and that it would be an unmitigated disaster if deterrence were to fail. They admit that neither superpower really wants war, but would prefer more serious negotiations for arms control to a steadily worsening arms race.

They are uncomfortable with President Reagan's rhetoric and his "ham-handed" dealing with the United States' European allies. They are worried about disarray in the Western alliance, but take courage in the comparable fragmentation of the communist world. They think the West, with all its weaknesses, is strong enough to deter any rash Soviet military adventures either in Europe or in Asia. They want deterrence, not defense. Their fear is that if war is to come, it is likely to be an unwinnable nuclear war resulting from mistake or miscalculation. They have no faith in the capacity of a computer or the infallibility of human judgment to keep the peace.

The interests of the United States in the Southwest Pacific and Indian oceans are to maintain peace and stability there, protect the sea lines of communication, and deny Soviet penetration into the area. The defense of these interests requires the capability to project U.S. military power throughout the area and the fullest support of the ANZUS allies.

Americans cannot afford to overlook or underplay the contributions of either ally to mutual security. Australia describes itself as a smallish, middle power committed to the West. Although greatly dependent on the United States, Australians do not see themselves as mere appendages of superpower deployment. They are ardently nationalistic and independent and insist upon being recognized and respected as such.

The government of Australia is conscious of its importance in regional and global defense. Since Australia lies near vital lines of communication between the Indian Ocean and the Southwest Pacific, its power can be projected in several directions. Its armed forces are small but highly professional. Its naval and air capabilities extend beyond its continental limits, significantly augmenting the United States' defense capability around Australia. Approximately two dozen military installations scattered over Australia are available to the United States for classified and sophisticated intelligence-gathering activities. Beyond its own territory, Australia provides a contingent for the multilateral force in the Sinai and the U.N. peacekeeping force in Cyprus. It participates in the Commonwealth military training team in Uganda and has offered supply supervisory forces should an agreement be reached in Namibia.

Both Australia and New Zealand contribute substantially to stability in Southeast Asia. By virtue of the Five-Power Defense Arrangement, their air units combine with those of Singapore and Malaysia in the operation of the Integrated Air Defense System (IADS). They are committed to the defense of Thailand in the event of external aggression and have assumed a leading role in seeking an acceptable solution to the problems of Kampuchea and Vietnam. They provide military assistance, including training, and enter joint exercises with the ASEAN members. They have a military presence in parts of Southeast Asia where Americans would not be welcome. Australians have excellent contacts in Indonesia in spite of differences over Papua New Guinea and Eastern Timor.

Both Australia and New Zealand carry on development assistance programs in conjunction with ASEAN. They have food surpluses, raw materials, and industrial technology that they grant to less developed neighbors. Consequently, they are identified with the advanced North rather than the less developed countries of the South in North-South disputes.

A comprehensive security system for the Pacific Basin depends upon the linkage of Australia and New Zealand with Japan and the Republic of Korea, with cooperation and low-key leadership from the United States. The economic linkage is healthy because of increasing trade and investments. The growing value of the security linkage is evidenced by the steady expansion of joint RIMPAC exercises involving both Australia and Japan. Australia and New Zealand are cautious in their attitudes toward Japanese rearmament. They are willing to let Japan protect 1,000 miles of sea-lanes, but they would object if Japan were to develop a nuclear capability and long-range bombers.

There exist differences of opinion between the ANZUS allies that demand therapeutic attention. While conservatives were in power in Canberra, they enjoyed a close relationship with Washington. When the Australian Labor Party (ALP) assumed office in March 1983, a certain strain entered the relationship. Accepting ANZUS as the sheet anchor of security and proclaiming itself as pro-U.S. and anti-Soviet as the conservatives, the ALP inclined toward a defense of Australian policy rather than the previous "forward defense." This seemed to indicate a withdrawal from operational integration with the United States. Once in power, however, Prime Minister Hawke appeared closer to his conservative predecessor than to the more radical elements in his party.

Some security issues between Australia and the United States must receive constant attention lest they deteriorate. Influential opinion groups in each country differ on the relative emphasis to be placed upon military factors on the one hand and the painstaking process of lifting living standards on the other as the allies work to strengthen the fabric of peace in the Pacific Basin. Some Australians and some Americans would prefer more economics and less defense in the whole range of ANZUS agreements.

The common fear of a nuclear holocaust raises conflicting ideas on how to avoid it. Australia has its peace organizations advocating a nuclear freeze or a nuclear-free zone in the immediate area. Although Australians generally welcome American military personnel, many are uneasy about nuclear vessels calling at their ports or overflights of aircraft presumably armed with nuclear bombs.

So far Australians and Americans have treated these problems with common sense and good will. The Australian government accepts the U.S. policy of "no confirmation, no denial" concerning nuclear-armed vessels and raises no objections to a limited number of discreet visits by nuclear-powered ships. Transit, but not basing, rights at Port Darwin have been granted B-52s. With regard to nuclear-free zones, Australia has walked a tightrope between the ideal and the practical. It objects to nuclear testing, stockpiling of nuclear weapons, and disposal of nuclear waste in the proposed free zones while admitting the United States' right of free transit of nuclear-powered or nuclear-armed vessels.

The sharpest U.S.-Australian disagreements center about the desirability and the consequences of U.S. military installations on Australian soil, particularly those at North West Cape, Pine Gap in the Northern Territory, and Nurrungar in South Australia. These installations are essential to the successful conduct of nuclear warfare by the United States. Successive Australian governments have agreed to host the Americans, believing Australian support makes the U.S. nuclear deterrence possible.

The opposition in Australia argues that these installations guarantee that Australia will become an immediate target in the event of a Soviet nuclear attack. In its view, these installations deny hope for a nuclear-free zone and infringe on Australia's sovereignty. Furthermore, they tie Australians too closely to unpredictable U.S. policies.

Before assuming power, the ALP stood for the removal of the installations. Since then it has relented to a certain extent. It advocates the removal of the most sensitive ones but, for the others, only a change in the rules for their operation. It wants more information about the installations made available to the Australian public, improved methods of consultation and control, access to the U.S. defense communication satellite, and greater participation in the intelligence-gathering process.

Although New Zealand does not host such strategic installations, it is more bitter than Australia in its antinuclear, antiarmaments protestations. Even though the two countries are usually considered together in analyses of their security policies, their individuality cannot be overlooked. New Zealanders are as nationalistic as Australians. They are far more concerned about the future of the South Pacific than the Pacific–Indian Ocean area. They perceive themselves more immune than Australia to the threat of outside aggression.

Conservative governments have been in power in New Zealand in 26 of the 32 years since the signing of the ANZUS treaty. Traditionally they have been pro–United States. The ruling National Party, together with the major opposition Labor Party, accounts for 80 percent of the parliament, but the majority party rules by a single vote. The size of the opposition and its emotional intensity should serve to warn of a possible divergence in the security paths of New Zealand and the United States. This could fray the entire ANZUS structure.

Vigorously condemning superpower rivalry, a high proportion of New Zealanders call upon both the United States and the Soviet Union to scale down their rearmament programs, reduce their nuclear stockpiles, and utilize their material riches for human betterment. A third of New Zealand's population, including church groups, labor unions, professional organizations, and ordinary concerned citizens, actively support a nuclear freeze or the creation of nuclear-free zones. Their aim is exclusively the avoidance of nuclear war. They deny categorically the efficacy of retaliation or a second-strike capability.

The government must trim its sails to the winds of public opinion. It supports the ideal of a nuclear weapons–free zone in the South Pacific, but shies from measures to bring it about. It denies permission for B-52 overflights and forbids entry of nuclear-armed vessels to New Zealand ports. It accepts, however, the U.S. formula of "no confirmation, no denial" and tolerates discreet visits of nuclear-powered ships. It fears the possibility that popular antinuclear, antiarmaments movements may take an anti-American turn.

The opposition Labor Party has passed resolutions to withdraw from the ANZUS connection, but currently merely advocates reconsideration of the whole range of ANZUS agreements. It wants more economic assistance as an alliance objective. It alleges that ANZUS currently is a lightning rod for nuclear attack and not a protective umbrella. It would use ANZUS as a forum to promote a nuclear weapons–free zone for the Pacific Basin. It also believes in a Pacific collective defense organization to parallel the concept of an economic Pacific Community.

The political climate in New Zealand is a clear indication that mutual security must rest on a broader basis than defense against the Soviet Union. To keep ANZUS alive and well demands consistent informed judgment, sensitivity, and common sense. The United States must recognize the special needs of its partners and attempt to satisfy them.

Australia, New Zealand, and U.S. Security Interests

Henry S. Albinski

The United States maintains extensive bilateral relations with Australia and New Zealand, but it views these two traditional friends and allies in a considerably wider context. Whether through the ANZUS treaty alliance or otherwise, the connection carries significant, security-related implications that reach well beyond the antipodes—into the eastern Indian Ocean, Southeast Asia, the South Pacific, and in some respects even farther afield.

This study is a synopsis of three dimensions of the United States' links with its ANZAC partners. The first summarizes U.S. interests and objectives in and around Australia's and New Zealand's strategic environments and how in principle these nations could be construed as U.S. assets. The second dimension deals with the capacity and willingness of the Australian and New Zealand governments to carry out policies consonant with U.S. objectives. The third assesses areas of foreseeable doubt, weakness, or breakdown in the continuation of traditional ANZAC contributions. The study closes with comment about the management of tripartite links.

Interests and Objectives of the United States

Underlying U.S. interests in the Indo-Pacific region are familiar: protection of strategic lines of communication, maintenance of political integrity within resident states and the avoidance of subregional conflict, and imposition of strategic denial upon the United States' foremost international rival, the Soviet Union. This implies the capacity to project and sustain military power in deterrent and, if needed, war-fighting roles.

The realization of objectives that underpin these interests naturally depends on a mixture of military, diplomatic, and economic measures. But the United States' resources are finite and often cannot effectively be husbanded without the consent and cooperation of sympathetic and, if possible, like-minded regional friends. In this sense, through a combination of location, makeup, resources, and behavior, Australia and New Zealand can be construed as substantial and irreplaceable assets.

One of Australia's and New Zealand's most impressive yet often overlooked assets is their insularity. They have no powerful and hostile neighbors and are far removed from potential sites of great power confrontation and regional conflict. They are substantially insulated from major threats. Their own security does not require the expenditure of scarce U.S. military resources, diplomatic credit, or economic subventions. Their abutment on Pacific lines of trade and communication invests them with additional value, both under normal conditions and in emergencies. Australia, moreover, is strategically placed to the south of the key maritime passageways connecting the Pacific and Indian oceans. The presence of a friendly power near such vital chokepoints is manifestly important.

The fulfillment of U.S. security objectives in the Indo-Pacific region requires active cooperation from among those prepared and able to contribute. Some of this assumes economic form. Japan's political steadiness and ability to maneuver a course between indifference to self-defense and a temptation to undertake regionally destabilizing rearmament depends in part on the availability of natural resources, which Australia has in abundance. The foodstuffs and industrial technology required by so many of their neighbors are available in Australia and New Zealand. If nearby wealthy and politically acceptable donors and trading partners are at hand for less developed countries, regional security and, ultimately, U.S. interests are fostered.

Political-diplomatic access often runs hand in hand with economic access. Because of historical indifference, geographic distance, and local resistance, the United States lacks effective entrée into a number of countries in the Southwest Pacific and Southeast Asia region. Hence, while favoring the individual and collective political, economic, and security viability of members of ASEAN, the United States has lacked intimate access to Malaysia and Singapore. Its relationship with Indonesia, the largest and probably the most strategically positioned member of ASEAN, has been qualified. More conspicuously, the United States has been tardy in establishing a major political and economic presence among the Southwest Pacific nations. The United States is not a member of the region's most prominent political grouping, the South Pacific Forum. Its superpower status engenders ambivalence, even unease, among the small island-countries.

Yet this region is the corridor for trans-Pacific lines of communications and incorporates the United States' Micronesian territories, which are moving toward autonomy and ties with the broader array of Pacific countries. Australia and New Zealand are themselves Pacific nations. They are in, not outside, the neighborhood. Their colonial records are clean, even admired. They are sophisticated nations, closely allied with the United States, yet middle and therefore far less intimidating powers. Their ability to exercise a role supportive of the United States can be useful.

The United States is beset by enormously complex and burdensome strategic responsibilities. The avoidance of general war is a pre-eminent consideration. The capacity to fight, survive, and, if possible, win conventional and nuclear war follows closely behind. The strategic balance in the contemporary global environment is acutely dependent on intelligence, surveillance, and command, control and communications (C^3) capabilities. The ANZAC countries, especially Australia, are particularly well sited in the Southern Hemisphere as land platforms from which such functions can be carried out.

On a regionally circumscribed basis, and especially since the Soviet occupation of Afghanistan, the United States has assumed inordinate military obligations in the Indo-Pacific region. The U.S. fleet is growing to 600 vessels. But this will take time, and even then resources will remain dispersed, especially for the Pacific Command. Problems on the Horn of Africa, the Persian Gulf, and in Southwest Asia have concentrated the United States' mind on the Indian Ocean and its littoral. As an Indian Ocean littoral nation, Australia is a natural object of attention for U.S. communication, transit, porting, staging, and other functions, as well as for Australia's military assets. In mid-ocean, the United States can utilize Diego Garcia. Working around the littoral, only Australia possesses in-place or developable infrastructural facilities, is politically constant, and—in contrast to South Africa—is not an international pariah. New Zealand is not an Indian Ocean littoral state, but it has a vital interest in the security of its trade routes.

The Southeast Asian scene poses its own difficulties for the United States. Southeast Asia has not yet accommodated the deep differences between Vietnam and the ASEAN community. Thailand regards itself as a front-line state. Sino-Vietnamese relations could deteriorate into a second and prospectively more regionally destabilizing conflict than resulted from the events of 1979. Backed by Soviet power, Vietnam can seriously threaten Thailand and challenge U.S. power in the Philippines and the surrounding seas.

Despite the recent renegotiation of the U.S. base agreement with the Philippines, the tenability of those facilities is questionable. In this setting,

Australia and New Zealand contributions can be salient. They might include the utilization of Western Australia for U.S. deployment around Southeast Asia and across the Indian Ocean, as a supplement or alternative to Philippine bases, and for Australia's and New Zealand's own deployments. They can include assistance to regional defense forces to foster a Western presence, as in Malaysia and Singapore, where comparable U.S. connections are absent.

In the South Pacific, Australian and New Zealand access to many of the island-countries alluded to earlier can be critical to U.S. security-political interests. Present Soviet naval deployments in the area are only occasional, and the United States wishes to keep the Soviet presence minimal and well monitored. The United States wants to avoid resident Soviet diplomatic representation in the region, Soviet assistance programs of scale, and most certainly Soviet military entrée via ship visits, landing rights, and defense arrangements. Australia's and New Zealand's traditional acceptance in the area puts them in a unique position to augment or replace U.S. efforts. They can and do make substantial contributions in the form of diplomatic brokerage, civil and defense assistance programs, and independent surveillance and other military tasks.

There are two additional ways in which the ANZAC countries further U.S. security interests. First, their participation in joint military exercises significantly improves U.S. readiness and fosters cooperative planning. Second, the ANZUS relationship has come to enshrine special meaning well beyond its tripartite membership. It has been publicized and is viewed by others as a remarkably intimate and durable association far exceeding the formal language of the treaty. Should ANZUS actually or in appearance become degraded, the adverse pan- and trans-regional implications for the United States' role as ally, guarantor, and, ultimately, crisis manager would be seriously debilitating.

ANZUS Cooperative Policies

After brief periods out of office, conservative governments were returned in Australia and New Zealand at the end of 1975. The New Zealand National Party, under Robert Muldoon, has since governed continuously. The Australian Labor Party (ALP) government, led by Robert Hawke, ousted the government of Malcolm Fraser in March 1983.

On a broad plane, conservative governments in the two countries have consistently and vigorously espoused the importance of close security and other ties with the United States. They have not regarded the United States, or ANZUS, as the full answer to their national security requirements and have not been averse to disagreeing with Washington. Still, they have defined ANZUS as something of a metaphorical sheet anchor of their security and have considered ANZUS's vitality as a test of the quality of their relations with the United States.

During a 1983 visit to Washington, Prime Minister Hawke got on very well with President Reagan. He argued that because of the many bonds between the two nations, "we will be together forever;"[1] that the United States enjoyed no closer relationship than that with Australia; and that "we regard our relationship with the United States as of fundamental importance."[2] The Labor Party remains firmly attached to ANZUS. It does not wish to amend the treaty's language or traditional objectives, but has expressed interest in a review. Its earlier questions about the treaty's de facto ambit seem to have been satisfied insofar as it has not asked for binding definition of where its provisions do, or do not, apply. Overall, the review will not likely result in much more than the adoption of new planning and coordination procedures.

Conservative governments in Australia and New Zealand have by no means held the Soviet Union accountable for the world's instability. But they have interpreted the Soviets as embarked on an expansionist course—mischievous, intrusive, and resorting to the full array of civil and military pressure to gain objectives. Australia under Prime Minister Malcolm Fraser was more outspoken than New Zealand under Prime Minister Muldoon, and until the Soviet intrusion into Afghanistan Fraser was in some respects more anti-Soviet than Presidents Ford or Carter. The ALP government has been somewhat less florid in its pronouncements, but little different in kind.

In Prime Minister Hawke's view, "On all the evidence the Soviet Union is an expansionary power and is prepared to use, either directly or through its surrogates, force of arms."[3] Labor has urged the United States to negotiate meaningfully on strategic arms control, but has not discounted the need for negotiation from strength. While condemning the Soviet presence in Afghanistan and its role in Polish affairs, the government has lifted sanctions imposed by former prime minister Fraser. These steps were in keeping with those of many other Western governments and in part with the United States itself, which rescinded its grain embargo. New Zealand's sanctions have remained in place. But early in its tenure the ALP government expelled a Soviet diplomat on spying charges since the government was in part interested in demonstrating its toughness to the United States and others.

Australia and New Zealand have cultivated excellent relations with the People's Republic of China for many years. During a visit to the two countries in April 1983, a senior Chinese delegation dwelt on its government's concern over deteriorating relations with Washington. Canberra undertook to transmit concerns and ideas between Beijing and Washington and to reduce misunderstandings. Australian foreign minister Bill Hayden remarked that China should not be encouraged to seek rapprochement with the Soviets since "it's in the interest of the Western world that the pressure be maintained on the Chinese border" to prevent larger Soviet deployments in Europe.[4] This was classical balance of power language, a "China card" formulation not scrupulously followed by a determined anti-Soviet Reagan administration. Even before the visit, New Zealand foreign minister Warren Cooper had spoken of the importance of China as a "strong ally" for the ANZUS powers and for Japan.[5]

Australia and New Zealand face the common dilemma of reconciling their own self-defense with their obligations as partners of the United States on a global scale. A useful opening question is whether their strategic doctrines permit or disavow diplomatic and military initiatives in places well removed from their own strategic environments. Part of the answer is structured by their size, location, and resources. If it chooses, Australia can be expected to do more than New Zealand. The tendency over the years within the two conservative governments has been to focus on the regional environment, in part meaning a pulling back from a forward defense posture. But diplomatic and military involvement in faraway places was never repudiated, especially when carried out in tandem with friends and allies. The outgoing Fraser government seemed, if anything, to be edging toward a more acknowledged mix between regional and outlying involvement.

Under whatever label, the Australian Labor Party has traditionally preferred a more "continental" or "defense of Australia" posture. The Hawke government's flat decision not to acquire an aircraft carrier to replace HMAS *Melbourne* was seen and explained as a conscious reduction of interest in distant deployment in keeping with concentration on a more modest strategic circumference. Labor's emphasis on increased self-reliance in defense could also imply less reliance on or expectations under ANZUS. The government has moreover stressed its interest in not stretching Australia's diplomatic resources much beyond the Asian-Pacific area.

But the government has chosen to extend Australia's participation in the Commonwealth Military Training Team in Uganda and has not repudiated the former government's offer to provide supervisory forces should an agreement be reached in Namibia. Under their conservative governments Australia and New Zealand contributed military personnel to the Sinai Multinational Force and Observers. The ALP was highly skeptical about the commitment and promised to review it on gaining office. It did and decided to maintain the contribution. Prime Minister Hawke's explanation closely parallels the reasons behind the original Fraser government decision: the need for regional stabilization in the Middle East, keeping radical—and by indirection, Soviet—influence at bay, and support for an intricate and significant initiative by Australia's U.S. ally. The operation in the Middle East is not under ANZUS auspices, but the alliance's spirit is in evidence far from Australia's and New Zealand's shores. There has also been a promise by Prime Minister Hawke to contribute what he personally can toward conflict resolution on a prospective Middle Eastern visit. Such an initiative, whatever its merits, could not possibly be interpreted as evidence of Labor's readjustment of focus to Australia's immediate surroundings.

Despite Canberra's decision to forgo a carrier replacement, both Australia and New Zealand retain a reasonable capacity for force projection—Australia through destroyers, frigates, and submarines, and New Zealand through frigates. Both nations possess an airborne as well as naval antisubmarine warfare capability. Australia is disbanding its fleet air arm, but has an F-111 strike capability and 75 F-18s on order. New Zealand's A-4s are likely to remain in service for some years. Australia's standing forces are much larger than New Zealand's (73,000 versus under 13,000) and better equipped, but both national forces are well trained and represent the most capable military establishments in their respective locales.

The United States has publicly nudged its ANZUS partners to carry a responsible share of the defense burden. It has been mindful of economic constraints in both capitals and especially of New Zealand's chronic balance of payments shortfall, which limits acquisition of expensive equipment from overseas. Neither Muldoon nor Hawke, however, appears disposed to impose real-term reductions on defense spending. Indeed, the ALP has long contended that it favors not less, or even less expensive, defense but rather a defense posture with somewhat different priorities from that of its predecessor. Various exercises continue with U.S. forces and with regional states. Without Australian and New Zealand (and Canadian) participation under RIMPAC auspices, it is doubtful that the Japanese Self-Defense Forces would have been politically able to steam far afield for bilateral exercises with the U.S. Navy.

Even more fundamentally, various forms of desired U.S. strategic access to Australia and New Zealand have largely been unimpeded. American spokesmen insist that unhindered port visits by U.S. vessels to Australia and New Zealand are strategically crucial to maintain effective peacekeeping and response capabilities. Collaterally, the United States regarded access by its vessels, regardless of their propulsion or armament, as a measure of ANZUS alliance viability. New Zealand under the National Party and Australia under both Liberal–National Party and Labor Party governments have welcomed such visits, not challenging the U.S. rule of "no confirmation, no denial" by demanding disclosure of potential nuclear weapon carriage. In Hawke's view, "if you have a relationship with the United States and you say that that relationship is fundamental, as we do, then you can't at one and the same time say you are going to deny access of the vessels to Australia."[6] Nor has the Hawke government threatened to reopen the arrangement under which unarmed American B-52s transit through Darwin on training and navigational flights. The United States has not signified any intention to request home porting or home basing privileges in Western Australia or stockpiling of nuclear weapons at Australian bases.

New Zealand houses American-emplaced astronomical facilities that have marginal strategic application, but Australia hosts numerous and strategically critical facilities. The Australian Labor Party accepts the Fraser government's position that the surveillance, electronic intercept, navigational, and C^3 installations such as Pine Gap, Nurrungar, and Smithfield are essential for Western strategic purposes, should not be compromised, and are worth whatever theoretical Soviet targeting risk that may result. The newest facility, an intelligence installation at Watsonia, Victoria, became operational after Labor's advent to office. There as elsewhere, valued cooperation with the Australian Defense Signals Directorate will continue. When in opposition, Labor threatened to shut down the naval signal station at North West Cape, Western Australia, unless Australia gained access to and a veto over potential nuclear firing orders transmitted through the installation. That move could have precipitated a serious rift in Canberra-Washington relations. But Labor shifted. It no longer demands renegotiation of the North West Cape agreement. Apparently with U.S. concurrence, it will settle for an Australian who would closely monitor relevant U.S. activities, but without direct access to message content from the signal station.

Regionally based U.S. requirements are also upheld by supportive ANZAC country behavior. In the Indian Ocean, independent New Zealand deployments are understandably rare. The Australian situation is different, especially in the eastern reaches of the ocean. Preparations are under way for a permanent Australian naval presence in Western Australia, and home porting for major units at Cockburn is a prospect. There is no sign that Labor will curtail inherited patterns of naval movement in the area. Moreover, airfield development plans in Western Australia are progressing, and P-3 deployments in the eastern Indian Ocean have not been scaled down. A brace of P-3s operates out of the Malaysian airbase at Butterworth, with considerable patrol time advantage over U.S. aircraft during deployments in the Andaman Sea and Strait of Malacca area. Wartime contingency plans regarding Australia's responsibilities for naval and air coverage of Indian Ocean approaches to Southeast Asian straits have been in place for over thirty years.

Australia does not always operate alone in the region. There is considerable operational advantage that accrues from the Australian air force's use of Diego Garcia, American air transit through the Australian Cocos, and reconnaissance flights through Darwin to the Indian Ocean. Exercises have been conducted in the Indian Ocean by the ANZUS partners and by Australia and the United States bilaterally. U.S. Marines have used Western Australia for amphibious maneuvers.

There is always some ambiguity whether such tripartite or bilateral exercises are under ANZUS aegis since the treaty refers to the Pacific exclusively. For domestic political and certain external reasons, Australia has been publicly ambivalent on this score, and New Zealand resisted any imputation of a formal extension of ANZUS into the Indian Ocean. In 1981, Prime Minister Muldoon claimed that New Zealand had "not been involved in any military presence under the ANZUS alliance outside the treaty area." There had been limited cooperation in the Indian Ocean, but "not under ANZUS aegis."[7] Disclaimers such as these are distinctions without difference and do not derogate tripartite regional cooperation by means favored by the United States.

ANZAC governments have, to U.S. relief, avoided pressing for denuclearization of the Indian Ocean. While he was Labor's foreign affairs spokesman in opposition, Lionel Bowen proposed a modest denuclearization plan for the Southern Hemisphere's Indian and Pacific oceans. But since attaining power, the ALP has focused on a nuclear-free zone in the South Pacific only. At the United Nations, the government has dropped Australia's earlier objections to the convening of an Indian Ocean conference on demilitarization. Although this disappointed the United States, Australia's position when and if the conference convenes will matter.

In Southeast Asia, both Australia and New Zealand are prominent and very much in step with regional objectives. They are deeply committed to the viability and security of ASEAN and its members, to the integrity of the sea lines of communication that traverse the area, and to a credible Western defense presence. Australia's regional defense cooperation program, through aid, training, and other means, is especially elaborate. Australian military personnel are in every ASEAN nation.

Australian and New Zealand forces are most conspicuous in Malaysia and Singapore because of the Five-Power Defense Arrangement (FPDA). A New Zealand infantry battalion is posted in Singapore. Australia and New Zealand maintain the Integrated Air Defense System (IADS) at Butterworth, canvassing Malaysia, Singapore, and their neighborhood. Periodic defense exercises undertaken on the initiative of the Fraser government have been continued under Labor. Clearly, the United States welcomes this Australian and New Zealand support for Malaysia and Singapore. Moreover, as one Australian defense official observed, "All noncommunist governments in Southeast Asia value the FPDA. There is a lot of feeling in ASEAN government and defense circles that Australia and New Zealand have such good links with the United States through ANZUS that in dealing with Australia, they are dealing with the United States by proxy. The difference is that Australia's military presence is acceptable whereas an American military presence would not be."[8]

Australia has close relations with its near neighbor, Indonesia. Through Irian Jaya it has a land frontier with Papua New Guinea, for whose well-being Australia assumes special responsibility. Indonesia's huge population, considerable natural resources, and strategic position invest it with exceptional standing in the ASEAN community. Australia has long sought to nurture its ties with Jakarta. Indonesia's forcible takeover of and subsequent practices in East Timor produced considerable resentment in Australia. The Fraser government gradually acceded to the fait accompli in Timor and, by the end of its tenure, was further strengthening relations with Indonesia, especially in the defense field.

In 1982 the ALP conference strongly condemned Indonesia over Timor. It demanded the withdrawal of Indonesian forces and a genuine expression of self-determination in Timor. Shortly after assuming office, the Labor government examined relations with Indonesia, and Hayden and Hawke held consultations in Jakarta. The Indonesian presence in Timor was accepted as irreversible. Not only was defense cooperation maintained, but under Labor a patrol boat was donated, and air and maritime exercises were staged with Indonesian forces. Hawke explained that the government had based its Timor decision on Australia's interests and the interests of "countries immediately concerned (especially Papua New Guinea), our ASEAN friends, and the United States."[9] All parties mentioned wished Australia essentially to leave well enough alone, which suited the pragmatic prime minister.

Australia's approach to Indochinese questions reveals similar pragmatism and indicates complementarity with U.S. positions. Deploring the Vietnamese occupation of Kampuchea, the Fraser government cut off civil aid to Vietnam in 1979. It derecognized remnants of the Pol Pot regime and abstained on the question of Kampuchean credentials at the United Nations. The Labor Party took office with a party commitment to resume civil aid to Vietnam. The formal rationale was familiar and plausible: it was unhealthy for Vietnam to endure international ostracism, increase its reliance on the Soviets, and be offered no incentive to disengage from

Kampuchea. But again the government backed off. There would be no resumption of aid until Vietnam exhibited considerable movement toward allowing a nonaligned Kampuchea to be free of Vietnamese occupation.

The government in Canberra consulted extensively with regional friends and outlying allies. It was prepared to be a channel of communications between Vietnam and the ASEAN nations, but would not undertake a formal mediating role. Australia's essential version of an Indochinese "initiative" for itself was welcome elsewhere, though skepticism about an early settlement in the region ran strong. The Hawke government was advised by the ASEAN community, China, Papua New Guinea, and the United States that restoration of civil aid would be unwise, and Japan had no intention of restoring its own aid program. Moreover, the consensus was against any Australian mediating effort. Australia felt that it could not offend so many nations with and for whom it had so many close political and security attractions. The argument from other capitals that Australian aid to Vietnam would convey the wrong signal and make Vietnam less disposed to seek a settlement was, of course, opposite to what Labor had deduced to be a reasonable gambit.

To Washington's satisfaction, the ANZAC powers have been especially active in the South Pacific. The effort has taken many forms. Civil and defense cooperation programs have been far in excess of those forthcoming from the United States. Exceptional Australian aid to and close political relations with Papua New Guinea have helped sustain the area's largest nation. New Zealand's political intelligence is especially respected by the United States. Both nations have on various occasions served as interlocutors and/or accommodators on legal and economic issues causing trouble between the United States and some Pacific island-nations. Australia and New Zealand used their access to dissuade a number of these countries from accepting Soviet diplomatic representation or economic assistance.

In the most overt strategic sense, the single most important contribution the United States has enjoyed has been Canberra's and Wellington's approach to regional nuclear issues. To protect sea lines of communication, facilitate naval passage and operations, and impose strategic denial on the Soviets, the United States has long been suspicious of nuclear weapons–free zone (NWFZ) proposals.

Australia and New Zealand have helped prevent a head-on clash between the United States and uncompromising free-zone supporters. The Fraser government freely admitted "we have ... made known to island governments on a continuing basis, both bilaterally and in multinational forms, our view that our mutual security interests could be harmed by actions which might restrict Western naval activities in the area."[10]

In part because of French testing in the region, the island-nations have long been uneasy about the nuclear factor. Various versions of a regional nuclear-free zone have been bruited about for some time, with the Fraser and Muldoon governments soft-pedaling such efforts. New Zealand has accepted the principle of a limited and defined zone, but has cautioned against implementation of proposals of persons who were "preoccupied by the ideal and [had] not examined the practicalities."[11]

Doubts about an ALP government's approach to the matter have apparently been dispelled. Hawke's words seem plain: Australia needs to "prevent nuclear testing, the storage of nuclear weapons, and the dumping of nuclear waste in the region. But referring back to the primacy we attach to the ANZUS treaty, I make it clear that the concept of a nuclear free zone is not intended to preclude the passage of nuclear-powered and armed vessels or air transit in the region."[12] The United States takes little if any exception to Australia's goals for such a nuclear-free zone. As Australia sets about promoting such a concept among the Pacific nations, its and New Zealand's credentials are enhanced by their long-standing and firm opposition to French testing. Without reputation, without entrée, their ability to argue on behalf of a modestly defined nuclear-free zone would be much reduced.

Problem Areas and Guidelines

Although Australia's and New Zealand's contributions to U.S. security objectives in the Indo-Pacific region are numerous and significant, it does not necessarily follow that such assets will be reliably available. It is useful to notice some of the possible problem areas, then suggest guidelines along which U.S. relations with Australia and New Zealand might profitably proceed.

From a U.S. security perspective, the Australian connection seems fit, even robust. The ALP government in Canberra has been reassuring. It is just possible, however, that the Hawke government's insistence on continuity in external affairs could erode the prime minister's own authority within his party and/or induce policy adaptations less in keeping with U.S. preferences. There are many vocal people, especially among Labor's rank-and-file members, offended by what they interpret as Hawke's carefree postponement or disposal of authoritative Labor policy on grounds of "changed circumstances" and outright pragmatism. Most of the parliamentary caucus is moderate and nonideological, but this might not indefinitely free Hawke to carry out policies exactly to his liking. If intraparty pressures build up, it will probably be through an accumulation of domestic as well as external policy grievances—grievances directed at style of governance and substance of policy. Some issues, such as uranium mining and marketing, arouse basic emotions. An issue such as Timor, though also emotive, is one more of conscience than of ideology and affects people well beyond the ALP. No immediate collision is forecast, but a watching brief seems in order.

Senior ALP party figures such as Hayden and Bowen, who earlier had voiced reservations about aspects of the defense relationship with the United States, changed their minds or fell quiet. Despite his reservations about visits by nuclear-powered or -armed vessels, Victoria premier John Cain acknowledges Commonwealth legal supremacy in determining whether such visits may occur. The new Labor government in Western Australia, where U.S. naval traffic is heaviest by far, has not interfered with the American presence. Survey data show overwhelming public support for ANZUS and a clear majority for port visits by nuclear-armed vessels. Hawke government policy on matters relating to U.S. defense policy and the U.S. presence in Australia will, however, as under Fraser, be the object of criticism from the Labor and non-Labor Left. In March 1983, some 150,000 people around Australia joined rallies on behalf of nuclear disarmament. Much of this sentiment was directed against U.S. policy and Australia's countenancing of it. There have been specific demonstrations against U.S. ship visits, but major incidents have been avoided. The disarmament and anti-U.S. movement could expand. Beyond some threshold, it could be more than a minor distraction for U.S. facilities and visiting forces and for Australian governments.

The nuclear issue and indeed the viability of security ties through ANZUS are, however, more pronounced in New Zealand. Developments there might not only degrade New Zealand's defense value to the United States, but potentially spill over into Australia and fray the alliance at large. That scenario derives from three considerations: the frailty and prospective loss of office by the incumbent National Party government; New Zealand public sentiment; and the possibility of an alternative government that, on present evidence, would not be as accommodating as its Labor counterpart in Australia.

Public reception of the government's defense policies has been mixed. ANZUS enjoys widespread support. The occasional visits of U.S. nuclear-powered vessels are approved. But nuclear issues have deeply divided the New Zealand public. There is a broad aversion to things nuclear, such as French tests in the Pacific and the presence of nuclear weapons in New Zealand or its Pacific neighborhood. The antinuclear movement is strong. There have been trade union shutdowns and significant public demonstrations protesting visits by U.S. vessels. New Zealand is a smaller, more isolated country than Australia. It is far removed from potential Indo-

Pacific flashpoints, and the sense of threat is low or indirect. Many New Zealanders fear being unnecessarily caught up in superpower rivalry. The New Zealand ethos is in general more placid, life quality–oriented and inward-turning than can be said of Australia.

At the organized political level, the result has been the evolution of defense policies held by the two main opposition parties that run strongly counter to those of the National Party government and are opposed in Washington. The Social Credit Party favors armed neutrality for New Zealand. The New Zealand Labor Party, effectively New Zealand's alternative government, holds a more complex and evolving position. In the writer's view, the impressions obtained by a U.S. congressional delegation visiting New Zealand in 1982 were misplaced. It was wrong for the delegation to report that National and Labor agreed that ANZUS was the "cornerstone of the nation's security," that "the overall importance and commitment to the ANZUS Treaty appears to transcend party politics," and that there were only "some differences" between the United States and Labor as to port calls by nuclear-powered vessels.[13]

The New Zealand Labor Party conference is on record urging withdrawal from ANZUS. Another party body, the Policy Council, sets authoritative policy, but the importance of the conference's feeling should not be belittled. Labor's last two leaders, Bill Rowling and David Lange, have accepted continuing membership in ANZUS. Lange has not downplayed the alliance as Rowling did and has not dwelt on restricting its coverage or championed its investiture with more economic content. Lange addressed the desirability of synchronizing New Zealand Labor policy with that of Australia's Labor government. While his thinking has shifted, he is not nearly as unconditional on matters affecting U.S. defense priorities and the alliance. He seems to favor port calls by nuclear-powered vessels, but has not publicly budged on opposition to nuclear weapons aboard visiting vessels. He has been severely chastized by party colleagues for his apparent acceptance of such visits.

From the U.S. vantage point, Lange appears more flexible than Rowling and would be easier to deal with as head of government. But basic problems remain. In 1982 a Labor member's proposal to ban nuclear weapons from New Zealand and its territorial waters was defeated in parliament by a single vote; all opposition party members voted in favor. The United States' "no confirmation/no denial" policy on the nuclear armament of ships and aircraft remains in place. Washington feels that the Darwin B-52 transit agreement with Australia as a model for ship visits to New Zealand is inapplicable, and the United States is unprepared to change the rules for New Zealand.

A Labor government in Wellington could therefore create severe U.S.–

New Zealand strains on a basic issue, one the United States regards as fundamental to its own strategic freedom of action and the vitality of the ANZUS alliance. Antinuclear and anti-U.S. opinion in Australia could gather force and confidence from a serious falling-out between New Zealand and the United States. Even in the absence of a change in official Australian policy, if only two of the three partners were operating the alliance sympathetically, ANZUS could well erode, and with it, its salutary impact beyond its membership.

Conclusions

The United States, Australia, and New Zealand, and their peoples are in a most meaningful way friends, partners, and allies. But nations devise policies tailored to their perceived interests, and these three are no exception. It has been analytically appropriate to evaluate Australia and New Zealand as U.S. assets. The discussion has not tried to pass judgment on the merits of U.S. objectives in the region. It is useful to acknowledge that these objectives and their supporting policies have changed little over several administrations.

The conclusion here is that Australia and New Zealand, with ANZUS as a bonding agent, have indeed been exceptionally valued security assets. Differences have and always will exist, and really nettlesome irritants may arise. Unless the United States radically reordered its security goals and policies, it could not avert such difficulties. But given the stakes involved, it should and often can temper the effects of such difficulties. The prescriptions are unremarkable, but worth underscoring. Style and substance in developing a measured response often merge. It is a combination of sensitivity, common sense, informed judgment, and priorities.

One area in U.S.-Australian and New Zealand relations that deserves cultivation on matters in dispute is explanation and persuasion and the avoidance of actual or perceived intrusion and browbeating. In 1982 when the New Zealand Labor conference was passing resolutions critical of ANZUS, the U.S. embassy in Wellington issued a statement declaring that "our reading of the New Zealand electorate gives them a lot more credit than some people [the Labor Party] apparently do for their understanding of global issues and their sophistication about things nuclear."[14] Rowling and others accused the United States of unwarranted interference and of arrogance. The line between candor and trespass is thin. But in an emotionally tense atmosphere, imprudence can embarrass and weaken friends and moderates and invigorate critics.

Second, the United States should be prepared to make allowances for the special interests and, at times, political requirements of the leadership in Canberra and Wellington. In light of widespread Australian skepticism when the proposal was raised, Fraser needed some concrete concessions from the United States governing terms on which B-52s would transmit through Darwin. Given its warm embrace of the alliance and of U.S. defense requirements, the Hawke government was entitled to a close hearing on its ideas about an ANZUS review and the assignment of an official to monitor activities at U.S. facilities in Australia. To Washington's credit, in these instances the response was neither dismissive nor condescending. Indeed, as when New Zealand lobbied hard in Washington to have pending U.S. treaties with Tuvalu, Kiribati, and with New Zealand regarding the Cook Islands ratified, the favor could be construed as being as much in United States' as in other parties' interests.

Third, the United States should be ready to move an extra distance in mollifying Australia and New Zealand on nonsecurity questions. Despite assorted commercial and legal differences with the United States, Australia and New Zealand have refrained from invoking linkage diplomacy. They have not insinuated that security arrangements might have to be reconsidered unless extraneous claims were satisfied. Granted the United States has to contend with its political constituencies, but it should extend economic concessions wherever possible. Australia and New Zealand both have negative trading balances with the United States and depend to a large extent on foreign trade. Their economies are troubled and not likely to rebound as fast as the American. It reinforces the climate of partnership when on special occasions the United States can be appreciative of their contributions to mutual security.

To return to essentials, the United States realizes exceptional security benefits from its Australian and New Zealand connections. The connections are not, and will not be, unpunctuated by differences and arguments. But at slight political and economic cost, the connections are manifestly worth sustaining.

Notes

1. Robert Hawke, remarks to the American-Australian Association, New York, June 16, 1983, cited by Mike Steketee, *Sydney Morning Herald*, June 16, 1983.

2. Robert Hawke, address at the National Press Club, Washington D.C., June 15, 1983, *Official Transcript*, p. 4.

3. New York interview of June 18, 1983, cited by Richard Bernstein, *New York Times*, June 19, 1983.

4. William Hayden, broadcast interview, cited by Michelle Grattan, *Age* (Melbourne), May 2, 1983.

5. Warren Cooper, remarks in Tokyo of March 16, 1983, cited in *Christchurch Press,* March 17, 1983.

6. Robert Hawke, Canberra press conference on June 1, 1983, cited by Michelle Grattan, *Age,* June 2, 1983.

7. Robert Muldoon, *New Zealand Parliamentary Debates,* June 10, 1981, p. 1467.

8. "The RAAF's Role in Southeast Asia," cited by Michael Richardson, *Pacific Defense Reporter,* October 1982.

9. Robert Hawke, interview with Ian Perkin and Wio Joustra, in *Australian,* March 29, 1983.

10. Senator Dame Margaret Guilfoyle, representing the minister for foreign affairs, Senate, *Commonwealth Parliamentary Debates,* May 18, 1982, p. 2079.

11. David Thomson, minister of defense, address to the Canterbury Officers Club, Christchurch, May 25, 1983, cited in *Christchurch Press,* May 26, 1983.

12. Robert Hawke, address at the National Press Club, Washington, D.C., June 15, 1983, *Official Transcript,* p. 10.

13. *Delegation Mission to New Zealand, Australia, Hong Kong, and Japan: A Report to the United States Senate by Senator Thad Cochran,* Senate, 97th Cong., 2nd sess., Document 97–27, 1982, p. 3.

14. U.S. embassy release of May 12, 1982, cited in *New Zealand Herald* (Auckland), May 13, 1982.

AUSTRALIA AND THE SECURITY OF THE PACIFIC BASIN

T. B. Millar

Over the two centuries of Australia's existence as a "European" country in the Southwest Pacific, slowly but surely and due to both internal and external factors it has advanced its sense of political and strategic independence. This has not been a simple continuum from total dependence to total independence. Politics and strategy are two lines—or groups of lines, like strands in a cable—that overlap, cross, and recross. Rhetoric has rarely coincided with reality, nor desire with accomplishment. The lion in some circumstances became the lamb in others. Nevertheless, since federation brought into existence a single state (albeit one still heavily overhung with the legal and psychological appendages of colonial status), Australia has assumed the role of a smallish middle power, largely independent in its capacity to make most political decisions but still dependent for its ultimate security on the support or protection of the U.S. superpower.

From its earliest days, Australia was a Pacific country. The initial settlements were on the continent's southeast corner, washed by the Pacific. A majority of the population, a preponderance of the decisionmakers in government, and the owners of wealth still live there, even if the great natural resources that determine Australia's economic well-being and international position lie in an archipelago of pockets spread across the 3 million square miles of the continent and an equal area of the Exclusive Economic Zone. Australian settlers spread out eastwards—as traders, missionaries, scavengers—until Australia became the dominant economic power in the Southwest Pacific.

Since the middle of the last century Australia has felt threatened by competing European powers operating in the Southwest Pacific and by peoples from the Northwestern and Western Pacific—Chinese, Japanese,

Indonesians, and, at several removes, Vietnamese. By the first decade of the century, Australia proposed to the British government a "Monroe doctrine" for the Pacific and received a dusty answer. In the mid-1930s it revived the notion in a different form, as a nonaggression pact. This also lapsed for want of international support as the world was preoccupied with Europe's second civil war in just over twenty years. But the intention of both proposals was the same: to have the United States exert its great power to keep the states of the vast Pacific perimeter in "international peace and security." This motion was given unplanned substance by the Pacific war of 1941–1945 and by the postwar regional security arrangements largely fashioned on the anvil of messianic U.S. anticommunism.

Australia and New Zealand were the only genuine and lasting allies of the United States in its postwar Pacific activities. South Korea and Taiwan sought only to be helped and protected against their stronger neighbors. Japan and Thailand wanted a one-way guarantee—a military umbrella traded in Tokyo and Bangkok against political embarrassment. The Philippines wanted help to defeat insurrection and as fat a fee as possible for the U.S. bases that help secure the region. Pakistan wanted defense against and a capacity to hit back at its subcontinental rival, India. Only Australia and New Zealand gave more than they received, paying their premiums on a U.S. insurance policy that might never mature, developing a web of relationships with the United States that went far beyond security, and becoming in the process important parts of a global Western defense, industrial, and cultural system, the main threat to which lay not in the South Pacific but in the new imperialism based in Eastern Europe.

In coming to terms with postwar Asia and its varying manifestations of nationalist sentiment, Australia has acknowledged them but clung to its Western roots and ties. How incompatible the two sets of pressure and attraction are remains to be seen. The strong trading and nascent security relationships with Japan are almost wholly compatible with both countries' links with the United States. Similarly, Australia followed the United States in coming to terms with the People's Republic of China, even if the situation was complicated recently by President Reagan's leaning toward Taiwan and by events in Kampuchea. Australia's links with ASEAN members and its deference to the association fit with their common anticommunism and ultimate dependence on the U.S. power. We thus have a rough balance of power in the Asian-Pacific region, and Australia is part of the status quo group, where its interests have always lain.

Yet largely because the two great protagonists are both Pacific and Atlantic powers, security in the Pacific cannot be separated from security in the North Atlantic and indeed the Middle East. The overall balance has become more complex than at any time over the past 30 years. The USSR has achieved a rough equivalence of nuclear power with the United States, prompting the Republican administration to engage in a combative rhetoric that many friends of the United States find uncomfortable. The West's strategic situation has also changed for the worse by the Soviet occupation of Afghanistan and its consequent closeness to the Gulf. The NATO alliance has been troubled by some ham-fisted economic diplomacy by the United States over interests rates and the Siberian gas pipeline, by dubious trade practices by the European Economic Community in its steel exports to the the United States, and by innate incompatible tendencies on both sides—in Europe, the belief that the the United States is trigger-happy and ready to fight a war to the last European; in the the United States, the belief that Europe is free riding on the U.S. security guarantee and prone to political accommodations with the Eastern bloc—a form of finlandization—for economic advantage.

The Western alliance—the conservative governments in Britain and West Germany notwithstanding—is thus in considerable disarray. Soviet propaganda against the NATO decision to upgrade its IRBM capacity in order to match the SS-20 deployments has been heavy and astute, whereas that by Reagan has been heavy but inept. The propaganda fostered the largest antinuclear protests ever held in the Western world. The antinuclear movement developed a higher intellectual and religious content through professional groups (doctors, lawyers, etc.), churches (both Catholic and Protestant), women's groups, and others organized to promote either unilateral nuclear disarmament (which would leave the West greatly vulnerable), a freeze on nuclear production (inspectable only in the West), or a declaration of "no first use" (more harmful to the West with its inferior conventional capacity). Although Britain and the Federal Republic of Germany are committed to installing the range of weapons, other member-countries are much more equivocal. In the United States the widespread public apprehension over nuclear weapons helped produce a greater readiness by the administration to consider a genuine process of negotiation and ease public confrontation of the USSR. There is a more reasoned debate on the subject, with prominent establishment figures in favor of various actions to reduce the danger of nuclear war and the scale of its preparations. The Reagan administration's problems with Congress over the MX missile publicly reflected these attitudes.

While the disturbance to U.S.–West European relations is much more complex, and while NATO is attempting to contain the disintegrative forces, we cannot ignore the forces.

The Soviet bloc also has its problems, of course, The Soviet Union is struck in a quagmire in Afghanistan. Poland, reflecting a serious disaffection with communist rule and Soviet control, has continuing underground activity despite martial law, and its loyalty in the event of an East-West war cannot be assumed. The whole of the communist bloc is experiencing severe economic difficulties, with a gross debt to the West approaching $100 billion.

Correctly or not, important officials in both the United States and the USSR believe that their relationship has noticeably deteriorated and the prospect of war has become closer since the Reagan administration took office. Yet it is hard to see a situation developing in Europe that would warrant, or would induce, either side to resort to force. The inevitable costs far outweigh any conceivable advantages. The two acts of arms control negotiations, dealing with strategic and intermediate-range nuclear weapons, offer a basis for a gradual relaxation of tension and confrontation. This may take some time to achieve, and the Russians are playing a dangerous game of threat and inducement to make Western Europe more accommodating to Soviet interests. The fear of nuclear war is heightened since the West European states are not prepared to match Soviet conventional strength. Yet none of the states of Western Europe is anywhere near comparable to Finland. The major NATO Europeans—Germany, France, Britain—are staunchly independent, anticommunist, and strongly armed. They would fight if attacked, as would U.S. forces in Europe. On the civil side, a Soviet attack anywhere in Europe would destroy important economic and technological benefits that the West offers the Eastern bloc. Wars are sometimes entered rashly, wantonly, or inadvisedly, but a war launched in Europe would involve an unprecedented degree of each of these.

Outside Europe and the North Atlantic, both superpowers have shown determination not to let a situation get out of hand. Thus the Russians have played a very subdued role in Africa, in South America, and in the Middle East, as they did in the Sino-Vietnamese war. The provision and apparent manning of surface-to-air missiles in Syria is an exception to this principle, but it is a very late intervention and may provide, from an objective viewpoint, a constraint on Israeli ambitions. It is assumed that the Soviets will take and foster targets of opportunity where they can—as in Central America, or if there were a second, pro-communist revolution in Iran, or a left-wing revolution in Iraq or Saudi Arabia. Here the U.S. Rapid Deployment Force, or Central Command, and the Carter-Reagan doctrine that the flow of Saudi oil is a vital U.S. interest constitute something of a deterrent to Soviet action in that region. A more powerful deterrent, so far as the Arab-Israel dispute is concerned, is that each American administration since 1948 has declared that it will not permit the destruction of Israel. It was the realization of this that prompted President Sadat to fly to Israel and to Camp David and thus to regain for Egypt in a single piece of diplomacy virtually all it had lost in four wars.

Australia contributes to the Western alliance system outside the Pacific in important ways. First, it is a host to major U.S. defense facilities: (1) the communications station at North West Cape, which communicates with submerged U.S. submarines in the Western Pacific and Indian oceans; (2) the ground station at Pine Gap in central Australia for an intelligence-gathering satellite; and (3) the station at Nurrungar, which, among other things, monitors Soviet missile launches. These facilities are widely believed to ensure that in a nuclear war Australia will be a target, but successive Australian governments of both major persuasions have taken the view that by providing more accurate communications and information, the facilities are an important part of the Western deterrent and thus make a nuclear war less likely. American submarines are serviced at the small Cockburn Sound naval base in Western Australia, and B-52 bombers use the air station at Darwin for staging (to or from Diego Garcia in the Indian Ocean), training exercises, and surveillance duties off the West Australian coast. Thus Australia is part of the process whereby the United States is able to deploy forces to protect Israel and the security of Western interests in the Gulf. The Royal Australian Air Force is part of the Integrated Air Defense System for Malaysia and Singapore, and Australian maritime reconnaissance aircraft stationed in that area patrol sections of the Indian Ocean. Through the Five-Power Defense Arrangement (with Malaysia, Singapore, Britain, and Australia) and its residual obligations under SEATO to the defense of Thailand, Australia contributes to the security of the junctions between the Indian and Pacific oceans and the few vital straits between them. Australia is also an important source of defense intelligence to its allies and friends. All these total—even without military forces in an emergency—a significant contribution to the security of the Western world.

In East Asia and the Western Pacific, the Soviet-U.S. balance has been shifting in several ways. With Soviet aircraft and naval shipping using facilities in Vietnam and a sophisticated communications station there, the Russians established a military presence in Southeast Asia that changed the strategic situation throughout the region. They have also engineered a favorable presence in Laos, where they are a welcome counterbalance to their allies, the Vietnamese. The Soviet Pacific Fleet is in some ways superior and in some ways inferior to the U.S. Seventh Fleet. Overall, the balance favors the United States, which has a three-service presence in South Korea, bases in Japan and the Philippines as well as at Guam and Honolulu, and access to bases in Australia. Even so the United States cannot ensure the security of its ships west of Honolulu. For a time one could speak of a de facto U.S.-China-Japan partnership against the Soviet Union in Eastern Asia, but since 1981 the Chinese have distanced themselves from the Americans and improved (without excess of zeal) their relations with the USSR. This does not represent anything like a return to the Sino-Soviet alliance of the 1950s: the differences and disagreements between the two great powers are too fundamental for that. Elsewhere, apart from North Korea and Indochina, there is almost no active sympathy for the Soviet Union anywhere in East Asia and the Pacific.

Whereas the balance in Europe may favor the Soviets in conventional arms and tactical nuclear weapons, it does not offer sufficient overall advantage to induce any Soviet military adventures. In the Arab-Israel dispute the United States has the major external role; in the Gulf the situation is fluid, but Russians respect the the United States' determination to keep oil flowing; in Afghanistan the Soviets are stuck in a war they cannot seem to win and cannot afford to lose. And in Asia and the Western Pacific, an improved Soviet position still leaves the USSR facing a largely hostile or at least unsympathetic de facto coalition of almost all noncommunist states, including those of ASEAN and, of course, of the ANZUS powers.

The regional strategic situation in Southeast Asia is weighted on the side of order and stability, although there are fragile elements. Those who fear a breakdown in international order in the region generally do so on the grounds that Vietnam, with Soviet support, may launch a large-scale attack against a Thailand supported by China. Why should it be so? It is not enough to say that by nature Vietnam is imperialistic and expansionist on its own behalf, or (a Chinese assertion) is the "Cuba" of Asia. The evidence suggests that the "dominoes" stop at the Thai-Kampuchean border. While Vietnam presumably wants to keep the border secure to deter Chinese reinforcements to the Khmer Rouge and the forces of Son Sann and Sihanouk and perhaps to support communist elements in northeast Thailand, a major Vietnamese war against Thailand would be counterproductive on all counts. It would range ASEAN, within which there is some sympathy for Vietnam and some fear of China, firmly against Vietnam. It would make Southeast Asia more strongly opposed to the Soviet presence in the area. It would bring renewed U.S. military aid to Thailand and defer indefinitely any attempts at rapprochement with or offers of aid by the United States or Japan to Vietnam. It would be a massive additional burden to a ruinous economy bailed out by Soviet aid acquired at considerable political cost. The Vietnam occupation of Kampuchea and Laos is nevertheless overtly imperialistic, and periodic Vietnamese forays across the border keep Thailand apprehensive and ASEAN uncertain what to do about it.

Australia is a factor in this situation and in others in Southeast Asia. It has given bilateral assurances to Thailand under the Southeast Asia Collective Defense Treaty ever since the Rusk-Thanat agreement in 1962. In the event of "aggression by means of armed attack" against Thailand, Australia will probably at least provide arms and equipment.

For several years, contrary to ASEAN and Chinese policies and pressure, the Australian government has viewed the rump regime of Pol Pot as too vicious to be supported even diplomatically and unlikely to become again the government of Kampuchea. Australia thus recognizes neither the Khmer Rouge nor the Vietnamese-installed government of Heng Samrin in Phnom Penh. The Labor Party government in Canberra, with more hesitation than its party platform warrants, watched quizzically and unsympathetically by the ASEAN members and China, has made approaches to Hanoi. It has two overlapping objectives: to encourage Vietnam to withdraw from Kampuchea and to promote better Vietnamese relations with the West so that Vietnam will not be so dependent on Soviet aid or offer such strategically significant compensation. Whether this is politically presumptuous for Australia or naive for its foreign minister—as some regional governments seem to think—it is a step in the only direction likely to bring greater stability to Indochina and its neighborhood.

It is not always easy to see what keeps ASEAN together. The association's economic objectives have barely been scratched. Its members have gained in international status by their common grouping—at little cost. Intraregional tensions have been swept under the carpet. But what is the carpet? When ASEAN was established in 1967, it was a common sense of insecurity and apprehension when Britain decided to withdraw from east of Suez and as the United States became deeply mired in Vietnam. The ASEAN states had too many dissimilarities in character, national interest, and external affiliation to form a security grouping, but to set up an economic arrangement was at least a common rope to cling to as the deck shifted under them. With the U.S. disengagement, ASEAN members have established bilateral defense arrangements with one another, and Australia is indirectly linked to these by its separate agreements with each. We will have to see whether a more stable Southeast Asian mainland (if it develops) contributes to the cohesion or to the disintegration of ASEAN. If there is no common fear, will there be a common bond?

Australia, by its contributions under the Five-Power Arrangement, its bilateral security links with ASEAN states, its membership in ANZUS, its own small but professional armed forces, and its lack of political ambitions is a positive force for peace and stability throughout the area. The only uncertainty is over the Australian-Indonesian relationship, stemming largely from Indonesia's bloody invasion of Timor in late 1976. Both Australian governments (of Mr. Whitlam and Mr. Fraser) straddled this event and derived the worst of all worlds by privately acquiescing in the takeover and publicly condemning it. Indonesia took umbrage at this and at the persistent unsympathetic reporting in Australian media. Relations are only now returning to a more even keel under strong efforts by both governments. Papua New Guinea, where both countries have interests and where political stability is still precarious, impinges on the Australian-Indonesian relationship in ways that are potentially destabilizing. Australia has no formal commitment to the security of Papua New Guinea, but it has a strong moral and psychological commitment. If in the unwelcome but conceivable situation of having to choose between supporting Papua New Guinea and supporting Indonesia, an Australia government would probably be compelled by electoral pressure to support Papua New Guinea.

During 1949–1972 Australia developed good trading relations with the People's Republic of China, but it had no diplomatic relations and indeed was generally unfriendly. Then the new Labor Party government of Mr. Whitlam quickly established formal relations, which have steadily prospered, even to the exchange of military attachés of senior rank.

The Australia-China relationship barely impinges on the security of the region. Australia is too remote from China to be relevant, too small to be influential. Each may give the other a nudge, wink, or frown, but unlike the Sino-American situation, no great issue now unites or divides them or hangs uncertainly on the horizon. Inasmuch as the Soviet presence in Vietnam is a strategic minus to the Western powers and noncommunist Southeast Asia, these (including Australia) are affected by whatever China does that will enhance that presence. Despite a common objective (the removal of Soviet power), China and Australia disagree over the means to attain it, and the United States has supported China in principle and in confronting Vietnam despite the obviously unfortunate consequences. Were China and the USSR to become partners once again, the whole international strategic balance would change to the great disadvantage of the West, and there is nothing Australia could do about it. But this seems an unlikely event.

Twenty years after World War II, Japan and Australia had become economically interdependent to a remarkable degree. Japan was Australia's largest customer, especially for a range of raw materials, and Australia was an important Japanese market for manufactured goods. Nearly another twenty years on, this relationship has been maintained. Both depend on the United States for their ultimate security and both engage in joint naval exercises with U.S. forces (the RIMPAC exercises).

There is a considerable literature on Japan's relations with the United States. Although U.S. bases in the Philippines are an important part of the defense of Western interests from Aden to Los Angeles (a fact on which

President Marcos trades without shame), the U.S.-Japan relationship is the key relationship in the strategic pattern of power in the Pacific. So long as Japan and the United States remain both economic and military partners, the long-term peace of the region is assured. A good Japan-U.S. relationship, preferably with Australia in partnership with both, is thus a vital interest of Australia.

The considerable trade between Japan and Australia would require protection in war. The two countries could not ensure this, assuming that the Soviet Union were hostile. Australia, in more muted but unequivocal tones, has joined the United States in urging Japan to be more strongly armed, including developing a capacity to patrol sea-lanes. The U.S. proposal is that Japan should safeguard maritime routes southeast and southwest (toward Southeast Asia and Australia) from Japan for 1,000 miles. To do this effectively in war would require increasing the Japanese navy by about a factor of three, which is politically unfeasible in the present climate. This distance takes Japan near the archipelagic states, whose wartime memories and national pride react adversely to a Japanese naval presence. With a naval strength much smaller even than Japan's, Australia could do little to safeguard its three major routes—north to Southeast Asia and Japan, northwest to Europe, and northeast to the United States.

The latter is also a major trading nation across the Pacific north (Japan is its largest overseas customer), center, and south and through the straits into the Indian Ocean. It would undoubtedly make sense for the United States, Japan, and Australia to operate jointly to safeguard merchant shipping in time of conflict and to prepare to do so in situations short of war. The United States has been promoting such activities, including other interested parties (especially Canada and New Zealand), for several years. (These five countries—the United States, Japan, Australia, New Zealand, and Canada—account for a large part of all trans-Pacific trade.) This raises the question whether there should be some wider alliance or semi-alliance structure for this purpose, a grand Pacific security grouping to protect shipping against hostile Soviet naval action.

However logical this may seem, probably none of the countries concerned would enter such an agreement. Australia, New Zealand, Canada, and Japan all have treaty arrangements with the United States, although Canada's lie within NATO (for the defense of Europe) and Japan's are for the defense of Japan, not of the region. Similarly Thailand (within what is left of SEATO), the Philippines, and the Republic of Korea have security arrangements designed for their protection but not for their participation in a wider collectivity. Other states such as Malaysia, Singapore, and Indonesia would have political problems in entering a formal treaty with the United States. They already feel that the United States would stand behind them if necessary, to protect *its* whole regional and global strategic interests. Australia's Labor government (since March 1983) has kept all the links established by its predecessors and will be part of whatever formal or informal arrangements the United States can engineer. It is not in Australia's interest to push its nonaligned neighbors into public declarations of dependence on the United States.

Australia and New Zealand, as neighbors of common heritage, are probably closer in most respects than any other two countries. Despite some hostility toward the United States in the New Zealand Labor Party, the policies of the two countries toward their partners in ANZUS and in the Five-Power Arrangement remain similar and compatible, as are their policies toward the micro-states of the Southwest Pacific. There Australia and New Zealand, as friendly neighborhood countries, can provide an anchor—economic and defense aid, and a general sense of security—that the United States by its remoteness cannot give. A tighter defense arrangement would probably create more problems than it would solve. Existing institutions, especially the South Pacific Forum, should meet any changes in the regional strategic balance. If there is a real challenge to the independence of any micro-state, especially on claims to the natural resources in its exclusive economic zone, some would wish a tighter link to the United States that they might not obtain, but might de facto be affected through the links of ANZUS.

One would like to recommend dramatic or even modest changes to institutions or other formal international arrangements throughout the Pacific that would ensure a wider sense of security in peacetime and a stronger factual security in the event of conflict. There appears no alternative to the patient search for consensus and cooperation, to the quiet exploration of informal agreement, and to the appropriate adjustment of institutions thereafter.

U.S. Installations in Australia: Agenda for the Future

Desmond Ball

The United States maintains in Australia more than two dozen installations concerned with military communications, navigation, satellite tracking and control, and various forms of intelligence collection, making Australia host to more such U.S. operations than any other country except the United Kingdom, Canada, and West Germany.

These installations have been the subject of major political controversy in Australia. They comprise the single most important U.S. strategic interest in Australia, but they are also the source and focus of most of the disquiet and opposition concerning the Australian-U.S. security relationship. The first part of this paper describes the principal U.S. installations in Australia, the second part outlines the major issues raised by these installations, and the third part discusses areas for future policy decision concerning these installations.

U.S. Installations in Australia

The exact number of U.S. installations in Australia is impossible to determine. In the first place, there is a definitional problem. All the important installations are officially known as "joint U.S.-Australian facilities" and involve Australian as well as U.S. personnel and funding. Indeed, some installations are manned and operated entirely by Australians, although the operations primarily benefit the United States. More important, however, is the extraordinary secrecy that surrounds these installations. The Australian public has never been given a list of all the defense, scientific, and intelligence installations in Australia. Even where a particular operation has been acknowledged, its function is usually described euphemistically only as "space research," "upper atmospheric studies," or "geological and geophysical research."

The most recent list of U.S. defense and scientific installations in Australia was provided by the minister of defense in answer to a question in the House on October 10, 1978. Listed were (1) Naval Communications Station Harold E. Holt, North West Cape; (2) Joint Defense Space Research Facility, Alice Springs, commonly known as Pine Gap; (3) Joint Defense Space Communications Station, Woomera, commonly known as Nurrungar; (4) Joint Geological and Geophysical Research Station, Alice Springs, commonly known as USAF Detachment 421; (5) TRANET Station 112 at Smithfield, South Australia; and (6) portable geodetic satellite observations posts, then operating at Perth and Townsville.

This list is far from complete. It excludes the National Aeronautics and Space Administration (NASA) satellite-tracking stations, such as Orroral Valley in the Australian Capital Territory, used to track and communicate with U.S. military and classified intelligence satellites; a network of five seismic stations operated by the U.S. Defense Advanced Research Project Agency (DARPA), at Hobart, Adelaide, Charters Towers (Queensland), Alice Springs, and Mundaring (Western Australia); a seismic research observatory at Narrogin (Western Australia); a U.S. Air Force solar observatory at Learmonth, (Western Australia); and an Omega VLF navigation station at Darriman in Gippsland (Victoria). On March 11, 1981, the Australian and U.S. governments agreed on the terms and conditions governing U.S. Air Force B-52 aircraft staging through the Royal Australian Air Force Base, Darwin, on navigation-training and sea surveillance flights over the Indian Ocean. About a hundred U.S. Air Force personnel and associated equipment support these operations, and some of these are stationed at RAAF Base, Darwin. Since 1979 the U.S. Navy has increasingly used HMAS Stirling at Cockburn Sound, Western Australia, as a replenishment and crew rest port for its ships patrolling the Indian Ocean, including aircraft carriers, nuclear-powered submarines, and missile cruisers and destroyers.

The three most critical U.S. installations are the naval communications station at North West Cape and the satellite ground control stations at Pine Gap and Nurrungar.

North West Cape, officially declared operational on September 16, 1967, is an important link in the U.S. global defense communications network. According to official brochures the base serves several purposes. However, its main function is to maintain reliable communications with submarines of the U.S. fleet in the Pacific Ocean and, in particular, "to provide communication for the U.S. Navy's most powerful deterrent force—the nuclear powered ballistic missile submarine." The very low frequency facility is the largest and most powerful of all stations in the United States' worldwide submarine communication system.

North West Cape also has an array of high frequency transmitters that are important to U.S. military operations in the Indian and Western Pacific Ocean areas and a ground station for the U.S. Defense Satellite Communications System (DSCS).

The Pine Gap facility, operational in 1969, is located nineteen kilometers (twelve miles) southwest of Alice Springs. The facility consists of seven large radomes and an enormous computer complex, currently being further expanded.

Pine Gap is formally administered by the U.S. National Reconnaissance Office (NRO). It was originally established as part of Project Rhyolite, which involves a few very large signals intelligence (SIGINT) satellites in geostationary orbit.

Nurrungar, located within the Woomera restricted area, about 480 kilometers (300 miles) northwest of Adelaide, is one of two ground stations for the U.S. satellite early warning system. Formally a detachment of the U.S. Air Force's Space Command, Nurrungar provides a real-time data link between the North American Air Defense Command (NORAD), the Strategic Air Command (SAC), and the National Military Command System on the one hand and the satellite early-warning system on the other hand. Data are derived from sensors aboard the geostationary satellites, which detect missile firings shortly after lift-off.

The Issues

These installations are the subject of intense controversy, and opposition to them remains widespread. The four principal areas of debate relate to the implications of operations at these installations for the global strategic balance, the possibility of Australia's becoming a nuclear target, a more independent Australian defense and foreign policy, and Australian sovereignty.

Implications for the Global Strategic Balance

At the global strategic level, the issue is between those who argue that the signals-monitoring and early-warning functions of Pine Gap and Nurrungar prevent any Soviet surprise attack and the North West Cape station preserves the deterrent capability of the U.S. submarine-launched ballistic missile (SLBM) force, thus reducing the possibility of any nuclear war—and those who argue that the capabilities of the United States' SLBMs enable them to attack Soviet nuclear forces in so-called counterforce operations and that satellite surveillance capabilities allow the United States to plan its strategic posture so as to engage the Soviet Union in a nuclear war rather than simply deter such a war, thus making nuclear war more likely.

Australia as a Nuclear Target

There is now widespread acceptance within the defense community of the argument that Australia's hosting of U.S. defense and intelligence installations is likely to involve Australia in a nuclear war in which not just the installations but (although much less likely) perhaps also Australia's military bases and facilities and even cities might be targets. In particular, it is generally accepted that North West Cape, Pine Gap, and Nurrungar would be priority targets in any strategic nuclear exchange, while RAAF Base Darwin and HMAS Stirling might be targets in some circumstances.

Still, it is argued that the effects of nuclear attacks against North West Cape, Pine Gap, and Nurrungar would be marginal given the isolated locations of these installations (although the fatalities from attacks on RAAF Base Darwin and HMAS Stirling could reach 150,000), and, in any case, Australia has a responsibility to accept the risks involved in supporting U.S. attempts to balance Soviet nuclear capabilities.

Implications for a More Independent Defense and Foreign Policy

In the 1950s and 1960s, when the critical decisions were taken to house the U.S. installations, Australian defense planners believed that because of its enormous size but limited budgetary resources and population, Australia could defend itself only with the active assistance of the United States and that the presence of the U.S. facilities on Australia's soil committed the United States to such assistance. Neither of these assumptions has been credible in the Australian defense community since the late 1960s. It is clear that the U.S. installations have constrained moves to a more self-reliant Australian defense posture and circumscribed Australia's diplomatic freedom of maneuver, especially regarding proposed regional arms control arrangements such as nuclear-free zones or so-called zones of peace.

The U.S. connection led to the development of an Australian defense posture that is not optimum from the Australian point of view and, indeed, has serious weaknesses.

With an annual defense budget of some $4 billion, of which only about 13 percent is devoted to new major capital acquisitions, Australian defense planners must choose between a force structure optimized for the defense of Australia, its maritime approaches, and its vital national interests and a structure designed for more distant operations in collaboration with U.S. forces. There are insufficient resources for a defense posture capable of satisfying both strategic concepts.

Infringements on Sovereignty

There are aspects of the U.S.-Australian intelligence connections and of the operations of some U.S. installations in Australia that led to Australian involvement in activities about which the Australian government has been neither informed nor consulted and in which their interests have not been appreciated.

One aspect of the intelligence relationship that infringes on Australian sovereignty is the opportunity for domestic intelligence operations provided by some intelligence facilities in Australia. This is especially the case regarding SIGINT operations, since the facilities are indiscriminate about the signals they intercept and record. There is evidence that the United States has monitored Australian communications. In some cases it would be difficult to avoid picking up local signals. SIGINT receivers tuned to wavelengths on the order of six centimeters would automatically intercept Australian voice messages and nonvoice information (facsimile material, teletype, telex, and other printer traffic) carried on microwave relay systems and domestic communication satellite links. Documents obtained by the *New York Times* in April 1979 revealed that Australian communications were included in the electronic intelligence intercepted by SIGINT satellites controlled from Pine Gap.

The U.S. facilities in Australia have been involved with external military activities several times without the knowledge or consent of the Australian government. North West Cape's high frequency transmitters were committed to the American mining of Haiphong and other North Vietnamese harbors in 1972. A Defense Department dossier, leaked at the ALP's Federal Conference in July 1973, asserted that satellites controlled through Australian ground stations were used to pinpoint targets for U.S. bombing raids in Cambodia. And during the Middle East War of October 1973, Pine Gap and Nurrungar, as well as North West Cape, were placed on alert on October 11, five days after the war began, and two weeks before the U.S. general alert of October 25.

Australian ground stations were apparently used to relay U.S. satellite intelligence about the Middle East conflict to the United States. At least some of this information was passed to the Israelis without the knowledge of the Australian government, whose avowed policy was evenhandedness. North West Cape was used on October 25 to communicate the general alert to U.S. installations and forces in the Indo-Pacific region. Only with this communication did the Australian government learn that *any* bases in Australia were involved in the alert. Australia was not even told this until the alert had been implemented.

In May 1978 it was revealed that the United States planned to upgrade the North West Cape satellite ground terminal; the minister for defense had not been informed.

Infringements of Australia's sovereignty occasioned by the operations at North West Cape have been of particular concern to the Australian Labor Party. As the present foreign minister, Bill Hayden, stated in April 1981:

> The question remains ... whether or not Australia exercises sufficient control over the operations of North West Cape to ensure that our authority and sovereignty is preserved.
>
> The answer is, no, we do not.
>
> The fact is that key U.S. communications from North West Cape cannot be monitored nor controlled by those Australians working there. Even the Americans at the station are unable to do this.
>
> Key messages are relayed in code through North West Cape from U.S. command centers elsewhere in the world. They are unintelligible to local U.S. staff even if they wished to monitor their contents.
>
> The most dramatic illustration of the use to which North West Cape could be put is the obvious one of relaying an order for a nuclear attack.
>
> At a lower level, it could be a series of commands directing offensive military operations in an area, and of a nature, that compromised our national interest.
>
> Eight years ago, during conflict in the Middle East, the United States relayed a message through North West Cape placing U.S. nuclear submarines on high levels of alert. Australia was not told beforehand.
>
> Australia has a sovereign right to be in ultimate control of affairs on her own territory. In these circumstances, we find present arrangements covering North West Cape unsatisfactory.
>
> We would seek to renegotiate the North West Cape Agreement to provide: first, that Australia's consent is mandatory for all orders to initiate military action which flows from the station; and second, that we be given firm and convincing assurances the station will not be used to send orders for a first strike nuclear attack nor to initiate a limited strike.
>
> If the United States would not accept these reasonable provisions designed to protect our national sovereignty, then we would ask them to wind down the operations of North West Cape as rapidly as possible.

The Agenda for the Future

The U.S. installations in Australia constitute one of the most critical issues of Australian national security policy. Unfortunately, the subject is also most complex and one of the most controversial; there are no easy answers for Australians concerned with what should be done about them. The installations differ enormously in their functions, relative importance, and implications for Australia's security. The balance sheet contains both positive and negative entries, many of the variables are uncertain, and the sum depends more on general philosophical attitudes toward the maintenance of any national security account rather than any calculation of costs and benefits.

The U.S. installations in Australia can be addressed from many directions. One is according to general function—scientific, intelligence, and more direct defense support, particularly defense communications. There are installations engaged principally in scientific activities, with relatively little defense relevance—as currently operated. These include the NASA satellite-tracking, communications, and data acquisition stations in the Australian Capital Territory and the new solar observatory at Learmonth. There can be little quarrel with hosting these particular operations, although given the economic and social problems, some might question the priorities evident in official science policy and research. However, even these installations have some military significance, sometimes potentially great military significance, the nature and implications of which have never been officially explained to the Australian public.

The second group of installations in Australia comprises those engaged in intelligence operations, although few of them have been officially acknowledged. They include the nuclear test–monitoring facilities and the satellite ground stations at Pine Gap and Nurrungar.

These intelligence operations are aimed against the Soviet Union, China, and countries in East, South, and Southeast Asia, including nominal allies of the United States and Australia, and may also include domestic intelligence. A wide range of strategic, political, legal, and moral objections can be raised against many of these operations; unfortunately, many are equally justifiable, and since most are technical collection systems that are generally indiscriminate, it is not possible to allow some and reject others.

The third group of U.S. installations in Australia provides communications, navigation, and other infrastructure support to U.S. military operations. This includes the naval communications station at North West Cape, the Omega navigation station, the TRANET navigation system, and a SOSUS-type antisubmarine warfare sonar system. Military operations supported by these installations include those of the Strategic Air Command; operations of NORAD, which is responsible for U.S. air defense; the operation of the U.S. FBM submarine fleet; operations such as the mining of Haiphong harbor (1972) and the bombing of Cambodia (1969–1972); and U.S. antisubmarine warfare operations against Soviet submarines. It is difficult to generalize about these military operations; while some (like the bombing of Cambodia) were insidious, others (such as NORAD operations) are essentially unobjectionable.

What, then, is to be done?

Removal of the Installations

The most radical proposal is that the United States dismantle its installations in Australia, either soon or when the relevant agreements come up for renewal. Unfortunately, there are many problems with this proposal. Does it include all "U.S. installations" in Australia and, if so, how are "U.S. installations" to be defined? Does it include scientific installations such as NASA satellite-tracking stations; installations also used by the Australian defense forces, such as the very low frequency and high frequency facilities at North West Cape; or installations that are important to monitor activities subject to arms control agreements, such as the seismic stations and, to a lesser extent, the Pine Gap facility?

Many of the installations must be located in Australia if their missions are to be fully effective and efficient. This greatly reduces Australia's freedom of maneuver over them. The United States would resist dismantling the facilities. Moreover, since most facilities have some worthy features, it would often mean throwing out the baby with the bath water. (For example, if Australia were to prevent the interception of microwave signals by stations in Australia, an immediate casualty would be the loss of access to Soviet missile telemetry so necessary to a viable SALT agreement.)

There may be two possible exceptions—the naval communications station at North West Cape and the Omega navigation station at Darriman, Victoria. Both of these could be located anywhere in a large area of the Southwest Pacific or eastern Indian Ocean with no degradation in the effectiveness of the respective communication and navigation networks as a whole. The U.S. FBM submarine communications system would be equally well served were the very low frequency station at North West Cape moved to the Marianas Islands, the initial choice of the U.S. Navy in the early 1960s. There is no technical reason why the Omega station should not be located on Macquarie Island or elsewhere in the Tasman Sea rather than in Australia. Communication and navigation systems of more direct relevance to Australia's interests and needs could then be installed in Australia. The technical performance of the U.S. systems would not suffer, and the United States could feel secure about the remaining installations.

Consideration might also be given the agreements and understandings concerning the U.S. operations at RAAF Base Darwin and HMAS Stirling at Cockburn Sound. Operations there ensure that, at least under some circumstances, two Australian urban centers—Darwin and Perth—are likely to be nuclear targets, a situation that would probably not pertain otherwise. In neither case are these operations of critical importance to the U.S. forces. Rather, the U.S. use of these establishments is based much more on convenience than necessity.

Prime Minister Hawke has reaffirmed that the United States can continue to use RAAF Base Darwin under the existing arrangements. However, an interesting possibility emerges with the upgrading of RAAF Base Tindal, located 15 kilometers south of Katherine and some 363 kilometers south of Darwin. Tindal is capable of handling all types of aircraft and will be the home base for 75 Squadron, which will transfer from Darwin when it is equipped with the new F/A-18A fighters. To transfer the B-52 operation to Tindal would not impair the effectiveness of the navigation-training and sea surveillance flights, but would ensure that any Soviet nuclear attack on the B-52 support facilities would not produce civilian casualties.

In the case of U.S. use of HMAS Stirling at Cockburn Sound, current arrangements might be modified to exclude visits of particular U.S. vessels that are likely to invite Soviet nuclear attention, that is, aircraft carriers and hunter-killer submarines. This would not interfere with visits of ships that have an operational role in this region, such as cruisers and destroyers, but only with those ships whose visits are matters of convenience, and would remove the only other likely situation in which an Australian urban center might suffer nuclear attack.

Commitment to Arms Control

The Labor government that came to power in 1983, particularly Foreign Minister Hayden, is strongly committed to arms control. Hosting the U.S. installations should provide Australia with a means not only of ensuring that their functions and missions contribute to arms control rather than to the destabilization of the central balance, but also of pressing the United States to act seriously and conscientiously with respect to arms control.

Several U.S. installations in Australia are involved in monitoring and verifying arms control agreements. The 747/DSP satellites controlled from Nurrungar and the NAVSTAR Global Positioning System (GPS) satellites tracked by the TRANET station at Smithfield are equipped with the Integrated Operational Nuclear Detection System (IONDS), which provides for rapid detection, locating, and reporting of nuclear detonations worldwide and thus contributes to monitoring any nuclear test ban. The seismic station operated by U.S. Air Force Detachment 421 at Alice Springs, together with the other seismic stations, is also involved in monitoring nuclear detonations. The Australian government has stated that it would "consider favorably any proposal that Australia be the site of one of the data centers which will need to be established to monitor a Comprehensive Test Ban Treaty by seismic means." Australia should then be able to increase its efforts to persuade the United States to resume negotiations on a comprehensive test ban treaty.

The signals intelligence received from the Rhyolite family of satellites controlled through Pine Gap serves many purposes, but through monitoring Soviet missile telemetry they provide perhaps the single most important means of monitoring Soviet missile developments and verifying Soviet compliance with strategic arms limitation agreements. Hosting the Pine Gap facility should give Australia a right to insist that intelligence derived from the operations of that facility should be used to support serious attempts to secure a viable strategic arms reduction agreement with the Soviet Union.

More generally, there might be some scope for using the installations to argue against the more destabilizing aspects of recent developments in U.S. strategic nuclear policy, but it would be a mistake to imagine that Australia's potential influence could ever have any significant effect on the U.S. strategic nuclear posture.

Australian Access to the U.S. Facilities and Their Operations

One of the disturbing features of the U.S. installations has been the lack of political control exercised by the Australian government over their establishment, operation, and maintenance. Indeed, until the mid-1970s the government was abysmally ignorant of the functions and missions of the major U.S. installations. It was not until early 1973 that the government asked Washington for "authoritative U.S. comment" on the roles of North West Cape and Smithfield regarding communication with FBM submarines and to the use of those submarines of the satellite navigation system.

In the cases of Pine Gap and Nurrungar, three of Australia's recent prime ministers, the only ones to address the issue, specifically stated that at the least, they were ignorant of major aspects of the operations of these stations. In December 1978 John Gorton stated: "I don't even know what Pine Gap is all about. I didn't then [1969]. I could have asked, but it didn't arise. I didn't ask about it." In May 1977 William McMahon stated that although when he had been prime minister he thought he knew the true functions of Pine Gap and Nurrungar, he was not now so sure: "I have increasing doubts that the Australian government knows the entire truth." Gough Whitlam revealed on a number of occasions that there were critical aspects relating to Pine Gap and Nurrungar that he was never told about. Whitlam told parliament on May 4, 1977, that the Australian government was unaware that information obtained by these facilities was made available to private U.S. companies such as TRW Systems Incorporated, that the first U.S. officer in charge of Pine Gap, Richard Stallings, was an employee of the CIA, or that Pine Gap was a CIA operation.

In October 1973 North West Cape, Pine Gap, and Nurrungar were placed on a higher alert status, and North West Cape communicated the U.S. decision to move to Defense Condition 3 to U.S. nuclear and conventional forces in the Indo-Pacific region, without informing the Australian government. As a result, an agreement was reached between Minister for Defense Lance Barnard and Secretary of Defense James Schlesinger on January 10, 1974, under which an Australian deputy commander was appointed to the North West Cape communications station. They also agreed that the United States would attempt to keep Australia more fully informed about operations and policy decisions relating to the station.

However, the procedures for implementing the agreement were evidently deficient, for the Australian press revealed in May 1978 that the United States planned to upgrade the satellite ground terminal at North West Cape and the minister for defense had not been informed. It took the minister for defense several days from the initial press revelations to determine that a new ground station was destined for North West Cape. His initial response was to indict the United States for not treating Australia "with the proper courtesy." He later stated that "there exists a difference of opinion between the United States government and the Australian government as to the procedures to be observed" in respect of consultation. Australia, once again, undertook detailed discussions with the United States to reach agreement on "improved procedures to meet the Australian government's needs."

Access to the U.S. installations and their operations needs to be considered at three levels: the appropriate degree of Australian access to the installations themselves, the nature of Australian representation in Washington, and the possibility of direct access to the various U.S. satellites controlled or monitored from ground stations in Australia.

Access to the Installations

Australian officials are now located at all the U.S. installations. At North West Cape the deputy commander is an Australian naval officer, and there are some 50 other naval and more than 200 Australian civilian personnel employed at the station. There are senior Australian defense representatives at both Pine Gap and Nurrungar, and some 225 and 200 other Australian personnel employed at these installations respectively.

However, there are important limits on Australian access to these installations. At North West Cape, Australians are excluded from the U.S. National Communications Room, which obviously constrains Australian ability to ensure that "the station will not be used to send orders for a first strike nuclear attack, nor to initiate a limited strike."

At both Pine Gap and Nurrungar there are national U.S. cypher and communication rooms to which Australians are not admitted. More importantly, Australians are also excluded from a critical section of the Control and Computer Building at Pine Gap. This building has three principal sections: (1) the Station-Keeping Section, responsible for keeping the satellites at geostationary altitude from drifting out of orbit and for aligning them toward areas of interest; (2) the Signals Processing Office; and, (3) the Signals Analysis Section. The Signals Analysis Section is staffed only by CIA and National Security Agency analysts; it includes no U.S. contract personnel and no Australian citizens. Many of the personnel in this section are linguists who monitor voice intercepts. Former staff at Pine Gap claimed that much of the material analyzed here is never passed to the Australian officers. It is imperative that there be Australian personnel in this section, not only to ensure that signals intelligence of interest is passed on, but also to build confidence that domestic Australian transmissions are not being intercepted and routed through this section.

Access in Washington

There is no Australian official in Washington specifically tasked with monitoring U.S. strategic policies, budgetary proposals, and decisionmaking that might affect Australia's interests through operations undertaken at the U.S. installations.

Following the 1978 controversy regarding a new satellite ground station at North West Cape, an agreement was reached between R. N. Hamilton, the first assistant secretary of the Strategic and International Policy Division of the Australian Department of Defense, and Michael H. Armacost, the deputy assistant secretary of defense (East Asia, Pacific, and Inter-American Affairs) under which the Pentagon was obliged to keep Australia fully informed of all likely and impending decisions with respect to the operations of the installations. In 1981 consideration was given to posting an appropriate defense officer to the embassy in Washington, with specific responsibility for monitoring these decisions; the officer was to be accredited to both the Pentagon and the other agencies involved in the operation of U.S. installations in Australia.

On June 13, 1983, in discussions in Washington with President Reagan and Secretary of Defense Weinberger, Prime Minister Hawke raised "the possibility of stationing in Washington a specific defense person whose responsibility it would be to liaise with the United States defense authorities so that we would have the capacity, in addition to that already existing, with the position of such a person, of having a fuller and more immediate knowledge of developments in regard [to the U.S. installations in Australia]." According to Prime Minister Hawke, "Secretary Weinberger believed that that was something that was worthy for further consideration at the official level and he gave me an undertaking that this proceed immediately." This matter was a principal subject of discussion when the minister for defense, Gordon Scholes, and the minister for foreign affairs, Bill Hayden, visited Washington for the annual meeting of the ANZUS Council in mid-July. They discussed with Secretary Weinberger two possibilities: (1) to place an Australian official in the Pentagon with direct communication with Canberra who "would be informed of any change in the strategic situation that might involve use of the facilities in Australia;" and (2) to place an official in the Australian embassy in Washington responsible for monitoring the use of the installations by the United States. Neither of these possibilities was acceptable. The most the United States would accept was an amendment to the 1974 agreement on North West Cape to the effect that the United States will liaise with a nominated officer of the Australian Defense Staff in the Washington embassy who will inform Canberra of "any change in the status of military preparedness or alerts which take place" regarding the North West Cape station.

This clearly does not satisfy the Australian point of view. There needs to be a senior Australian official in the embassy tasked solely with the responsibility of monitoring and reporting on decisions and developments that might affect Australia and its interests. The purview of this official must be broader than the Department of Defense. Although the National Reconnaissance Office is formally located in the Pentagon, comprehensive monitoring of decisions and developments concerning Pine Gap would also require accreditation to the CIA, most particularly the Foreign Missiles and Space Center of the CIA's Directorate of Science and Technology, and the Defense Special Missile and Astronautics Center, which is jointly maintained by the Defense Intelligence Agency and the National Security Agency.

Access to U.S. Satellites

The Australian Defense Forces would benefit greatly from access to U.S. defense communications satellites. The United States maintains at least two defense satellite communications system satellites and one fleet satellite communications satellite within range of its ground stations in Australia. The defense satellites have six channels, operating in the super high frequency (SHF) band. Australia should request that one of these channels be reserved for use by the Australian Defense Forces and should procure a ground terminal to provide a quasi-independent defense satellite communications capability for the Australian Defense Force.

Informing the Australian Public

Finally, it is imperative that the Australian public be told as much about the general purposes and functions of the installations as is compatible with genuine security requirements. The extraordinary secrecy the government has imposed on the installations, together with the deception and dissembling it has practiced, has little to do with any genuine security requirements. The target of this secrecy is not Australia's (or the United States's) adversaries but the Australian public.

Most of what the government has attempted to keep from the Australian public is available in the public record in the United States. While the Australian government refused to acknowledge the presence of National Security Agency personnel in Australia, the worldwide operations of this agency have been discussed in U.S. congressional and executive reports since the mid-1970s, and their presence at North West Cape was mentioned in official U.S. Navy testimony in 1972. Other instances in which information relating to U.S. installations in Australia has been *officially* disclosed in the United States but not available to the Australian public include the following: the installation of the AN/TSC-54 satellite ground terminal at North West Cape in 1967; the Pentagon's plans for replacing this with an AN/MSC-61 ground terminal; the use of NASA satellite-tracking and communications facilities in Australia for defense communications; the U.S. Defense Intelligence Agency's control of the geodetic observation stations in Australia 1961 until 1972; various military uses of the Omega navigation system, disclosed in numerous congressional hearings; the extent of the wartime SIGINT exchange arrangements between Australia and the United States; the likelihood that VLF communications stations such as Cutler (or North West Cape) are priority nuclear targets. The list could be extended. In these cases, the information was presented to the U.S. Congress, subjected to security sanitization, and officially released. It should be part of the public record in Australia.

As a general principle, information generally available to the intelligence agencies of the Soviet Union and other national adversaries should also be made known to the Australian public. There may be particular exceptions to the principle. There have perhaps been instances where something may have been put on the public record accidentally, and officials have thought it best not to draw attention to the matter; there might also have been instances where officials would prefer not to confirm particular reports since such confirmation might free hostile intelligence collection and assessment resources for application elsewhere; and there might be cases where official confirmation of information might lead to demands for even more information. However, the general principle that the Australian public should know as much about U.S. operations in Australia as do Soviet intelligence agencies remains determinate.

The platform of the Australian Labor Party declares that "Labor will make known to the Australian public the general purpose of the bases and any change to these." A resolution calling for a statement describing the general purposes and functions of the installations was passed at the ALP National Conference in July 1983, and Mr. Hayden declared at the outset of his visit to Washington in mid-July that agreement on "a joint public statement on the 'general purposes and functions' of the bases at Pine Gap and Nurrungar would be a matter of high priority during his visit." Unfortunately this attempt was frustrated by Secretary Weinberger, although Mr. Scholes later stated that "we have agreed that those discussions will continue and I will be reporting back to the government and we will then determine what the next steps will be in that process and exactly what approach we are going to take from there."

The major U.S. installations in Australia—North West Cape, Pine Gap, and Nurrungar—are potentially consequential. In accepting the potential risks entailed in hosting these installations, the Australian public is entitled to an official statement of the "general purposes and functions" of these installations. The statement need not be much different from the descriptions earlier in this paper. Without an official statement, informed and authoritative public debate on these installations and their implications for Australia's security is not possible. And that debate, on such a controversial and critical subject, is essential in a democracy.

THE INTERESTS AND POLICIES OF NEW ZEALAND

Richard Kennaway

New Zealand has a very unusual strategic position. It is a small, geographically isolated, but comparatively wealthy country situated in an area with low regional instability and minor global strategic significance. Yet traditionally it has had close political, economic, and cultural links with a major power—whether Britain or the United States. In terms of a recent academic paradigm, it is a country with low system linkage (little significance in the context of great power rivalry) but high partial linkage (close bilateral relations with a major power). Rather curiously, the authors describe this combination as "an ideal type . . . rarely if ever found in practice."[1] It is not surprising, therefore, that the perception or evolution of national security interests in New Zealand may appear somewhat unusual in a global context.

Traditionally New Zealand has reacted to this unusual strategic situation in very orthodox fashion by following an alliance strategy. The logic of the strategy has been that (1) because of its small size, New Zealand is unable to provide effectively for its own defense; (2) in an uncertain world it is nevertheless essential for some defense provision to be made, both to deter possible aggression and to defend New Zealand if deterrence fails; (3) the only viable strategy therefore is one of alliance with a major power that broadly shares New Zealand's interests and values; and (4) in order to maintain the alliance framework, New Zealand must be prepared to contribute as effectively as its capabilities allow to the overall alliance goals and strategies, even where its own interests are not directly involved. Until World War II, the major ally was Britain. For the next 30 years, both Britain and the United States were important in New Zealand's dual-alliance framework. In recent years, the major stress has been on the defense relationship with the United States and Australia.

So far, New Zealand governments of different political complexions have followed the broad traditional strategy. The two main political parties, National and Labor, held with different degrees of emphasis that the alliance should be maintained. Alternative strategies have been favored only by the minor parties, Social Credit and Values (as well as the small Socialist Unity [Communist] Party), which between them, until 1981, gained no more than 20 percent of the vote and two parliamentary seats. In the 1981 election, Social Credit gained 20.65 percent of the vote, but its questioning of the traditional strategy was rather muted.

Recently, however, this questioning has intensified. The Labor Party, which gained more votes than the National Party in the last two elections, recently enjoyed a substantial lead over National in public opinion polls (though most of the extra support has been at the expense of Social Credit). It is engaged in an internal debate on alliance issues that may lead to a significant policy change. Social Credit, whose support has apparently declined since 1981, is now giving more emphasis to attacking traditional alliance strategy. Even in the National Party, there has recently been more debate on alliance issues. Outside the political parties, there has been a rapid growth in "peace groups" and nuclear free–zone committees. In view of this evolution of opinion and policy, it would be unrealistic to give a single perspective on "the interest and policies of New Zealand." Therefore, this paper will analyze the evolution of the various perspectives and consider the main reasons for the intensified debate.

National Party governments, in office for 26 out of 32 years since the ANZUS Treaty was signed, are the strongest supporters of the traditional strategy. The Muldoon government, in office since December 1975, remains clearly within this tradition. The 1978 *Defense Review* put great stress on ANZUS as the essential element of New Zealand's security, and "the ultimate guarantee of security in the region."[2] There is no prospect that the 1982 *Defense Review,* now in preparation, will mark any significant change.

In accordance with this overall strategy, the Muldoon government has given great weight to alliance considerations in formulating its policies. It took an early decision to accept visits by U.S. warships in 1976 subject to the provisions of the New Zealand code for nuclear-powered shipping, without inquiring whether the ships were nuclear-armed. Subsequently there have been six visits by nuclear-powered ships. Although the crews have generally been hospitably welcomed in New Zealand ports, the visits have been marked by considerable political protest and strikes. Similarly, the government has effectively shelved the implementation of a nuclear weapons–free zone

(NWFZ) in the South Pacific against the wishes of its alliance partners. Coincidentally, the Muldoon government took office on the day that the United Nations General Assembly passed a resolution (by 110 votes to 0, with 20 abstentions) endorsing the principle of a South Pacific Zone. Approval for the principle as a long-term goal has never been withdrawn. However, no steps have been taken to implement the zone since the South Pacific Forum meeting at Rotorua in February 1976, which agreed that the principle of freedom of navigation on the high seas would be respected and compatibility with existing security arrangements maintained.

Nevertheless, alliance and nuclear matters have recently been a topic for significant debate even within the National Party. A backbench National MP, Marilyn Waring, who has long supported NWFZs, recently strongly attacked visits by U.S. warships in a public letter to the United States ambassador. She was persuaded not to support a bill introduced in 1982 by a backbench Labor MP, Richard Prebble, which would have barred such visits, and may yet support a similar bill introduced by the Social Credit leader, Bruce Beetham, which has been referred to a select committee. She claims a good deal of support within the party, and since National only has a one-vote majority over Labor and Social Credit combined, her position is influential. Further, although a resolution strongly supporting ANZUS was passed, nuclear issues were a major topic for debate at the recent National Party Annual Conference. Another National MP, Douglas Kidd, who chairs the Parliamentary Disarmament Committee, has now put forward another "nuclear peace zone" plan giving weight to ANZUS obligations. The debate continues.

Even under a National government, there have still been some differences of emphasis between New Zealand and its alliance partners in recent years. The New Zealand governments generally have held the view that the security aspects of the alliance should not be overemphasized. It devoted a lower proportion of GNP to defense than its alliance partners. It was reluctant to extend alliance commitments to the Indian Ocean after the Afghanistan crisis in 1980 and rather grudgingly agreed to make a commitment there "as resources permit."[3] Conversely, it has been anxious for increased linkage between the security, economic, and political aspects of the relationship. New Zealand warmly welcomed the recognition in the 1977 ANZUS communiqué that "the health of the economies of the three partners is of concern to each, for it affects their capacity to play the responsive and responsible role... which is our common desire."[4] Mr. Muldoon reminded Vice-President Bush on his visit to Wellington in 1982 that the alliance aims of strengthening the fabric of peace in the Pacific area could not be carried out by military activity alone, but also involved "the slow painstaking processes of... endeavoring to shift living standards."⁵ Rather paradoxically, perhaps, the recent ANZUS review initiated by the new Australian Labor government resulted in the regional scope of ANZUS being reaffirmed in a manner much in accordance with New Zealand's perceptions. In any case, the minor differences in emphasis involved no questioning of the basic strategy.

The evolution of Labor Party policy potentially raises more fundamental questions. Official policy continues to hold that the alliance should be maintained, being broadened to emphasize nonmilitary factors. The policy also includes a commitment to promote a NWFZ actively and to oppose visits by both nuclear-powered and nuclear-armed vessels. It declares that Labor will use the ANZUS forum to promote the objective of a nuclear-free Pacific.

Clearly this policy could involve some tension between New Zealand and its alliance partners. The ANZUS treaty does not require members to accept visits by particular types of vessels or aircraft operated by alliance members. The other alliance members might well feel, however, that a complete ban on visits by a large and growing proportion of the United States fleet was a strange way for New Zealand to fulfill its commitment to "maintain and develop the parties' individual and collective capacity to resist armed attack."

In any case, the Labor Party will have to reconcile two different initiatives for change. Ever since the 1950s resolutions have come forward at Labor Party conferences that New Zealand should withdraw from ANZUS (or from all military pacts or alliances with nuclear weapons states). For many years such resolutions were invariably rejected. On four occasions recently, however, in 1977, 1980, 1981, and 1982, the party conference passed resolutions favoring withdrawal from military alliances, and it is expected that a similar resolution will be passed at the conference in September 1983. Indeed, the new leader of the party, David Lange, stated that the visit to New Zealand by the USS *Texas* shortly before the conference had made such a resolution inevitable.⁶ In 1981 the party's Policy Committee, which drafts the official policy for the election manifestos, did not feel bound by the conference resolutions. It will be interesting to see, however, if further resolutions can be ignored.

A very different initiative to change came in March 1983 when Lange proposed that party policy be amended to permit visits to New Zealand ports by nuclear-powered, but not nuclear-armed, vessels. He received considerable criticism within the party for this initiative. More recently he stated that under his proposal the ships and aircraft of nuclear powers could visit New Zealand only if the prime minister received assurance that no nuclear weapons were carried.⁷ Furthermore, nuclear-powered ships would still be banned until strict safety conditions could be devised for preventing environmental hazards. He hoped that party policy would be amended to allow visits by nuclear-powered vessels under these conditions. He also suggested that Pacific nations may have to accept that both nuclear-powered and nuclear-armed ships may travel through the international waters of a South Pacific NWFZ as the price for its early acceptance. Again, the debate continues.

The Social Credit Party strongly supports a policy of armed neutrality for New Zealand. It moved to this position with hesitation. In its 1978 policy it favored "responsible neutrality," although its main emphasis was on financial policy. In 1981 Social Credit stated that it would maintain the commitment to ANZUS pending production of a special paper on the range of global options open to New Zealand, but there was also support for a "nuclear armament free zone" and for re-examining military agreements in the light of independent diplomacy. Since 1981 the party again became more strongly committed to the policy of armed neutrality. It is confident that the resistance that New Zealand could mount from its own resources, both by passive resistance and guerrilla warfare, would ensure that the costs of occupation would far outweigh any returns to an invader. The party also sees its defense policy as contributing to the wider objectives of an economically and culturally self-reliant and independent New Zealand. It believes a neutral New Zealand could act more credibly in international peace initiatives such as disarmament conferences and contributions to United Nations peacekeeping forces. It attacks current Labor Party policy for suggesting that support for a nuclear-free zone is compatible with continued acceptance of ANZUS and declares that "New Zealand cannot be both party to a nuclear pact and an initiator of a non-nuclear zone."[8]

The Values Party has now virtually disappeared into political oblivion, having gained only 0.19 percent of the vote in the 1981 election (as against a peak of 5.19 percent in 1975). It was, however, the most consistent proponent of the strategy of unarmed neutrality for New Zealand since 1972. Although its political success was insignificant, its views had a certain influence. It has long taken the view that "New Zealand security lies not with defense pacts with great powers, but through friendship and cooperation with other nations in the Asia-Pacific region."[9] From this perspective, alliances are not so much an aid to deterrence as an incentive to attack because of the danger that New Zealand could be drawn into conflict outside its immediate interests. It therefore favored leaving ANZUS, dismantling New Zealand's armed forces, and replacing them with "a multipurpose civilian defense and social service organization" that could contribute to United Nations peacekeeping forces or provide social and technical assistance overseas. It was also among the earliest and strongest supporters of a NWFZ in the South Pacific, and its attitude toward the nuclear arms race of the superpowers was to dissociate as strongly as possible from any involvement.

There has been a rapid growth in nonparty groups concerned with nuclear issues. A visit to New Zealand by Dr. Helen Caldicott in April 1983 stimulated great interest. Many local authorities, including the Auckland, Wellington, and Christchurch city councils, declared their districts to be NWFZs; there are now 30 such zones covering 900,000 people, or 30 percent of population.[10] A petition with over 50,000 signatures favoring a South Pacific NWFZ was presented to parliament and received by MPs of all three parties. Church, student, medical, and trade union groups gave increased attention to the issue. There were two marches by 20,000–30,000 people in Auckland and smaller marches in other centers. The protest fleet that sailed out to greet the USS *Texas* in Auckland on August 2 was described by its commanding officer as the "largest he had seen in his nineteen years on nuclear ships."[11]

How can one account for such increased questioning of the traditional strategy that New Zealand has followed for so long? The basic explanation is twofold. First, in the security field, concern about the conventional dangers with which ANZUS was most clearly designed to cope has declined, while concern about other dangers to which the traditional strategy is less relevant has increased. Second, New Zealand, partly for historical reasons, traditionally looked to its major alliances for contributions to a wide range of objectives—idealistic/identity and economic objectives, as well as security—and there was increasing concern about these aspects.[12] In this context, there are five main reasons for the change, of which the first two (and in part, the third) relate mainly to security.

Perhaps the most important single factor for change is that there has been no immediate, direct conventional threat to New Zealand's security since 1951. Various potential direct threats have been perceived from time to time—from Japan in the early 1950s, from the Sino-Soviet bloc throughout the 1950s, from China during the Vietnam war, and from the Soviet Union since 1975. The 1978 *Defense Review* confirmed, however, as previous *Defense Review*s had, that no direct threat to New Zealand's security existed, and none was foreseen within ten years unless there was a major shift in the global balance.[13] Although international relations have deteriorated since 1978, few people see any immediate threat and none for the near future. It could be argued that the absence of threat was evidence for the success of ANZUS. Even if New Zealand had been nonaligned, with benefit of hindsight it is hard to envisage that any direct threat to New Zealand would have occurred. The international environment was not prone to make long-distance, unprovoked attacks on isolated small countries, whether aligned or nonaligned. In any case, since no direct threat occurred, New Zealanders tended to become less concerned about the security aspects of the alliance. Additional security benefits are likely to be more highly appreciated only when some potential direct threat seems imminent. Clearly there has been a widening divergence here between New Zealand's and the United States' perspectives.

The second factor was increasing concern about possible nuclear threats and dangers, relative to which the traditional concepts seem irrelevant or even counterproductive. The peace groups in many cases adopted the slogan "ANZUS Makes New Zealand a Nuclear Target." They take the view that U.S. defense-related installations and occasional visits by U.S. warships increased the possibility of New Zealand's being threatened and that the alliance is more likely to act as a lightning conductor than a nuclear umbrella.

Their arguments are oversimplified. Short of major nuclear holocaust, the possibility of a nuclear attack against New Zealand seems remote. In the current international environment, countries are no more prone to make long-distance, unprovoked nuclear than conventional attacks. Certainly the "nuclear pawn" theory of the early 1960s, which suggested that a superpower might be tempted in the absence of general hostilities to launch an attack on a small ally of its rival to demonstrate its power or to acquire a bargaining advantage, seems no more plausible now than twenty years ago.

In New Zealand, U.S. defense-related installations are of minor and declining significance. The former Aerospace Defense Command Tracking Station at Mt. John closed by the end of 1983. The former naval communication unit at Harewood has been downgraded to other purposes, mainly connected with the United States' presence in Antarctica. The naval observatory transit circle facility under construction at Black Birch will be of very limited and indirect military significance, though the naval appropriation request to Congress referred to its function of obtaining the location of stars in the Southern Hemisphere "with the increased accuracy required for military purposes."[14] It is hard to envisage that any of these installations could plausibly be regarded as nuclear targets.

Similarly, visits to New Zealand ports by U.S. nuclear warships are short and infrequent and do not include visits by long-range, missile-carrying submarines that form part of the strategic deterrent. Although considerable publicity was given to a report casting doubt on the overall safety record of the United States' nuclear-powered ships, careful checks were carried out by the National Radiation Laboratory since visits to New Zealand resumed in 1976, and no increased radiation was detected.[15]

It also seems too simple to argue, as the New Zealand minister of defense did, that because the ships that make friendly port calls to New Zealand are not part of the strategic deterrent, "therefore they do not bring with them the slightest risk of nuclear attack on the port which offers them hospitality."[16] One can hardly believe that all other potential military targets are exempt from nuclear attack. Although Soviet "negative security guarantees" (assurances not to use nuclear weapons against countries that do not have nuclear weapons on their territories) may not be too credible, they would presumably be invalidated by the presence of tactical and strategic nuclear weapons. It seems reasonable that in certain circumstances New Zealand, as an ally rather than as a nonaligned state, would be slightly more likely to rate as a target. Indeed, a U.S. spokesman was quoted as expressing gratitude for New Zealand participation in ANZUS on the grounds that it shows such total support "that we [New Zealanders] are prepared to accept, in the event of nuclear war, a proportion of the nuclear devastation that would otherwise be concentrated on the United States."[17]

In short, in relation to a possible nuclear attack, the traditional alliance concepts no longer operate in the traditional way. Protection becomes much less relevant. There is no defense, and no effective "action to meet the common danger" against a nuclear missile on its way toward New Zealand. The only relevant traditional concept therefore is deterrence—conflict avoidance by threat of retaliation against a potential aggressor. The consequences of that retaliation would be so awesome that it hardly seems plausible or desirable for the United States even to threaten to react to an attack on New Zealand by using nuclear weapons.

The third major factor is the growing concern in New Zealand about the proliferation of nuclear weapons in the arsenals of both superpowers and the consequences of that proliferation. The U.S. government is strongly convinced that the Soviet Union pulled ahead in some significant way and that it is therefore necessary for the United States to catch up. It even holds that further proliferation of nuclear weapons is an essential prerequisite to effective arms control. For many governments and individuals otherwise sympathetic to the United States, however, a significant perception of danger arises not from the alleged lead that one side or the other may have gained in the nuclear weapons race, but rather from the proliferation of the weapons themselves, whoever owns them. The existence of the weapons stockpiles and the diversion of the resources involved is seen as creating enormous dangers, especially since the safeguards against use of the weapons depend on the fallible technology of computers and detection systems and the imperfect judgment of individuals operating the systems. These dangers are not specific to any one country. No one can say exactly what the effects in the Southern Hemisphere would be, how far global ecosystems would be affected, or how far New Zealand would be insulated by distance and isolation from the worst effects of nuclear catastrophe. The impact of a nuclear holocaust on national security could still be devastating, however, even for those countries against which no weapons were directly targeted.[18] This is another potential danger in relation to which the traditional concepts underlying ANZUS are no longer appropriate.

The fourth reason for increased questioning is the increased awareness of and enthusiasm for nuclear weapons–free zones. For many years a wide cross-section of New Zealand opinion supported the concept, at any rate as an ultimate ideal. In 1963, the Labor Party conference passed a resolution "that the Southern Hemisphere, by international agreement, become a nuclear free zone." In the same year Prime Minister Sir Keith Holyoake of the National Party, while expressing reservations about the practicalities, stated that "though the South Pacific is a vast zone, it is too small for me. I want to see the whole world a nuclear free zone, by means of an all-embracing disarmament agreement."[19] During the 1960s and early 1970s, however, the main focus of attention was on the more limited aim of opposition to French atmospheric tests in the Pacific. It was only in July 1975 that the nuclear-free zone concept surfaced again, when Labor Prime Minister Bill Rowling put forward a plan for a NWFZ in the South Pacific at the South Pacific Forum in Rotorua.

There is no necessary incompatibility between the alliance and a NWFZ. Rowling emphasized that it should be developed in consultation and cooperation with alliance partners. Equally, Rob Muldoon, while strongly stressing alliance factors, has not gainsaid the introduction of a zone as an ultimate ideal. The United States has not been completely opposed, provided that certain conditions were met, such as adequate verification and nondisturbance of existing security arrangements. Public opinion polls in New Zealand generally showed support both for the alliance and for the introduction of a zone.[20] Nevertheless, there are still potential tensions between the two ideals. It remains to be seen how far practical terms can be negotiated that both satisfy the zone proponents and are compatible with the alliance. An increasing body of opinion views the development of the zone concept as the most important contribution that New Zealand can make both to national and to global security.

The fifth factor for increased questioning is economic. The major threats to New Zealand's well-being over the past 30 years have been economic rather than military—from the British application to join the European Economic Community to continued agricultural protectionism in the major developed countries. Although New Zealand's ANZUS partners are also major trading partners, the ANZUS relationship has been of limited significance in this regard. New Zealand's negotiators have often claimed the relevance of alliance membership in seeking economic benefits, but they were seldom very successful. It was only in 1977 that an ANZUS communiqué specifically recognized the relevance of economic factors to the alliance.[21]

Recently, the economic benefits of the relationship were more evident since it helped New Zealand obtain political backing to avert quite serious protectionist pressures in the U.S. Congress. There were also potential costs, as in 1979–1980, when it appeared that President Carter would press New Zealand to impose sanctions, first against Iran to protest the seizure of the hostages and then against the Soviet Union in protest against its incursion into Afghanistan. The requests were not pressed, and no major costs were incurred, but as Iran and the Soviet Union were New Zealand's fifth and sixth largest export markets that year, the potential costs were high.

New Zealand perceptions of national interests and policies are being intensively reconsidered. This reconsideration, and this paper, focused mainly on the New Zealand–United States security relationship. (In the general debate, New Zealanders, like Australians, often forget that ANZUS is a trilateral relationship.) It has been the main argument, however, that security interests cannot be adequately considered in a purely military context.[22] The increased questioning is, in part, perhaps a reaction against the tendency to overemphasize the military aspects.

If the need for increased concern with wider political aspects is recognized, then perhaps a wider political framework is also necessary. The exclusive trilateral framework has been greatly valued by New Zealand and Australia and still has a useful part to play for some purposes. Although the Asian and Pacific Council failed to adjust to changing political realities, and despite the obvious difficulties, it may be time for a new Asian-Pacific political organization within which the broader national and regional interests can be considered in their new contexts.

Notes

1. C. E. Morrison and A. Suhrke, *Strategies of Survival: The Foreign Policy Dilemmas of Smaller Asian States* (New York: St. Martin's Press, 1979), p. 294.

2. New Zealand Ministry of Defense, *Defense Review, 1978*, p. 16.

3. *N. Z. Foreign Affairs Review*, 30, no. 1 (January–March 1980): 11.

4. Ibid., 27, no. 3 (July–September 1977): 29.

5. Ibid., 32, no. 2 (April–June 1982): 24. See also *International Security in the Southeast Areas and Southwest Pacific Region* (St. Lucia: Queensland University Press, 1983), p. 25.

6. *Christchurch Press*, July 8, 1983.

7. *Christchurch Star*, July 7, 1983.

8. Press statement by Dick Ryan, Social Credit spokesman on defense, February 22, 1983. See also D. Davis, "Armed Neutrality: An Alternative Defense Policy for New Zealand," *N.Z. International Review*, 8, no. 1 (January–February 1983).

9. *Beyond Tomorrow: 1975 Values Party Manifesto* (Wellington, 1975), p. 49.

10. N.Z. Nuclear Free Zone Committee, *Newsletter*, August–September 1983.

11. *Christchurch Star*, August 3, 1983.

12. Richard Kennaway, *New Zealand Foreign Policy, 1951–1971* (Wellington: Hicks Smith, 1972), pp. 14–17, 144–47.

13. New Zealand Ministry of Defense, *Defense Review 1978*, p. 13.

14. U.S. Congress, *Military Construction Appropriation for 1982: Hearings*, 1:1237-140; quoted in G. E. Tweddle, "The U.S. Military Presence in New Zealand," (Christchurch: University of Canterbury, M.A. thesis, 1983).

15. Report by D. Kaplan for Fund for Constitutional Government, quoted in *Christchurch Press*, July 12 and 21, 1983.

16. New Zealand Ministry of Defense, *Report for the Year Ended March 31, 1982*, A.J.H.R. G.4 (Wellington, 1982), p. 6.

17. Quoted in R. Northey, "The Alliance: The Ever-Present Danger," in *N.Z. International Review*, 5, no. 6 (November–December 1980): 4.

18. Cf. New Zealand Commission for the Future, *Future Contingencies: Nuclear Disaster* (Wellington, 1982).

19. *N.Z. External Affairs Review*, 13, no. 5 (May 1963): 31.

20. J. Henderson et al., *Beyond New Zealand* (Wellington: Methuen, 1980), pp. 243–47.

21. *N.Z. Foreign Affairs Review*, 27, no. 3 (July–September 1977): 29.

22. For a similar argument in the European context, see M. Howard, "Reassurance and Deterrence: Western Defense in the 1980s," *Foreign Affairs*, 61, no. 2 (Winter 1982–83): 309–24.

IV
SOUTHEAST ASIA

INTRODUCTION

Claude A. Buss

Of the four Asian subregions in the Pacific Basin—Northeast Asia, the Southwest Pacific–Indian Ocean area, Southeast Asia, and China—it is Southeast Asia that calls for most skillful diplomatic management in formulating effective security policies for the United States, its allies, and friends.

In Northeast Asia the immediacy of the Soviet threat effectively joins South Korea and Japan with the United States in planning for mutual security. In the Southwest Pacific the Anglo-Saxon cultural background and political heritage of parliamentary democracy in Australia and New Zealand give them a certain sympathy with the United States in security matters despite differences in perceptions of the Soviet threat. In Southeast Asia, because of the diversity and complexity of the area, it is difficult to generate anything approaching consensus on priorities of national interests or common measures for their protection.

Southeast Asia is the home of many races, religions, and tongues. It is an important area not only because of its strategic location and its valuable resources, but also because of the vitality of its 300 million people. Since more than 70 percent of its wealth is still in agriculture, the frightening disparity between the very rich and the very poor is most apparent in the metropolitan areas. With a rapidly expanding, highly trained middle class in each country, its destiny is tightly linked with the market economies of the Western world. In spite of a rapidly increasing population, the nations of Southeast Asia consistently register an impressive GNP growth rate.

With the exception of Thailand, the nations of Southeast Asia have only recently emerged from long periods of imperial rule. As new nations in a complex world, each is obliged in its own way to grapple with the fundamental problems of statehood set forth in the Preamble of the U.S. Constitution: "to form a more perfect union, establish justice, insure domestic tranquility, provide for the common defense, promote the general welfare, and secure the blessings of liberty to ourselves and our posterity."

Their struggles for development and modernization are deeply influenced by their history and strategic environment. Apart from Brunei and Burma, Southeast Asia is organized into two antagonistic groups of states: the Indochinese states of Vietnam, Kampuchea, and Laos identified with the Soviet Union and the ASEAN states of Indonesia, Malaysia, Singapore, Thailand, and the Philippines backed by the United States. The traditional fears of China—the overseas imperialists and Japan—though not entirely erased, have been replaced by their respective attitudes toward superpower confrontation. To the Indochinese states, the Soviet Union holds the promise of a better future; the United States represents the threat; to ASEAN, the reverse is essentially true.

The concept of a sharply defined bipolar world, however, has never been popular in Southeast Asia. No one accepts the proposition that either the United States or the Soviet Union is totally good or totally evil. Both have imperfections. Southeast Asians suggest that the superpowers spend as much energy in self-improvement as in the quest for an acceptable balance of military power.

Opinions about the United States and the Soviet Union vary from country to country, from individual to individual. No opinion or statement represents a consensus, but each provides an insight into problems that must be considered in the decisionmaking process.

Both the United States and the Soviet Union are interpreted in dual roles: each symbolizes an ideology, and each is a superpower. The ideology of communism has little appeal in Southeast Asia, where it is far more a cloak for Soviet hegemonism than a utopian social theory. It has no attraction as an economic or social model, but as a great power the Soviet Union is recognized and respected for its growing strength. Southeast Asians observe, however, that the Soviet Union is inclined not to use its power for the protection and welfare of Asians but rather to attain its own objectives: guaranteeing maritime passage for its merchant ships between Vladivostok and the Black Sea, containing China, and seeking to counteract the U.S. position in Asia. Particularly since Afghanistan, the raw power of the Soviet Union is looked upon with distrust.

The ideological image of the United States is essentially good. Its association with democracy and freedom is sufficiently imprecise to allow Southeast Asian countries to interpret the United States as loosely as they please. No one pretends that the United States is perfect or an embodiment of either ideal. However they may criticize the United States, the Southeast

Asians respect, even envy, U.S. economic achievements and the attractiveness of its way of life.

As a superpower, the United States is not feared as a potential aggressor. The members of ASEAN view the U.S. military presence as the best hope for preventing war. After Vietnam, and until the last years of the Carter administration, they feared U.S. abandonment of their interests in Southeast Asia. The implications of "No More Vietnams" and the Nixon Doctrine were somewhat ominous. Contemporary Southeast Asians are inclined to warn Americans against being too militaristic, too prone to use force, in crisis management and conflict solution. They want Americans to reduce excessive arms expenditures and to set aside more of their wealth for economic assistance to the less developed nations of the Third World.

Southeast Asians are not blind to the fateful consequences to their own area should the superpowers engage in hostilities anywhere in the world. They do not want to be more closely tied to either side in a superpower confrontation. They demand the dignity of dealing with the United States and the Soviet Union on every occasion in accordance with their own interests and their own independent spirits. They want to set up their own ideals and pursue them in their own way at their own pace.

The Southeast Asian allies and friends of the United States are less concerned about the threats to security deriving from their immediate strategic environment. Their attention is riveted on the situation in Indochina. To ASEAN, the first step to peace in the region is a satisfactory solution to the threat from Hanoi.

A sharp distinction must be drawn between ASEAN as an organization and the policies of each member-state. ASEAN, the organization, is often given more credit than it deserves. It represents the ideal in regional cooperation and enjoys an image of unmitigated success. Its reputation rests on the dynamism of its members and their willingness to act together to face a common threat. Each member-state of ASEAN is proud of its independence and insists on its right to care for its own national interests while cooperating in the regional organization. In the confrontation with Vietnam, each has its own view of the best solution for the problem.

The intentions and capabilities of Hanoi cannot be judged without reference to the supporting role of the USSR and the ultimate relationship between Vietnam and the PRC. It is the total Soviet support of Vietnam that makes the Indochina problem so critical to future stability in Southeast Asia. By the treaty of 1978 the Soviets and Vietnamese agreed to consult together to take effective measures to safeguard their security if attacked. This paved the way for Soviet access to the Camranh naval base and gave new military strength to the Vietnamese army, "the third largest army on earth."

The Vietnamese have become absolutely dependent on the Soviets for military and economic assistance. Neither nation is satisfied with the relationship. It is too costly for the Soviets, too humiliating for the Vietnamese. The future looks worse, rather than brighter. The Soviets cannot increase their help. Even with outside assistance, the leadership in Vietnam must prove its ability to cope with its horrendous internal problems.

ASEAN's relations with Vietnam benefit from the rift in current Vietnam-China relations, but this may not be a likely long-term situation. So far, China has been no more adept with dealing with Vietnam than Vietnam has been in dealing with China. A less hostile relationship would be mutually beneficial. Furthermore, Vietnam-China relations cannot be divorced from either Vietnam-USSR or China-USSR relations. An improved atmosphere among all sides of the triangle would probably better the long-term prospects for peace in Southeast Asia.

Kampuchea is the eye of the storm. There will be no peace in the area without an equitable solution of the Kampuchean question, and no solution can be divorced from the historical factors of Sihanouk, the French connection, the Vietnam war, and U.S. bombings. Vietnam expected a quick victory in Kampuchea and bogged down in a protracted conflict. Vietnam's dilemma is whether to apply more force in Kampuchea and push for an Indochinese federation or accept a negotiated settlement covering Kampuchea and Laos.

Thailand, the next domino in the path of possible Vietnamese expansion, is the ASEAN state with the most vital interest in Kampuchea. The Thais fear that Vietnam, backed by the USSR, will rely upon force. They prefer to reach an understanding with Vietnam that will keep Kampuchea a buffer state. They would not object to Vietnamese hegemony in the Indochinese peninsula, provided their leadership were based on the will of the people.

From a different location, Singapore insists that a united front is essential against the Soviet Union and its Vietnamese satellite. Singapore would have Vietnam withdraw from Kampuchea and would prefer an independent government at Phnom Penh. It would like to mobilize world opinion against Vietnamese aggression and to retain U.S. backing for its policies.

Indonesia and Malaysia are more anti-Chinese than their other ASEAN colleagues. They want a coalition government in Kampuchea, possibly including representation from Vietnam but certainly without the domination of the Chinese-backed Pol Pot. They see Vietnam as a possible buffer against China, and they want to wean Vietnam from its Soviet backers.

Apart from blunting the threat from Vietnam, the member-states of ASEAN identify their greatest security need as the strengthening of their own state structures. In the realm of political stability, this means wiping out insurgencies and satisfying the legitimate needs of opposition groups. Where an authoritarian regime exists, it calls for peaceful succession. In pursuit of economic development, a reasonable balance between outside help and self-reliance is essential. Economic development implies social change, risking communal violence in plural societies and intensified class struggles where an agricultural society is inching toward a newly industrialized status. If state policies keep up with the constant economic and social changes, minor instability is an acceptable price to pay for progress.

As the largest member of ASEAN and spokesman for the Third World in North-South relations, Indonesia is unhappy lest it be overlooked or undervalued in the analysis of Southeast Asia's security problems. Since independence, it has been identified with a free and active foreign policy. Dedicated to national resiliency, it is nonaligned but not neutral. It identifies itself with other new nations in Asia, the Muslim Middle East, and Africa. A Muslim country, it is not attracted by godless Marxism. It is not too worried about the Soviets as it still has confidence in the superiority of the U.S. Seventh Fleet. On the other hand, it has little enthusiasm for the Western imperialist world, which let Indonesia down in its struggle for West Irian. It has clashed head-on with the United States over the containment of communist China and U.S. cooperation with Israel. It is willing to cooperate more closely with the United States and Japan, but will not budge from its basic free and active foreign policy. Although it is dedicated to the ideal of a zone of peace, friendship, and neutrality (ZOPFAN), it cannot but tolerate the military presence of the United States in the Philippines. It does not want any closer association or alliance as the price for more U.S. assistance. It wishes the United States would be more sympathetic to such nonmilitary security problems as the new international economic order and the Law of the Sea.

Malaysia is close to Indonesia in language and religion and, in many respects, follows parallel international security policies. A great difference is that Malaysia, with Singapore, the United Kingdom, Australia, and New Zealand, participates in a five-power defense arrangement and an integrated air defense system. Malaysia, too, accepts the ZOPFAN ideal. Malaysia is far more interested in stockpiles of tin and rubber than in closer military ties with the United States. Like Indonesia, its national priorities are to build up national resiliency, put down insurgencies, prevent communal violence, and promote economic development.

Thailand has a comparable list of priorities regarding its security problems. The Thais want to play their own game, stressing internal development regardless of the extent of their support for either ASEAN or ZOPFAN. They do not want war, they dislike the Soviets, and they do not want to be an unsinkable U.S. aircraft carrier. They seek mutual interests with everyone, whatever their ideological differences. They seek détente with China, their traditional threat, and they are not too interested in the Pacific Basin.

The Thais are always smiling, but pragmatism is the reality behind their smiles. They love power—so long as it does not threaten—and tend to follow the leader. In analyzing the current balance of power, they view economics as an important ingredient of power, and they see power increasingly diffused in the world. It is no longer concentrated in the hands of the United States and the Soviet Union. The relative power of the United States is declining, and it is considered unreliable. Nevertheless, it is greater than that of the Soviet Union and therefore more attractive to Thailand.

Of the members of ASEAN, the Philippines is perhaps closest to the United States in its search for mutual security. The era of "special relations" has given way to a relationship between equals, rooted in a treaty of mutual defense, U.S. use of Philippine bases, and extensive programs of military and economic assistance. Contacts between individual Americans and Filipinos are more effective than public policies in binding together the United States and the Philippines.

Differences remaining between Americans and Filipinos are clearly seen in the arguments over the Philippine bases, primarily Clark Air Base and Subic Bay. The rental for U.S. use of these bases, amounting to $1 billion over the next five years, together with the peripheral economic benefits from the U.S. presence in the Philippines, accounts for about 5 percent of the total Philippine GNP. This income is welcome to the government and to the Filipinos who depend upon it.

Opponents of the bases agreement argue that they infringe Philippine sovereignty. They are of no special value for the security of the Philippines in nuclear war and serve largely to protect the military and economic interests of the United States. The opponents further claim that both countries would be better off if the bases were abandoned and the Americans would withdraw.

In light of the conference discussions, certain conclusions emerged that should be considered by policymakers concerned with security in Southeast Asia. It is elemental that ASEAN stay unified. A solid core of democratically inclined, free, and independent nations is needed for stability and growth. They are entitled to more economic and military assistance, when they are prepared to absorb it. For Americans, there is every need to keep the Philippines and Thailand as close as possible, but there is little need to get the other members of ASEAN (Indonesia, Malaysia, and Singapore) to make statements or overtly to move closer to the United States. The United States must respect their yearning for ZOPFAN and recognize the necessity of something less than a zone of neutrality or a nuclear-free zone if it is to conduct its military operations at the peak of operating efficiency.

With regard to Japan, the Republic of Korea, Australia, and New Zealand, the United States should encourage them to offer more help to Southeast Asia in matters of trade, aid, and investment. With particular reference to Japan, there is general consensus in Southeast Asia granting Japan a larger role in the protection of Southeast Asia and the sea lines of communication leading thereto. This role, however, must remain within the framework of the U.S. alliance and not lead to Japan's building a highly sophisticated and massive military machine.

U.S. officials must recognize the legitimate needs of the Soviet Union as a Pacific power and not pass up opportunities for peaceful solutions of conflicts. The United States must avoid playing the China card or driving the Soviet Union to a more adventuresome military policy. It must remain strong at home and keep its commitments and capabilities, its activities, its rhetoric, in line. A credible military presence or projection of military power in Southeast Asia is the strongest factor in holding ASEAN together, yet the United States must avoid going too far with its military activities lest it create new tensions and misunderstandings. A low-key approach goes with a high profile, and a velvet glove with a big stick.

The United States' ASEAN allies insist that it not spend too much money building up either Japan or China but rather spend it on ASEAN. Rather than induce Japan to protect Southeast Asia, the United States should help ASEAN members develop the ability to protect themselves. It must listen sympathetically and be sensitive to the economic, political, and cultural problems. It should continue to oppose Vietnam. It should remain in step with ASEAN but seek openings for better relations with Vietnam, should an opportunity present itself.

Four decades of protecting national security interests in the Southeast Asian sector of the Pacific Basin reveal alternations of pride and humiliation, frustration and achievement. In the aftermath of World War II, Southeast Asia was a mass of frightened, discouraged, hungry people. American help went far to bring order out of chaos. By 1955 the newly independent nations were assured of continued existence, and the threat of a communist-dominated Southeast Asia region was dispelled. By 1965 a U.S. dream for a noncommunist Vietnam appeared a possibility. After a decade of hostilities, that dream was shattered, but so was the international communist monolith. In 1975 Vietnam took its place as the last of the great independent nations in Southeast Asia. In 1983, with its allies and friends, the United States is on the way to a balance of power that promises another decade of peaceful change in the Pacific Basin.

THE SECURITY SITUATION IN INDOCHINA

Douglas Pike

This paper addresses Indochinese security in terms of the Association of Southeast Asian Nations (ASEAN); that is, in terms of the status and meaning of its security with respect to the ASEAN-Indochina relationship. This consideration is part of a broader context—the general security of the Pacific Basin. Where does Indochina fit in the grand geopolitical scheme?

The first part of this paper discusses the major factors in Indochinese security. Five can be identified: the war in Kampuchea, the Sino-Vietnamese cold war, the Soviet presence in Indochina, internal conditions in Vietnam, and the intra-Indochina relationship among Vietnam, Laos, and Kampuchea. Part two examines Vietnam in rather orthodox security terms as a threat potential. Part three offers conclusions and judgments.

Kampuchea

The war in Kampuchea is the focus of Indochinese insecurity. Kampuchea may not be the sole cause of the area's instability, but, as the eye of the storm, it certainly contributes to it. Nor can there be a significant return to regional stability until the Kampuchean situation is resolved.

The Vietnamese are in Kampuchea, bogged down in a protracted conflict largely because of miscalculation and poor judgment by their ruling Politburo. The invasion of Kampuchea, during Christmas 1978, was meant to "solve the Pol Pot problem," as it is expressed in Hanoi. The expectation was that this would take about six months at the most. The Politburo had other means to rid itself of Pol Pot, and there was some experimentation with these earlier in 1978. But the Hanoi leaders were convinced that what was required was the quick military fix—to solve the Pol Pot problem with Moscow-style warfare. When the war became protracted, after Pol Pot adopted the strategy of the Viet Cong and North Vietnamese against Americans in South Vietnam, the Vietnamese army cast about for a new strategic response. It was dual-edged.

The Vietnamese army sought a cheaper kind of counterinsurgency, ways of pacifying Kampuchea with fewer casualties. The effort sought to make use of high technology warfare—greater use of long-range artillery, more air strikes, and more mechanized warfare rather than costly ground sweeps and combat in difficult terrain. This tactic tended to be self-defeating. It allowed continued insurgent existence, gave them time and space, and followed something of a law in insurgencies: if guerrillas don't lose, they win. In any event, clearly this part of the strategy has not been successful. The Kampuchean insurgents are, if anything, stronger now than when they began in 1979—not powerful enough to defeat the People's Army of Vietnam (PAVN), but of such prowess as to make their destruction cost more than PAVN generals are willing to pay. This may not last, but they hold the balance at the moment as the guerrilla bashing persists and the PAVN attempts to grind down the insurgents with minimum sacrifice.

The second strategic response by the Hanoi generals was an attempt to create a viable surrogate force from Khmer stock by building from nothing a People's Republic of Kampuchea Armed Forces (PRKAF). PAVN cadres discovered that army building is the slowest of tasks, marked by constant setbacks such as a desertion rate that has approached 50 percent a year. Yet they persevere and presumably, given enough time, will eventually accomplish their mission.

At times Hanoi has shown signs of faltering, indicated by signals of interest in an outcome in Kampuchea other than military. Some observers believe these to be mere tactical maneuvers, and so far they have come to naught.

As far as can be seen—not more than a year at most—Hanoi will pursue its present strategy and probably will accomplish nothing decisive. If there is a major change of war policy by Vietnam, it is more likely to result from changes within the leadership in Hanoi rather than from developments on the battlefield.

Sino-Vietnamese Face-off

The second major factor to evaluate in assessing the current Indochina security situation is the cold war between Vietnam and China that began in 1979. It was triggered by Vietnam's invasion of Kampuchea, although its roots are much deeper. It also began as the result of blunders by the Hanoi Politburo and to a lesser extent by the Chinese leadership. At one point the confrontation bloomed into a shooting war, a month-long border war in 1979, which ended inconclusively. Since then the face-off has remained a cold war that threatens to become a hot war.

In part what is involved is a struggle for regional power by Vietnam and China. And in part, perhaps a more important part, it is a redefinition of the relationship between the two. Hanoi's leaders believe that as a result of their Vietnam war victory, the centuries-old Sino-Vietnamese relationship—that of pupil to teacher—must be replaced by a new association of greater parity. China does not acknowledge any need for basic change, holding that Hanoi's victory was a matter of luck and U.S. indecisiveness, and thus there is no need to redefine the relationship. The argument may strike the Westerner as rather abstract, but there is more reality here, Asian-style, than in such finite issues as the future government of Kampuchea.

Chinese leaders believe they know how to deal with Vietnam and how to influence it, the essence of centuries of experience. Further, they believe the United States and others do not know how to cope with Vietnam. The Beijing formula involves sustained, unrelieved pressure of every sort that can be mounted. The Vietnamese understand only force, say the Chinese, and anything but force is misread in Hanoi as weakness. Any gesture or offer to compromise differences, the Chinese add, merely reinforces the Hanoi leaders' conviction that they were right all along and need only continue their implacability to eventually get what they want. There appears to be merit in the Chinese policy approach, based on past history, although three years of the Chinese method has yielded none of the results the Chinese desire.

China seems determined to continue its effort to influence Vietnamese behavior, although we cannot be certain, for Chinese foreign policies in the past 35 years have been characterized by sudden, dramatic reversals. A changed Sino-Vietnamese relationship may come as a by-product of the current sporadic talks between Moscow and Beijing on issues between them, one of the knottiest being Vietnam. However, it is difficult to envision a marked change in Chinese policy toward either the USSR or Vietnam until there is some resolution of the Kampuchean problem.

Soviet Presence in Indochina

Vietnam and the USSR are locked into an unusually intimate relationship, linked by a military alliance in all but name. It is a relationship born of Soviet opportunism and Vietnamese dependency. The USSR, it seems clear in retrospect, rushed rather incautiously into the geopolitical vacuum that developed in the region following the Vietnam war. Moscow moved first and thought afterwards. It perceived an opportunity and seized it, only later realizing the full meaning and ultimate consequences. One outcome was to drive Soviet stock throughout noncommunist Southeast Asia to its lowest point in decades. Benefits accrued to Moscow, but they were not unalloyed.

For Vietnam, the genesis of the relationship was more elemental. Because of leadership errors, Vietnam was short of food—a 20 percent shortfall of rice in some years. Without Soviet assistance there would be rice riots in Vietnam. And Hanoi needs weapons—to defend itself against China and for its war in Kampuchea. For these it is totally dependent on the USSR, for there are no arms factories in Vietnam. As Vietnam's economic malaise deepened in the late 1970s, it was increasingly dependent on the Moscow dole. Lately, the tide appears to have turned. Food production is back to the 1976 level, but Vietnam's population has increased since then (about 2.5 percent each year since 1976). The USSR supplies Vietnam with all its defense needs, in effect underwriting its annual defense expenditures, estimated at 50 percent of the total state budget. It also supplies Vietnam with all its petroleum and most of its chemical fertilizers. Moscow extracts from Vietnam as much as it can in exports, but Vietnam has little to offer. The result is one of the worst trade imbalances in the world.

There is reason to believe that the Kremlin is dissatisfied with the cost-benefit ratio of the present Soviet-Vietnamese relationship. Soviet admirals might not concur, although the value of Camranh Bay to the Soviets is debatable, but other leaders seem to believe the USSR got the worst of the bargain. The Soviet reaction to this estimate, however, is not to alter the relationship but to rationalize it and make it more equitable for the USSR. Several far-reaching measures have been taken since 1981, passing certain defense burdens to the Vietnamese and changing the import-export pattern, for example.

The strategic importance of Vietnam to the USSR is a matter for debate. There are advantages for Moscow and no compelling reason why it should abandon the present alliance, especially if it can be made more cost-effective.

What could alter the present relationship and cause distancing, or conceivably even a rupture, are developments on the Vietnamese side. The Vietnamese do not like their dependency on the USSR, nor do they particularly like the Russians. But there is little they would want to do about the association until they become economically self-sufficient and until the

China threat subsides. Even then there would be less chance of a breach in relations than of arranging a more orthodox association.

Internal Factors

Vietnam's basic internal condition is grim, a compound of social malaise, economic stagnation, and failed leadership. If Vietnam's behavior were influenced by internal troubles, as in most countries, it would have turned inward several years ago to concentrate on problem solving to the exclusion of external adventurism. But Vietnam has never been governed by laws of political science operative elsewhere.

The overriding problem in the country is a socioeconomic decline that set in about a year after the end of the Vietnam war and has grown steadily worse. Among Hanoi-watchers, the dispute over interpretation of Vietnam's condition is whether it has hit bottom and is bumping along there.

The essential reason for this economic failure—which is important to understand since in its cause lies the suggested remedy—is the inability of the ruling Politburo to make the right decisions and implement the correct policies. Management of Vietnam is in the hands of the fifteen-man Politburo (and among these, the so-called "circle of five" is dominant), who are unchallengeable politically. There is no regional challenge to them, as in China, or institutional challenge, as in the USSR. They hold all the power, and that is part of the problem. These men, who ran the long war, are of a singular mind-set. They are implacably determined, some would say fanatic, and exactly the leaders needed for a long war against a formidable foe. However, they have the wrong mind-set to run a country at peace, and they have proved totally unequal to Vietnam's needs. Peace requires different kinds of thinking about different kinds of problems. This Politburo, in dealing with Pol Pot, China, economic development, ethnic Chinese in Vietnam, ASEAN, and the United States, made one bad decision after another and, when its mistakes became evident, piled new bad decisions atop the old, compounding the errors.

The result, most apparent on the economic front but evident throughout the society, was near total economic stagnation. Getting the economy going again is the central problem. The problem should not be insurmountable, but apparently is beyond the capabilities of Vietnam's leaders. A social malaise, part of the problem, manifests itself among ordinary Vietnamese not by counterrevolution, but by evasions and manipulations to cope with the system rather than depose its leaders. The men of the Politburo can count themselves fortunate.

Opposition to the regime in Vietnam, the resistance, is ubiquitous, low level, poorly led, and even more poorly organized. Many of the original elements, holdouts from the army of South Vietnam, have been penetrated and badly decimated. Others, chiefly the Montagnards, still appear to give Hanoi some concern.

To succeed, the resistance must organize the latent hostility throughout Vietnam. It must mobilize and motivate people through an organizational weapon. Success or failure of the resistance will not turn on public attitudes—if public opinion were the determinant, the regime would have fallen years ago—but on the organizational skills of resistance leaders. The struggle must be more organizational. But the men in Hanoi have won all their victories by using just such organizational strategy, and they are particularly adept in counterorganizational or organization-slaying strategies. The history of their antiresistance campaign has been characterized by ingenious use of counterorganizational techniques to disorganize and frustrate the resistance.

Based on history, it is difficult to be other than pessimistic about prospects for the resistance. The worldwide record is that communism is a one-way street, and a country that goes communist never throws out the communist government. What is past is prologue but, of course, not always. Therefore, it cannot be stated flatly that the resistance has no chance. The recent history of Vietnam is a succession of "impossible" events, and it would be a foolish prophet who would rule out a civil war in Vietnam that could topple the present regime.

A more likely development, if there is a traumatic change of leadership in Hanoi, would be one effected by upper-level party cadres or senior military officers. Even this seems remote. There will be changes in leadership of course, and this is under way, the slow generational transfer of power. This could be speeded up, even precipitously, by the demise of two or more of the inner "circle of five." A power struggle could then develop in which some faction, in the party or the military, would move to install a new set of leaders. This would not be an anticommunist government, nor would it arise from the general population. It would be more in the nature of a palace coup d'etat.

Intra-Indochina

The final factor in this survey concerns the nature of the ultimate association to emerge in Indochina among the three Indochinese systems—Vietnam, Laos, and Kampuchea. The central issue is whether there is to be eventually a federated (or confederated) arrangement, clearly the intent of the present Hanoi leadership (and probably also any future Hanoi leadership), or whether it will be some arrangement far short of this. Hanoi's pursuit of this objective seems determined but not immediate. Its invasion of Kampuchea was not to further federation, nor do Hanoi's leaders believe that federation can be accomplished with bayonets. They seem willing to wait until even the next century to accomplish the goal, providing events in the three states always move in that general direction.

A single Indochina has various meanings within the region. China appears to have most at stake since it would then face a single element (rather than three) with something of a historical antipathy toward it, one totaling more than 60 million people. China and the rest of Southeast Asia eventually will have to face the question of the ultimate political configuration on the Indochina peninsula, specifically the acceptable limits of integration of the three societies by Hanoi. It is a vast and difficult problem, which is one reason it has never been faced squarely. It also is why Kampuchea is so important. Is a federated arrangement, or even a confederated arrangement, acceptable? China gives every indication of blocking it. ASEAN, certainly Thailand, stands against it. Hanoi is determined to establish some sort of single structure, although it is in no hurry. Sooner or later, the issue of federated/confederated Indochina must be addressed both by Hanoi and its neighbors.

To a large extent, the future political structure in Indochina is caught up in a broader consideration, the growth of regionalism in Southeast Asia. (As used here, *regionalism* means regional system, a matrix of institutions above the nation-state level to which there is attachment, identity, perceived purpose, and value.) In the past decade we have seen the rise of ASEAN and the forced development of a Federation of Indochina. These regional groups, in differing ways, are in their infancy, but they clearly have a history pushing them, and both have a future. For the United States, the problem is that there are regional groups and regional groups—theirs and ours. What gives impetus to one will lend impetus to the other. The United States and other outsiders almost certainly will be obliged to consider Southeast Asia in terms of regional dynamics and regional institutions.

Vietnam as a Security Threat

The People's Army of Vietnam (PAVN) is a formidable military force—the third largest army on earth. It has more than a million men in its "full military" component and at least two million in its paramilitary forces. Most soldiers have considerable battle experience, not only from the Vietnam war but also from recent combat in Kampuchea. However, PAVN's prowess can be overstated, for there are a number of technical limitations at work as well as some political-diplomatic inhibitions.

Party theoreticians in Hanoi write extensively in their journals about "ASEAN and history." The consensus is more or less standard Marx. The two regional groups, ASEAN and communist Indochina, are viewed as symbols of the great global struggle between the forces of progress and reaction, between socialism and capitalism. In this context, the official Hanoi belief is that the governments and societies of ASEAN are neither legitimate nor durable. Sooner or later these systems will be swept away, cast onto the trash heap of history, as it is phrased, and replaced by a new form, the people's republic. Within this view the doctrinal debate is whether Vietnam should (or need) assist this process. Should it help history along, or should it allow the wave of the future to come when it will? The Hanoi Politburo is preoccupied, if not beleaguered, by economic stagnation, the ever-present China threat, and the war in Kampuchea. It is in no position to contribute much to converting ASEAN into a set of people's republics. But the impulse is there, as latent force, always ready to surface. The peoples of the ASEAN region should make no mistake about it, entertain no illusions—Hanoi regards them and their systems as the ideological enemy.

The challenge that Vietnam can offer ASEAN is threefold: direct military threat, indirect military threat, and what might be called the psychopolitical threat.

The ASEAN countries, for the foreseeable future, have little to fear from Vietnam in terms of direct military threat. The exception is Thailand. PAVN lacks the naval and air power to project force over long distances, say, into Indonesia. The USSR is enlarging these two arms, but an analysis of the air and naval augmentation suggests that the risk to the region is not appreciably increased.

PAVN could invade Thailand almost at will. The Thai army is small and lightly equipped (chiefly to deal with insurgents) and could not stop a tank-led blitzkrieg invasion by an armed force that totals more than three million. But although Hanoi's legions could occupy Bangkok in a matter of days and quickly fan out across the country, this quite probably would trigger a widespread Thai insurgency against the invaders; in effect, a "super Kampuchea." There are other compelling reasons why Vietnam should not invade Thailand and probably will not (short border incursions, even some lasting a week or so, are another matter). The Chinese probably would act militarily; ASEAN almost certainly would aid Thailand at some level; Moscow would disapprove, perhaps even strongly; and Vietnam could not be sure of the U.S. reaction. Further, there are elements within the leadership of Hanoi, including important factions in the military, that would regard such a move as sheer "adventurism." They represent a highly significant opposition. Thus, many forces work against a Vietnamese attack on Thailand, but again, there is no certainty.

The indirect military threat to ASEAN posed by Vietnam is aiding and abetting local insurgencies in the various countries. This is a difficult threat to evaluate. Some observers believe that the age of the guerrilla is over, although it is unlikely that Hanoi shares this conclusion. Shortly after the end of the Vietnam war, the PAVN High Command reviewed the insurgent and potential insurgent forces of Southeast Asia, focusing on the three Thai insurgencies, and were unimpressed by their findings. In any event, they did not fund these or other regional insurgencies from the stocks of military supplies they captured in the South. It seems clear that Hanoi has ruled out promoting guerrilla wars, possibly because it sees itself as vulnerable to such activity.

The third threat Hanoi could offer lies in that grey area between war and politics and might be called psycho-political. This challenge is an extension of Vietnamese ideological thinking and is partly military (that is, security-oriented) and partly socioeconomic. It has been evolved by Hanoi party doctrinaires in detail, but is still in draft form. The basic strategy is to induce and coerce ASEAN countries to cut their ties to the capitalist world (and the multinational corporations, which Hanoi deems even more odious) in exchange for regional harmony the only way ASEAN can ever attain it. Hanoi would offer amicability and help in establishing a stable region if ASEAN would alter its present links with Western/Japanese capitalism. Party theoreticians in Hanoi worked out an ideological rationale for this—a doctrine that synthesizes nationalism and collectivism. It holds that no nation can call itself independent if it maintains close economic ties with external capitalism. Nor can it claim neutrality in the struggle between the two great competing world systems. However, the rationale does not require choosing a particular brand of Marxism and permits neutrality in the Sino-Soviet dispute. The rule would be collectivism at home (or not, as a nation chose) and nationalism abroad (defined as being economically nonaligned). The great enemy then would not be capitalism per se, but economic interdependency. The "carrot" in this strategy would link the Third (or Fourth) World nations of Southeast Asia into commodity blocks (as with rubber or tin production). The "stick" would be a bellicose, intransigent, ever-threatening Hanoi, willing and able to perpetrate regional instability.

In the late 1970s much was made of this strategic approach in Vietnamese journals. After Vietnam's troubles escalated, not much more was heard of it. Whether it is resurrected at some opportune moment will depend largely on the leaders who eventually take over in Hanoi.

Judgments and Conclusions

The Indochina-ASEAN relationship appears to have entered a period of flux and change. Almost daily come new overtures from various capitals, rumors of breakthroughs, good offices proffered by some third party. Hanoi has been particularly active in scattering gestures of reasonableness in the direction of ASEAN, China, and even the United States. Its motives have been variously interpreted as opportunism, mistaken perceptions of weakened opposition, tactical efforts to force short-term concessions, or genuine desire to improve relations. The dynamic scene underscores the difficulties in determining a trend of events and making projections and predictions.

One conclusion seems self-evident. Kampuchea will remain the touchstone of regional instability, and a stable region requires resolving the issue to the satisfaction of all with a major stake in it.

Three scenarios suggest themselves as most probable for Kampuchea in the next year or so. They are, in ascending order of probability: (1) a negotiated political settlement in which a new governing structure in reached, agreeable to all parties; (2) successful "pacification" of Kampuchea by PAVN (that is, elimination of the insurgency or its confinement in the Cardamon mountains) and the creation of a viable military force from the PRKAF; and (3) continued warfare, with the issue unresolved in any decisive way. The chief variable here is the Hanoi leadership; a change in the Politburo could trigger a marked change in policy toward Kampuchea. The other major dynamic factor is China and the possibility that it might suddenly change its strategic position with respect to Kampuchea and Sino-Vietnamese relations. But in the absence of these developments, the most likely prospect for Kampuchea is more of the same.

The second conclusion is that regional stability demands a rapprochement between China and Vietnam, that this is not likely in the near future, but that eventually it will take place. Confrontation and cold war were never intended by the Hanoi Politburo, but resulted from its miscalculation and bad judgment. The same is true of the Chinese. China is too large and close to Vietnam to permit hostility to continue indefinitely. However, given Soviet backing, Vietnam's position is not untenable and Hanoi's leaders seem prepared to wait for a decade, if necessary, for improvement. China seems determined to press on with its policy of "bleeding Vietnam." It seems convinced it knows better than others (certainly the United States) how to deal with the Vietnamese and is impatient with the advice of outsiders. However, Chinese foreign policy since 1948 has seen cycles of seeming implacability abruptly give way to an entirely new approach.

Thus, a sudden change in the Hanoi-Beijing axis, or the Hanoi-Moscow-Beijing triangle, is always possible. More likely, however, is the prospect of very slow improvement in Sino-Vietnamese relations.

A third conclusion is that we probably have witnessed the limits of intimacy in the Soviet-Vietnamese relationship, and the most likely prospect is a distancing process. There is little reason to believe that the fundamental nature of the relationship will change. The only probable exception may be the result of a significant change in the relations between the USSR and China; that is, an end to the Sino-Soviet dispute, itself unlikely.

A fourth conclusion is that the Vietnamese internal scene will probably improve only slowly, at an uneven pace, and be marked by considerable trauma if two or more of the major figures pass from the scene. The key factors—a stagnant economy, an out-of-touch, anachronistic leadership, a failed foreign policy that has left Vietnam surrounded by enemies and very nearly friendless (save only for the USSR and Cuba)—are conditions that develop slowly and usually change only at glacial speed. The Vietnam agricultural front has improved, but recently ideologues in the party stepped up the doctrinal battle and threaten even the modest gains made so far.

Outsiders can contribute only marginally to helping Vietnam, assuming they have reason to do so. The kind of trouble Vietnam is experiencing is the lonely sort that can be rectified only by the Vietnamese themselves. This same self-contained characteristic applies to the resistance in Vietnam; in the end it will stand or fail on its organizational, mobilization, and motivational abilities, not on actions or support by outsiders.

Vietnam, as far as ASEAN is concerned, is a security sword cutting both ways. A sick Vietnam is a weakened and preoccupied Vietnam, hence less of a threat to its neighbors but also unstable and unpredictable. Therein lies an inescapable dilemma for ASEAN, whether to help or hinder Vietnam's national development since in the first instance it increases threat potential and in the second perpetuates a potentially explosive condition.

The meaning for ASEAN, the final conclusion, is that in unity there is strength, in solidarity there is security. The truly great danger ASEAN faces—and the United States by extension—is disunity, disarray, a coming apart. As long as the ASEAN states are internally cohesive and firmly bound, Vietnam is not inclined to move against them. But if weakness develops, for example, a series of coup d'etats in Bangkok, the Vietnamese might be tempted to strike by the lure of opportunity, even against their better judgment. Anarchy is the true enemy of ASEAN, but if these countries remain ordered and firmly joined, they have little to fear from Vietnam.

The Power Balance as Seen from Jakarta: A Projection for the 1980s and Beyond

Lie Tek Tjeng

Indonesia's political and strategic thinkers are not exactly happy with current projections of the Asia-Pacific power balance for the final decades of the twentieth century.

Indonesians could not fail to observe with some satisfaction the world's growing attention to ASEAN as a regional organization—a supplier of raw materials, area of investment, and a market with about 300 million people, all strategically located between the Pacific and Indian oceans. Yet they cannot but feel dismayed to observe the current projections of this vital Asia-Pacific region for the rest of this century, centered primarily on the interplay between the United States, the USSR, the PRC, and Japan, without taking ASEAN into account.

Realistic Indonesian political and strategic thinkers do not deny the important roles of the four powers in determining the basic pattern of Asia-Pacific developments; however, they feel that realistic projections should also pay attention to the views and aspirations of local powers, like those of the Republic of Indonesia.

This paper presents an Indonesian perspective,[1] focused on its national aspirations that determined its Weltanschauung and basic orientation of its foreign policy since 1945. This paper could contribute to a better understanding and appreciation of Indonesia's position in world affairs and contribute as well to a better understanding and appreciation of the Third World's views and aspirations that play a growing role in world affairs.

The Background and Manifestation of Indonesia's Free and Active Foreign Policy

Nationalism and anticolonialism were the driving forces of modern Indonesia that culminated in the Proclamation of Independence in 1945, the ensuing War of Independence (1945–1949), and the struggle for West Irian, unified with the republic in 1963. They determined the basic orientation of its foreign policy, still valid today. As defined by the respected Dr. Hatta, Indonesia carries out a free and active foreign policy that does not take sides in the cold war and actively works for world peace.[2]

Godless Marxism is an alien ideology to the majority of Indonesians—excepting, of course, those who embrace this ideology like the Marxists and Communists—who accepted the Pancasila philosophy (admittedly, not a few Indonesians have been attracted to some former socialist ideals).

The protracted struggle for West Irian[3] made it practically impossible for any realistic politician to contemplate siding with the West—primarily the major colonial and/or ex-colonial countries like England, France, the Netherlands, and Belgium under U.S. leadership—in the cold war.[4] It was natural, if not inevitable, that Indonesia identified itself with the new nations in Asia, the Muslim Middle East, and Africa that became independent of Western domination after World War II. Even though Indonesia's free and active foreign policy was not pro-communist or anti-West in the 1950s, its manifestation clashed head-on with the United States' basic policy in the Asia-Pacific region.

Following the outbreak of the Korean War in June 1950 and before the emergence of the USSR as a naval power, the PRC became the United States' main enemy in the Asia-Pacific region. The United States recognized the Chiang Kai-shek government in Taiwan as the sole legitimate government of China, refused to recognize the PRC, and tried to mobilize China's neighbors in its containment-of-China policy.[5]

Indonesia, like Burma and India, had a one-China policy that recognized Beijing; besides, Indonesia consistently refused to join SEATO, created in 1954 to contain the PRC. There was also a clash of personalities between the flamboyant Sukarno and the legalistic John Foster Dulles. Indonesian-U.S. relations steadily declined in the 1950s because of Indonesia's growing dissatisfaction and irritation with the United States' reluctance to support Indonesia's claim to West Irian, which Sukarno made his national objective, and Sukarno's fateful decision to use the cold war in unifying West Irian with the republic.

Indonesia's leftward drift steadily pushed it toward the communist camp and was halted only by the failure of the September 30 Movement in

1965. The policy of the New Order, under Suharto, centered on economic development and cooperation with the West, including Japan. The New Order only rectified the leftist deviations of the old order, but did not deviate from Indonesia's basic free and active foreign policy orientation bequeathed by the founding fathers less than 40 years ago. This was based on the realization that accepted national aspirations cannot be set aside without causing unwanted repercussions.

Indonesia—after the secession of East Pakistan and the formation of Bangladesh—has the world's largest Muslim population, with some 90 percent of its inhabitants being Muslim.[6] In contrast to its Western-trained and Western-oriented elite, the majority of Indonesians who attended traditional and/or religious schools emphasizing the teaching of the Holy Koran and Arabic, are oriented toward the Arabic Middle East.[7] Hence their sympathy with the struggle of their fellow Muslims against Western colonialism or domination in the Middle East.

There are emotional ties between Indonesian nationalists, particularly the 1945 generation, and the Arab countries in the Middle East. As one of them has summarized it: "The Arab countries headed by Egypt were the first to unreservedly support our declaration of Independence when we ourselves were not sure whether this would be successful. How can we but be pro-Arab?"

Indonesia's adherence to its free, active foreign policy orientation was also manifested in its one-China policy. Following the anticommunist wave, particularly the anti-Chinese wave that swept the country after 1965, many thought that Indonesia would join SEATO and recognize Taiwan. However, this did not take place, even though Indonesian-PRC relations were frozen.

Although significant differences were noted between Sukarno's and Suharto's Indonesia, these should not be interpreted as a change in basic principles accepted in 1945 as the national aspirations of the Indonesian people.

The Background and Basic Motivation of ZOPFAN

The Kissinger visit to Beijing in mid-1971 and President Nixon's visit to China in February 1972 officially ended the Sino-American cold war and decisively changed the basic pattern in the Asia-Pacific region.

The Sino-American hostility throughout the cold war in Asia (1950–1972) that determined the basic pattern of Asian developments made way for a realignment in which the United States and the PRC counted on each other in the Asia-Pacific region to balance the growing power of the USSR, newly emerged as a global naval power.[8]

This sudden and total reversal of the United States' basic attitude toward the PRC profoundly shocked the Asian countries that, until then, had been mobilized to contain "communist China."[9] These political developments decisively influenced the acceptance of ZOPFAN (Zone of Peace, Freedom, and Neutrality) in November 1971 by the foreign ministers of ASEAN (established in 1967).

The Philippines, Thailand, Malaysia, and Singapore meanwhile found that reliance on the West, particularly the United States, did not give them peace but only invited Chinese reaction that supported local communist parties and subversive antigovernment forces.[10] They drew the inevitable conclusion that they should no longer rely on an outside power.

Their disillusion with the United States, preceded by Indonesia's traumatic experience with the communist world in 1965, led to their common acceptance of ZOPFAN as ASEAN's orientation, and this seemed justified by developments in the 1970s following the communist victory in Indochina in 1975 and the United States' lack of interest in Southeast Asia for the rest of that decade.

Conclusions

The New Order under General Suharto made economic development the national objective, but Indonesians realized that they had no alternative but the West—including Japan—for assistance and cooperation.[11]

However, cooperation with the West, especially the United States, should take full account of Indonesia's free and active foreign policy orientation and of the fact that, in the eyes of many Muslims, the United States is the "protector of Israel."

Indonesia and the United States often belong to different, or even opposing, camps, as in the North-South dialogue, efforts to establish a New International Economic Order, OPEC, and the Law of the Sea Treaty, even though Indonesian attempts to play a moderate role are appreciated by the United States.

Indonesia's long-term concern is the PRC rather than the USSR. Within this frame Vietnam is considered a viable buffer state that should be prevented from being used against ASEAN. Hence, Vietnam should not be pushed further into the Soviet embrace but should be weaned away, if possible.

Indonesia's political and strategic thinkers are concerned by the steady growth of Soviet naval power and the emergence of the USSR as a global power since World War II. They were somewhat "alarmed" in the late 1970s when, following the Vietnam debacle, the United States withdrew from Southeast Asia; however, they were reassured after seeing U.S. determination to remain a Pacific power. Generally, Indonesia's political and strategic thinkers believe that the U.S. Seventh Fleet has an edge over the Soviet Pacific Fleet, especially after the addition of the new nuclear carrier and renovated battleship units.

Indonesian political strategists do not think it wise to step up U.S.-Soviet confrontation in the Indian and Pacific ocean areas or accelerate the arms race that they think will ensue if Indonesia and/or ASEAN joins the United States.

Many Indonesians who remember the Japanese occupation in World War II are not enthusiastic about an accelerated Japanese rearmament program, even though they realize that a growing military role for Japan seems inevitable. Hence their desire that Japan's rearmament be paralleled by efforts of the ASEAN countries to step up their national and regional resilience to prevent a further widening of the gap between Japan's Self-Defense Force capability and that of the armed forces of the ASEAN countries.

With regard to scenarios in the Asia-Pacific region, Indonesians would like to see strategists sketch the roles that the Southeast Asian countries, particularly the ASEAN countries, are expected to play. Indonesia's political and strategic thinkers believe that Southeast Asian security should primarily be the responsibility of the Southeast Asian countries and the ASEAN countries should not be compelled to take sides as the *sine qua non* for assistance to build up their capability to patrol and guard their territories, seas, and skies.

In case of an imminent or real attack that the ASEAN countries cannot handle themselves, they will, of course, call on their friends for assistance. However, Indonesia's strategists feel comfortable with the power balance now shaping up in the Asia-Pacific region; hence they feel no need to insist on an accelerated Japanese rearmament that could only reawaken fears of the revival of Japanese militarism among its Asian neighbors and its own people or an official linking of ASEAN as the United States' ally that could cause unwanted domestic repercussions in some ASEAN countries.

Notes

1. This is the personal view of the author as a scientist and an Asia-watcher and does not necessarily represent the viewpoint of the Indonesian Institute of Sciences or of any other institution with which he happens to be affiliated at present.

2. See *Foreign Affairs* 31 (April 1953).

3. As former armed forces chief of staff and Christian church leader, retired Lieutenant General Simatupang said, "There are only two Southeast Asian countries that had to fight to get their independence; one is Indonesia, the other is Vietnam." This contrasted sharply with the peaceful decolonization of the ex-British or ex-American colonies and should be seriously taken into account in trying to really understand the basic orientation and course of Indonesian politics.

4. As an example one could cite here the fall of the Soekiman cabinet in the early 1950s, caused by Foreign Minister Soebardjo's willingness to sign the MSA agreement, though with some modifications. For details, see Herbert Feith, *The Decline of Constitutional Democracy in Indonesia* (Ithaca, N.Y.: Cornell University Press, 1962).

5. Distinguishing Chinese communism from Soviet communism was not necessary as long as there was a Sino-Soviet bloc; however, this became vital with the Sino-Soviet split.

6. Unlike Pakistan or Saudi Arabia, Indonesia is not a Muslim country.

7. The Dutch scholar Boeke mentioned the dual economy of the Dutch East Indies, now Indonesia. Dualism is not limited to the economy, but also extended in other basic fields like education, culture, politics, etc.

8. To understand the reason for this basic change, see my article "Sino-Soviet and Sino-Japanese Relations: A View from Jakarta," *Pacific Community,* July 1975.

9. As one young Thai scholar said to his American audience during a lecture-tour by ASEAN scholars in 1982, "I grew up in the Cold War atmosphere, when we Thais were constantly told that Chinese communism is our enemy number one and the root of all evil in Asia, if not the world. Suddenly we were told that we should become friends with Peking."

10. See my paper, "China's Policy Towards Southeast Asia: A View from Jakarta," written for the German-Indonesian Conference held by the Institute für Asiakunde and the Indonesian Centre for Strategic and International Studies in Bali, July 1982. This paper will be published by the Indonesian CSIS.

11. Even communist countries looked to the West and Japan, rather than to the USSR, as more promising for assistance and cooperation in development.

The Interests and Policies of Malaysia: A Study in Historical Change

Chandran Jeshurun

The current phase of political stability and regional security in Southeast Asia should be viewed against the tumultuous background of the past. Traditionally, the countries of this part of Asia devised intricate relationships among themselves as well as accommodating the power and influence of large neighbors through lord-vassal and tributary linkages. These historical balance-of-power mechanisms are unable to function as effectively as in the past due to two new variables: the emergence of new, independent nation-states and the intrusion of external great power interests.

Although the newly emerging states all faced the common tasks of nation building and economic development, it was stability and security that became the primary goals. The nations of Southeast Asia are not only divided by ideological differences and great power conflicts, but even more by traditional rivalries and ethnic diversities. Since the Vietnam war the region has witnessed the somewhat unusual spectacle of conflicts within the communist camp being played out by their proxies on the mainland. Among the noncommunist states there remain the endemic problems of communist and separatist insurgencies and socioeconomic development where state policies cannot keep pace with the growing aspirations of the populace. It is not surprising, therefore, that several of the nation-states of Southeast Asia have become ardent advocates of nonalignment as one of the few viable foreign policy options left for them. The interests and policies of one such nation-state, Malaysia, will be examined against this general background of political and security developments.

Malaysian strategic thinking about national security and regional stability has evolved over the 25 years since independence. Its founding fathers acknowledged that the new nation must provide for its national defense and security by entering into a form of military alliance with the departing colonial power, the United Kingdom. Thus came into being the Anglo-Malayan (Malaysian after 1963) Defense Agreement (AMDA) in 1957 whereby the United Kingdom pledged itself to come to Malaysia's aid if there arose any threat of external aggression. Before long Australia and New Zealand became formally associated with AMDA, and the concept of Commonwealth defense was born. Admittedly, Malayan leaders were not blind to the larger political and strategic motives that obviously governed the policies of their Commonwealth partners. Nor were they unaware of their own military weakness, for, apart from some seven battalions of infantry with small supporting units and a fledgling armored reconnaissance force, they had no navy and air force to speak of. Politically, too, the government in power had to justify its defense policy before its own constituency as there was no great enthusiasm among pre-independence politicians for the former colonial power, least of all when it involved an unequal military alliance.

Nevertheless, the existence of AMDA did allow the Malayan government to embark upon needed rural socioeconomic development programs without the crippling burden of a heavy defense budget. Simultaneously, modest but systematic plans were approved for building an independent naval and air force capability. Most significantly, Malaya avoided entanglement in the SEATO strategy of containing Communist China and its allies in mainland Southeast Asia. This was achieved at the same time as the successful termination of the Communist Party of Malaya's twelve-year-old insurgency, known as the Emergency, in 1960.

With the formation of the Federation of Malaysia, including the Borneo states of Sarawak and North Borneo (Sabah) and the island of Singapore, some aspects of earlier strategic thinking had to be revised in light of enlarged national security and defense responsibilities. Sukarno's Indonesia had adopted his policy of *Konfrontasi* in opposing the United Kingdom's decolonization process. The Philippines, which had hitherto demonstrated a certain willingness to participate in regional cooperation by joining Thailand and Malaya in the Association of Southeast Asia (ASA), laid claim to Sabah. Brunei decided not to join the federation, and Singapore, which joined in 1963, seceded in 1965 due to insurmountable political differences. Malaysia capitalized on the Commonwealth defense umbrella in combating Konfrontasi and expanding its own forces, aided by military funding, training facilities, and weapons transfers provided by the United Kingdom in particular.

The mid-1960s constituted something of a watershed in Malaysian strategic thinking due to the changes in Britain's East of Suez defense policy. Malaysia was left to cope with Indonesia, the Philippines, and independent

Singapore. But it was the Nixon Doctrine in 1969 that most troubled Malaysian and regional strategic planners. After much fervent diplomacy by both Malaysia and Singapore, a Five-Power Defense Arrangement (FPDA) was concluded that linked them strategically with the United Kingdom, Australia, and New Zealand. The terms of the new FPDA formula were more vague and less reassuring than the earlier defense treaty.

In providing for its security after the proclamation of the Nixon Doctrine and in the absence of the old Commonwealth defense umbrella, Malaysia was compelled to undertake specific measures in the fields of diplomacy and military preparedness. Uncertain about the future roles of the United States, China, and the Soviet Union in Southeast Asia, Malaysia was obliged to look out for itself. Malaysia decided to participate in the anticommunist forum for Asian and Pacific Cooperation (ASPAC), only to pull out of it rather unceremoniously in 1973. Furthermore, anticipatory moves were made to adjust its diplomacy to the new security situation in Southeast Asia by establishing diplomatic links with communist bloc countries, beginning with the USSR and Eastern Europe in 1968 and culminating with the Democratic Republic of Vietnam in 1973.

Although there was no inherent anti-U.S. element in this new, more evenhanded diplomacy, Malaysia had by then abandoned its absolute dependence on the Commonwealth defense strategy. To further emphasize its desire to accommodate the interests of other powers likely to play a role in regional security, Malaysia took the bold step of opening diplomatic links with the PRC in May 1974. It paid more attention to the possibilities of greater regional cooperation through the Association of Southeast Asian Nations (ASEAN), comprising Indonesia, Malaysia, the Philippines, Singapore, and Thailand, founded in 1967.

The ASEAN ploy was by no means a solution for Malaysia's strategic planning. Nevertheless, it produced a number of intriguing options for regional stability and a new kind of diplomatic equilibrium. One of the earliest ASEAN-sponsored moves to pre-empt subordination of regional interests to great power demands was the Malaysian initiative of 1971, which resulted in the Kuala Lumpur Declaration, in which the five member-states of ASEAN espoused the goal of creating in Southeast Asia a Zone of Peace, Freedom, and Neutrality, or ZOPFAN. None of the signatories deluded themselves into thinking the major powers would underwrite such a neutralization proposal, but they derived a certain satisfaction from the prestige gained from their bold, independent initiative.

Malaysia has moved with some circumspection in adopting Indonesia's theory of national and regional resiliency as its diplomatic creed. Seeking to maintain internal stability and to develop sufficient economic and military strength to counter potential threats to its security, Malaysia *is* proudly self-reliant. This is illustrated by the growth of its armed forces and its strong support of the FPDA.

Resilience has exposed differences in individual perceptions of common problems within ASEAN. The organization has suffered because of the pressure that each member-state tries to exert to promote its individual interests. The Vietnamese have not been averse to exploiting such strategic variables, and Malaysia does not always agree with the ASEAN stand on a number of issues. Malaysia has found it necessary, and sometimes expedient, to work independently of the regional cooperative effort.

Much of Malaysia's cautious and circumspect attitude toward big power linkages in regional security stems from the perceived weaknesses and disadvantages of the SEATO experience. Malaysia traditionally adopted a policy of guarded suspicion in dealings with major powers such as the United States, in part because of lack of faith in security arrangements that appeared to be safeguards for outside interests in Southeast Asia. The anxieties and uncertainties Malaysia experienced in relating to the post-SEATO U.S. strategic and diplomatic goals in the Western Pacific were exemplified by the wide-ranging fluctuations in U.S.-PRC relations. It would have been logical for Malaysia to seek self-reliance when the United States seemed to be withdrawing from its military and strategic role in Southeast Asia after 1975. Such responses were detectable in the reactions of other regional states. Often they amounted to no more than posturing or assertions of national pride. They were short-lived, as events in the Indochinese states under Vietnam's tutelage created a new strategic order in Southeast Asia.

The appearance of this new order, and the threat it contained, prompted many Southeast Asian states to depart from the ideals of ZOPFAN to call for a residual U.S. capability in the region. In the Malaysian case, the acceptance of a U.S. air and naval presence is determined not alone by the rapport between Vietnam and the Soviet Union, but by the perception in Kuala Lumpur of an enlarging Soviet interest in the loosely organized land and sea mass of the region. The USSR-Vietnam relationship may provide the reason for a more receptive attitude toward the U.S. military presence, but it does not constitute the stimulus for this accommodating policy.

Insufficient attention has been focused on the relations of individual states in the region with the USSR, for, as with Malaysia, the nature of those relations has a vital impact on regional perceptions of U.S. security interests as well. Although Malaysia's ties with the Soviets are relatively recent and have undergone some ups and downs since 1968 when formal diplomatic links were established, the Kuala Lumpur government has always been studious in observing the U.S.-USSR strategic relationship.

This pragmatism often is misinterpreted within and outside the country as either an attempt to play one side against the other or a blatant demonstration of anti-U.S. tendencies. One of the rationales for Malaysia to establish relations with the Soviets was the economic factor, as the Soviet bloc had become an important market for the export of primary commodities such as rubber. In the early 1970s the government of the late Tun Abdul Razak toyed with venturing into joint efforts in major development projects such as hydroelectric dams, although this was subsequently dropped, presumably due to the high security risks involved. But an undeniable denominator in the whole question of the country's relations with the major powers is the apprehension about the long-term interests of the PRC—an enigma in which the saliency of proper relations with the USSR cannot be ignored.

Are the two other major interested parties in the Western Pacific, the PRC and Japan, disposed to play a constructive role in regional security? For a while it appeared that China would emulate the United States and avoid as far as possible any entangling involvements in Southeast Asia. That prospect was soon dismissed after the Vietnamese invasion of Kampuchea, if not earlier, due to the undisguised support of the Beijing government for the Khmer Rouge regime at Phnom Penh. The open Chinese hostility to Vietnam gave rise to collective efforts by ASEAN as well as to individual initiatives of member-nations to work toward a political solution of the Kampuchea issue. Hitherto, hopes of breaking the China-Vietnam stalemate over Kampuchea have proved illusory, but Malaysia has been quietly supportive of some third-party intervention to surmount the seemingly intractable obstacle. Together with other Southeast Asian parties, Malaysia has discussed such possibilities with the Burmese.

As for Japan, things could not look brighter in view of the present Malaysian government's "Look East" policy, which is a personal crusade of Prime Minister Dr. Mahathir Mohamad to launch the nation into an embryonic industrialization phase. Kuala Lumpur is divided on the issue of Japan's playing a more direct role in regional security. To some policymakers, the prospect of a Japanese security role is considered so novel as to make it, for the moment, theoretical and irrelevant. Some would prefer to put off consideration of the need for a Japanese role so long as there is a U.S. military alternative generally acceptable to the regional states. Others hesitate to treat seriously the possibility of a strategic role for Japan in the belief that innate role-expansion tendencies by the Japanese are inimical to peace and strategy in the region.

Malaysia has demonstrated a bold readiness to come to terms with the Vietnamese. Even before the debacle over Kampuchea in 1978, Malaysia had developed substantial bilateral links with Hanoi, especially in such areas as economic reconstruction. Largely due to constraints imposed by the coordinated ASEAN response to Vietnamese aggression, Malaysia has temporarily abandoned many of the bilateral projects worked out with Vietnam. In the tricky diplomatic arena, the two parties have consistently maintained a dialogue without giving the appearance of challenging the formal ASEAN position.

Behind these bilateral links between Malaysia and Vietnam lies the still unknown factor of Hanoi-Washington relations. Part of the problem of a dialogue between ASEAN and Vietnam is the tendency of individual member-nations to conduct their own diplomacy. Although a smaller nation and thus at a disadvantage in coping with great power interests, Malaysia is determined to give priority to its own national and regional interests in arriving at some modus operandi with Vietnam.

In keeping with apparently clearheaded attitudes toward its security and defense needs, the Malaysian government has embarked on evolving a national strategy. Based on the recent past, Malaysia, like its ASEAN partners, is faced with internal and external security threats. The Communist Party of Malaysia (CPM) insurgency has naturally absorbed the bulk of its military planning, and both the Malaysian Army and the Royal Malaysian Air Force (RMAF), to a lesser extent, have been deployed to counterinsurgency warfare roles for the past thirty-five years. There is no doubt that the military solution of the insurgency threat has been long realized. However, given the tactics of the CPM, its ability to find more or less permanent refuge in the northern jungle terrain of Peninsular Malaysia and short-term sanctuary across the border in southern Thailand, it is highly improbable that Malaysia envisages extinction of the insurgent forces.

The current military and Royal Malaysia Police strategy is aimed at containing the CPM guerrilla remnants and preventing them from breaking out and spreading into the heavily populated regions along the west coast of the peninsula. A similar situation prevails in Sarawak, where the Rejang Area Security Command (RASCOM) in its Third Division concentrates forces of brigade strength to prevent a revival of the communist threat there. Malaysia has also developed somewhat unique bilateral security cooperation with the neighboring states of Thailand and Indonesia.

Of the two border states, Malaysia had a longer history of cooperation with Thailand. Begun as an expediency by the British during the height of the Emergency in the late 1950s, the practice of border security cooperation was actively cultivated by Malaysia and Thailand in the 1960s. Not only was a formal agreement reached between the two parties providing for across-the-border operations and intelligence sharing, but the bilateral security cooperation was institutionalized with the General Border Committee and Regional Border Committee that met at regular intervals.

These joint efforts against the communist insurgents on the common border reached a peak in 1979–1980 with a series of large-scale combined operations. Despite their cooperation, the two countries differ markedly in their respective perceptions of their security problems. The Thais see activities of the PULO (Pattani United Liberation Organization) separatists in southern Thailand as merely an irritation. The Malays see the border insurgency as a threat to the territorial integrity of their nation. The heavy concentration of Malaysian ground and air forces in that region is undertaken with regard to the sensitivities of Thai national pride.

Such defense plans in the interests of one party are unlikely to be discussed bilaterally, or even within the ASEAN forum, and it has become the vogue for local military commanders on both sides to issue unilateral statements at variance with cordial joint statements emanating from the meetings of the Regional Border Committee. One cannot, therefore, escape the impression that there exist a number of gray areas in Malay-Thai border relations that the respective governments find convenient to relegate to the level of unofficial communication. There is always the danger that political experience will bring surface disagreements. In the spirit of ASEAN solidarity and the common interest in defusing sensitive issues Malaysia has proposed, and the Thais have responded favorably, to elevate their border arrangements to formal diplomatic exchanges in accordance with international law.

Bilateral border security cooperation arrangements were worked out between Malaysia and Indonesia for the common border between Sarawak and Kalimantan. While there is less difficulty implementing joint operations with the Indonesians, due to the lower level of insurgency in that region, Malaysia has nevertheless developed a much wider range of military collaboration with Indonesia, especially naval patrols and air exercises. Not only because of the common responsibilities both countries share in the protection of sea-lanes in the Strait of Malacca but also due to the predominant Malaysian interest in protecting communications across the South China Sea with Sabah and Sarawak, the Kuala Lumpur government has given priority to maintaining close military ties with Indonesia, its archipelagic neighbor.

As part of this strategy, Malaysia has joined Singapore in the Integrated Air Defense System (IADS) within the FPDA framework. Malaysian troops have exercised jointly with those of Australia and New Zealand in both those countries and on Malaysian soil. A logical extension of such cooperative strategies is that eventually both Malaysia and Singapore would conduct joint military maneuvers.

A major development in Malaysian strategic planning occurred after the Vietnamese invasion and occupation of Kampuchea. This was the publicized military determination to develop a Malaysian armed forces capability for engaging in conventional warfare. For the first time Malaysian strategic planners conceded the need for diplomatic initiatives as well as higher military capability to face the new perceptions of threat. The new role envisaged for the Malaysian armed forces was, however, limited to threats within Southeast Asia. It was assumed that the intervention of any external power would provoke a major conflict involving the big powers. Between 1975 and 1979, Malaysian defense expenditures increased by 50 percent annually, whereas from 1979 to 1982 the increase was at a phenomenal rate of almost 200 percent. The recession in 1983 resulted in substantial trimming-down of the army's budget, while major increases in the allocation for the Royal Malaysian Navy (RMN) and the Royal Malaysian Air Force (RMAF) were left more or less untouched.

Malaysian strategic thinking has undergone a fundamental change, placing more emphasis since 1979 on the development of the two hitherto junior services, the navy and the air force. The construction of new bases at strategic locations and the orders placed for aircraft and naval vessels clearly pointed to a perception of external threat. Indeed, it was widely speculated in late 1982 that the next chief of defense forces, a position formerly an army monopoly, might well be the chief of navy to reflect the new strategy. Malaysia will likely continue the priority given air and naval defense and offensive capabilities, while the army will likely maintain its present strength but develop specialized units, such as armored columns.

In articulating national threat perceptions in Southeast Asia, particularly in terms of external aggression, there is an ambiguity in the current situation as well as increasing relevance for the Pacific community as a whole. The military role of the big powers is fundamental. For Malaysia, the vastly increased Soviet naval presence in the Western Pacific and its regular appearance within Southeast Asian waters is of primary concern. The pattern of Soviet-Vietnamese military cooperation clearly points to the need for a countervailing force to neutralize the USSR's conventional capability.

Malaysia shares the ASEAN consensus as to the desirability and credibility of the U.S. forces in the Western Pacific. Nevertheless, controversy surrounds the potential of the United States' contribution to stability in the region due to differing perceptions of the PRC's long-term interests and the perceived goals of Japanese policy. These factors must be considered by ASEAN members as they make judgments about some balance of power in the vast sweep of territory bordering the Pacific.

A more immediate concern of Malaysia is the emergency of a regional balance of power to cope with the anticipated expansion of the Vietnamese sphere of influence. Although no one seriously questions the superiority of the Vietnamese war machine, there is evidence that the regional states, including Malaysia, are steadily upgrading and expanding their armed strength. Although strategic plans vary from state to state, they must be based on the common premise that ground forces of the big powers will not be deployed.

Nor can there be any certainty about China's military forces, especially its ultimate achievement of a navy with a blue-water capability. Of no less significance will be how Japan provides for its own defense and security, a process well under way. Faced with such important considerations of the security scenario in the Western Pacific, and without any certainty regarding the respective roles of the USSR and the United States, Southeast Asian nations such as Malaysia refrained from enunciating a clear-cut security perception and preferred, instead, to work quietly within regional frameworks such as ASEAN.

Most discussions of Southeast Asian regional security have invariably alluded to the prospect of an ASEAN military pact. Malaysia has a fairly long experience of bilateral military cooperation with at least three of its ASEAN partners. Nevertheless, on the basis of the record of combined operations alone (for example, the 1979–1980 Malay-Thai campaigns), it does not seem plausible that an effective ASEAN force could ever be deployed without considerable and lengthy combined exercises.

Observers have noted the trend over the past decade toward increasing standardization of equipment, weapons, and, most important of all, command and control functions among ASEAN member-states. Joint bilateral exercises are regarded as dress rehearsals for the ultimate forging of ASEAN military forces. Yet, discrepancies in the sizes as well as the roles and missions of individual ASEAN member-states' armed forces do not augur well for further military unity. For smaller nations like Malaysia and Singapore, the strategy of allying their forces with larger, more powerful, or more militarily experienced forces is not likely to appeal because the strong nationalist postures of ASEAN member-states (even in nonmilitary matters) highlight the obstacles that an ASEAN military pact would encounter. Malaysian strategic planning for regional security in Southeast Asia is clearly based on the premise of either unilateral or, at best, bilateral responses to a common external threat.

There is a distinct change in attitude toward the prospect of joint military exercises, particularly air and naval, with U.S. forces in the Western Pacific. Although such collaborative plans do not include Malaysian elements, it is plausible that the changing professional standards of the armed forces, coupled with the training backgrounds in U.S. military establishments that characterize the new leadership of the army and air force in particular, will conceivably lead to Malaysia's availing itself of the opportunities, and admittedly the disappointments, inherent in joint exercises with U.S. forces. Malaysia, in its own way, is indicating its willingness to cooperate in fashioning a balance of power designed to preserve peace not only in the ASEAN region, but in the Pacific Basin as well.

National Security in the Pacific Basin: A View from Singapore

Obaid ul Haq

It is instructive to see how the Republic of Singapore—the smallest member of ASEAN—has viewed its security situation and to study the policies its political leaders have adopted to secure, maintain, and promote a climate of security and stability for Singapore and the region in which it is situated. How does a strategically situated small country in a turbulent area of the world ensure its security and territorial integrity? What options are open to it?

In 1970 S. Rajaratnam, Singapore's seasoned foreign minister, spelled out the formula of his island-republic's security as

> . . . a judicious mixture of well-trained and well-equipped defense forces, friendly alliances, wise foreign policy, and giving as many countries as possible a tangible stake in the security, prosperity, and integrity of Singapore.[1]

This formula is still useful in the analysis of Singapore's strategy of survival. Singapore depends on multilateral underpinning for its security. While relying on its own resources and strength in the first instance, Singapore must base its security on a political and military configuration of forces that is favorable to the maintenance of territorial status quo and inhibits and deters violence against and interference in the affairs of other countries.

In order to achieve this favorable configuration of elements in Southeast Asia and the Asia-Pacific regions, Singapore needs a balance of great power interests and policies. This is conducive to the existence of an independent, reasonably secure, and viable Singapore. It also provides a hedge against threats and challenges that might arise from the region itself. Such a condition actually has existed over the past two decades.

Singapore, like many other small and medium powers, relies on the international climate to underwrite its security in the long run. But to give operational significance to regional factors and great power relations in creating a climate of stability and confidence and to provide time for the mobilization of forces working for stability, Singapore needs to have adequate self-defense capacity.

The possession of an adequate and a credible defense capability will allow a small country to prolong the period of resistance long enough to mobilize international support in its own defense. Moreover, by dimming the possibility of a quick victory and cost-free military adventure, it may deter others from taking liberties with its territorial integrity. In addition, the acquisition of such a credible defense has enabled Singapore to participate in and benefit from collective defense arrangements established with Malaysia and traditional Commonwealth friends.

Singapore's defense system had to be built from virtually nothing. In August 1965 when Singapore became independent, it had only two infantry battalions—trained primarily for internal security operations. Moreover, two-thirds of the soldiers in these units were not Singaporeans. It had no air force or navy to speak of.[2]

Singapore's defense buildup, launched in late 1965, was pursued with the zeal and determination that have become the hallmark of the island-republic. The need to acquire a credible defense assumed a desperate urgency when the British government announced its plan to withdraw its troops from Singapore and Malaysia in the 1970s. This change in British policy coincided with the Nixon Doctrine of 1969, which announced, *inter alia,* a curtailment of U.S. military commitments on the Asian mainland.

In the early 1970s Malaysia and Singapore negotiated a new defense agreement with their traditional Commonwealth partners—Britain, Australia, and New Zealand. The new agreement—called the Five-Power Defense Agreement—did not contain any definite commitment to the defense of the two Southeast Asian signatories; it merely provided for joint consultation in case of threat to the security of Singapore and/or Malaysia.

The Five Powers also reached agreement on the creation of a Joint Air Defense Command to be located at Butterworth, Malaysia. Operational since 1971, this unit provides a valuable service for both Singapore and Malaysia.

With the withdrawal of British and later of Australian troops, only a small contingent of New Zealand forces remain in Singapore. This is the residue of what in the 1950s and 1960s was a formidable base.

The value of the Five-Power Defense Agreement lay primarily in its psychological import. In 1978 Prime Minister Lee Kuan Yew observed:

Whether it [the Five-Power Defense Agreement] will continue to have any relevance depends not simply on Australia and New Zealand, but on the United States, her policies, and posture in the Pacific and Indian oceans ... As long as the United States is seen clearly to be a force in the region, these residual token forces are not irrelevant as tokens.[3]

Singapore must depend on external conditions and powers for its long-term security and territorial integrity. Its own resources are too meager to ensure this fundamental objective. The island-republic needs external help and cooperation, especially that of great powers, not simply for its physical security but also for its economic survival. In Singapore's case, foreign policy and international economic relations are so close that, in the judgment of one study, "Singapore's economic policies are the most important expression of its external politics because while external aggression is unlikely, economic stagnation and depression would without doubt end the island's quest for political independence."[4]

This need for international support and multilateral underpinning has been an important element in the thinking of Singapore's senior leaders. They rested their quest for independence on securing this international backing. They proceeded on the assumption that the young republic did not have to bargain away its independence in order to secure such support. Singapore can offer services and assets that a large number of states, including all major powers, would find useful.

Singapore's dependence on external developments is so crucial that it requires its leaders to pay continual attention to the international scene and to the shifts in great power policies. It requires a facility in reading and responding to nuances in great power policy pronouncements.

A realistic security and foreign policy must reckon with certain basic factors that cannot be wished away. One such factor is the existence of great powers and their rivalries and conflicting interests in Southeast Asia; countries of the region cannot ignore or escape the impact of these rivalries on their societies and on regional international relations. They have neither the will nor the power to force the great powers from the region. Expulsion of great powers, even if it were possible, would not lead to peace and stability in the area; if past experience is any guide, it might lead to greater insecurity, more conflict, and more blatant use of force. It would leave small countries to the tender and uncertain mercy of their bigger neighbors. Lee Kuan Yew once said, "Asian solution to Asian problems [in the Indonesian Confrontation period] would have meant the end of Malaysia and Singapore."[5] It is, therefore, in the interest of Southeast Asian nations "to seek a multipolar presence in their region as a more agreeable alternative to a single-power dominance."[6]

If the countries of Southeast Asia can put their houses in order—both domestically and regionally—and avoid confrontation among themselves, they can use their collective strength not to oppose the great powers but to negotiate realistically with them and enter into mutually beneficial relationships.

Singapore's leaders have consistently maintained that isolation from the great powers is not a feasible foreign policy option for Southeast Asian countries. On the one hand, they lack the power to expel external influences and on the other, they need the cooperation of the great powers to achieve political, economic, and security objectives.

The great powers, by their simultaneous presence, can impose on each other the need for restraint in pursuing their interests. In this way they can neutralize and check the vaulting political and military ambitions of one another. Moreover, such a configuration of power will have a salutary restraining influence on any overly ambitious regional state, which would have to reckon with the reactions of the great powers.

It has been the considered view of Singapore's leaders that U.S. power and presence in the Pacific and in Southeast Asia is the centerpiece of the multipolar balance. An isolationist United States or even a weakened or disinterested United States will create serious disruption in the world balance of power. If there is a loss of nerve and weakening of political will in the United States, it will adversely affect the climate of stability and security and heighten fears and tensions in the Asia-Pacific region.

Looking at the international scene from one of the busiest crossroads of the world, Singapore's leaders became deeply concerned about major trends and developments in great power relations in the post-Vietnam, post-Watergate period. At a time when the United States was withdrawing militarily from the Asian landmass and curtailing its commitments in Asia generally, the rise of the Soviet Union as a naval and military power was seen as a major threat to the stability and security of Southeast Asia.

Lee Kuan Yew had little faith in the policy of détente and feared that although it might lull the West into complacency, it would not restrain the Soviet Union in pursuing its expansionist policies. The Soviet Union will play from strength, and its strength lies, according to Lee, not in economic performance, where it has constantly and embarrassingly lagged behind the free-market economies. Its strength lies in its military power and its capacity to produce and supply sophisticated weapons to its friends and allies. "A disturbing consequence of the Soviet effectiveness in the instrument of war as compared with the implements of peace," Lee averred, "is that her interests are better served in crises than in peace."[7] The implication is that the Soviet Union will seek to exploit trouble spots where they exist and create ones where none existed before.

The rise of Soviet power in the 1970s coincided with the decline in U.S. military strength. The setback to the United States' power in Southeast Asia, however, did not represent any inherent and permanent weakness. As Lee Kuan Yew suggested:

> If the President and Congress can speak in one voice on basic issues of foreign policy and in clear and unmistakable terms, then friends and allies know where they [the Americans] stand, and others will not pretend to misunderstand when crossing the lines from insurgency into open aggression. Then the world will see less adventurism.[8]

However, in the period of uncertainty about U.S. resolve to stay involved in Asia, Lee Kuan Yew was groping for acceptable alternatives to an exclusive U.S. role. He floated, among others, the idea of a joint naval task force consisting of the United States, Western European, Australian, and Japanese units to balance the increasing Soviet naval buildup in the Pacific and Indian oceans.[9] But the proposal did not receive enthusiastic response from any quarter. Lee has considered a limited development of Japanese Self-Defense Forces as making both economic and strategic sense.[10]

He has welcomed the developing relations between the People's Republic of China and the United States. In an interview with the *Asian Wall Street Journal,* he said, "Helping China to modernize ... may create a more stable world balance of power ... Imagine how unequal the balance of power would be if China were on the side of the Soviet Union."[11] The fears of U.S. withdrawal have been largely allayed by the advent of the Reagan administration, which has been welcomed by all countries in Southeast Asia that regard the presence of U.S. power as indispensable to the stability and security of Asia.

In the post-Vietnam period, direct military involvement of the United States, especially in the form of bases on mainland Asia, is not a practical proposition. Singapore's leaders are cognizant of this situation. What they expect of the United States is the maintenance of a strong naval presence to counter growing Soviet naval power in the Asia-Pacific region and extension of military and economic aid to those countries of Southeast Asia that face externally fomented communist insurgency and aggression.

Singapore's leaders consider Vietnamese expansionism and aggression as particularly ominous for the ASEAN states. They have said explicitly that a resurgent Soviet Union directly emboldened its Southeast Asian ally—Vietnam—to embark upon a policy of regional hegemony. Without Soviet support, Vietnam would not have been able to persist in its policy of conquest and occupation in Kampuchea.

A significant change has taken place in the attitudes of Singapore, Malaysia, Indonesia, the Philippines, and Thailand toward their regional organization—ASEAN. And this was particularly noticeable in the case of Singapore. In the early years of its existence, the activities of ASEAN were largely confined to noncontroversial social, cultural, educational, and economic matters. Since 1975, however, Singapore has joined other ASEAN members in submerging their internal differences and confronting a triumphant Vietnam as a united and cohesive group. ASEAN's unity has strengthened the bargaining position of member-states vis-à-vis its communist neighbors and the extra-regional powers.

In recent years, ASEAN has become a major fulcrum and a focus of Singapore's strategy of survival. The regional organization has become one of the most important elements in the thinking and calculation of Singapore's leaders. The accent on ASEAN unity has become a persistent and prominent theme in the pronouncements of Singaporean leaders. Lee Kuan Yew redefined the formula for Singapore's strategy of survival thus:

> Our future stability and prosperity depend on taking the right decision now. These decisions include those to increase ASEAN solidarity and cooperation, to have better relations with the West, and to refuse to take sides between the contending communist powers.[12]

Singapore's leaders, like those of other ASEAN states, are acutely aware that the conditions in their area are closely linked with those of the Asia-Pacific region. They have welcomed and encouraged growing economic and trade ties with other countries of the Asia-Pacific region, but as a group ASEAN has not shown any enthusiasm for the concept of the Pacific community. Members of ASEAN, which have made a considerable political, psychological, and even emotional investment in the formation and growth of their organization, are wary that membership in a wider community may dilute, if not impair, their far-from-firm unity. A broadly based Pacific community may well accord with the political and strategic interests of its major proponents—Japan, the United States, Australia, and, of late, South Korea, but it may not serve the collective interest of ASEAN or the individual interests of its members, including Singapore.

Notes

1. *Straits Times,* December 16, 1970.
2. See Goh Keng Swee, "National Service and Defense Policy," in *Towards Tomorrow* (Singapore: National Trade Union Congress, 1973), p. 56.

3. Quoted in *Far Eastern Economic Review*, May 12, 1978, pp. 20–21.

4. Erik C. Paul, "The Viability of Singapore: An Aspect of Modern Political Geography" (University of California at Berkeley, Ph.D. diss., 1973), p. 312.

5. Lee Kuan Yew, *Prime Minister's Speeches, Press Conferences, Interviews, Statements,* mimeo. (University of Singapore, October 9, 1966).

6. S. Rajaratnam, *The Mirrow* (Information Division, Ministry of Culture, Government of Singapore), 12, no. 28 (July 12, 1972): 1.

7. For the text of this speech, see *Straits Times,* June 9 and 10, 1977.

8. Lee Kuan Yew, *Prime Minister's Speeches,* Interview in Kingston, April 30, 1975.

9. Asian Research Bulletin, quoted in Kawin Wilairat, *Singapore's Foreign Policy: The First Decade,* Field Report no. 10, Institute of Southeast Asian Studies (1975), p. 98.

10. *Straits Times,* October 7, 1978.

11. Reproduced in ibid., February 25, 1979.

12. Ibid., January 28, 1979.

THAILAND'S INTERESTS AND POLICIES

Sukhumband Paribatra

I discovered only a few days ago that I would be making a presentation. I hope that you will understand if my presentation lacks the polish, substance, and depth of those who have the honor of speaking before this distinguished audience.

The list of participants reads like a "Who's Who" of political science, strategic studies, and international relations, with an even longer list of achievements that are true reflections of their intellectual vigor and discipline. Making a presentation on brief notice before such an audience is, I assure you, a daunting one.

My distinguished ambassador to the United Nations is present. My interpretation of Thailand's interests and policies is not an orthodox one, certainly not one of which the Ministry of Foreign Affairs would approve. I hope that after this provocative presentation, I will still have a country to go back to.

Briefly, allow me to put forward my analysis of what Thailand's interests and policies have been and are and try to relate them to the themes and issues discussed in this conference.

Thailand was the ASEAN country most directly affected by the failure of the United States in Vietnam. Consequently there has evolved among Thais and foreign students of Thai affairs a "before-and-after" syndrome much loved by dieticians and beauticians.

After 1975 Thailand ended the policy of mono-emphatic dependence on the United States—the policy of being the first, but by no means the last, "unsinkable aircraft carrier" of the United States. Since then, Thai foreign policy has been "omnidirectional," seeking linkages, dialogues, and mutuality of interests with all countries, whatever the ideological divides. Then,

Thailand tried to turn its back on entanglement with the great powers' rivalry and the balance of power politics that such rivalry entails. Instead, by emphasizing its connection with ASEAN and by subscribing to the concept of ZOPFAN, it tried to espouse a greater notion of "neutrality" and conduct its policies in accordance with what can be termed "a balance of interests." At least until 1978–1979 Thailand diverted itself from a singular preoccupation with external threats, and the internal dimension and manifestation of such threats, to a much sharper and more sustained focus on internal development.

All analyses seem to confirm the age-old belief that Thais are a flexible people, bending to the winds of change with complete equanimity. Thai diplomacy remains a "weathervane" diplomacy. With certain reservations I believe such analyses are correct, but only phenomenologically correct. They do not go to the heart of the matter and do not adequately explain what Thai leaders, from time immemorial, have attempted and quite frequently succeeded in achieving. They do not explain a strong, tenacious thread of logic and continuity that has underlined Thai policies, past and present.

I shall present what I believe is Thailand's conception of its own interests and rationale for its policies. Thai leaders have always focused on their country's internal developments and internal power structure and alignments. Put another way, their aims have been, except for a few instances, to mobilize internal resources of the country for private or public ends. The historical focus on internal affairs was made possible by geographical factors, most of the Thai resources being available in the compact and rich central plain. Wars there have been, but most for self-defense, for control over buffer or tributary states for self-defense, or for gaining a specific resource—people—for internal development.

Thai foreign policy has generally aimed to mold an external environment most conducive to internal development and certain internal power alignments. The means generally used has been diplomacy, sometimes devious and Machiavellian, sometimes brilliant, sometimes too clever by half, but always pragmatic. Thais have never sought to impose their Weltanschauung, or belief systems, on the external environment. They are not crusaders by choice or inclination.

What external environments have the Thai leaders generally felt to be conducive for internal developments and internal power alignments?

For Thai leaders, the environment must provide security from landbased threats from the north, west, or east. For them, seaborne threats do not have the same immediacy or significance. Next, the environment must permit Thais to securely exploit external resources, that is, raw materials made into finished products for internal purposes. To achieve that environment, the Thais have generally avoided playing one great power against another in a "flexible" manner; rather they have promoted a mutually beneficial attachment to a hegemonic power—China, Britain, Japan, and the United States. Failing that, they have tried to promote an overwhelming correlation of forces to buttress their external position.

Throughout history, one element has been clear. Thais love power. They find power seductive, alluring, irresistible, and even fascinating so long as the source of that power is not an immediate, tangible threat.

By 1975 the Thais found the external environment much changed: (1) U.S. power declined and could not be relied upon; (2) power in the international system became diffused; (3) economics grew important in relation to politics; (4) the landbased threat (China) weakened and became preoccupied with its conflict with the USSR and Vietnam, united, strong, evidently ambitious, and supported by the growing might of the Soviet Union.

Thai leaders tried to manage the external environment by attaching great significance to the U.S. connection, re-emphasizing their commitment to the Manila Pact and Rusk-Thanat communiqué. They also tried to promote an overwhelming correction of forces—military, political, economic—to buttress their position and ensure their security and well-being. Such has been the rationale for their relationships with China, Japan, the countries of ASEAN, Australia, New Zealand, the European Economic Community, the newly industrializing countries, and the oil-exporting Arab countries.

Deep down there is no starry-eyed belief in neutrality, or "omnidirectionalism," or idealism. The ASEAN countries seem to have become one another's ventriloquists. The Thais have made the correct motions and said the proper words of idealism, but it would be wrong to assume that Thailand's attachment to ASEAN is based on anything but a down-to-earth calculus of self-interest. In the land of smiles, behind those smiles is a pragmatic, hard-nosed realism. The present trend seems likely to continue. It will not change unless the United States, the West, and the noncommunist world weaken significantly against the Soviet challenge, which, for the Thais, is manifested in the Vietnamese threat.

What does the Pacific Basin community concept mean to the Thais? Not much. The acronym PBC is almost unknown, and it is likely most of them would believe it a new kind of synthetic material or aspirin. It is not a matter of disinterest or lack of information. It is largely a question of what the concept offers in terms of real benefits. The realization of the concept seems far in the future, and its benefits remote and uncertain. However, should the concept develop and PBC is thought to confer economic benefits and enhance Thailand's security environment, the Thai leaders would be interested immediately. When the chips are down, the Thais want to be standing next to the one with the biggest pile of chips.

The foregoing is an attempt to analyze Thailand's interests and policies as they had been and are. Realism is the key, and indeed realism seems to be the underlying theme of this conference up to this point. For this reason I have found my own countrymen and indeed the discussions a little lacking in inspiration.

I am a Thai and hence by definition a realist. But I think that into the Thai Weltanschauung, and into the discussions here, a certain amount of idealism should be injected with emphasis on dialogue, identifying/implementing areas of cooperation, consultation among like-minded countries, and away from confrontation and the focus on rivalry.

In the past we in the "noncommunist" world have fallen into the trough or quagmire of negativism with such notions as "anticommunism," "containment," "flexible response." I do not suggest that we attempt a rollback. But I do believe that it is time, both here and in my country, to discuss ideals in a positive way, to stand up and carry out positively these ideals, and let everyone who does not subscribe to these ideals and objects to them do the worrying, fretting, constraining, or responding.

THE POLITICS OF PHILIPPINE SECURITY

Salvador P. Lopez

During the first two decades after the Philippines became independent in 1946, the foreign policy of the republic could be defined in terms of a simple formula: close alignment with the policies of the United States on the assumption that the fundamental objectives of the two countries, in domestic as well as in international affairs, were essentially identical. Manuel Roxas, first president of the republic, set forth that policy in his inaugural address on May 28, 1946, and committed the Philippines "to the cause and the international program of the United States of America." During the proclamation of the independence of the Philippines on July 4, he declared: "We are fortunate to have as the guarantor of our security the United States of America, which is today the bulwark and support of small nations everywhere in the world."

If the rhetoric sounds dated, President Roxas was speaking as the newly elected first president of a bleeding nation as it staggered to its feet amid the rubble of war. The new republic badly needed assistance to bind the wounds and rebuild the lives of its people. And the nation had to meet these urgent necessities while assuming the responsibilities of independence. Then, and in the context of the warm sentiments evoked by the wartime alliance between the two countries, most Filipinos could acknowledge without embarrassment the close identification of the foreign policy of the Philippines with that of the United States. That identification was especially close in the area of national security and mutual defense.

This policy remained relatively unchanged until the administration of Ferdinand E. Marcos, sixth president of the Philippines. In May 1975, in the third year under martial law, President Marcos formulated six foreign policy objectives for the guidance of his administration. Those provided for intensified support of ASEAN, closer identification with the Third World, support of Arab countries in their struggle for peace in the Middle East, continued mutually beneficial relations with Japan, establishment of diplomatic relations with China and the Soviet Union, and a continuing healthy relationship with the United States compatible with the emerging realities in Asia. These guidelines have basically remained unchanged.

Foreign Policy Guidelines

For the first time since independence, President Marcos reordered the diplomatic priorities of the republic. One of the most important initiatives he took was to commit the Philippines to the cause of the less developed countries (LDCs) of the Third World, where live the poorest three-fourths of mankind.

Calling for closer identification with the Third World presented no difficulties since the Philippines has long been identified with the Afro-Asian group in the United Nations and enjoys good relations with Latin America. It has consistently supported the liberation of colonial peoples and was an active member of various U.N. agencies whose purpose is to accelerate economic and social progress in the developing countries. In 1976 Manila was the site of a meeting of the Group of 77, and the U.N. Council on Trade and Development met there in 1979. At the Cancun summit of 1981, President Marcos was a leading spokesman for the Third World. He sought and obtained observer status for the Philippines at conferences of the Group of Nonaligned States.

The Third World commitment was shown in the strong support the Philippines gave to the Charter of Economic Rights and Duties of States approved by the U.N. General Assembly on December 12, 1974. Specifically, the charter emphasizes the collective responsibility of the developed, industrial countries towards the LDCs regarding trade, aid, and transfer of technology, as well as in other economic and financial matters, and the duty of LDCs to strengthen cooperation among themselves to bring about a new international economic order. Having voted for the charter, the Philippines is obliged to re-examine its laws, treaties, rules, regulations, practices, in the domain of trade, industry, economics, and finance to bring them in harmony with the purposes and principles of the charter.

Regarding the Middle East, the Philippines first supported the Arab cause in the General Assembly in 1947, when it opposed the partition of Palestine in committee, only to reverse its vote in plenary session under pressure from Washington. Subsequently, the Philippines pursued an even-handed policy by supporting Arab demands for the return of territories seized by Israel during the wars of 1967 and 1973 while supporting the right of Israel to exist as a state. In 1974, after the oil crisis, President Marcos placed the Philippines squarely behind the Arab cause. However, the guideline is worded to cover a solution to the Arab-Israel dispute that the Philippines had previously supported and that recent developments seem to favor; namely, the restoration to the Arab states of certain territories occupied by Israel, recognition by the Arabs of Israel as a state with secure frontiers, and recognition of the rights of the Palestinian people.

Philippine relations with Japan are good and can only become better, provided, as the guideline stipulates, these are mutually beneficial, especially in the area of trade relations. The Philippines has an important stake in the security of Japan. Should Japan lose the protective umbrella of U.S. military power, it might be compelled to develop a military capability that could include nuclear weapons. Japan as a nuclear, or even a major, military power would be unacceptable to the Philippines and the members of ASEAN. Yet, Japan is understandably concerned about its security in the face of a potential threat from the Soviet Union. The Philippines is trying to comprehend Japan's predicament. At the same time, the Philippines expects Japan to understand the problems resulting from its position as the Philippines' second most important trading partner—a position that gives Japan powerful leverage to benefit or to prejudice the Philippines economy and the well-being of the Filipino people.

Windows to the Socialist States

President Marcos's visit to Beijing in June 1976 resulted in the normalization of Philippine relations with the People's Republic of China. It took President Marcos ten years to pry open long-barred windows that give on the socialist states of the world. He relaxed travel restrictions between the Philippines and the socialist states. Next he encouraged the development of economic and cultural relations between them. Then he authorized diplomatic relations between the Philippines and the socialist states of Eastern Europe. The logical final step was the establishment of diplomatic relations with the two great socialist powers: China in 1976 and the Soviet Union in 1977.

The policy of caution has been necessary. Since World War II a widespread communist rebellion led by the National People's Army (NPA) has drawn inspiration and support from Moscow and Beijing. Later, an armed separatist struggle was mounted by the Muslim National Liberation Front (MNLF) with outside support from some Arab States channeled through Sabah, in North Borneo. Concurrently, the Philippines was a leading member of various alliances and security arrangements. There developed a system of "special relations" with the United States. Time was needed to enable Filipinos to disengage from the habits of the past and to assess the new political and ideological alignments emerging in the region as a result of détente and the U.S. withdrawal from Indochina.

The Philippines had to reorient itself as speedily as possible to the emerging political realities in the region. That required a frank re-examination of its role in Asia, and its responsibilities as an Asian nation and member of the Third World. This, in turn, called for the normalization of relations with China and the Soviet Union and a continuing review of its relations with the United States.

As early as 1964, as the secretary of foreign affairs in the administration of President Diosdado Macapagal, I urged a review of policy toward the Soviet Union and the socialist States of Eastern Europe, the first high official of the Philippine government to do so. I considered a modification desirable in the national interest if it enabled us to develop a new foreign policy leverage, reduce our excessive dependence upon the United States, and broaden our options in international affairs.

The considerations that were adduced to support a major shift in Philippine foreign policy have subsequently been shown to be essentially valid. However, the power equation in East and Southeast Asia has radically changed since then: Soviet influence has grown; the United States has barely held its own. Japanese economic supremacy, with its built-in potential for political and military power, has been firmly established, and Japan continues to prosper. China is trying to achieve more rapid development through modernization and security through a precarious balancing act between Washington and Moscow. An assessment of the developing power equation in the region would seem to justify the Philippine decision to initiate diplomatic overtures to Beijing and Moscow.

The normalization of relations with Beijing is basically desirable since a vast and important country like China cannot be ignored in fashioning a workable system of regional or international security. The Philippines had to come to terms with China.

A cautious policy toward China is clearly incumbent on all its neighbors, including the Philippines. It should be a guarded policy of friendship similar to that observed by most Latin American countries toward the United States—friendly, yet not so intimate that it risks being crushed in the embrace of its giant neighbor. A policy of caution would be doubly desirable for the Philippines, having regard to its large Chinese population and its proximity to Taiwan.

On general grounds of prudence, the Philippines is observing a policy of equidistance between Beijing and Moscow.

The Filipino Dilemma

The Filipino is torn between the opposing tropisms of ideology and geography: he is in Asia, but not of it; he wants to belong to Asia, but is aware he is not fully accepted by his fellow Asians. There is something frenetic about his efforts to prove his Asianness; he is even willing to listen to the cultural nationalists and purists who urge him to discard the Western trappings of his life and Western influence on his mind and soul.

In a paper published in 1966 entitled "Realities of Philippine Foreign Policy," Dr. Onofre D. Corpuz noted "a kind of indecisive tension between the country's ethnic and physical geography on the one hand and its modern historical connections on the other." He added that while "the former pulls us toward the world of Southeast Asia, the latter draws us toward the Western, United States–dominated world." Dr. Corpuz drew attention to a pendulum-like swing in Filipino attitudes, first toward the West and then toward Asia. During the first three decades of this century, the Filipinos, reacting to the relative leniency of U.S. rule, developed a strong feeling of friendship for the United States. In the 1930s they were drawn, in response to the menace of Japanese aggression, to the "Asia-oriented" idea of a union of Indonesians, Malayans, and Filipinos, largely inspired by the Malaya Irredenta movement, which had a powerful hold on the imagination of the young Filipino students and patriots. During the war and the enemy occupation, Japan's anti-U.S. propaganda impressed some Filipinos, and although its effects on Filipinos were nullified by Japanese arrogance and brutality, it laid a new emphasis on closer relations with Asia. According to Dr. Corpuz, the collapse of the U.S. presence during the Japanese occupation also compelled the Philippines to begin the long-postponed task of finding its new place in Asia. This was, however, offset by the heroic Filipino-U.S. resistance on Bataan and Corregidor, the return of U.S. forces in 1944, and the heavy dependence of the Philippines upon the United States for its security and for assistance in postwar rehabilitation, which revived and sustained the U.S. presence anew.

The "close and special ties" that bound the Philippines to the United States—ties that, in Dr. Corpuz's phrase, were "too close for comfort and too special for self-respect"—flourished after independence in 1946 and were forged during the terms of Manual Roxas and Elpidio Quirino. The Military Bases Agreement, the Military Assistance Pact, and the Mutual Defense Treaty were products of this period. Philippine-U.S. bonds were perhaps strongest during the early 1950s when Ramon Magsaysay served, first, as secretary of national defense and then as president. The SEATO Alliance was established under the Manila Pact of 1954. Yet, also during the Magsaysay era the slogan "Asia for the Asians" was coined, and its underlying philosophy clearly enunciated.

President Marcos strongly supported the creation in 1967 of the Association of Southeast Asian Nations (ASEAN). It was expected that ASEAN, the third attempt at regional organization by the same states that set up ASA and Maphilindo, plus Singapore, would get off to a flying start. However, the ASEAN Declaration, adopted in Bangkok on August 8, 1967, largely remained a paper declaration of good intentions for seven years. On February 24, 1976, the heads of the five member-states finally met in Bali and forged two important documents: the Declaration of ASEAN Concord and the Treaty of Amity and Cooperation in Southeast Asia. In a third document, it was agreed to establish a Permanent Secretariat at the ASEAN Headquarters in Jakarta.

The pace of cooperation among the member-states to achieve their declared political, economic, social, and cultural objectives accelerated after the Bali summit and even more so following the Kuala Lumpur summit of 1977. The most hopeful initiatives were in three areas; namely, measures to facilitate mutual assistance to meet critical shortages of food and energy resulting from natural disasters and major calamities, establishment of large-scale industrial projects based on the principle of complementation, and preferential trading arrangements among themselves. Indicative of its increased capacity for concerted action was the decision of ASEAN to conduct dialogues with third countries (Australia, New Zealand, the United States, Japan, and Canada) and with regional and international organizations: the European Economic Community (EEC), the United Nations Development Program (UNDP), and the Asian Development Bank (ADB).

On the other hand, the ASEAN political objective of establishing a "zone of peace, freedom, and neutrality" in Southeast Asia was momentarily set aside. Southeast Asia is too large and important in a material and strategic sense to be exempted from the designs of competing, ambitious powers. Its best hope of peace and security lies in maintaining relations of equal friendship with all countries, particularly with the great powers whose interests intersect or collide in the region. This would appear to be the only prudent policy for ASEAN.

Yet, the five members of ASEAN could have different perceptions of their political future and their relations with the great powers in the region. The continental members of ASEAN (Thailand, Malaysia, and Singapore) are exposed to ideological and military pressures to which the seaward members (Indonesia and the Philippines) are comparatively immune. To all ASEAN members, but especially to Thailand, the existence of a strong and resurgent Vietnam poses a threat of imponderable magnitude.

ASEAN has made encouraging progress since Bali and Kuala Lumpur. But progress has tended to slow as the organization moves steadily onto the stage of practical action and comes to grips with the hard realities and the detailed problems of regional consensus and cooperation. Despite repeated denials, the members of ASEAN cannot avoid facing up to the problems of common defense and security.

One should guard against facile comparisons between ASEAN and the EEC. The latter is composed of highly industrialized countries with pluralistic social structures and ideologically homogeneous political systems. They achieved political maturity and stability over a long period. They developed a capability for intraregional trade through regionwide tariff reductions. The ASEAN nations can approximate the success of the EEC only as they industrialize and diversify their primarily agrarian economies and achieve a requisite degree of economic integration.

Consistent support for the United Nations and active participation in its work were long accorded high priority among the foreign policy concerns of the Philippines. This was appropriate for a country that was allowed to participate in the San Francisco Conference of 1945 and had the unique distinction of becoming a charter member of the United Nations even before achieving independence. In return for the privilege, the Philippines continued through the years to devote a substantial portion of its political and diplomatic resources to the activities of the United Nations and its specialized agencies.

Although the United Nations has lost much of the luster of its early years and had its power eroded and its influence diminished by the competing forces of regionalism and nationalism, it serves as a useful center for planning the establishment of a more rational world order, as well as a forum where the nations of the Third World can pursue their struggle for development. The Philippines consistently supported U.N. decisions to speed up the process of decolonization and to set up more equitable aid and trade arrangements for developing nations.

The developing, precarious balance of power in Asia and the Pacific rests on the United States, the Soviet Union, China, and Japan. A certain caution may be necessary in using the classical concept of "balance of power" to describe the situation in Asia: (1) because the four powers are clearly unequal in industrial and/or military capability and therefore the assumed equilibrium of power is hardly justified; and (2) the situation is evolving so rapidly that the relative stability that a balance of power presupposes does not exist. Although it is tempting to draw a parallel between the balance of power in Europe and the North Atlantic and the balance of power in Asia and the Pacific, the differences are too important to be glossed over. In Asia and the Pacific, SEATO, the only multilateral military alliance worthy of the name, was dismantled long ago; nor is there a communist alliance in the region comparable to the Warsaw Pact in Europe. On the contrary, the two great communist powers in Asia continue in potential if not actual opposition to each other, while the lesser communist states around them—North Korea, Vietnam, Cambodia, and Laos—maintain a discreet policy of equidistance toward Moscow and Beijing as best they can.

There is a clear need in the region for a provisional balance of power that would help preserve the peace, however precarious. The détente between the United States and the Soviet Union, broken after the Soviet invasion of Afghanistan, has not been restored. There is an urgent need for them, which they recognize, to negotiate an agreement on limitation of nuclear armaments, realizing that in the nuclear standoff that exists between them, neither would gain from the further escalation of nuclear capability. An escalation would increase the danger of nuclear war by accident or miscalculation without increasing their security.

The United States is obviously pleased with the coolness in the relations between the two communist giants and would prefer not to see a reconciliation. China would like a failure in détente and suspension of any nuclear negotiations between Moscow and Washington, suspecting that they might otherwise plot to divide the world between them. Yet China can hardly wish to see the military and ideological rivalry between the two superpowers explode into war because its catastrophic consequences would not spare China. Japan is a close political, economic, and ideological ally of the United States; it has a certain empathy for China even as it suffers from a historical emotional block with respect to the Soviet Union.

This is the emerging balance of power in Asia and the Pacific, with the operative word being "emerging." While the balance of power in Europe remained static after World War II, held firmly in place by the stabilized confrontation between NATO and the Warsaw Pact, the balance of power in Asia and the Pacific is dynamic and flexible. The NATO–Warsaw Pact power balance is momentarily disturbed by the dispute over the deployment of U.S. medium-range nuclear missiles in Western Europe. Nevertheless, the European balance of power has retained its essentially bipolar character and is likely to offer no surprises. By contrast, the Asian balance of power is multipolar and therefore uncertain and unpredictable. The risks of destabilization, of unhinging the fulcrum of the balance, are far greater in Asia than in Europe.

The American Bases

A review of Philippine-U.S. relations is a necessary consequence of the emerging balance of power in Asia and the Pacific as much as it is the logical counterpart of Philippine foreign policy reorientation toward Asia. The major sticking point in a review would concern the future of the U.S. bases. While the basic Philippine objective is to strengthen Philippine authority and jurisdiction in the bases, there is an underlying Philippine assumption that failure to satisfy national demands might oblige President Marcos to ask for the abrogation of the bases agreement in advance of 1991, when its term expires. On the other hand, the ultimate position of the United States regarding the bases would depend on a final determination regarding an alternative defense line in the Pacific. This would depend on the evolution of Soviet-U.S. relations, the outcome of disarmament negotiations, and the resolution of Japanese security.

The Philippines has shown that it will not be satisfied with cosmetic changes in the military bases agreement. A decision to have a Filipino commander in each base, to fly the Philippine flag over them, to recognize Philippine jurisdiction over certain specified offenses committed therein, or to increase the "rental" for their use are concessions to national dignity that, however belated, do not go to the heart of the matter. The central issue will be that the continued presence of U.S. military bases on Philippine soil, under existing conditions, constitutes a perpetual charge and infringement on Philippine sovereignty. If it is argued that this has not happened in England, Germany, Japan, Spain, or Turkey, where U.S. bases are also located, the answer would be that none of these countries had been a U.S. colony.

The future of the U.S. bases in the Philippines is relevant to whether such a shift in Philippine foreign policy could, or should, lead to a policy of nonalignment. Nonalignment would call for the termination of existing mutual defense and military assistance arrangements between the Philippines and the United States. The Filipino people would need to rethink the whole problem of national security. One view is that the sudden abrogation of these arrangements might so weaken the U.S. military posture in the Western Pacific that the emerging quadrilateral balance of power in the region would be seriously disturbed. A radical and precipitate shift from alliance to nonalignment would pose an imponderable danger for the Philippines, as well as for the region as a whole. By joining the ranks of the nonaligned at this juncture, the Philippines might unwittingly help to precipitate the very danger of conflict it is seeking to prevent by nonalignment.

Therefore, while the Philippines has wisely forged new links—economic, cultural, diplomatic—with China and the Soviet Union, it must also carefully consider under what terms and conditions it can maintain existing ties and mutually beneficial relationships, including security arrangements, with the United States and the West. The whole purpose, after all, is not to substitute one hegemony for another, but to broaden the options available to the Philippines and strengthen its hand in international affairs.

Another view is that while the U.S. bases in the Philippines were originally intended to safeguard the common security interests of the two countries, they no longer serve this purpose. With the establishment of relations between the Philippines and China and between the Philippines and the Soviet Union, there no longer is an imminent threat of aggression from the only two powers whence such a threat could come. Nor can it be said, as it can be said of the U.S. bases in Europe, that Clark Airbase and Subic Bay Naval Base serve a clear purpose of regional security. NATO is still very much alive, but SEATO is now dead.

The rationale for termination of the bases agreement is basically this: it no longer serves the common security interests of the two countries, although it may serve the interests of the United States as a superpower. But it is argued that the bases are required to maintain the new balance of power in the region. With the growth of Soviet naval capability in the Pacific and in the Indian oceans, the security of Southeast Asia and the waters around it becomes critical, and the United States' abandonment of Subic Bay Naval Base and Clark Airbase would dangerously unhinge the power balance in this part of the world.

According to this view, the risks attendant upon U.S. withdrawal from the bases in the Philippines are exaggerated. Despite Vietnam, or perhaps because of Vietnam, the United States remains a formidable power in this part of the world, and this is not lost on the Soviet Union. The construction of U.S. bases in the Marianas and Micronesia and the strengthening of U.S. bases in Japan, South Korea, and Australia would enable the United States to maintain a military presence of sufficient credibility to deter any other power from dominating the region.

The case for the Nixon Doctrine, proclaimed as a consequence of the U.S. withdrawal from Vietnam, is that the countries in the region should rely mainly on their own resources for their defense and security; if they should at any time require assistance, the United States would extend such assistance as it is in its interest to do so. However erratic and uncertain they may be, the moves of President Marcos to bring the Philippines closer to a policy of neutrality and nonalignment is a logical response to the Nixon Doctrine.

Since the military-strategic argument is not persuasive, the U.S. bases can be seen to serve another, more credible purpose; namely, to support and protect U.S. economic interests in the Pacific Basin.

In his book *The Imperial Republic,* Raymond Aron explores the relationship between military supremacy and economic expansion. He asks: "Is the United States defending the free world or a world open to a free economy?" Aron recalls that in the polarized system that prevailed during the cold war, the United States "defined its national interest not in the restrictive sense—the physical security of its people and the stability of its institutions—but in the broad sense—securing a milieu favorable to its ideas, goods, and investments." According to that definition, "free world and world with a free economy tended to merge into one another." Therefore, "free world" does not necessarily mean a world dedicated to the principles of liberty, equality, and democracy, like the United States itself, but a world that is freely accessible to U.S. ideas, goods, and investments.

In the Philippines, the continued presence of U.S. bases would not be in the long-range interest of promoting or preserving the United States' political, economic, and cultural influence. They tend to encourage anti-American feeling among Filipinos, fed by incidents in the bases and by the challenge they pose to Filipino nationalism and Filipino dignity. American policymakers must decide whether it is more important for the United States to keep the bases than to keep the good will of the Filipino people and whether any bases would be useful if located in an increasingly hostile environment.

All the East and Southeast Asian countries other than the Soviet Union and Vietnam want the United States to keep the bases in the Philippines. Of course they do. The presence of the bases relieves them of the necessity of building their own or offering bases on their soil to the United States, which they will never do.

The assumption that both the Philippines and the United States will need the bases to defend their common interests for the indefinite future contains a sinister element: since the Philippines, like its Asian neighbors, would feel threatened by the resurgence of Japanese military power, it would be compelled to ask the Americans to remain in the bases to counter that threat. That would be a replay of a script they have seen before: continued U.S. bases or another Japanese invasion.

The assumption that the bases protect the Philippines takes no account of the advent of nuclear weapons, which may have changed all that. Nuclear missiles sited on the territory of the superpowers may deter them from attacking each other directly. But deterrence would not necessarily apply to nuclear weapons emplaced in foreign bases. Thus, nuclear weapons emplaced or stockpiled in Clark or Subic might tend to draw rather than deter a nuclear attack should one superpower decide to start a "winnable" theater nuclear war.

These are some considerations that make U.S. withdrawal from the bases a consummation devoutly to be wished, and not by Filipinos alone. The United States may eventually achieve technological breakthroughs or other alternative strategies that would enable it to dispense with the bases in the Philippines.

With U.S. withdrawal from the military bases, the Philippines would become sovereign for the first time in more than four centuries. The Filipinos would know what it is to live in the pride and dignity of genuine independence. Relations between the Philippines and the United States and between Filipinos and Americans would become more salutary.

The fear expressed that this would mean giving up the United States' friendship for friendship with another power or powers is unfounded. The Filipinos would never accept a relationship with any power that would derogate from Philippine sovereignty and independence. They would be foolish to reject U.S. bases in order to submit to domination by another power. The recent statement of President Marcos that he would negotiate with the Russians if the Americans should decide to abandon the bases was said in a moment of irritation and anger. It should be read in that light.

Global Context of Philippine Security

This is the global context in which the Philippines will pursue its goals of development and security. Policy will be conditioned by a growing pressure for new relationships and structures based on the interdependence of peoples.

At the turn of the century, two basic arrangements for the maintenance of international peace—balance of power and collective security—will yield ground to a third; namely, world order *cum* world government. It was once hoped that the United Nations would serve as a useful way station to achieve a new international order, the threshold to some form of world government. But the United Nations has become the ultimate refuge and bastion of the modern nation-state. Only if it returns to its original vocation as the prefiguration of a new universalism can the United Nations serve as midwife to a new international order, a true union of mankind.

Albert Einstein, whose mathematical genius gave the world the original formula for nuclear power, was so appalled after Hiroshima that he became an earnest advocate of world government. He was laughed at by the scholars and social scientists who regarded him with contempt and told him, in effect: "Dear Dr. Einstein, please stick to your math and your physics and leave the science of politics to us!" But was Einstein wrong in believing that only some form of world government, wielding commensurate authority over the nations, could tame the nuclear weapon?

Meanwhile, as the Philippines evolves new relationships of mutual benefit with its neighbors in Asia, with the developing countries of the Third World, and with the socialist states, it must also establish on a more equitable basis its relations with the industrial powers of the West. Only as it finds its proper place and plays its appropriate role in bilateral, regional, and international affairs would the Philippines qualify as an effective participant in the interdependent world.

The Philippines, granted independence in 1946, ushered in the worldwide liquidation of colonialism. By achieving true freedom, sovereignty, and independence as it enters the twenty-first century, the Philippines should make a useful contribution to a new world order born of the "global fairness revolution" and based on the principle of "equal shares" in a regime of "global interdependence."

DISCUSSANTS

Guy Pauker

At the outset the chairman of this session, Charles Wolf, asked us to address four questions:

1. Is the more or less unalloyed picture of success and effectiveness attributed to ASEAN entirely warranted?
2. If so, to what is it attributed?
3. Can ASEAN serve as a model for other forms of regional organizations inside or outside the Pacific Basin?
4. What are the forecasts for ASEAN's future development?

Does the reality of ASEAN correspond to the image or the myth of ASEAN? No, it does not. ASEAN united in 1967 in order to overcome such local conflicts as *Konfrontasi* involving Indonesia, Malaysia, Singapore, the Sabah dispute between the Philippines and Malaysia, and other more localized problems, such as the far Malaysian border. Between 1967 and 1976 ASEAN was primarily a prime ministers' club, very useful in that it provided a venue for regular exchange, but not achieving very much. ASEAN was jolted by the fall of South Vietnam and the rest of Indochina. The 1976 summit meeting led to a much more structured organization promising cooperation of all sorts except security.

Looking back at the years since ASEAN's foundation, the "sweet sixteen" period of organization was given an important boost by the Kampuchean crisis. Had the Kampuchean crisis not occurred, ASEAN would have had to invent it. It gave ASEAN an opportunity to show its solidarity as an instrument for international diplomacy, including an extremely valuable constructive role in the United Nations in the past four or five years. Much of the mystique of ASEAN is due to the demonstration that it can work very closely as a diplomatic instrument for international order and stability. By the same token, if one looks at the reasons for which ASEAN was initially and allegedly created—namely, economic and cultural cooperation—the bottom line is almost invisible. Economic cooperation, for very understandable reasons, has been very hard to achieve with countries at the stage of development in which arguments for protection of infant industries and domestic markets are still very valid. And cultural cooperation is difficult, if not impossible, because the masses of these countries have such varied and antagonistic ethnic and cultural backgrounds. So much for the first question.

Recognizing that ASEAN is probably one of the most successful regional groups in the world, let us address the second question: To what is ASEAN's success attributable? This was already answered in part, but ASEAN is an increasingly significant political success story. A high degree of political cooperation has been achieved among countries that less than two decades ago had considerable problems among themselves. A very perceptive statement was made by the Singaporean foreign minister at the Prime Ministers' Conference in Bangkok at the end of June 1983. When asked about ASEAN's contributions to the economic development and political stability of the region, he replied substantially as follows, "In my view the biggest contribution of ASEAN has been the way we have presented to the rest of the world a picture of ASEAN cooperation and neighborliness. We work together on many different projects, we try to speak with the same voice, and we have created an image of ASEAN as a symbol of stability." He went on to say, "We have some differences of view, as anywhere else in the world, but we do not highlight our problems or air our differences in public. We try to solve our problems quietly." He pointed out that this favorable image has been a great advantage because ASEAN is a free trade economy and depends very much upon foreign investments and foreign markets. When international investors look at the ASEAN region they have confidence in the members' stability and growth. This helps in each state's efforts to improve the lot of their people. In sum, ASEAN's contribution to the economic development of the area is less remarkable than the image of confidence that is projected to the rest of the world. In this situation, everybody benefits.

Let me comment on the final question, where is ASEAN going? ASEAN is moving toward becoming a security organization, under the pressure of Soviet deployment in Southeast Asia. This is not necessarily imminent, but the trend is noticeable. The defense establishments of ASEAN are very interested in standardization of weapons and equipment, exchange of training opportunities, and joint exercises on a bilateral or multilateral basis. Obviously, ASEAN is increasingly security-oriented.

ASEAN has stuck together more than anything else because of the glue of a U.S. presence in the area. If the United States were not the stabilizer in Southeast Asia and the Western Pacific, the divergencies would grow wider between those who perceive that the Soviet Union is the greater threat to the region and those who in the long run entertain more fears of the Chinese.

To throw something controversial into the hopper for the remaining discussion, I suggest that if the United States were to disappear as a stability factor from the area, the Soviet Union would suddenly become a much more welcome presence than we would ever assume possible. With all due respect to our friends, whose feelings may be hurt by this, if many had to choose between submission to China or Japan and the acceptance of the Soviets as the guarantor against them, they would prefer the Soviets. Fortunately, the U.S. presence in the ASEAN region is by far the preferred solution to their unwelcome dilemma.

Sean Randolph

Lie Tek Tjeng's remark, that the United States might make projections about the Pacific Basin without taking ASEAN into account, should not cause worry. Reviewing statements of policy since 1976, there are an increasing number of references to ASEAN and U.S. support of ASEAN, with greater fervor behind the words.

In the next five to ten years we will see a consolidating focus in the U.S. view of East Asia, looking at Japan, China, and ASEAN as the three principal bases of U.S. policy. Australia and New Zealand should also be included in any discussion of East Asia and the broad Pacific region. Within this context, an independent security role for ASEAN is entirely possible.

What ought the U.S. role be in relation to ASEAN? All the papers have referred to this topic in different ways. Lie's paper avers the United States should consider Indonesia's basic free and active foreign policy and that Southeast Asian countries should have primary responsibility for their own security. Chandran refers to Malaysia's vociferous foreign policy of handling its foreign affairs single-handedly. On the other hand, some Southeast Asians refer to the vital U.S. presence in the area, calling it an anchor for regional equilibrium. They are not consistent. That there is a certain schizophrenia in ASEAN policy is understandable in the sense that all the countries would like to be recognized for their increasingly responsible roles in the area but, to a greater or lesser extent, would like to have the United States there too.

This varies within each country, of course. The Thais would like to see the United States prominently visible at their backs. The Indonesians, and some others, want to see the United States as present but comfortably over the horizon, not too visible. There is no reason why the United States cannot do both. These are not inconsistent. From the U.S. perspective, though, whatever its approach to the individual countries in the area, the overriding verity is that ASEAN as a group does not act as a single entity, and the United States must respect this. This is where the United States must put "skillful diplomacy" into play.

The United States has much in common with the ASEAN countries. It respects their economic achievement, and it can extol them out as models for others. The United States and the ASEAN states have increasingly overlapping security interests. Yet they have some very real differences, especially on Third World issues, the Law of the Sea, and commodities. With that said, ASEAN is the linchpin of U.S. policy in Southeast Asia. There are differences, but the United States can and should live with those differences. The key ingredient from the U.S. standpoint is the attainment of a very careful balance.

Despite the similarity of views, the key to ASEAN's success has been its independence. The United States should avoid the temptation to press too close to ASEAN and should reassure its ASEAN friends that it is very sensitive to this caveat. The United States respects ASEAN's independence and its integrity. It is neither in ASEAN's nor in the United States' interest to have it identified with the United States informally or in a more formal arrangement. Washington has no desire for a formal or informal security arrangement with ASEAN.

From the U.S. perspective, the key is a readiness to do the kinds of things ASEAN would like the United States to do—maintain a consistent and reliable security presence in the area and be ready to step in when called upon. An example of U.S. readiness was shown last April when it expedited supplies of military equipment to the Thais to help in their border fighting. The United States cooperates in the economic area. The crux, then, is that it should demonstrate leadership and a constructive attitude only as far as the ASEAN countries want it to go. The natural trend of events will create an overlapping of interests without the United States' forcing its views upon the ASEAN states.

Looking beyond ASEAN, to the broader region of the Pacific Basin, we read the same need to strike a proper balance. While recognizing the growing acceptance of the Pacific Basin concept, the United States is sensitive to the necessity of restraint in discussing a formal collective defense structure. Looking forward to more and better cooperation both in ASEAN and the Pacific Basin, the United States' policies must be based on the evolution of the infrastructure of common interests.

Chandran Jeshurun

My comments are essentially impressionistic, based on what I have listened to during the earlier sessions, and because they constitute a response to the wider implications of security in the Pacific Basin.

Ambassador Birabhongse of Thailand sounded a warning on the growing gap in the levels of economic growth and development becoming frighteningly apparent in the Western Pacific. This vital economic factor was put another way by Admiral Inman when he spoke of the danger of growing economic frustrations experienced by some nations in that region. Admittedly, he was thinking primarily of the lopsided situation emerging in Indochina in his analysis of future security problems. Nevertheless, the nations of Southeast Asia, particularly the members of ASEAN, are equally troubled by an almost uncontrollable unevenness in economic growth, and the causes for that need to be examined frankly. The main sources of discontent in Southeast Asia are directly associated with trading patterns between ASEAN and several of the important countries of the Pacific Basin. The situation is even more untenable for those of us in Southeast Asia striving against odds to preserve our democratic forms of government when most of our economic woes seem to result from policies pursued by our Pacific Basin associates. Thus, the misunderstandings between Malaysia and the United States over the release of stockpiles of tin and rubber by the General Services Administration dampen the prospects for greater understanding of the common goals both countries share in the Pacific Basin concept.

The countries of Southeast Asia are proud of their independence and therefore jealously guard what they consider their fundamental rights in any cooperative ventures for a regional order. Too often in the past the United States has underestimated this self-pride among the smaller nations of the Western Pacific and arbitrarily acted on issues such as economic relations and human rights without due recognition of the larger issues at stake. Thus, whereas there might be commonly shared perceptions among the United States, Japan, South Korea, and Southeast Asia on a host of vital questions in the Pacific Basin concept, it should be understood that within the subregion, the agenda of priorities might be somewhat differently arranged. No one would deny that national and regional security looms large in our national policies. By the same token, however, the pace of national economic and social development is such as to require a concentrated and sustained commitment, particularly since time is not in our favor. With the turn of events in Indochina since 1975, Southeast Asia needs the understanding and patience of its natural friends and allies in the Pacific Basin to enable it to form a core of democratically inclined, free, and independent nations. In this there is undoubtedly much that the United States, Japan, and others can contribute, given the opportunities that exist.

In conclusion, it must be stressed that Southeast Asia, and more especially, the members of ASEAN, are aware of the increasing role the USSR is aspiring to play through a cleverly devised strategy in which naval superiority appears to be the main element. It is in our backyard, the South China Sea, and our front doorstep, the Strait of Malacca, that most of the regular movements of the Soviet Pacific Fleet take place. The *Minsk* has not been as close to anyone's waters in the Pacific as to those of the ASEAN members, and we are, consequently, actively monitoring its activities to assess the security problems likely to arise. The other nations of the Pacific Basin who happen to be our friends should at least allow us the dignity of dealing with the situation before a major international problem emerges.

Birabhongse Kasemsri

The first highlight is the Kampuchean situation. The Vietnamese invasion makes it clear to us that there indeed has been a serious violation of international legal principles and laws, including the Charter of the United Nations. It has created a pretext for outside powers to intervene within the region, with attendant complications that pose lasting obstacles to the realization of ZOPFAN, or the establishment of a zone of peace in Southeast Asia. It has made tangible the Vietnamese trick, which has security, political, and socioeconomic and psychological implications.

In the excellent paper presented by Dr. Douglas Pike, there is one exception—regarding the concept of the Indochinese federation. He says that Vietnam's "invasion of Kampuchea was not to further federation, nor do Hanoi leaders believe that federation can be accomplished with bayonets. They seem willing to wait until even the next century to accomplish the goal, providing events in the three states always move in that general direction."

There came a point when Vietnam, at least the Hanoi Politburo, felt that to follow Ho Chi Minh's testament represented the course with the least resistance. So the idea, the concept of Indochinese federation, did swing the Vietnamese leaders to the use of force to accomplish their goal, given the need for decisive action at that point, before the opportunity slipped away. To back this view are the historical events that preceded 1975, back to the 1930s, and events subsequent to Pol Pot's taking over the regime, the power in Phnom Penh, and assuming governmental control. This also explains Vietnamese determination to stay the course in Kampuchea.

There is another point in Dr. Pike's statement—that China gives every indication of blocking the federation idea now and in the future. ASEAN, certainly Thailand, stands against it. It has been, and is, the Thai government's policy *not* to oppose such a scheme or idea if it can be implemented voluntarily. If the federation or confederation could be achieved with the consent of the peoples of the three countries, we would accept the consequence. But the reality is different. There has been use of force, aggression if you will, to coerce Kampuchea, and that relationship is based on unequal status between the three, with Vietnamese domination in the forefront.

The Thai government's policy and attitude towards the situation in Laos may convince you of the correctness of our statement. ASEAN came into being as a grouping based on consent of the member-countries, and ASEAN is the cornerstone of Thailand's foreign policy. So why should we oppose a similar grouping if it were to come about voluntarily?

The second highlight concerns the important economic and social dimensions of security and calls attention to the positive economic roles that can be played by Japan, the United States, Canada, Australia, and New Zealand.

The third point is that there must be a clear perception of the real defense needs of countries in the region as opposed to promoting major power rivalries in the region, which can only exacerbate the situation and even induce some regional countries to a different course of action in the long run. There is a need for great powers to consult with the countries in the region to determine their real defense needs. And there must be an increased readiness by the major powers, especially the United States, to respond to such needs. The Reagan administration has been forthcoming in its response to the needs of Thailand.

The fourth point to be highlighted, on a strategic level, is the question of Soviet threat versus what Dr. Teller referred to as the United States' defensive capability concept. Would it prove adequate to meet the Soviet threat? More important perhaps, could it avoid a nuclear confrontation? The reality of the Soviet threat is there. The modalities being used may create a desperate situation in which nuclear confrontation could not be avoided. Projection of power from fortress America may be a good deterrent.

The fifth point is that ASEAN can help promote the PRC's constructive role in regional peace and development. It may cause fears, real or imagined, on the part of some of our friends, but ASEAN has effectively found a balance: Thailand's "gravitation" toward China. So it is a question among ASEAN states to which we attach so much importance; otherwise we would need to look elsewhere for support, not necessarily military but economic and social. With unity, ASEAN is viable and provides good options and valid alternatives.

Finally, we should consider the relevance of other issues. These would include, first, the legal framework for avoidance of conflict and peaceful settlement of disputes within the region. And as you know, the Pacific area, of which Southeast Asia constitutes a major portion, is geographically expansive, and most of it is the Pacific Ocean itself.

Second, the Law of the Sea could play an important role because there are many elements that could be sources of conflict. Overlapping jurisdiction of claims, questions of passage through the straits and the sea-lanes to the straits, the rights of landlocked states to mineral resources in the seabed, fisheries, and scientific research with its quasi-military aspects. These are sensitive issues, but they could be potential sources of conflict. We have within the region an anomalous situation since the United States refused to sign the convention of the Law of the Sea, and it may have a long-term impact.

Third, there is a clear need to strengthen international agreements concerning the use of clinical or biological weapons in the area. Thailand, as a frontline state, feels the impact of this.

Fourth, and last, is the refugee problem. There is need for greater responsibility sharing. There was a great deal of tension from the influx of land refugees, as well as the boat people fleeing their homelands. And there was much bargaining, great differences among our friends on the question of responsibility sharing. We consider sound the basis of international agreement and understandings, including what we call the corollary at Geneva: that the policy of first-refuge countries depends on the willingness of the resettlement countries to assume their own obligation and eliminate the residual problem for countries of first asylum. Thailand and the other ASEAN countries, as well as Hong Kong and certainly Australia and the United States, can be regarded as countries of first asylum, but insofar as the United States, Australia, Canada, and others are concerned, they are regarded as countries of resettlement.

Stephen Jurika

I take a slightly different view of the Philippines than Ambassador Lopez does, and I would like to establish very briefly my own credentials. My mother is buried in the Philippine National Heroes Monument, my father in San Carlos Cathedral in Manila, my sister nearby. We had lived there for a long time and operated a multinational company out of the Philippines. We were part of the oligarchy there that Mr. Lopez also belongs to—same family, only much more money.

The Philippines is an archipelago in search of identity. The only language in which people can communicate from one end to the other is English. There are 57 dialects, a relatively primitive communications system, a censored press, martial law and its successor (which is basically martial law without the declaration), government by edict. This does not make for a cohesive Philippine nation. The oligarchy has been running it for a long time, although the oligarchies have changed. More recently the old landed aristocracy has given way to technocrats and bureaucrats.

The United States, I should remind you, is the only postcolonial power in all Asia that planned on independence when it took over its colony. Independence was granted on time in spite of four years of World War II. The United States was the only nation that attempted to plant in its colony the seeds of democracy and the democratic process, a process that is sadly missing throughout the islands.

Now I am interested in security, Philippine security as well as U.S. security, and the United States would like to retain those bases in the Philippines. The Filipinos are ultra-sensitive about pride and dignity, and this can destroy really fine relationships on diplomatic and economic fronts. Philippine sovereignty is not being infringed. The Bases Agreement of 1947, with its subsequent modifications, and the defense agreements between our two countries have been changed, amended, altered to the point where the Philippines has the same relationships with the United States as the NATO members in Europe. We have a Philippine commander on the bases. The Philippine flag flies from the flagpole at the same height as the U.S. flag. Jurisdiction over off-base, off-duty offenses is vested in the Philippine government. Agreements freely entered into can scarcely be seen as a "trampling of sovereignty."

If in 1991, the terminal date of the bases agreement, the intrinsic demands for security in the Philippines are found to be separate from those of the United States—if our interests are neither coincident or parallel—then by all means I think the Philippines in its sovereign right should demand that its own security aspects be paramount. But the United States has the same obligations to look after its own vital interests. If the agreement continues to be desirable, it should be renewed. Otherwise, forget it.

The fact is that U.S. imperialism does not exist anymore. I have been in and out of the Philippines for almost 75 years. I lived there; I went to school there—I have Filipino friends by the hundreds. There is no one more companionable than a Filipino when it comes to having a good time, going to a party, or going out to the big plantations. On the other hand, they are extremely difficult to deal with sometimes, and it is our own damn fault! Let me point out why difficulties arise. Filipinos are 5'4" to 5'6" tall—we have gone into meetings with Americans 6'2" to 6'4" tall with MPs or people behind them, equally tall, in crisply starched uniforms, brass sparking, gold braid sparkling. The Philippine military officer does not have the money to buy the latest uniforms and do all these things on their own, and they are resentful. And I would be too if I were a Filipino. If I were dictating U.S. negotiations with Filipinos, I would meet in civilian clothes, pick people no taller than 5'7" or 5'8" or 5'9," and I would treat the Filipinos exactly as equals. If we want them as partners, we must treat them like partners! On the other hand, when their "dignity" is affronted, make certain they may not expect "special relations" and continued military aid and economic concessions. Reciprocity—as equals—should become the basis for U.S. negotiations.

James Gregor

I have an almost irrepressible urge to defend Ambassador Lopez because he has been abused. But I will constrain myself and continue the abuse. To suggest that the United States is responsible for all the disabilities of the Philippines is exaggerating a bit. The suggestion that the United States was charged with the obligation of establishing equity in income distribution in the Philippines simply misunderstands the task of the United States in the Philippines. Most of the internal structure predated the Americans and as a consequence, the actions of the Philippine legislature. With respect to how that legislature was chosen, this was largely a function of decisions made by the caciques.

The United States did not really install the Marcos dictatorship, but this assumption activates students in universities to demonstrate. The United States knew very little about what Marcos was planning, and U.S. representatives were as surprised as anyone else when martial law was imposed. To talk about the United States–Marcos dictatorship is obviously an abuse of Americans' disposition to listen to almost anything.

The suggestion that U.S. support of authoritarian countries has led to all kinds of disasters may very well be true in some arcane sense. But to suggest that Cuba, Nicaragua, and Iran are in some sense or another the consequence or result of U.S. foreign policy is to stretch the truth beyond credible limits. To suggest that whatever came after the revolutions—

Cuba, Nicaragua, and Iran recommend themselves to us—is a further abuse of our intelligence. That Castro is to be preferred to Batista, that Khomeini is to be preferred to the Shah of Iran, that the Sandinistas are to be preferred to their predecessors, is stretching it a bit. They had rotten systems, and what they got afterwards were obscene systems. If what Ambassador Lopez wants in the Philippines is a post-Marcos regime that parallels that of Cuba, Iran, or Nicaragua, he is welcome to it. I did suggest that he take up residence at my home if there is such a change, and he, I think, is disposed to accept.

Now, to support liberal and democratic forces—yes. Where are they? If someone is to suggest that there are liberal democratic forces the United States can support in the world, I am an advocate of their support. My suspicion is that whatever forces advertise themselves as "liberal democratic" turn out to be less democratic than the authoritarian regimes for which they substitute. Now in that sense, I am a bit cautious. Oppositionists advertise themselves as liberal and democratic, and this is particularly notorious in the Philippines, given as they are to histrionics. There everybody is a democrat, including the New People's Army and the Muslim insurrectionists.

This brings us to a more serious part of our discussion. There are bases in the Philippines. Those bases are important. Can the United States do without the bases? Yes, it can survive without the bases! The United States will survive without almost anything. But without those bases it would be more difficult for it to stabilize Southeast Asia. Placing those bases in Yokosuka, in Pearl Harbor, or in the Marianas is not a reasonable alternative. In the first place, that would increase the length of time to get to critical areas; second, the costs are exorbitant; third, the Philippines enjoy a considerable benefit from those bases. Very briefly, let me tell you what they are. About $300 million is disbursed from those bases annually, which, given the multiplier effect, probably produces about 5 percent of the Philippine GNP. About 40,000 Filipinos are employed on those bases, and the Filipinos are trained with up-to-date technological skills that radiate out into the entire area. To suggest, as the ambassador does, that the Filipinos object to those bases is to stretch the truth beyond all reasonable means. Surveys conducted among the general population show that they do not resent the bases, and the closer you get to the bases the more they support them, primarily because of the economic spin-off in the presence of those bases.

As far as the United States is concerned, any alternative to those bases would work considerable hardship on its ability to intervene in a critical area. Because of the presence of the Soviet Union, all Asian countries would prefer to have those bases in the Philippines than anywhere else. It just happens that they are at Subic and Cubi Point and are essential to U.S. logistics and refurbishing. Most of the Asian nations welcome their presence. If the United States were to withdraw them, it would destabilize the area critically to the disservice of Asia in general, Southeast Asia, and the Philippines as well.

One thing to be remembered is that the Philippines, in the long term, may have considerable problems in the waterways of the South China Sea. Remember there are 127 atolls, cays, sandbars, small islands, a variety of other pieces of territory in that general area over which the PRC claims exclusive rights. Now the Philippines has some of the islands in the Spratly collection. It has also extended control over Scarsborough Reef, and the PRC insists that there is a conflict of territorial interests in that area. As the PRC extends its war capabilities, as it has recently (as you will recall, on May 21, 1980, they retrieved a capsule from a long-distance missile about 4,000 miles from the Chinese mainland using a flotilla of eighteen ships and helicopters), the territories in the South China Seas will become increasingly subject to the demands of the Beijing government.

The Philippine government has a requirement to maintain its own defensive perimeter, for it has extended itself to Palawan. It now has recoverable oil supplies in Nido, off Palawan, and that is going to cause some concern and stress. The Philippines cannot defend itself, and its commitment to national defense is relatively small, actually the smallest in the Asian community. It does need the support of a power that has the capability of projecting itself into the area—not only against the Soviet Union, but against any contender.

The Philippine bases are a major stabilizing feature in Asia, and in Southeast Asia in particular, and no Asian country anticipates withdrawal from those bases. I think that the demand made by the Marcos opposition that those bases be withdrawn is a little bit of a fevered consequence of whatever they drink in the Philippines. It does not have any substance in international relations. It should be dismissed just for what it is—hyperbole. It is used to embarrass the Marcos government. The Marcos government is getting $1 billion over the next five years. The United States is paying rental for those bases, and the rental is comparable to what it pays for bases in Turkey, Greece, or anywhere else. The treatment of those bases is similar to those in the NATO countries, and the United States is not infringing upon the sovereignty of the Philippine Islands at all.

The relationship between the Philippines and the United States has improved considerably over the past decade or so. The United States is now striving assiduously to restore democratic rights in the Philippines, which is in its ultimate interest, but those democratic rights are—as the ambassador seemed to recognize—associated with free enterprise. The United

States cannot impose equity, it cannot impose equality of income, but it can be instrumental in assistance. There are illustrations in the Pacific where the United States has instrumentally improved conditions for the general population. I refer to the ROC on Taiwan, where you have the best family equity in Asia, bar none, and an economic rate of growth that has been spectacular over the past three decades. There is no reason why the Philippines cannot embark on that kind of program under the umbrella of U.S. protection and with capital investments from the United States, which now comprise about half of investments in the Philippines.

In that sense, I do think that there is some merit to Ambassador Lopez's remarks. The Philippines is a very attractive place, it has a right to dignity, it has a right to independence, and it has a right to the United States' admiration and commitment.

Salvador P. Lopez

I think that I have contributed some excitement to this conference. I was afraid that it was going to be very dull from beginning to end, so I am glad that I have been able to make that contribution.

You know the trouble with colonialism? It is so much better to talk about it with the colonist than with the colonized. It is nicer, so much more pleasant. You can stand at the top of the stairs and talk to us below. But the fellow down below is something else. And we Filipinos have been there for 400 years! I hope that gives you an idea of why I feel as I do. And why many Filipinos feel as I do. We want you to get the hell out of there!

Now, one more thing. I did not say that we should take care that whoever succeeds Marcos might be worse. I am precisely suggesting that you do something so that a Khomeini will not succeed Marcos in the Philippines. You can give us your help.

Now, what of the liberal democrats in the Philippines? They are all over the place. You are not looking hard enough. You are looking only at the fellows in front, and that is the reason you are in trouble.

V
CHINA

INTRODUCTION

Claude A. Buss

Of all the variables that determine the future of peace and stability in the Pacific Basin, none is weightier than the political and economic course to be followed by the People's Republic of China (PRC, or China). To anticipate China's twists and turns, to respond to them, and to influence them in a favorable direction is the greatest challenge facing the United States, its allies, and friends in terms of their own security.

After Mao Zedong's victory on the mainland in 1949 and the conclusion of the Sino-Soviet alliance in 1950, communist China became the main enemy of the free world in Asia. After the fighting in Korea, the primary objective of U.S. diplomacy in Asia was to contain communism. More specifically it was to contain the PRC, backed by the USSR, with an alliance system including Japan, the Republic of Korea, the Republic of China (ROC, or Taiwan), Australia and New Zealand, and the Southeast Asian countries of Thailand and the Philippines.

The Sino-Soviet split profoundly altered the strategic situation in the Pacific Basin, but China was unable to act independently in external relations as long as Americans in Vietnam were perceived as the enemy. China's current policies date from the Nixon détente, the death of Mao, and the accession of Deng Xiaoping. In foreign affairs, China now acts in complete independence, seeking its own place in the world, testing the international order while working out its domestic problems. The uncertainties of China are central to any analysis of politics and security in the Pacific Basin.

The papers and discussions of the conference addressed a series of questions regarding China's future. How secure is the regime of Deng Xiaoping, and what might be expected of its successor? What are China's prospects of accomplishing the Four Modernizations? To what extent will China become a factor for stability in the East Asian region? Can communist China come to terms with the capitalist West? How can relations with China be managed to preserve a satisfactory global balance? Should any steps be taken to improve relations between the United States and its friends and allies on the one hand and China on the other?

Questions about relations with China, however, cannot be answered on the limited basis of bilateral relations between Washington and Beijing. If the total security of friendly nations in the Pacific Basin is to be strengthened, due consideration must be given to the interests and policies of U.S. allies and, above all, to the security and welfare of Taiwan. It is incumbent upon Washington to cooperate with Beijing only in ways that will not hurt its friends or create new tensions that would undoubtedly result from a strengthened China.

During nearly ten years at the helm, Deng Xiaoping has guided China in a manner that might have been considered treasonable in the early days of the revolution. There is no indication that his successors will revert to anything approaching the fanaticism of the Cultural Revolution, but it could happen. The new generation of leaders appears calm, more bureaucratic than revolutionary, and solidly in control of the party, the government, and the military establishment. Because followers of the Gang of Four are alive, one can never be sure that China will pursue its present policies. Were China to alter its course or fail in its struggle to solve its basic problems of overpopulation and insufficient food, the security of the anticommunist world would suffer. A confident, prosperous China is far more important to peace and stability than a suffering, chaotic China.

China shares with the United States the strategic interest of opposing the "hegemonism" of the Soviet Union. This does not mean that China is unreservedly on the U.S. side or totally opposed to reconciliation with the Soviets. China is convinced that neither superpower can achieve superiority over the other. In China's view, the global rivalry between the United States and the Soviet Union is the main cause of turmoil in the world and the greatest threat to world peace. It needs and wants a prolonged period of international stability to concentrate its energies on domestic development. China thinks that the superpowers are not super any longer since so much nonmilitary power has passed into the hands of Germany, Japan, and the Arab world.

Until 1981, China perceived the Soviet Union as the most immediate threat to its national security. Seeing Soviet troops on their borders and witnessing the process of encirclement in Korea, Mongolia, Vietnam, and Afghanistan, Chinese leaders admonished their people to dig their tunnels deep and store grain everywhere. They equipped and deployed their armed forces, anticipating an attack from the Soviet Union, and developed a small nuclear retaliatory capability. The antagonism between the Soviet Union and China serves U.S. interests well, as long as it stops short of all-out war.

There is no need for the United States to be nervous about the attempts of Beijing and Moscow to move closer together. An agreement to talk is a far cry from an agreement to agree. A friendlier attitude toward the Russians may be welcome to the Chinese. It would placate the foes of Deng Xiaoping, who think he is too pro-American, and it sends caution signals both to Hanoi and Washington. The United States need not construe possible improvements in Sino-Soviet relations as necessarily adverse to its national interests. These improvements must be judged on their contribution, if any, to peace and stability in the region.

It is not safe to assume that China needs the United States more than the United States needs China and that therefore China will always be dependent for its security on the United States against a challenge from the Soviets. It is dangerous to underestimate China's potential power. It is not helpless and, regardless of outside help, counts on its ability to drown any invader in a sea of blood. Its strength grows as its modernization programs progress. China has its disagreements with the United States and is unhappy about minor irritants that crop up. It has misgivings about Americans in Korea as it once had about the presence of the U.S. military in Vietnam, but it does not see the United States as a threat to its security.

China is ambivalent in its estimates of the United States. It looks to the United States for technical, economic, and certain military assistance. Yet as a communist country, it will not receive much sympathy from the arch-capitalist United States. No matter how much the two countries' strategic interests converge, the Chinese know that the Americans will never jeopardize New York to protect Beijing. Their current judgment in looking at the United States and the Soviet Union is "a plague on both your houses."

Another factor in determining the most effective policies for dealing with China is the status of China's relations with other nations and peoples in the Pacific Basin.

Curiously, China's greatest difficulties are with its communist neighbors. It does not want the USSR to become as dominant in North Korea as the Americans are in the South. It owes Kim Il-sung (and possibly his successor) a certain support as a heritage of the Korean War. China does not want another war on the Korean peninsula and would prefer to see a peaceful reunification of the two Koreas. Because every conciliatory gesture China makes toward South Korea stirs criticisms in the North, it will be interesting to see if China enters the 1988 Olympic games in Seoul.

China's war with Vietnam was a fruitless experience for both participants. Most grievously for China, it solidified the Soviet alliance with Vietnam and provided the excuse needed for the Soviets to project their military power in Southeast Asia. The active Chinese interposition in Kampuchea and its unwillingness to forswear support of local insurgencies have quickened ASEAN fears of a Chinese move to the south. Neither Indonesia nor Singapore has established diplomatic relations with Beijing.

China's relations with its noncommunist neighbors have been less troublesome. It has behaved in a correct but restrained manner toward the Republic of Korea. It did not hesitate to negotiate directly with Seoul for the return of a hijacked civilian airplane with its passengers and crew. It permits substantial trade through the backdoor of Hong Kong. Only the North Korean objection prevents China from adopting U.S. proposals for cross-recognition of the two Koreas.

China and Japan both appear to be generally pleased with their relationship since the Peace and Friendship Treaty of 1978. They have resolved the knotty problem of Taiwan, and Japan's economic assistance is proving vital for much of China's progress in modernization. Neither China nor Japan wants a drastic change in the prevailing security arrangements in the Pacific Basin. China would represent an ominous threat to Japan if it were to turn again toward the Soviet Union, and Japan would be a potential menace to China were it not for Japan's U.S. connection. China is confident that Japan's military expansion will be controlled within the parameters of the Japan-U.S. mutual security treaty.

To the south, China's major preoccupation is to work out with the United Kingdom an acceptable status for Hong Kong after 1997. Hong Kong is not another Falkland Islands. The problem is to preserve Hong Kong's dynamism under Chinese sovereignty. China may have no great difficulty setting up a special administrative district, but it may not be easy to maintain a convertible currency, promote trade, curb taxes, and preserve an unchanged legal system. Hong Kong is the source of 30 to 40 percent of China's foreign exchange earnings.

The last, and possibly the most perplexing, question addressed by conference participants before making suggestions for China policy was "What reasonable steps might be taken by the United States, Japan, and others to assist the Republic of China (Taiwan) in safeguarding its national interests?" It was assumed that the ROC is too valuable an ally, or friendly nation, to sacrifice on the altar of better relations with China.

Taiwan is justly proud of its political stability, economic prosperity, and its goodwill throughout the world. It has a 40-year record of achievement. Its per capita income has grown from $70 to $2,600 per year and is expected to reach $6,200 by 1990. Although the most spectacular growth has been achieved in industrialization, the good life of Taiwan's cities is shared by the rural areas. Outside of Japan and Singapore, Taiwan enjoys the highest level of living in Asia.

Taiwan possesses a strategic location and is an "unsinkable aircraft carrier," in General MacArthur's phrase, off the east coast of China. It has significant military power. Its trade and tourism with the United States, Japan, ASEAN, and the island-states of the Pacific flourish. It does more trade with the United States than the PRC. Based on the three principles of Sun Yat-sen, which are consistent with the ideals of freedom and justice, the government of the ROC is determined to play a positive and active role in contributing to the security and prosperity of the Asia-Pacific region.

History reveals the obstacles to the reunification of Taiwan and the mainland. Taiwan was restored to China at the end of World War II—but which China? Sovereignty over Taiwan is disputed between the People's Republic of China and the Republic of China. Both sides insist on the right of settling the dispute by themselves, without benefit of outside interference. Taiwan is small and prosperous, totally opposed to absorption into the communist system of the mainland. Beijing, on the other hand, is envious of Taiwan's prosperity and frustrated by its inability to reunify the fatherland. Repeated offers of special treatment have been scornfully rejected.

However, the future of the Republic of China is not just a bilateral issue between Beijing and Taipei. The United States, and at least some of its allies, has been involved from the beginning. The Americans were tied to Chiang Kai-shek at Nanking, and they followed him to Taipei. Their advice, encouragement, and assistance contributed mightily to his success. The United States and the Republic of China were joined in a Treaty of Mutual Defense in 1954, after the cessation of hostilities in Korea. The great shift in U.S. policies toward Beijing and Taipei dates from the Nixon overtures to Mao Zedong.

In the Shanghai communiqué of 1972, the United States and the PRC recorded their respective views about the future of Taiwan. The United States acknowledged that all Chinese on either side of the Taiwan Strait maintain that there is but one China and that Taiwan is a part of China. But the United States did not then recognize or deny the sovereignty of the PRC over Taiwan, nor has it since.

Then in 1979, as part of the price of normalizing relations with the PRC, the United States terminated its treaty with the ROC and withdrew its military forces from Taiwan. The U.S. Congress, chagrined over the decisions of the president, passed the Taiwan Relations Act, guaranteeing the continuation of commercial, cultural, and other unofficial relations and committing the United States to make available to the ROC arms of a defensive character.

In a joint communiqué of August 17, 1982, China declared its fundamental policy to be to strive for a peaceful solution to the Taiwan issue. For its part, the United States affirmed that its arms sales should not exceed, either in qualitative or quantitative terms, the level supplied in recent years and that it would gradually reduce its sales of arms to Taiwan, leading to a final resolution. The United States linked its commitment to a continuation of efforts by the PRC to reach a peaceful solution.

This historical sketch indicates steps that must be taken to strengthen the Taiwan government as it seeks a more secure position in the Pacific Basin. Controversies are rooted in a commitment to abstain from the use of force, the problem of sovereignty, and the sale of arms. Taiwan does not want the United States even to discuss these matters with Beijing, fearing that the United States' good intentions to be helpful would only add to Taiwan's risk of losing the gains of the past 40 years.

Taiwan was particularly distressed that the United States crumbled before Beijing's pressures to withhold sales of F5Gs and F/16/J79s to Taiwan. The ROC wants the United States to supply it with whatever modern weapons it can use and pay for, to train the Chinese on Taiwan in their use, and to continue at least joint studies or unofficial conversations on such matters as naval cooperation and protection of the sea lines of communication. The ROC government suggests that for the United States and Japan, it would be strategically unwise to trade something reliable (the ROC) for something uncontrollable (the PRC).

The problem of Taiwan is the darkest cloud on the security horizon of the Western Pacific. The United States must be careful not to let impatience drive it to seek a quick-fix solution. A generation or two might be required for Chinese on both sides of the Taiwan Strait to compose their differences. It is perhaps wisest for the Americans and their allies to relegate the problem to the back burner while poised to help whenever the Chinese indicate their readiness to move ahead.

A bloody battle for reunification is scarcely in the cards; yet there is little hope for agreement through direct negotiations. No one wants Taiwan to disappear into the maw of mainland China, and no one wants to see the current antagonism cause war. The best hope is that in time Marxism-Leninism, as practiced by Beijing, may become more compatible with Taiwan's version of Sun Yat-sen's principles.

It was clear throughout the conference that the PRC would not replace Japan as the center of U.S. and allied security policy in the Pacific Basin. Nothing in the discussion of China policy cast any doubt upon the necessity of maintaining a strong U.S. military presence in the entire region and giving unmistakable signs of the United States' commitment to forward military defense for the protection of its national interests.

The PRC's posture of independence suits U.S. interests because there is no longer need to deploy U.S. forces in the Pacific against a perceived Chinese threat. The United States must find the balance between playing the China card and driving China into another alliance with the Soviet Union. It is better to have China tilt toward the United States rather than toward the Soviets. It will serve U.S. purposes best to help integrate the Chinese into the international system and the political life of the Pacific Basin. Their cooperation can be of inestimable value in solving the long-range transnational problems of population control, protection of the environment, raising the living standards of the Third World, access to scarce raw materials, further rationalization of international trade and finance, and limitations of armaments.

During the conference many practical suggestions were offered for the better management of the United States' relations with China. It should consult with the Chinese continuously on common geopolitical objectives. It should take every advantage of mutual interests in Western Europe, the Persian Gulf, or Afghanistan and freely discuss with them differences in such places as the Middle East, Southern Africa, and some underdeveloped areas in the Third World.

Immediately after the resumption of normal diplomatic relations with China, the United States tended to be euphoric in contemplating strategic cooperation against the Soviets. Progressively it made available to the PRC dual-use equipment, then nonlethal military support equipment, and finally opened the possibility of supplying the Chinese with certain categories of lethal weapons. Most of all, the Chinese want to build an industrial establishment to produce their own weapons systems. For this they need access to U.S. high technology, and in this sphere the United States needs to be unusually prudent.

Making China too strong militarily—for example, assisting it in developing its offensive or nuclear capability—would create new tensions among the United States' allies, including Japan. There are grave doubts about China's capacity to utilize sophisticated weaponry and its ability to adapt its massive army to modern warfare. The United States cannot supply enough war matériel or training to the PRC to make it a significant factor in the balance of power in the Pacific. The most that can be anticipated soon in a military way is cooperation in military education and training, permission to observe each other's military exercises, exchange of intelligence, and, possibly, exchange of naval visits. There is no possibility of a U.S.-PRC alliance, a three-way U.S.-PRC-Japan pact, or a four-way U.S.-PRC-Japan-ROK understanding.

The critical need in the United States' China relations is to shift emphasis from the strategic to the economic, scientific, and cultural aspects. The

United States should do what is necessary to ensure that the PRC will devote its energies to growth and modernization in a peaceful, supportive environment in Asia. Economic frustration, like the uncertainties of succession, could make for future instability, causing Chinese leaders to resort to external adventures to divert the people from their internal hardships.

It is in the United States' interest to contribute to China's economic health and prosperity. Some things can be done by Washington; others must depend on the private sector. China needs access to U.S. schools and business establishments for the education and training of its scientists and technocrats. It needs U.S. loans and investments to develop agriculture, industries, mines, renewable energy resources, offshore oil and gas deposits, and its potential in high technology. Approximately 10,000 Chinese students are now in the United States, and between 1979 and 1983, the U.S. government concluded with the Chinese 21 agreements on scientific exchanges and technology transfers.

Americans can profit immensely by paying more attention to the psychological idiosyncrasies of the two countries. The Chinese lack an understanding of the U.S. system, and Americans do not always appreciate Chinese peculiarities. But Americans dare not disregard Chinese sensitivities or fail to insist upon respect for their own. American distrust of them is reciprocated by Chinese distrust of Americans. Americans find the excesses of their system repugnant, and they fear that Americans' extreme permissiveness will undermine their fundamental values. Exaggerated rhetoric on either side benefits no one. On the other hand, benign neglect would destroy the gains of the past decade.

Most of all, the United States must not get out of step with its allies in dealing with China. Everything said in the discussions of Northeast Asia, the ANZUS, and ASEAN regions must be considered in making China policy. U.S. allies have their special concerns with China that must be respected. They are pleased that the United States has resumed normal diplomatic relations, but they dislike the emotionalism that creeps into U.S. judgments about China. They think of China as a sprawling giant that, at best, can become nothing more than a regional power. Conscious of the dangers stemming from China's long-term ambitions in the East Asia–Pacific region, they want to ensure their views are fully considered before assigning to China an expanded role in the national security interests of the United States, its friends, and allies in the Pacific Basin.

CHINA'S ROLE IN PACIFIC BASIN SECURITY

Jonathan D. Pollack

Among the states of East Asia and the Pacific, the greatest uncertainties and imponderables attach to China. No nation in the postwar international system has shifted its political and strategic position more frequently or more sharply; this pattern of change contributes both to the attention accorded China and to the repeated doubts over the prospects for stability in China's internal and external roles. The inability to define and maintain a consistent, long-term policy course reflects China's recurrent political and economic debates and East Asia's centrality in the conflicts and crises of the postwar era. Lacking the geographic and political neatness of the postwar division of Europe and faced with major internal upheavals throughout the region, East Asia became the major battleground involving U.S. military forces during the 1950s and 1960s, with China cast by Washington as the principal villain. Without a consensual framework for major power interactions in the region—indeed, with China's political legitimacy directly challenged by the United States—it seems little wonder that the first decades of communist rule in China were characterized by instability and international conflict.

By any measure, China's politics and prospects in the early 1980s represent a distinct improvement over the past. The Chinese no longer challenge the legitimacy of the international order that long sought to exclude them. Under the aegis of Deng Xiaoping, China has undertaken policy changes that less than a decade ago would have been judged ideologically treason-

---

Views expressed in this paper are the author's own and are not necessarily shared by the Rand Corporation or its research sponsors.

ous and politically suicidal. Indeed, despite repeated expressions of concern about the stability of the Deng leadership in China, Deng has now held power longer than any U.S. president since Eisenhower. The Chinese have also begun to come to terms with the economic, political, and technological price paid for two decades of internal turmoil and strident, exclusionary external policies. The largest questions confronting leaders in Beijing for the remainder of this century concern the resiliency of their policy framework and the adaptability of their political and economic institutions. Can a Leninist organizational system permit sustained economic growth without engendering widespread societal and political upheaval? Will the mechanisms of central state power permit the devolution of authority required to spur individual initiative? Can China adapt to the technological and economic advances of the West and of its neighbors in the Pacific Basin, without generating visceral or excessively nationalistic policies?

An additional set of issues concerns the prospects for stability and security in the West Pacific. How fully will China contribute to the realization of these goals? What will be the effects of China's modernization effort on Chinese attitudes and policies toward its neighbors? How is Soviet and U.S. conduct in the region likely to influence Chinese thinking and policies? To address these questions, this paper will briefly explore four interrelated issues: (1) China's strategic significance and power prospects; (2) the PRC's orientation toward the superpowers, especially in relation to U.S. and Soviet policy within the region; (3) China's relations with the regional communist powers (Vietnam and North Korea); and (4) China's strategy toward its noncommunist neighbors.

Assessing China's Strategic Role

Scholars and practitioners alike remain deeply divided in their judgments about China's impact on the contemporary international system.[1] The intellectual debate about China's power potential and security role remains very skewed since these differences reflect policy debates in the West about China's political and strategic importance. The range of opinion is wide and contradictory.

1. China is a regional power that poses no threat to its neighbors; with sufficient assistance from the West, it will become a credible major power supportive of U.S. goals and interests in East Asia.
2. China is militarily weak and backward and therefore not a credible collaborator with the West in restraining the exercise of Soviet power.

3. China is weak and highly vulnerable to Soviet political and military pressure; thus Beijing has no alternative to relying on U.S. power for enhancing its security.
4. China may appear weak, but its long-term objective is to be the dominant power of the Asia-Pacific region, thus setting limits on Western identification with China's underlying power ambitions.
5. China adheres resolutely to its foreign policy principles; it will never work behind the backs of its friends for short-term expediency.
6. The Chinese are perpetually changing their policy course; thus the West must deal cautiously with China, lest any assistance (especially in the military area) work against Western interests.
7. The Chinese are discerning, unsentimental practitioners of realpolitik; the United States can deal with China precisely because of this strategic acumen.
8. Chinese diplomatic practice is marked principally by duplicity, chicanery, deception, and flattery; its leaders possess neither scruples nor strategic vision and will not long remain committed to their present alignment with the West.
9. China is weak and divided internally; thus the West cannot depend on the orderly development of its society, polity, and economy.
10. China may be relatively weak and backward; but in the larger, longer picture it will be a powerful, more advanced society with whom the West must maintain close relations.

China seems almost an international chameleon; it is all things to all people. Yet the very divergence of the debate reflects China's strategic significance. If the Chinese devote their minds and energies to playing a major international role, it is impossible for a state of such size, numbers, and absolute economic and military power not to assume substantial political and strategic importance. The unresolved issues concern the dimensions of this role and its implications for international security and stability in the Pacific Basin.

Judgments about China in terms of pure power capabilities are therefore misleading. Compared with its noncommunist neighbors, China is economically and technologically backward, but that does not make China strategically insignificant. Similar arguments can be made about the Soviet Union. The Soviet Union's economic performance and per capita GNP lag well behind that of the major European powers, the United States, and Japan, but this does not call into question the Soviet Union's credentials as a superpower. Similarly, the Chinese have repeatedly been at the forefront of great power rivalries and conflicts, beginning with the Sino-Soviet alliance and China's entry into the Korean War. For two decades, the United States deployed naval, air, and strategic forces against China. For the past decade and a half, the Soviet Union has committed major ground, air, naval, and strategic forces against the PRC. The superpowers have never doubted China's strategic importance, especially in relation to China's likely wartime behavior.

An additional issue concerns power potential. Despite China's relative underdevelopment, the Chinese economy already generates substantial resources for national needs, including defense. Strategically unimportant nations do not produce more than 5,000 combat aircraft or test and deploy ICBMs. Dwight Perkins has demonstrated the logic of a compound interest model of national power.[2] If China sustains economic growth rates comparable to those attained in its first three and a half decades, and if China is prepared to commit approximately the same portion of its GNP to its defense effort as it did in the 1970s, then by the year 2000 China will allocate approximately $100 billion in current dollars to defense expenditure. Nor are issues of technological sophistication and skilled manpower insurmountable obstacles, especially in view of the availability of advanced technology and the present opportunities for training skilled manpower in the West.

However, China is now at an international crossroads. Its embroilment in some of the postwar era's principal geopolitical conflicts elevated the PRC to major power status, but it also exacted a substantial political and economic price. Chinese leaders realize their economic prospects are far better served by the avoidance or amelioration of external conflict and confrontation. This has led China to attempt to diminish tensions with its neighbors, including the Soviet Union. Even in the absence of major change in Beijing's political and military rivalries with Moscow and Hanoi, Chinese policies toward both the Soviet Union and Vietnam are far less strident and confrontational than in the late 1970s.

In relation to noncommunist Asia, the PRC has decided that its interests are better served by accommodation than by confrontation. China must make up two decades of lost time; yet it is still struggling to devise a system of incentives and rewards essential to technological innovation and economic growth. If China is to achieve sustained progress in re-establishing its educational system, modernizing its factories, developing its energy resources, improving the standard of living of its citizens, and training more technically proficient managers and workers, it cannot do so on the basis of exclusionary policies or in an atmosphere of acute international tension.

Thus, China's leaders acknowledge that their development efforts will require "a peaceful international environment." Heightened tensions in either Asia or the Pacific or major war would dramatically affect the PRC's economic and political prospects for the remainder of this century and beyond. Above all, the Chinese recognize that their security prospects will continue to derive from their relations with the superpowers and the role of Soviet and U.S. power in the region.

China and the Superpowers

Notwithstanding Beijing's ritualistic attacks on "the hegemonism of the two superpowers," the Chinese understand that U.S. and Soviet power set these two states apart from all others and that China cannot afford the risks and uncertainties of excessively provoking either or both. Although China has at times adopted "a plague on both your houses" mentality (notably during the 1960s), a strategy of isolation and estrangement from Washington and Moscow is inherently dangerous for Beijing's security interests. The Chinese also understand that close alignment with either global power at the expense of the other is not a workable long-term strategy. As the Chinese noted in their polemical exchanges with Moscow in 1963, China's position as junior partner in the Sino-Soviet alliance placed the PRC on "the frontline of the struggle against American imperialism," effectively precluding extensive Chinese economic and political dealings with the noncommunist states along its periphery.

U.S. policy toward the PRC in the 1950s and 1960s reinforced this isolation. The United States's strategy toward China had two broad objectives: the political and military encirclement of China (implemented by the forward deployment of U.S. naval and air forces and the establishment of bases and alliances throughout the West Pacific) and prevention of the consolidation of communist control in Southeast and Northeast Asia. For both economic and security reasons, China had no credible alternative but to focus its attention on Asia rather than the Pacific. To diminish the direct U.S. threat to Chinese security and territorial sovereignty, China dealt largely with the other Asian communist states and parties. One can speculate about the "what if" questions had North Korea not invaded the South, but the sequence of events on the Korean peninsula between June and October of 1950 froze the regional security environment for the next two decades and precluded meaningful Chinese relations with most of its noncommunist neighbors to the east and south.

The Nixon initiatives toward China unfroze this pattern. China's initial efforts to overcome the diplomatic and economic isolation of the Cultural Revolution also contributed to the process, but it was the United States' strategic reassessment in Asia that propelled this change. China could now begin to deal more fully with its neighbors, unconstrained by U.S. political and military opposition. Even if the Nixon administration sought to improve relations with Beijing largely for broader strategic reasons, the implications were more regional than global. For the first time, China could look to the Pacific, even as it remained principally an Asian power.

Changes in Soviet foreign and military policy since the mid-1960s, however, further transformed the East Asian political and strategic landscape. The United States' retrenchment was accompanied by Soviet advancement, with China the proximate cause in both cases. The buildup of Soviet ground and air forces, principally facing China's northeastern provinces, made China's relations with the USSR as much a security issue as an ideological or political one. The steady expansion and improvement in Soviet naval and strategic capabilities during the 1970s underscored the Soviet Union's emergence as a two-front power. Even if other factors helped spur the Soviet buildup in the East (specifically, U.S. forward-based naval power and the U.S. base and alliance system in Northeast Asia), Moscow had signaled its determination to remain an Asian power. Unlike the Americans, who were deployed principally in the Pacific and had avoided major conflict with the Chinese since the Korean War, the Soviets posed an immediate, land-based challenge to Chinese security. Moreover, Moscow had built up its military assets in Asia without diminishing its force levels in Europe.

This ominous strategic pattern found Washington and Beijing moving toward an informal security coalition in the late 1970s and early 1980s.[3] China seemed closer to aligning with one of two superpowers than at any time since the Sino-Soviet alliance. These dealings were based on mutual need. China, militarily vulnerable and technologically and economically backward after two decades of internal political convulsion, confronted a growing Soviet presence to the north (the Sino-Soviet border), east (the Soviet Pacific Fleet), south (in Indochina), and west (in Afghanistan). The United States, having designated the Persian Gulf a vital strategic interest following the fall of the Shah and the Soviet invasion of Afghanistan, urgently needed stability on other vital fronts. Moreover, the Chinese kept large numbers of Soviet and Vietnamese troops committed along the PRC's northern and southern borders. Although the Chinese could not prevent Soviet expansion in the Third World and had no incentive to initiate hostilities, they did complicate Soviet force planning and diminished U.S. military requirements in the Western Pacific. In addition, the Chinese provided tacit support for the U.S. political and military presence in the region. It was a reasonable bargain for both states, but it did not constitute the beginnings of a Sino-American alliance. China's leaders had an almost neuralgic aversion toward any moves that might impinge upon their freedom of action. They further recognized that higher levels of Sino-American security association might needlessly provoke the Soviet Union, possibly leading to heightened tensions in Northeast Asia.

No matter how grandiose China's united front rhetoric, the Chinese sought to restrain the Soviet exercise of power, not goad Moscow into pre-emptive action against the PRC. Collaborative actions with the West were intended to complicate Moscow's consolidation of its geopolitical gains in both Southeast and Southwest Asia, diminish Soviet pressure against China, and temper or deter further Soviet actions in areas of instability. An informal security coalition with the West also made possible a significant infusion of advanced technology for China's industrial and military modernization. The United States had thus accorded China an independent political and military weight. Such strategic calculations proved worrisome to various Asian states since they appeared to portend a much larger Chinese political and military role in East Asia, seemingly sanctioned by the United States. These concerns were understandable but somewhat exaggerated. The United States may have acquiesced to China's military moves against Vietnam, but a larger strategic design for Sino-American relations was still lacking. Not only did China express repeated wariness about entering into an overly encumbering relationship with the United States, but also opinions in Washington remained deeply divided over the wisdom of and prospects for a coalition between the United States and China.

The latter issue remains a complicating factor for both nations. From the time of the initial Nixon-Kissinger breakthroughs with Beijing, the Chinese have learned a great deal about the vicissitudes of the U.S. political process. These uncertainties have found expression in a number of areas, notably the Taiwan arms sale issue and debates over technology transfer to the PRC. Fundamentally, these issues reduce to several critical factors: How important is China to U.S. strategic and regional interests? Does China need the United States more than the United States needs China? In the absence of a Chinese capability to project its military power, what can the United States expect from China in dealing with a multifront challenge from the Soviet Union?

With the renewed suspicions and tensions between Beijing and Washington in the early 1980s, relations deteriorated sharply. For a period in 1982, the increasingly strident atmosphere of Sino-American relations threatened to undermine the China's acceptance of the U.S. political and military posture in the Western Pacific. Both states stood to lose by such differences. Indeed, the only state that benefited by this instability was the USSR since it no longer had to weigh as seriously the possible effects of its behavior on U.S.-Chinese relations.

During 1983, however, U.S.-Chinese relations returned to a steadier footing. The previous U.S. emphasis on China's strategic potential was supplanted by a recognition of China's role as a modernizing, regional power. Although Washington still recognized areas of strategic convergence with Beijing, it is Japan, not China, that is the economic and strategic centerpiece of U.S. Asian policy.[4] Although the Chinese resented being characterized in regional terms, such a revised course indicated to Beijing that the United States did not intend to use China as a pawn in the U.S.-Soviet global rivalry. It also shifted the focus of the United States' China policy toward America's role and interests in China's modernization, in particular the issue of technology transfer. The visit of Defense Secretary Caspar Weinberger in September 1983 signaled China's readiness to resume the aborted defense dialogue with the United States and recognize the continuing congruence of U.S. and Chinese interests. It was followed by the reciprocal visits of Premier Zhao Ziyang to the United States in January 1984 and of President Reagan to China in April 1984, thereby underscoring the determination of both states to avoid a damaging deterioration in relations.

These developments, however, did not portend the reconstitution of a Sino-American united front in East Asia. The Chinese repeatedly conveyed that their security interests were better served by standing somewhat apart from the United States rather than closely aligned with it. This posture presumed that the challenges to PRC security were manageable. During fall 1982, the Chinese had consented to the initiation of Sino-Soviet consultation at the vice–foreign minister level. Beijing had held out the prospect of improved Sino-Soviet relations if Moscow demonstrated a willingness to diminish the Soviet threat to China. Such overtures, however, had also been intended as a demonstration of China's capacity to deal independently with the Soviet Union (thereby sending an important signal to Washington) rather than from any expectation that a new leader in the Kremlin would be more forthcoming than his predecessor. Indeed, China consented to these discussions only after reaching agreement with the Untied States in August 1982 on an explicit formula for continued U.S. arms sales to Taiwan.

In undertaking these negotiations, the Chinese had concluded that Moscow would be more likely to normalize relations with China if Sino-Soviet interstate relations were separated from the broader Sino-Soviet security rivalry. Indeed, the Soviet Union had long sought to decouple its political and economic ties with the Chinese from their larger strategic differences. As one leading Chinese strategist argued:

On the one hand, China opposes [the superpowers'] hegemonism and on the other, China will maintain and develop relations with both of them on the basis of the five principles of peaceful co-existence. China is seeking to achieve the normalization of relations between itself and the Soviet Union, and all this requires [!] is for the Soviet Union to eliminate threats to China's security.[5]

This argument is somewhat disingenuous since the future of Sino-Soviet relations cannot be separated from the broader strategic context governing the Moscow-Beijing relationship.[6] It is possible that in the atmosphere of crisis in the late 1970s, the Chinese feared major Soviet advances in both Southeast and Southwest Asia, but Moscow's inability to consolidate its position diminished Chinese anxieties. Some leaders in Beijing apparently believe that Moscow will search for opportunities to diminish the multiple demands and pressures it now confronts, especially with the renewed heightening of the Soviet-American global competition.

These expectations were not met. A more correct tone was established in Sino-Soviet relations during 1982 and 1983, including higher levels of trade, increased scientific, cultural, and athletic contacts, and a noticeable decline in polemics between Moscow and Beijing. But the Soviet Union proved unyielding on what the Chinese described as the larger obstacles to improved Sino-Soviet relations (the Soviet military presence along the Sino-Soviet border and in Mongolia, including the SS-20s deployed east of the Urals, Soviet support for the Vietnamese occupation of Kampuchea, and the Soviet occupation of Afghanistan). By early 1984, the Soviet Union had deployed 135 SS-20s in Asia, an increase of nearly 40 since early 1983.[7] A steady enhancement in the Soviet military presence in Vietnam included the stationing of TU-16 bombers in Vietnam in late 1983 and the conducting of joint Soviet-Vietnamese amphibious maneuvers along the Vietnamese coast in April 1984. In Afghanistan, Moscow stepped up both the scale and intensity of its actions against the guerrilla resistance.

At the same time, Moscow conveyed its unhappiness over the renewed warming in Sino-U.S. relations, explicitly criticizing the results of President Reagan's visit to China. In early May, harsh Soviet commentaries on renewed tensions along the Sino-Vietnamese border were followed by Moscow's abrupt postponement of the impending visit of First Deputy Premier Arkhipov to Beijing, who would have been the highest-level Soviet visitor to China since the border conflict of 1969. Thus, the prospects of China's defining an independent foreign policy course acceptable to both Moscow and Washington remain doubtful.

Indeed, although the Chinese argue that Sino-Soviet relations and Sino-American relations are separate issues, the Soviet-American competition exerts a powerful influence on PRC security strategy. Having previously criticized the United States for its alleged appeasement of the Soviet Union, the Chinese now seem uncomfortable with an excessively confrontational atmosphere in U.S.-Soviet relations, especially heightened tensions within China's immediate security environment. In an ironic postscript to the PRC's earlier calls for strengthened U.S. resistance to "Soviet hegemonism," China has again criticized "American hegemonism," arguing that the United States is now engaged in an effort to recover from its strategic setbacks of the 1960s and 1970s. According to the Chinese, the Reagan administration's defense strategy overemphasizes the augmentation of U.S. military power, thus slighting the development of a peacetime political coalition to oppose Soviet actions. Yet the U.S. defense buildup also enables China to describe the present superpower balance as a stalemate, thereby providing the PRC greater maneuverability in defining a foreign policy course apart from both Washington and Moscow.

In the view of Chinese strategists, a renascent "American hegemonism" is more illusion than menace and largely irrelevant to the long-term political, military, and economic directions of the international system.[8] Those Western strategists credited with "farsightedness" recognize that the prevailing direction in international politics is toward the diffusion of power. In this view, both superpowers will appear much less "super" and will need to solicit others rather than dominate them. The intermediate forces within the international system—China, Japan, the Western European states—will begin to assume a larger political and strategic role in a multipolar international system.[9] These arguments, however, tend to neglect the intersecting great power interests in areas of more immediate concern for regional states such as China. The West Pacific and Northeast Asia are far too important strategically and economically to expect either superpower to relinquish its role in the region. The Chinese understand very well that it is only the inability of "either [superpower] to achieve overwhelming superiority . . . [that] enables many countries in the intermediate zone to win more freedom of action."[10]

China and the Asian Communist States

Among its six East Asian communist neighbors, China enjoys reasonably good relations only with North Korea. Do leaders in Beijing ponder the irony that their major security challenges emanate exclusively from other communist powers, while their major economic partners are all capitalist states? As China looks increasingly to the Pacific to stimulate economic growth, on the Asian mainland the PRC remains deeply enmeshed in major military rivalries to its north and south.

The principal difficulty for Asian communist leaders is that they have yet to define a nonconfrontational approach to interstate relations. Even with North Korea—the only state with which China maintains a treaty entailing military obligations—relations with Beijing have been subject to intermittent strains. These internecine conflicts benefit the noncommunist powers of Asia since the communist states remain preoccupied with their mutual rivalries and antagonisms. In a long-term sense, however, it is difficult to see how the Pacific Basin nations will gain by continued polarization and conflict on the Asian mainland.

China's dealings with both Vietnam and North Korea are rooted in complicated histories that, in the latter case, remain virtually unknown in the West. (The profound deterioration of Sino-Vietnamese relations in the late 1970s provided a wealth of information from both Hanoi and Beijing about their past dealings.) Among the three states, none has, in its own estimation, fully achieved its original political-military goals: a unified national communist state for Beijing and Pyongyang and the effective control of all of Indochina by Hanoi. All three leaderships are proud, nationalistic, and fiercely independent. The largest issue for the Chinese is whether to accept these traits as a more or less permanent state of affairs, with leaders in North Korea or Vietnam owing China no particular deference or loyalty.

China's record on this issue is mixed. Relations between Vietnam and China deteriorated steadily throughout much of the 1970s, but especially after Hanoi's armies overran the South in spring 1975. The Chinese assert that this shift was caused exclusively by Vietnam's arrogance and inflated territorial ambitions, abetted by Hanoi's close alignment with Moscow. Absent such a strategy of "regional hegemonism," Sino-Vietnamese relations would never have deteriorated. The bitter antagonism expressed by both leaderships raises the issue of whether either state was capable or desirous of maintaining decent relations after the fall of Saigon.

Although leaders in both capitals have at times sought to convey hints of flexibility and a willingness to settle their differences, the troop redeployments brought about by the border hostilities of 1979 remain essentially intact. Despite periodic tensions since that time, neither side has wished to resume major hostilities. However, as developments in spring 1984 demonstrate, the antagonisms between China and Vietnam run very deep and are unlikely to diminish appreciably in the foreseeable future.

Although it is impossible to prove, leaders in Beijing have probably been chagrined by Hanoi's determination to "stay the course" both in Kampuchea and with respect to Sino-Vietnamese differences. Vietnam has become increasingly dependent on the Soviet Union for military and economic aid and must now compensate Moscow by allowing regular access to the prized facilities at Da Nang and Camranh Bay, but there is no evidence of crisis in Hanoi. The Chinese, with their military reputation tarnished in the unexpectedly costly border war of 1979, show little desire to replay that conflict, even though they continue to place the Vietnamese under military pressure. Yet the confrontation and conflict along the Vietnamese border (and the heightened Soviet encirclement to the south that it engendered) pose risks to China's broader effort to secure "a peaceful international environment." China continues its pressure along the border and aids the anti-Vietnamese forces in Kampuchea, but the pressure is not unrelenting. So long as both sides find the political, military, and economic costs bearable, only two possibilities seem likely to alter the status quo: a major realignment of the political and military forces in Kampuchea or a major political or strategic shift in the Hanoi leadership. In the absence of such changes, both states are stalemated. The options for each are limited, and the enhanced Soviet role provides a different context than a few years ago.

China's relations with North Korea are somewhat different. Beijing takes its ties to Pyongyang very seriously. The nightmare vision of North Korea becoming a "second Vietnam," although extremely remote, must nevertheless worry the Chinese, especially in the context of the succession to Kim Il-sung. Beijing's grudging willingness to endorse the arranged succession suggests that China's alternatives were limited and unpleasant. The visit of Kim Il-sung to Moscow in May 1984—his first official visit to the Soviet Union in more than two decades—also creates the possibility of Soviet–North Korean ties improving from their virtual nonexistence at present. China has not voiced any concern about this possibility, but leaders in Pyongyang have been displeased by China's growing unofficial ties with South Korea and may view Kim's trip to Moscow as an opportunity to diversify their sources of political support.

The security dimension of Sino–North Korean relations is also very different. The Korean peninsula remains the one location on the Asian mainland where the United States still deploys military forces. To the Chinese, there is an uncomfortable parallel between U.S. support for South Korea and continuing U.S. ties with Taiwan. Yet the Chinese share with the United States a fervent desire not to see a resumption of hostilities in the Korean peninsula. Chinese officials will acknowledge a common U.S. and PRC interest in stability in Korea or at least a continuation of the status quo. China's deliveries of combat aircraft to the North during 1982 indicate a continuing PRC concern with the balances of forces, perhaps prompted by the recent augmentation of U.S. air power in the South. But the Chinese cannot do anything that poses a major risk to their close political relationship with North Korea, lest renewed differences with Pyongyang provide the Soviet Union a larger opportunity on the peninsula.

Thus the possible enhancement of U.S. defense collaboration with the Republic of Korea causes concern in Beijing since it complicates Chinese efforts to move toward diminished tensions on the peninsula in a manner acceptable to the North. Here as well, China's room for maneuver is limited, and the potential consequences of deteriorating Sino–North Korean relations exceedingly unpleasant to contemplate.

The real test of Sino–North Korean relations, however, most likely must await the death of Kim Il-sung. Will the Chinese seek to persuade North Korea to redirect its political and economic policies, much as China did after the death of Mao? Will China then be prepared to incur greater risks by accepting the reality of two Korean states? And how would these changes influence Chinese perceptions of the U.S. military role in Northeast Asia? The continuing division of the Korean peninsula typifies China's bifurcated political world—the intersection of China's involvement in decades-long Asian conflicts with new opportunities in the Pacific Basin.

China and the Pacific Basin

The largest issues faced by the states and societies in the Pacific Basin in relation to China concern the PRC's efforts at accommodation with its noncommunist neighbors. China's relations with Japan, South Korea, Taiwan, and Hong Kong represent separate and special cases; yet they share common characteristics. The latter three societies hope that China will accord them a recognition and respect that parallels what has developed between China and Japan over the past decade. The outlook for regional stability is bleak if the delicate, complicated issues between China and its immediate neighbors are mishandled.

The Chinese confront several competing choices. They recognize the political, economic, and security benefits they enjoy by virtue of closer ties with the Pacific nations and diminished tensions with the United States. They also appreciate the potential implications of a reversion to a regional security environment where U.S. and Chinese objectives are in fundamental conflict. One Chinese authority has noted that "if China and the United States regress to a similar kind of opposition and aggression to that which existed between them during the 1950s and 1960s, then the consequences for the Asian-Pacific region and the rest of the world will be very serious and difficult to predict."[11] Yet the Chinese do not acknowledge that their actions could contribute to such a retrogression.

The handling of the Taiwan and Hong Kong issues, in particular, will reveal a great deal about the long-term directions of Chinese policy. To the PRC, these issues represent two of the final, unresolved questions blocking the unity of the entire Chinese state. The Chinese are turning to powerful, emotive symbols of patriotism and nationalism to achieve at least symbolic reunification of Hong Kong and Taiwan with the mainland. By promising substantial autonomy and latitude for existing political and economic systems, the PRC leadership seems to believe that it has made offers no reasonable party could refuse.[12] These proposals virtually preclude coercive means to achieve reunification, and they tacitly acknowledge that the mainland's economic system is wholly inappropriate for either Taiwan or Hong Kong.

Such overtures are intended principally to demonstrate China's sincerity and reasonability to the United States and Japan, for these two states are the linchpin of Chinese strategy in the Pacific Basin. It is impossible to determine whether Deng and other Chinese leaders believe that their appeals will be greeted positively by the people of Hong Kong and Taiwan. Deng may believe that in conjunction with the political and economic reforms under way within China (in particular China's recently announced plans to expand greatly the special economic zones in the coastal regions), the differences between the mainland, Hong Kong, and Taiwan will gradually narrow, thereby ultimately permitting reintegration of these separate systems.

Even as Deng implies a "live and let live" attitude, he also understands that there are limits beyond which he cannot pledge China's forbearance. But he also understands that any recourse to a more coercive strategy would be fundamentally destabilizing to political and economic relations in the Western Pacific. So long as China maintains a compelling need for good relations with the United States and Japan, one can only hope this will temper and restrain China from considering alternative approaches.

Such issues, however, cut both ways. The United States, pressed with major defense responsibilities on multiple fronts, can ill afford to consider again preparing for conflict contingencies involving the PRC. In this sense, policymakers in Washington confront the singular opportunity of a China focused principally on its internal economic reconstruction, generally supportive of U.S. regional goals, and opposed to the expansion of Soviet power. For the interests of all in the Pacific Basin, it is an opportunity that must not be squandered.

The Asia-Pacific region today represents a major success for U.S. political, economic, and strategic policies, and China is a principal factor in that success. Despite the intermittent difficulties of managing relations with the PRC, there is an enormous disparity between the strident, confrontational, xenophobic China of the 1960s and early 1970s and the nation that now admits to compelling economic and technological needs from the West, without the Soviet Union representing a credible alternative. Yet there are continuing issues over which scholarly and governmental opinion remain divided. At the risk of some oversimplification, are the Chinese in such straits and with so few options that the present status of U.S.-Chinese relations will remain more or less intact no matter what U.S. policy toward Beijing is? Or does benign neglect, or worse, endanger the gains of the past decade, in particular China's role as a stabilizing regional force, to the consequent disadvantage of U.S. allies and friends in the Pacific?

There are reasonable prospects for greater policy continuity in China, but there are also imponderables. Displaced and disgruntled politicians may be eagerly awaiting Deng's passage from the scene; they may well include some within the military ranks and other elements of centralized state control who look with great disfavor on many of the economic and political developments of recent years.[13] Some may be far more suspicious than Deng about the benefits of close association with the West. Others may take seriously the notion of the United States as a resurgently hegemonic power that will seek to dominate Northeast Asia to the detriment of Chinese interests. Consideration of such uncertainties must occupy a central place in any analysis of politics and security in the Pacific Basin, especially in view of the many different roles China has assumed in prior decades. These questions nevertheless are of a very different order from the ones posed in the past. They suggest how far we have come with China—and how far we still have to go.

Notes

1. For my own views, see "China's Potential as a World Power," *International Journal*, Summer 1980, pp. 580–95; "China in the Evolving International System," in Norton Ginsburg and Bernard Lalor, eds., *China: The Eighties Era* (Boulder, Colo.: Westview Press, 1983); and "China and the Global Strategic Balance," in Harry Harding, ed., *The Three Chinas: China's Foreign Relations in Historical and Contemporary Perspective* (New Haven: Yale University Press, 1984).

2. See Dwight Perkins, "The International Consequences of China's Economic Development," in Richard Solomon, ed., *The China Factor* (Englewood Cliffs, N.J.: Prentice-Hall, 1981), especially pp. 132–35; and "The Economic Background and Implications for China," in Herbert Ellison, ed., *The Sino-Soviet Conflict: A Global Perspective* (Seattle: University of Washington Press, 1982), especially pp. 100–110.

3. For a detailed assessment, see Jonathan D. Pollack, *The Lessons of Coalition Politics: Sino-American Security Relations*, R-3133-AF (Santa Monica, Calif.: Rand Corporation, February 1984).

4. For an excellent interpretive synthesis, see Richard Nations, "A Tilt Towards Tokyo," *Far Eastern Economic Review*, April 21, 1983, pp. 36–40.

5. Pei Monong, "China's Future Role in Asia," *Shijie Zhishi* [World knowledge], no. 10 (May 16, 1983), in *Foreign Broadcast Information Service Daily Report–China [FBIS-China]*, July 22, 1983, p. A-6.

6. For a detailed analysis, see Jonathan D. Pollack, *The Sino-Soviet Rivalry and Chinese Security Debate*, R-2907-AF (Santa Monica, Calif.: Rand Corporation, October 1982).

7. U.S. Department of Defense, *Soviet Military Power*, 2nd ed. (Washington, D.C., March 1983), p. 34; 3rd ed. (April 1984), p. 50.

8. For a discerning Chinese discussion of these issues, see Zhang Jingyi, "Analysis of the Reagan Administration's Military Strategy," *Renmin Ribao* [People's daily], May 5, 1983, in *FBIS-China*, January 10, 1983, pp. B-1–6.

9. See Zong He, "Changes and Development Trends in the International Situation," *Shijie Zhishi*, no. 11 (June 1, 1983), in *FBIS-China*, July 21, 1983, pp. A-1–5.

10. Cheng Bifan, "U.S.-USSR Contention in the Sea of the Western Pacific," *Renmin Ribao*, January 19, 1983, in *FBIS-China*, January 20, 1983, p. A-2.

11. Pei Monong, "China's Future Role in Asia," p. A-6

12. See Derek Davies, "A Leap into the Dark," *Far Eastern Economic Review*, May 3, 1984, pp. 14–16; Michael Weisskopf, "Taiwan's Role in a United China Would Be Equal, Deng Pledges," *Washington Post*, July 19, 1983; idem, "New Proposals from Peking Being Offered to Taiwan," *Washington Post*, July 30, 1983; and David Bonavia, "The Bait for Taiwan," *Far Eastern Economic Review*, May 3, 1984, pp. 14–15.

13. For one very suggestive interpretation, see Susan L. Shirk, "The Domestic Political Dimensions of China's Foreign Economic Relations" (Paper delivered at the annual meeting of the International Studies Association, Mexico City, April 5–8, 1983).

THE INTERESTS AND POLICIES OF THE REPUBLIC OF CHINA

Tun-Hwa Ko

This is a brief analysis of security policies of the Republic of China on Taiwan. What are its national interests? What are the roles it is trying to play in the international arena? What are its major problems? What might be its future? What may the United States and the rest of the world do for Taiwan?

The opinions expressed here are those of the author. They do not represent any official view. This does not imply, however, that these views would not be shared by other colleagues and scholars in Taiwan.

The Republic of China on Taiwan

The ROC has exercised control of the islands of Taiwan and Penghu, plus a number of offshore islands such as the Matsu, Kinmen, and Tungying groups of Fukien province. In the South China Sea (or Nanyang, in traditional Chinese) between the Philippines, Malaysia, and Borneo, there are still some islands under the juridical control of the ROC. Tai-pin, the Chinese name of the largest, is garrisoned by ROC troops, has a strong defense capability, and good facilities for surveillance.

Since the ROC withdrew from the United Nations, it has maintained substantial contacts in cultural, trade, and other relations with more than a hundred nations, in addition to those nations that have had diplomatic relations with the ROC.

The economic success of the ROC has contributed to its political stability in recent years because most people desire political stability and continued economic prosperity. In recent years the ruling party in Taiwan expanded the scope of general elections to three important bodies: the National Assembly (to elect the president); the Legislative Yuan (the powerful legislative body); and the Control Yuan (the watchdog).

There is much broader political participation by the Taiwanese. The distinction between the "Taiwanese" and the "mainlanders" is artificial and has been perceived mistakenly by some foreign observers. The distinction has also been seized upon by a small group of politically ambitious people who want to exploit the "gap of origins."

Ethnically, all Chinese in Taiwan are of the same origin. The distinction between them is nothing like the difference between a black and a white American. People from different provinces of China speak different dialects or, more accurately, use different pronunciations of the same Chinese words and sentences. Having lived for more than thirty years in Taiwan, they all speak good Mandarin, with the same accent. Thanks to the good language programs in the elementary schools and due to television and radio, the way the Chinese people speak the Chinese language has been regularized. Now the young Chinese in Taiwan tend to speak Chinese like television newscasters. The young generation, all born in Taiwan, are not aware of the distinction between mainlanders and Taiwanese. By intermarriage, the differences are gradually disappearing.

The ruling party has spared no effort to recruit more Taiwanese into the higher echelons of the government and party apparatus. Seventy percent of KMT members and local organizers are now Taiwanese. At the provincial level, thirteen of the seventeen ministers are Taiwanese.

Another unique point about the ROC on Taiwan is that it enjoys a large measure of goodwill throughout the world. Although it has "family troubles" within the Chinese world, it has no external enemies.

Taiwan is situated in a very strategic location. It straddles an important link between the Indian and the Pacific oceans and between Northeast Asia and Southeast Asia. Shipping coming from the Indian Ocean to the Pacific Ocean, or vice versa, must pass through either the Bashi Channel or the Taiwan Strait. Taiwan has significant bases and forces to keep watch on such shipping. Other islands controlled by the ROC are also in good positions to keep a close watch on ships nearby.

Taiwan was one of the advanced bases used by the Japanese for their invasion of the Philippines. During the Vietnam war, Taiwan provided important logistic support for U.S. operations. Bases and fleets are still important multipliers in seapower equations.

Taiwan is now important not only to itself, but also to friendly nations and to its adversaries. In strategy, the retention or the loss of important strategic key terrain is of great importance to all contestants. Nonavailability of Taiwan bases to the noncommunist or the free democratic world could destroy the continuity of Asian sea lines of communication and break Western security links between the Indian and Pacific oceans.

Use of the Taiwan military installations by communist nations to project power into the Western Pacific region would, for all practical purposes, neutralize U.S. use of the Philippines and Ryukyu bases.

ROC's National Interests and Policies

The Chinese people have a deep sense of history. A Chinese is aware of his long history and the highly developed Chinese civilization, of which he is justly proud. For the past 150 years or so, the Chinese have been humiliated by the West and by their own backwardness in modern science and technology. They suffered from the rule of the Manchu government before 1911.

The Revolution of 1911, reflecting the popular demands of the Chinese people, called for: (1) the independence of China and no more humiliations by foreign powers; (2) freedom and democracy; and (3) the well-being of the people. The Chinese people have struggled for these ideals since 1911.

In spite of the Japanese invasion started in 1931 and the civil war after World War II, these goals of Dr. Sun still remain the national objectives of the ROC on Taiwan, where they have been partially achieved.

Now the ROC, facing threats from its main adversary—the PRC—and facing the stern realities of the outside world, seems to have adopted the following policies. They might not have been collected officially; yet in essence they are expressed in public writings.

1. To build up Taiwan as a model province for the reconstruction of all China.

2. To remain in the free, democratic camp of the family of nations and to defend its values and principles.

3. To oppose communism and military expansionism.

4. To coordinate more with neighboring countries in regional defense, and to play an indispensable role in the Pacific Basin.

5. To base the further growth of Taiwan on a sound and prudent economic program.

6. To encourage more participation from the private sector in the decisionmaking process, in national economic enterprises, and in political reform.

7. To increase defense capabilities by better planning, better quality of men and weapons, better training, and higher morale.

8. To improve research and development to strengthen the defense capability of the country.

9. To improve the mobilization systems and civil defense.

10. To utilize nuclear power only for peaceful uses, not for making bombs.

11. To expand substantial contacts with more friendly nations in trade, cultural exchange, and other relations.

12. To improve the educational system, produce better citizens, better scholars, and expertise in all fields (including the natural and the social sciences).

13. To preserve and promote what is good in traditional Chinese culture and life.

The Problems of Unification and the Future of Taiwan

The PRC leadership has never ruled out the use of force to unify China. Being Marxist and communist, the PRC can be counted upon to use military force only after the other means (political, economic, and psychological) have been tried. PRC leaders would try to isolate and squeeze the ROC before launching a military attack. They are not ready for an overseas invasion because favorable conditions needed to ensure their success by military means have not been created.

Under the circumstances, their policy is characterized by a number of "united front" initiatives toward Taiwan. As soon as the United States and the People's Republic of China "normalized" relations on January 1, 1979, the PRC sent a message to compatriots in Taiwan to strive for peaceful reunification of the Motherland. The funeral of Soong Qing-ling (widow of Dr. Sun Yat-sen) provided an opportunity for an invitation to the president of the ROC. More significantly, on the eve of the October National anniversary, 1981, Ye Jianying put forward a nine-point program for reunification with Taiwan by which Taiwan would keep its armed forces and capitalist economy and participate in a government of national unity. Before Liao Zhengzhi died in 1983, he wrote a personal letter to the president of the ROC earnestly urging reunification.

The united front approaches have been ignored or rejected by the government and people in Taiwan.

Some in Taiwan feel that the PRC is addressing public opinion in the United States rather than aiming at Taiwan. The PRC knows that while the living standards in Taiwan are so much higher than those of the PRC, no person in Taiwan would support negotiations with China. People on Taiwan are afraid of losing what they have so laboriously and successfully obtained during the past 30 years.

The story of Tibet also discouraged the people of Taiwan from having faith in negotiating with the PRC. In May 1951, a seventeen-point agreement was signed under duress, absorbing Tibet into the People's Republic of China. The document guaranteed to honor the existing political system, the religious beliefs of the people, and the status of the Dalai Lama. What happened? The People's Liberation Army moved into Tibet. By 1956 a bloodbath had started. The Chinese bombed monasteries and villages and put thousands of Tibetans to death. In the following years there was great destruction of the scriptures and other symbols precious to Tibetans. Suppression of religious worship and certain death caused Tibetan refugees to flood into India and other neighboring countries, including the Dalai Lama, who had to escape. Although the PRC since 1979 has tried to convince the world that the Tibetan people are allowed religious freedom, the Dalai Lama has not returned to his native land.

Unification by direct negotiation between the two parts of China is now unacceptable. The ROC's long-range national objective is to carry out the unfinished tasks of the revolution led by Dr. Sun Yat-sen in 1911. The official line in Taipei on unification is that unless the Chinese Communists agree to exchange their Marxist-Leninist views for the three principles laid down by Dr. Sun Yat-sen, negotiation for reunification is inconceivable.

No matter why negotiations for reunification are not acceptable, the real question is What will be the future of Taiwan? As to that future, nobody knows. Not the ROC, nor the PRC, nor anybody can tell.

Using imagination and rationality, one can nevertheless guess about the future. Taiwan and mainland China might remain separated for a long time, or Taiwan might become a separate political entity affiliated with mainland China in certain aspects. Taiwan might become a fully independent state, or it might be conquered by China. Taiwan might be reunited with China under conditions totally unperceived today, or the ROC might recover the mainland. Who knows?

From earliest times there has been only one China, culturally and genetically. This does not mean China has been always politically united. Throughout history China has been divided, united, then divided again, almost in cycles. China has been divided into two parts, three parts, many parts, but to the Chinese people there remains always only one common heritage—that is, our Chinese Culture.

Wars waged in China had actually taken on forms unlike those waged in European theaters. Very few decisive battles were fought with bloody and total annihilation of enemies. People in the different "warring states" of China were essentially the same ethnic Chinese, who did not hate each other when their "kings" went to battle. Victories and defeats of the contestants were more often decided by political issues than by bloody encounters.

When China was divided, it was usually by terrain features, mostly the big river valleys. But now, as at the end of the Ming dynasty, China is divided by the Taiwan Strait.

For more than 35 years the Republic of China has been, de facto, an independent political entity. Proving valuable in maintaining the general peace and order of the world, it is a fact of international life that might continue for a long time.

The PRC Is Not a Western Security Asset

Some people might think that China, with a population of 1 billion, a land area of 3.5 million square miles, and regular armed forces of more than 4 million officers and men and with large natural resources, must be a great asset to Western security. Because of China's geographical location and its historical border dispute with Russia, people think China has tied down about fifty Soviet divisions along its border that otherwise could have been deployed elsewhere. This view underlies the policies of U.S.-PRC normalization.

Nothing could be more dangerous than policies based on the premise that the PRC is a Western strategic asset in countering threats of the USSR. The concept of the PRC as a security asset is wrong because:

1. The PRC has not tied down Soviet troops along the Chinese border. The Soviets are not only defending against the Chinese, but protecting the Soviet Far East against the United States and its allies, particularly the Japanese.

2. Soviet forces were there long before the PRC-U.S. normalization.

3. Soviet Far Eastern forces were not moved from the European theater, but were created in the region. During the buildup of the Far Eastern forces, the European theater forces were also increased.

4. The USSR, in any case, must be ready to fight a two-front war.

Resource-rich Siberia is under development and must be protected. Soviet troops, missiles, aircraft, and the Pacific Fleet have been growing. The PRC has not stopped this growth and could not have stopped it.

5. Since the U.S.-PRC rapprochement in 1972, the USSR's power and expansion have increased all over the world. The U.S.-PRC linkup seemed actually to have furthered Soviet expansion, as seen by the closer relation between the USSR and Vietnam and Vietnam's invasion of Kampuchea.

6. The PRC has always avoided total commitment to either superpower. It would remain neutral in the beginning, if either superpower tried to knock out the other.

7. The PRC is not and does not want to become a security asset to anybody, even though it may want each superpower to think it can be used for its own benefit.

8. If the PRC should decide, for the time being, to remain substantially friendly toward the United States, it would be its own decision and made out of its conviction that for the immediate future, the combined strategic weapons inventory of the United States, France, the United Kingdom, and the PRC is at least in parity with that of the USSR, deterring the Soviets from risking a confrontation. Therefore, it is safe for the PRC to remain in such a position, buying time needed for its own modernization program.

Arms Sale and the "Sovereignty" Issue

Why was the PRC so fussy about the ROC's request to buy F5Gs from the United States? The F5G is not actually an aircraft the ROC really wants because it needs a better performance aircraft to replace the F5E. The ROC should ask for the F16A or F20A, or other better performance aircraft. The request for F5Gs was refused on the grounds that there was no need for the ROC to purchase newer aircraft. The reason for denying the F5Gs to the ROC was not sound, but was made under PRC pressure.

The PRC is aware that a small number of F5Gs will not change the military balance over the Taiwan Strait. The PRC production rate of aircraft is about 400 per year or the same number of aircraft as in the entire ROC Air Force fighter fleet. The PRC has more than enough MRBMs and IRBMs to neutralize Taiwan's airbases without having to bomb the runways or carry out a fighter sweep.

The PRC's protest of the U.S. arms sale to Taiwan is based not on the relative combat effectiveness of the opposing forces, but on the sovereignty issue. "Sovereignty" has been a term the PRC found useful and used as a "control rod" (like that in a nuclear reactor) to create just enough heat to harass the United States since the Geneva negotiations in 1954. With "sovereignty," the PRC could generate the right amount of heat in U.S.-PRC negotiations to put the United States in an awkward position. It is a negotiating technique used frequently by communist countries to create a deadlock at the beginning of long negotiations.

Taiwan is fundamentally different from Hong Kong. There is still a British colonial government in Hong Kong, but Taiwan is ruled by Chinese only. The government in Taiwan was founded by the Chinese constitution created by representatives of the whole country, including the communist parties after World War II. There is no foreign power on Taiwan; so there is no intervention by a foreign nation in any part of China.

As a free country, the United States can sell to and buy from any country, including weapons. The United States should stand firm on trading with any part of China, and it should decide on what to sell and buy. If arms sales to Taiwan are a genuine infringement on the sovereignty of the PRC, then soybean sales, or any sales, to Taiwan should also constitute an infringement. If the United States feels guilty intervening in another nation's sovereignty to the extent of stopping its support of Taiwan, then it would be accused of violating sovereignty by its policies of occupying Korea and supporting Israel.

In international law, there is no consensus on the definition of the word "sovereignty." Each nation has its own interpretation of the term. The Soviet Union is said to treat sovereignty as partial or conditional. The brotherly socialist states do not have complete sovereignty, thus enabling the Soviet Union to intervene.

Authorities on international law should form a committee or study group to develop the concept of "sovereignty" to suit the contemporary international milieu. Then, when the PRC uses the "sovereignty" issue as a control rod, the matter could be referred to the international committee for study, thus permitting negotiators to move to other meaningful subjects without delay or without giving the Communists another easy victory.

Suggestions for U.S. Policies in the U.S.-ROC-PRC Relationships

Some premises might be usefully restated for the sake of suggesting U.S. policies in the U.S.-PRC-ROC relationship.

Although the future of Taiwan cannot be predicted, it is likely to remain separated from China for a long time. The dynamism of the Taiwan economy, its strategic location, and forces in being make it clear that Taiwan has an important role to play as a link between Northeast and Southeast Asia.

The PRC is independent, flexible in choosing its own strategies vis-à-vis the USSR, the United States, and the Third World, and maintains its own ideology as a Marxist-Leninist state. Its economic growth is slow. The ROC was a faithful ally in World War II and decided to remain in the free, Western, democratic camp.

In strategy, it is not prudent to trade something reliable (the ROC) for something uncontrollable (the PRC). It is not wise for the United States to sacrifice Taiwan on the demand of the PRC for any reason. Tactically, it is a mistake to give up defensible grounds to an enemy even before it attacks. Taiwan is defensible and is determined to defend itself. There is no need for the United States to grant another victory to the Communists. Taiwan has no enemy outside China. Nobody wants to see it "sink." To keep Taiwan's status quo means "no new major crisis."

Strengthening Taiwan's air force and navy will keep the collective sea lines of communication safe in the Bashi Channel and the Taiwan Strait.

The ROC would like to have the United States adopt the following policies to preserve mutual security interests in the Pacific Basin:

1. Keep the Taiwan Relations Act intact.
2. Make no further concessions to the PRC's demands concerning Taiwan.
3. Encourage informal, cooperative studies on such matters as lines of communication and naval cooperation in the Pacific Basin.

With American creativity, it should not be difficult for U.S. policymakers to keep Taiwan "afloat" while conducting negotiations with the PRC.

Conclusions

The Republic of China on Taiwan is economically prosperous and politically stable. It has attained the qualifications of a separate political entity. It has no enemy outside the China mainland.

There is but one cultural or ethnic China. The traditional Chinese culture and way of life is being preserved in Taiwan better than in any other part of China. The world's largest and richest collection of Chinese artifacts is housed in Taiwan. The national goals set by Dr. Sun Yat-sen in

1911 are independence, democracy, and a good quality of life for the people. These are what the ROC is struggling for.

The PRC is not a Western security asset.

Taiwan's defense capability must be maintained to prevent a crisis that might otherwise occur in the Western Pacific. A stable Taiwan is good for regional stability. The United States and the Republic of China should carry on arms sales programs on mutually agreeable terms.

Finally, it must not be overlooked that if the PRC or USSR used Taiwan military installations to project their power into the Western Pacific region, they would, for all practical purposes, neutralize U.S. bases in the Philippines and the Ryukyus. Western security links between East and West Asia could be broken, and the important sea line of communication between the Indian Ocean and the Pacific Ocean would be at risk. Basic wisdom dictates the necessity of friendship and cooperation between the United States and the Republic of China.

Economic Development and Security: Perceptions and Policies of the Republic of China

Shirley W. Y. Kuo

From the national view, successful economic development is an essential factor for security, as human betterment is at the base of social and political stability. From the regional view, close economic cooperation among nations is an efficient means for elimination or reduction of conflict. The economic development of the Republic of China on Taiwan and its underlying perceptions and policies will be examined in these contexts.

Human Betterment

The Principle of the People's Livelihood, a doctrine of Dr. Sun Yat-sen's, is the guiding principle of economic development in the Republic of China. It is defined as "the existence of society, the welfare of the nation, the life of the masses . . . If most of the economic interests of society can be harmonized, the majority of people will benefit and society will progress."[1]

Guided by this principle, the actual objective of economic development is the conquest and harnessing of nature in the service of mankind. Successful economic development should be defined as advancing human betterment through rapid growth, price stability, full employment, more equitable income distribution, diffusion of education, proper sanitation, convenient transportation, adequate housing, prevention of pollution, and settlement of problems of the elderly, labor, poverty, and so on.

An assessment of the performance of Taiwan's economy over three decades reveals that rapid growth was accompanied by stable prices, successful labor absorption, and improved income distribution.

In a developed country where the production of goods and services is in excess of the people's basic needs, a higher growth rate advances the standard of living. However, in an underdeveloped country where not enough food can be produced to support basic needs, higher growth makes life possible. At the close of World War II, per capita income in Taiwan was about U.S. $70. The per capita income has increased rapidly, reaching U.S. $2,543 by 1982. Real gross national product grew at an average annual rate of 9.2 percent over three decades. The goods and services produced in 1982 in Taiwan were eleven times greater than those produced in 1952. Rapid growth has brought significant improvement in people's lives.

The reduction of unemployment is a good way to combat poverty and social unrest because unemployment means zero wage income. Unemployment in Taiwan, which stood higher than 6 percent in the 1950s, was reduced to less than 3 percent by the end of the 1960s. The significance of near-full employment is not only that jobs will be available for everyone, but also that real wages rise with increasing productivity. During the 1960s, the labor force was rapidly absorbed by the lower-wage industries in which unskilled labor constitutes a relatively large portion. As a result, the wage rate of unskilled labor rose more rapidly than that of skilled labor, making possible a greater increase in the incomes of lower-income families.

Taiwan's economy enjoyed very stable prices in the 1960s, increasing at only a 3 percent annual rate on the average. Although prices rose rapidly in 1974 and in 1979–1980 due to the oil crises, inflation was stemmed immediately after each crisis. For 1983 the inflation rate is low; the wholesale price index recorded a negative 2 percent growth in July, and the consumer price index increased by only 2 percent.

Income distribution in Taiwan has been among the most equitable in the developing world[2] and is improving. During 1964–1981 the income share of the poorest 40 percent of families rose progressively from 20.3 percent to 22.6 percent. The income share of the richest 20 percent of families declined from 41.1 percent to 37.0 percent. The equitable income distribution, amid rapid industrialization and urbanization, was realized because of Taiwan's successful land reform, its special topographic features, its emphasis on balanced growth, and its decentralized industrial development.

Successful land reform was implemented during 1949–1953. Reduction of rents and higher yields resulted in an increase of more than 80 percent in average farm incomes. With two-thirds of the island being mountainous and most of the arable area concentrated on its west coast, economic activities in Taiwan are heavily concentrated in one-third of its area. The four largest cities, Taipei, Taichung, Tainan, and Kaohsiung, are rather evenly spaced to form balanced urban centers. The government advocated balanced growth, and the interdependence of agriculture and industry was strongly emphasized.[3] Policies aimed at improving equity between rural and urban regions were manifested in an emphasis on rural irrigation, electrification, education, transportation, and other rural construction. As a result, the irrigation system was diffused over most of the cultivated area. Electrification was extended to every home. Education was spread and promoted, not only to males but also to females. Excellent road and rail networks spread all over the island. The mileage of rural roads rapidly increased. Technical assistance through the Joint Commission on Rural Reconstruction and through farmers' associations was enhanced. Thus were laid sound foundations for a marked spatial dispersion of economic development. Past industrial development was extremely rural-oriented to provide the advantages of easier acquisition of raw materials, rural laborers, and cheaper land. Thus, the relatively dispersed character of Taiwan's industrialization led to the proportion of industrial establishments in the five largest cities being only 34 percent of the total in 1951, a figure that remains virtually unchanged in 1971, and to the proportion of persons employed in manufacturing in the cities actually declining from 43 to 37 percent between 1956 and 1966.[4]

The rapid rate of employment generation, leading to full employment in 1971, provided unskilled labor with job opportunities. Newcomers and unemployed individuals were absorbed by the nonagricultural sector, particularly light manufacturing industries. Thus the rapid absorption of unskilled labor contributed substantially to the rise in relative incomes of lower-income families, urban and rural. Moreover, an increasing share of off-farm income in the total income of farm families impeded ever-widening income gaps between sectors. A typical farm family received 79 percent of its income from nonagricultural activities in 1979. During 1966–1969, while per-family income in both farm and nonfarm sectors showed a considerable increase in all income brackets, nonagricultural income was the major source of increased farm-family income.

Economic development brought significant social welfare benefits. The literacy rate increased to 90.2 percent in 1981, up from 45 percent in 1946. Over the same period the percentage of school-age children in primary schools increased from 78.6 percent to 99.8 percent. In 1968, nine years of education was made compulsory. Transportation construction was intensified during 1974–1978 through implementation of the "ten major projects." Living space per head increased to 17.9 square meters in 1980, and the share of dwelling investment in the GNP increased to 4.5 percent in 1980 from 1 percent in 1952. The wide-scale diffusion of public utilities increased in scope far more than can be measured in terms of income. For example, electrification grew to 99.7 percent in 1980 compared with 33 percent in 1949.

All these are the result of economic development, and this achievement was the cornerstone of social and political stability in Taiwan over the past three decades.

Contribution to Defense Ability

The agricultural share in the GDP dropped from 32 percent to 7 percent, and the industrial share increased from 22 percent to 50 percent. Particularly since 1971, capital- and technology-intensive industries such as metals, electronics, and machinery, closely related to defense industries, were a dominant share of light industries. This shift from agriculture to industry and from labor-intensive light manufacturing to more capital- and technology-intensive manufacturing is conducive to defense ability.

The improvement in financial ability is the third force. The Taiwanese economy has had a trade surplus for more than ten years. As a result, its financial credibility is high. Despite the heavy defense burden, the government budget has had surpluses for more than ten years. The tax burden of the economy has been relatively low, as total taxes have equaled less than 25 percent of the GNP.

Thus, with the rise in per capita income, upgrading of the economic structure, advancement of technology, and improvement in financial conditions, the people of the Republic of China on Taiwan have contributed much of themselves to making their country safer.

Perceptions and Policies

That tells the success story of Taiwan. An essential factor contributing to this success was an "institutional environment" favorable to the exercise of private entrepreneurial talent. A second factor can be traced to the resource aspect: capital and labor. The success story of the ROC is traceable, partially, to the availability of resource inflows from abroad, particularly from the United States, that augmented the nation's import and investment capacity. Thus with a liberalized, externally oriented policy in the 1960s, Taiwan was able to expand manufactured exports rapidly due to the advantages of its abundance of inexpensive, diligent, and educated labor.

The remarkable, impressive trade and industrial growth achievements of the developing countries in the Pacific Basin indicate that it will remain among the most dynamic regions in the world in the 1980s and the 1990s. This optimism is reinforced by the two biggest economies in the free world, the United States and Japan, in this region.

The cooperative features among countries in the region are obvious if we examine the shares of trade conducted by one country with other countries within the region. Trade between the other states of the Pacific Basin and the United States, which has a more global orientation than any other country in the world, equaled 36 percent of total U.S. exports and 50 percent of total U.S. imports in 1981. The corresponding export and import figures for other countries were Japan, 49 percent and 44 percent; the Philippines, 71 percent and 57 percent; Thailand, 51 percent and 62 percent; South Korea, 59 percent and 60 percent;[5] and the Republic of China on Taiwan, 53 percent and 60 percent.

Economic cooperation can be firm only if it is based on the mutual interests of the countries involved. The trade of the Republic of China with countries in the region shows some complementarity. Trade between the ROC and the United States and Japan shows that the ROC has been exporting relatively labor-intensive, light manufacturing goods in exchange for machinery and manufactured intermediate goods.[6] Since the United States and Japan are in a better position to phase out labor-intensive goods and ought to concentrate on their capital goods sector in which they are known to be most competitive, this pattern of trade well fits the national interests of the trading parties.

The trade between the ROC and ASEAN and ANZUS countries (excluding Singapore) shows that exports of the ROC to these countries have been concentrated in manufacturing goods, which comprised 85 percent of all exports to this group in 1982. Imports from these countries (excluding Singapore) have been mainly raw materials and resource-oriented semifinished products, which comprised about 80 percent of all imports in 1982. This evident complementarity between the trading parties reveals sound mutual interests and forms a firm foundation for economic cooperation.

However, the competitive character of trade is unavoidable. Particularly in the 1980s, the weakening of some industries in the developed countries vis-à-vis the competition from the newly industrializing countries and the near-NICs has aroused protectionism, even though it is against long-term development. More and more nontariff barriers have been imposed. Import quotas and so-called voluntary export quotas have often been applied, mainly to exports of labor-intensive manufactures. On the other hand, newcomers in the international market have been accelerating their exports of cheap-labor products.

To pursue further growth, the Taiwanese economy has been undergoing a transition from light industries to skill- , technology- , and knowledge-intensive industries so that its trade goods can be tailored to the new world market. This is a way of avoiding conflict. For further advanced development, intermediate inputs, parts, and machinery and equipment will still have to be imported from developed countries. Technology should be transferred. Raw materials and semifinished products ought to be imported from other countries. This indicates that the close ties of the Republic of China with other Pacific Basin countries will be further tightened in the future as a way of promoting mutual interests.

Notes

1. Dr. Sun Yat-sen, *The Three Principles of the People.*

2. H. B. Chenery, M. S. Ahluwalia, C. L. G. Bell, J. H. Duloy, and R. Jolly, *Redistribution with Growth* (London: Oxford University Press, 1974).

3. T. F. Ho, *A Biography of Mr. Chen Chen* (Anti-Communist Publisher, 1965), pp. 172–75.

4. Gustav Ranis, "Industrial Development," in Walter Galenson, ed., *Economic Growth and Structural Change in Taiwan: The Postwar Experience of the Republic of China* (Ithaca, N.Y.: Cornell University Press, 1979).

5. Chong-yah Lim, "Trade in Manufactures: A Singapore Perspective" (Paper presented at the Korea Development Institute Workshop on Pacific Cooperation Task Force on Trade in Manufactured Goods, Seoul, Korea, June 28–July 1, 1983).

6. Shirley W. Y. Kuo, *The Taiwan Economy in Transition* (Boulder, Colo.: Westview Press, 1983).

The Republic of China and the Pacific Basin: Policy Perspectives in the 1980s

Yung Wei

In the 1980s the Asian-Pacific region is confronted with challenges in economic development and political security. The increasing Soviet military presence in the area, the unresolved Afghanistan situation, and the continuing conflict in Indochina all add to the anxieties of leaders of Asian and Pacific countries. The "normalization" between the United States and mainland China has not returned normalcy to the region. On the contrary, there is still worry among leaders of Asian-Pacific nations over future development in China and its effects on the external behavior of the Chinese Communists.

How can states in the Pacific region manage their foreign relations to minimize the probability of involvement in another military conflict in the region? How can they strengthen their national defense without overtaxing their economies and without being thought to harbor aggressive designs by neighboring states? How can they be assured a steady supply of oil and nuclear fuel so that their economies will not be threatened? What arrangements can they develop to safeguard trade routes, particularly the crucial sea-lanes and straits, amid increasing Soviet naval power in the Pacific and Indian oceans? What workable schemes and approaches can the noncommunist states in the Asian-Pacific region adopt to promote cooperation among themselves? These are but a few key questions confronting the leaders of this region and their allies.

To resolve some of the questions, various schemes of international cooperation have been developed in the past two decades. Yet these schemes have centered basically around economic cooperation, even a deliberate avoidance of any discussion of issues relating to national security. Still, national security in the shifting balance of power in the Pacific region is definitely a paramount concern among Asian leaders.

This paper will suggest answers to these questions by examining the factors that affect the security environment of the Asian-Pacific region. Following the analysis, several conceptual schemes for cooperation are presented. The role of the United States in international cooperation in this region will be a major subject of analysis. Finally, policy perspectives of the Republic of China, concerning the security and prosperity of countries in the Asian-Pacific region, will be examined.

The Security Environment

Since World War II the Asian-Pacific region has been one of the most turbulent areas in the world. In less than three decades this region was ravaged by five regional, but internationally significant, wars: the Korean War, the Vietnam war, the Indian-Pakistani war, the war between India and mainland China, and, most recently, the conflict between Vietnam and mainland China. In addition, intensive and sometimes prolonged internal wars between governmental troops and insurgent forces have been waged on the Chinese mainland, in Malaysia, the Philippines, Indonesia, Thailand, and Kampuchea. Based on these unhappy experiences, the nations in the region have every reason to be sensitive and concerned about their future security.

The major challenges to the security of the Asian-Pacific region include the increasing Soviet military presence in the Pacific and Indian oceans, particularly its naval forces; the problem of energy supply as well as nuclear fuel; the instability of the Korean peninsula; the continuing conflict in Indochina; and the future course of the PRC.

The increasing Soviet military force has been keenly felt from Northeast Asia to the states around the Indian Ocean. The Soviet naval fleet and maritime fleet has increased significantly in recent years. The expanding activities of the Soviet navy in the channels surrounding Japan, Taiwan, the Philippines, Indonesia, and Malaysia have created deep concern among the littoral nations. For this reason the recent military exercises conducted by U.S. forces and its allies throughout the Pacific are generally welcomed.

The countries of Northeast Asia are highly industrialized, yet have poor energy supplies. All depend upon the importation of energy resources, primarily oil from Middle Eastern countries and, increasingly, nuclear fuel from the United States and other Western countries. The maintenance of a sure supply has become one of the most pressing problems in this region.

The conflicts in Indochina remain potential dangers to noncommunist countries in Southeast Asia. The possibility that the Soviet Union and communist China may escalate their conflict concerns many countries in this area, particularly Thailand. If the escalation occurs, the communist states of Southeast Asia might gain military superiority regardless of the outcome of a limited war in Indochina. Furthermore, this competition on land may lead to rivalry in the South China Sea and Indian Ocean, which would be detrimental to the noncommunist countries.

The Future Course of Mainland China

As for developments within mainland China, all the nations in the Pacific region are deeply concerned. Despite the much publicized so-called Four Modernization plans, economic development on mainland China has fallen far behind the original goals. Some modification of the goals and strategies of the development plans were made, reflected in the reports to the Sixth People's Congress. But there are still many problems in the economic development and political readjustment of mainland China. Given the advanced age of Deng Xiaoping, the residual influence of the Cultural Revolution group, and the inability of the Chinese communist system to fulfill its promise to raise the living standard of the Chinese people, the possibility of political instability is high in the post-Deng era. Some analysts point to the new constitution as a safeguard of systematic change, but in a regime that has undergone numerous, abrupt, and drastic changes in its governing structures and policies and where a new constitution is only a political manifesto of the winning faction, promises and plans lose their meaning as guarantors of policy continuity.

Should there be a renewed economic setback and political upheaval, the possibility of using external issues to divert people's attention from internal difficulties is always there. This possibility, coupled with the possibility of rapprochement between communist China and the Soviet Union, should restrain any government of the free world from entering into closer relations with communist China, particularly in the areas of military and militarily related technology transfers.

The relationship between the United States and communist China causes all nations in the region to be deeply concerned. Defense analysts in Japan mention that Taiwan is important to Japanese security because if Okinawa is the southernmost Japanese territory, then Japan is no farther from Taiwan than Japan is from South Korea. Given the importance of the sea passage east of Taiwan, Japan does not want to have Taiwan fall into hostile hands.

The short-lived euphoria of ASEAN over the potential utility of communist China as a counterbalance against the Soviet Union has died down. Mainland China has neither the ability nor the desire to be a protector of the national security of Southeast Asian states. Given the reluctance of the Chinese communist leaders to disassociate themselves from the insurgent forces in the region, there is increasing consensus among Southeast Asian states to consider both the Soviet Union and mainland China as security threats. This may explain their increasing desire to cooperate with the United States and ANZUS states in concerted military exercises.

Policy Perspectives of the Republic of China

The Republic of China (ROC) has basically overcome the shock of severance of diplomatic ties with the United States. Trade between the two countries has increased from U.S. $9.03 billion in 1979 to $13.3 billion in 1982. The ROC is encouraging more purchases of U.S. goods to narrow the imbalance of trade, now in ROC's favor. The ROC has become the nineteenth leading trading nation of the world, and the seventh largest trading partner of the United States. Tourism flourishes between the United States and the ROC. The resumption of Pan American flights to Taipei testifies to the importance of Taiwan in tourism and trade in the Pacific region. Concerning the ROC's relations with other Pacific states, significant progress has been made without fanfare. A major effort has been made to improve relations with ASEAN nations. The visit of Premier Sun to Indonesia indicated interest on both sides in increasing substantive relations. Improvement of relations with Japan resulted in frequent visits to the ROC by members of the Japanese parliament and leaders of the ruling Liberal Democratic Party.

The ROC has also made great efforts to expand its relations with island-states in the Southern Pacific, establishing diplomatic ties with Nauru, Tonga, Western Samoa, and the Solomon Islands. In addition, trade and cultural affairs sections were established both in Sydney and Auckland to expand relations with Australia and New Zealand. Government and business leaders also are quite interested in various activities aimed at increasing cooperation in the Pacific region. Business leaders, scholars, and occasionally officials have participated in various Pacific Basin conferences, including those organized by PBEC, Pacific Community Canberra Seminar, PEC, PCC, and the Pacific Forum. Without question the ROC wants to make sure it will be a part of any major activities in this area.

The ROC is determined to play a positive and active role in the Asian-Pacific area. Given the strategic location of Taiwan in the West Pacific and on the major sea-lanes and routes, coupled with its economic dynamism and political stability, the ROC will remain an asset to the prosperity and security of the free Pacific nations. Despite diplomatic setbacks in the past decade, the government of the ROC has never wavered in its firm commitment to the democratic camp.

The Chinese Communists have made numerous "peace offensives" against the Republic of China. The more notable include the nine points offered by Ye Jianying and the more recent five points expressed by Deng Xiaoping. But the crucial factor remains that for a communist regime that changes its "constitution" like discarding used cars, where political leaders often become "traitors" overnight, and where policymakers often break promises to their own people, assurances and promises to the outside world are empty words.

The government of the ROK has repeatedly declared that it will never give up its goal of eventually reuniting China under the Three People's Principles, that it will not negotiate with the Chinese Communists, and that it will retain a constitutional form of government. It has adopted realistic domestic and foreign policies. In the domestic arena, the ROK recently adopted a ten-year plan for the Taiwan region that incorporates policy goals and strategies in social, economic, cultural, and educational development for the next decade. These goals are included in the annual policy programs of various ministries and agencies. It is projected that by 1989, the total GNP will reach U.S. $125 billion and per capita income will reach U.S. $6,200.

The ROK has also developed an overall plan for foreign relations. Despite the ROC's diplomatic ties with only 23 nations, it has developed "substantive" ties with more than 126 nations and areas of the world. Generally these are quiet, but in the aggregate very important.

The Republic of China and the United States

Of all the diplomatic relations of the ROC, those with the United States are the most important. The reasons are found in political, economic, and security arenas. Politically, the ROC and the United States share basic ideological and national goals. The ROC's plan for reuniting China under the teaching of Dr. Sun Yat-sen is basically consistent with democracy and freedom as proclaimed by every American administration. Economically, the United States is a major trading partner of the ROC, and the trade will increase as time passes.

The most important relationship between the ROC and the United States is in the security arena. It is the ROC's hope that the United States will adopt a policy that will include the following points:

1. Do not recognize the Chinese communist claim of "sovereignty" over Taiwan.

2. Continue supplying the ROC with adequate defensive weapons, including training of personnel using these weapons.

3. Fully implement the provisions in the Taiwan Relations Act and not yield to Chinese communist blackmail or pressure for the revision of the act.

4. Take a firm position, not forcing the free Chinese on Taiwan either to yield to Chinese communist conditions for "unification" or to negotiate under Chinese communist military threat.

5. Refrain from giving assistance to elements of the Taiwan separatist movements. This movement can bring only disaster to the 18 million people in Taiwan by provoking the Chinese communist regime on the mainland to use force against Taiwan.

6. Help the ROC upgrade its scientific and technological standards, and support the ROC's effort to further develop its economy and build various economic networks to enlarge contacts with all nations of the world.

7. Assist the ROC government to improve its international status and maintain, as well as increase, its membership in international organizations.

The Republic of China is determined to remain an active member of the Pacific community, working with all the friendly noncommunist nations to increase prosperity and security in the region. Given the steadfast policy of the government, the vitality of its economy, and the resourcefulness as well as the perseverance of the people of the ROC, with the cooperation of all freedom-loving Pacific nations we have confidence that this goal can be achieved.

Recent Trends in Chinese Foreign Policy

Ralph H. Clough

The first three decades of the People's Republic of China (PRC) have been turbulent. Successive political campaigns in the 1950s culminated in the disastrous Great Leap Forward. The 1960s brought the chaos of the Cultural Revolution, and the 1970s saw two fierce struggles for power, one ending with the death of Lin Biao and the other with the fall of the Gang of Four. Domestic turbulence was matched by external crises: the Korean War, confrontations with the United States in the Taiwan Strait and Vietnam, conflict with India, clashes with Soviet forces at Zhenbaodao, and the brief but bloody incursion into Vietnam. Relations with the Soviet Union swung from alliance and comradeship in the 1950s to tense military confrontation on the border and Chinese denunciation of the Soviet Union as the main threat to world peace. Relations with the United States ranged from war in Korea to efforts to join the United States in a united front against Soviet expansionism. Deploring the turbulence of the past, China's leaders proclaim the need for stability to carry out the Four Modernizations.

Unless some unexpected international crisis occurs nearby, the 1980s will be relatively calm for China in both domestic and foreign affairs. The revolutionary generation is passing, and the new leaders are more bureaucratic, technocratic figures. No charismatic personality capable of inspiring strong loyalty and fierce opposition and able to mobilize the masses to strike down his enemies has appeared. Reacting against the injection of politics into every sphere, the people are more difficult to manipulate with parades and slogans. Leaders tinker with the system, making incremental changes, but they would meet strong resistance instituting radical changes such as Mao attempted.

China's leaders need prolonged stability, not only to consolidate their position and manage the transition from Deng Xiaoping to his successor or successors, but also to regain lost ground in economic development and build an industrial base to modernize China's defenses. Not until the opening of China to the world in recent years could numerous Chinese in influential positions go abroad and learn from firsthand observation how far China lagged behind the industrialized nations. Only a large and growing influx of technology and other knowledge over a long period will enable China to narrow the gap. Deng and his colleagues understand the problems well. They adopted a long-term strategy of expanding technical, scientific, economic, and cultural relations with advanced industrial countries. They see this opening to the outside as vital to meet China's defense needs and the rising expectations of the Chinese people. The longer it continues, the more difficult it will be to re-encage China in a closed, xenophobic system.

Premier Zhao Ziyang, in a November 1982 report to the National People's Congress, forecast the integration of China into the world economy.[1] By 1985, he said, China's foreign trade would increase by 51.8 percent, an average of 8.7 percent annually during the current five-year plan, substantially exceeding the projected growth rate in agricultural and industrial production. He urged the effective use of foreign loans, encouragement of direct investment, and participation in joint ventures by foreign businessmen. He stressed the important role of coastal cities in expanding foreign economic and technological exchange. Guangdong and Fujian should continue their special roles, he said, but Shanghai, Tianjin, and other coastal cities should expand their use of foreign funds and their roles in world markets.

Zhang Aiping, newly appointed defense minister and former director of scientific and technological work in the military, in an authoritative March 1983 article in *Hong Qi,* outlined China's need for defense modernization, the obstacles in the way, and a long-term strategy to attain the goal. He noted that a country the size of China cannot rely on purchasing weapons abroad or on copying foreign weapons. It must develop a modern industry of its own capable of designing and producing adequate modern weapons. Zhang emphasized that while industry is being modernized, the nation should avoid excessive diversion of funds to military purposes that would slow the modernization process. In his stress on production of nuclear weapons, Zhang implied that he considered strengthening China's fledgling nuclear retaliatory capability the quickest and most cost-effective means of deterring the Soviets from employing their greatly superior nuclear capability against China. China must buy time to further its industrial and defense modernization. As Zhang put it, China must "use the present international atmosphere of relative peace to develop as quickly as we can new types of weapons and equipment to strengthen the modernization of national defense."[2]

China and the Superpowers

Since its founding, the PRC's principal foreign policy preoccupation has been its relationships with the superpowers. Only the Soviet Union and the United States are capable of seriously threatening China. Moreover, since the break with the Soviet Union in the early 1960s, the Chinese have characterized the global rivalry between the United States and the Soviet Union as the main cause of turmoil and the greatest threat to world peace. During the 1970s they attacked the Soviet Union as the most aggressive and dangerous of the two superpowers, but since 1981 most of their authoritative public pronouncements have dropped this explicit distinction.

Chinese public statements, however, do not conceal that Deng and his associates view the Soviet Union, not the United States, as the primary threat to China's security. Ever since the Soviet buildup on China's frontier culminating in the clash at Zhenbaodao and the withdrawal of U.S. forces from Vietnam, the Soviet menace has been the prime concern of China's defense planners. In Hu Yaobang's report to the Twelfth Party Congress in September 1982, he denounced the buildup of Soviet forces on the Sino-Soviet and Sino-Mongolian borders, Soviet support for Vietnam's invasion of Kampuchea, and Soviet military occupation of Afghanistan as "grave threats to the peace of Asia and to China's security." Hu's attacks on U.S. policies toward Taiwan and Israel do not refer to these policies as threatening China's security.[3]

Although Chinese leaders have not ceased to regard the Soviet Union as the principal security threat, they have altered their views on the immediacy of the threat and the appropriate tactics for dealing with it. They long ago discarded Mao's slogan, "Dig tunnels deep and store grain everywhere," and have converted to other uses many of the air raid shelters dug after the Zhenbaodao conflict. China's acquisition of a small nuclear retaliatory capability and its growing relationship with the United States reduced concern over an early Soviet military attack on China. Deng's willingness to order Chinese forces to invade the Soviet Union's ally, Vietnam, in 1979 demonstrated his confidence that Soviet military action against China was unlikely. Minimizing the risk by announcing in advance his intention to limit the scope and duration of the incursion, Deng brashly tweaked the nose of the Russian bear.

Although the Chinese perception of a Soviet threat to their security became the principal cause of strain in Sino-Soviet relations, ideological differences over relations within the international communist movement add to that strain. The Chinese no longer attack Soviet domestic policies as "revisionist" now that China has adopted policies, such as the use of foreign funds, that it formerly condemned in the Soviet Union. The Chinese attack the Soviets for arrogating to themselves the right to interfere in the affairs of other communist parties. Hu Yaobang stated that "the practice of one Party compelling other Parties to make their policies serve its own Party and state policies, or even resorting to armed intervention in other countries . . . can only undermine the very foundation of the international communist movement." He reminded his listeners that "our Party has suffered from the attempt of a self-elevated paternal party to keep us under control."[4]

Resumption of political talks with the Soviet Union in 1982 suggest that the Chinese see advantages in a relaxation of Sino-Soviet tension. Privately, they speak pessimistically of prospects for Soviet modification of policies that the Chinese see as creating a threatening encirclement of China. Nevertheless, talks with the Soviets serve other useful purposes. Less tension would help create the stable international environment China needs to pursue its long-term economic development. Expanded trade and cultural exchanges with the Soviet bloc further the reduction of tension and contribute to Chinese development. Sino-Soviet talks create uneasiness in Hanoi, thus adding to strains between the Soviets and Vietnamese. In addition, they counter criticisms by some Chinese and some Third World countries that Deng's policies of 1979–1980 were tilting China too far in the direction of the United States.

The recent modification of China's posture toward the Soviet Union probably was also intended to warn the U.S. government not to take China for granted. The notion of maneuvering for advantage within the U.S.-Soviet-China triangle doubtless influences the Chinese, as it does the Soviets and Americans. The potential effect on any third party—of policies adopted by the first and second parties toward each other—is only one factor considered in adopting the policy and not necessarily the most important one. To focus exclusively on triangular maneuvering to explain the policies of the three powers toward each other produces skewed and misleading conclusions.

As the weakest party in the triangle, China's capacity to influence the superpowers is limited. The Chinese can create uneasiness in the United States by making friendly gestures toward Moscow. Some Americans would then urge the U.S. government to make concessions to Beijing on disagreements between the two countries to prevent China from moving closer to the Soviet Union. This is a tricky game for the Chinese, however, for they could easily overplay their hand. If many Americans were convinced that China was moving closer to the Soviet Union than to the United States, the U.S. government would be less, rather than more, likely to make concessions sought by the Chinese.

The Chinese are ambivalent about their relationship with the United States. Close relations offer many advantages, both in terms of China's development and its position relative to the Soviet Union. Yet Chinese leaders learned from their association with the Soviet Union in the 1950s the danger of becoming too close to and too dependent on one of the superpowers. So sensitive have the Chinese become that Hu Yaobang expunged from the record the intimate Sino-Soviet cooperation of the early 1950s. "We have shown the world by deeds that China never attaches itself to any big power or group of powers," declared Hu.[5] No doubt he meant that China had not, for the past two decades, attached itself to any big power and will not in the future. Hence, the constant stress on the *independence* of China's foreign policy.

To say that China conducts an independent foreign policy does not mean that China's leaders have freedom of choice in making foreign policy decisions. Like leaders of other countries, including the superpowers, they are subject to many constraints. Neither does an independent Chinese foreign policy mean a policy of equidistance from the superpowers. Whether China leans more closely to the Soviet Union or the United States depends on its leaders' calculations of China's national interests and their own domestic power positions at the time.

The 1980s favor China's continuing relatively close relations with the United States, although China's leaders probably cannot regard a close *military* relationship with the United States as a realistic option for China for several reasons.

First, it would alarm the Soviet Union without producing the massive flow of new weapons required to give Chinese forces greatly increased capability against superior Soviet military power. China could not afford to buy the weapons required, and the United States could not provide them by grant or loan without greatly increasing the U.S. budget deficit, which has already become a prospective heavy burden. Moreover, the United States hesitated to furnish China some of the dual-use technology to modernize China's defense industry.

Second, a U.S. commitment to assist in China's defense could not be relied on. Would the United States risk Los Angeles or New York to prevent a Soviet nuclear attack on Beijing or Shanghai? Or would the United States use its military connection with China as a bargaining chip in its global rivalry with the Soviet Union rather than in the long-term effort to strengthen China's position in the strategic triangle?

Third, China's leaders are reasonably confident that China can deter a large-scale Soviet military attack during the several decades needed to build a modern defense industry. The size and population of China are daunting, and China's small but growing nuclear retaliatory capability discourages possible resort to nuclear weapons to offset the Soviet manpower disadvantage. Soviet inability to subdue Afghan resistance must give pause to military planners considering contingencies involving military force against China.

Despite their rejection of a close military relationship with the United States as neither feasible nor desirable, China's leaders favor a productive and expanding Sino-American relationship that would retain limited cooperation in the military area and improve prospects for coping with Soviet pressures or obtaining Soviet concessions. Soviet threats to China's security and the Soviet tendency to resort more to the stick than to the carrot in foreign policy counsel the advisability of good working relations with the other superpower.

More important than an existing or potential military relationship is China's access to U.S. technology for modernizing and expanding its industry, including its capability for producing military hardware. The United States has far more to contribute than any other country because of the size of its market, its broad range of advanced technology, the capability of U.S. firms to help develop China's resources—such as offshore oil—and the extent, openness, and variety of American educational and training opportunities.

The euphoria of 1979–1980, when Americans and Chinese welcomed the normalization of relations, was excessive and could not last. Exaggerated expectations produced disappointment. High-flown rhetoric on ceremonial occasions lauding friendship between the Chinese and American people masked profound differences between the two societies and divergencies in the foreign policies of the two countries. Leaders on both sides, pressed by domestic critics of their policies and forced to cope with knotty problems that cropped up in the relationship, took a more reserved view of its benefits.

Some problems in Sino-American relations are similar to those that the United States has with many other countries, such as the dispute over quotas to be allocated to Chinese textile imports. Others, such as the Hu Na defection case, grow out of differences in political systems and lack of sensitivity or understanding in handling the problem. Still others arise from an ambivalence within the U.S. government and among Americans over whether U.S. interests will be served by creating a strong Chinese military force. Some Americans stress the need to strengthen China to make it a more effective partner to counter Soviet expansionism, while others are skeptical of the feasibility of U.S.-PRC military cooperation against the Soviets. They fear that Chinese military power might be used in ways inimical to U.S. interests. The result is debate over the sale to China of technology that would strengthen its military capability, including dual-use technology ordered for civilian purposes, but which could be diverted to weapons or military production. Secretary of Commerce Malcolm Baldrige, on a June 1983 trip to China, announced an easing of restrictions on the sale of dual-use technology that would increase such sales but not end either the debate among Americans or Chinese dissatisfaction with their inability to purchase all the U.S. technology they want.

Another source of strain in U.S.-PRC relations is widespread concern among conservative Chinese that excessive U.S. influence in China would undermine the communist system by introducing subversive and decadent ideas. They viewed with alarm the enthusiasm with which many young people greeted the normalization of relations with the United States and the popularity among them of things American. They quickly squelched the dissident movement symbolized by Democracy Wall, which criticized China's lack of Western-style democracy and respect for human rights. They attributed the spread of corruption in the economic system to the infiltration of decadent bourgeois culture from outside China.

The contradiction between the need for Western technology and the fear of Western adulteration of Chinese values is the theme of a persistent and unresolved debate among Chinese since the nineteenth century. In urging expansion of foreign trade, import of advanced foreign technology, and increased use of foreign capital, Hu Yaobang warned: "In no circumstances must we forget that capitalist countries and enterprises will never change their capitalist nature simply because they have economic and technological exchanges with us. While pursuing the policy of opening to the outside, we must guard against, and firmly resist, the corrosion of capitalist ideas, and we must combat any worship of things foreign or fawning on foreigners."[6] The resultant efforts to prevent bourgeois contamination by limiting contacts between Chinese and foreigners and by sharply restricting social science research in China by foreign scholars have somewhat dimmed the early American enthusiasm for relations with China.

The primary obstacle, however, to closer relations between China and the United States is the dispute over Taiwan. The United States has made important concessions to China three times: in the agreement on the Shanghai Communiqué in 1972, in the normalization agreement of 1978, and in the joint communiqué of August 1982. In each case, the Chinese withdrew from the maximum demands to reach agreement, but served notice that the issue would not be resolved until the United States no longer stood in the way of the PRC's recovery of sovereignty over Taiwan.

The Chinese made what they considered a generous offer to the authorities in Taiwan in Ye Jianying's nine-point proposal of September 1981. Taiwanese authorities promptly rejected it. Beijing's difficulty is that, with its lower standard of living, more repressive society, and history of recurrent political upheavals, it has little to offer to attract the Taiwanese or give them confidence that promises made would be kept.

Chinese leaders must find it difficult to swallow that the people of Taiwan see serious risks and few advantages from reunification with the mainland on Beijing's terms. Consequently, they blame the Taiwan Relations Act and U.S. sales of arms to Taiwan for encouraging the Taiwan authorities to reject negotiations. In the August 1982 joint communiqué, worked out in ten months of difficult negotiations, the United States pledged that arms sales to Taiwan would not exceed those of recent years—either quantitatively or qualitatively—and that they would gradually be reduced. This agreement temporarily eased tension over the issue. It is almost certain, however, that the Chinese will raise the issue again and press the United States to set a date to phase out arms sales to Taiwan.

In the August 1982 joint communiqué, the PRC declared its fundamental policy to be to strive for a peaceful solution to the Taiwan issue. PRC leaders are undoubtedly serious in their desire to recover sovereignty over Taiwan peacefully. Using military force to conquer Taiwan would be an embarrassing admission that the PRC was unable to convince the authorities and people of Taiwan of the advantages of reunification. It would also be extremely costly militarily and would leave the PRC too seriously weakened to face Soviet threats to its security. It would severely damage PRC relations with the United States and Japan and slow down its economic development and defense modernization. Moreover, a Taiwan with a war-crippled economy and a sullen, hostile population would be more of a burden than an asset, perhaps for a long time. Thus, a military attack on Taiwan in the near future is improbable.

Despite increasing Chinese criticism of the United States, especially on the Taiwan issue and technology transfer, substantive relations between the United States and China expanded. The United States became China's third largest trading partner after Japan and Hong Kong. The two countries exchange hundreds of official delegations every year in a variety of fields. American firms have been awarded contracts to help develop a large coalfield and to explore for offshore oil in the South China Sea. Some 10,000 Chinese students and scholars are studying in the United States, more than in any other country. Between 1979 and 1983, the United States and China signed 21 agreements on cooperation in science and technology. President Reagan's science adviser, George A. Keyworth, visiting Beijing in May 1983, described this program as "the most successful scientific and technical cooperation in the world."[7]

These trends demonstrate the value placed by the Chinese on the American connection in spite of their dissatisfaction with some aspects of it. When the Chinese government banned imports of several American commodities in retaliation for U.S. quotas on Chinese textile imports and canceled several planned cultural exchanges in retaliation for the United States' granting political asylum to Hu Na, the retaliations were carefully selected to express Chinese irritation forcefully without seriously damaging the fabric of U.S.-PRC relations. The manifold benefits to China of the U.S. connection, together with the Soviet threat to China's security, probably will result in further enhancement of Washington-Beijing relations, even though Taiwan casts a cloud on the relationship.

Japan, Korea, and Hong Kong

Japan, economic powerhouse of the Western Pacific, is China's most important neighbor. A friendly state, it could make a unique contribution to China's economic development. Were it to turn hostile and become militarized, however, it could pose a serious threat, especially if Japanese industry and military potential were allied with the Soviet Union. Even a neutralized Japan, no longer linked to the United States and subject to intimidation by Soviet military power, would increase the threat to Chinese security. Consequently, the Chinese have a strong interest in the continued health of the U.S.-Japan security relationship and the Japanese self-defense capability.

The Chinese are ambivalent concerning the appropriate level for Japanese military power. They see the Japanese threatened, as they are, by the steady strengthening of Soviet forces in Northeast Asia, including the emplacement of SS-20 missiles and Backfire bombers near their territory. They support Japan's claim to the Northern Islands seized by the Soviets at the end of World War II. They worked hard to persuade the Japanese to sign a peace treaty and friendship treaty in 1978, embodying a clause opposing hegemonism, which Moscow (and Beijing itself) regarded as an anti-Soviet action. On the other hand, while accepting the need for a Japanese defense force to counter the Soviets, Beijing does not, like Washington, urge the Japanese to accelerate their defense buildup. On the contrary, the Chinese feel uneasy whenever signs of a revival of Japanese militarism appear. In 1982 they stridently denounced the Japanese attempt to soften the description in Japanese textbooks of their aggression against China. Pointing out that "Japanese militarism unleashed one war of aggression after another against China, inflicting colossal calamities on the Chinese people and grievous damage on the Japanese people themselves,"

Hu Yaobang warned that "some forces in Japan are whitewashing the past Japanese aggressions against China and other East Asian countries, and are carrying out activities for the revival of Japanese militarism."[8]

The textbook dispute was resolved prior to Prime Minister Zenko Suzuki's visit to China in September 1982. While it temporarily soured the atmosphere between the two countries, it did not interfere with the main business between them—the economic relations essential to China's modernization program. Japan is China's principal trading partner, chief foreign participant in the giant Baoshan steel mill project and other new plants, co-operator in the production of offshore oil in the Bohai Gulf, and provider of needed scientific, technical, and managerial training for Chinese. Japan's proximity, the long experience of the Japanese in dealing with China, and Japan's ability to provide a wide range of industrial products at competitive prices will ensure its continued predominance in the China market. The reluctance of Chinese leaders to become dependent on a single country, however, will limit the production of the market allocated to Japan and enable Americans and Europeans to secure substantial shares.

Chinese policy toward Korea is shaped by two fundamental concerns: (1) prevention of renewed conflict on the peninsula, which would drag China into a confrontation with the United States and Japan and gravely jeopardize its progress toward modernization; and (2) rivalry with the Soviet Union for influence in Pyongyang. Thus, the Chinese must formally back the North Korean position on the unification of Korea and the withdrawal of U.S. forces from South Korea, while discouraging Kim Il-sung from attempting to unify Korea by force.

Maintaining friendly relations with North Korea is more important than ever for China since the Soviet alliance with Vietnam. Soviet predominance in North Korea would constitute another link in its chain of military encirclement of China, particularly if it could use warm-water ports in North Korea for the Soviet navy. The Chinese have several advantages over the Soviets in competing for influence: the historical and cultural affinity between Chinese and Koreans, common interests as developing nations, participation of Chinese soldiers in the Korean War, and Kim Il-sung's fear that the Soviets might some day try to set up by force in North Korea a government more to their liking—as they did in Czechoslovakia and Afghanistan. The Chinese government is at a disadvantage, however, being unable to compete with the Soviets in providing North Korea with modern technology and weapons.

Beginning with Premier Zhao Ziyang's visit to Pyongyang in December 1981, the Chinese sought by a series of high-level visits to cement their relations with North Korea. Deng Xiaoping and Hu Yaobang made an unusual secret visit to North Korea in April 1982 for Kim Il-sung's seventieth birthday celebration. Kim was received in China in September 1982 with great fanfare and conducted personally by Deng Xiaoping on a tour of Sichuan. Recently, Kim's son and designated successor, Kim Chong-il, is reported to have visited China. There are other signs that the Chinese overcame their distaste for cults of personality and dynastic succession to curry favor in Pyongyang.

The growing importance of South Korea in global economic and political affairs made it increasingly difficult for China and the Soviet Union to comply with North Korea's insistence that they have nothing to do with South Korea. North Korean protests appear to have caused the Chinese to reduce their backdoor trade with South Korea, which had reached significant proportions in 1981. But the recent hijacking of a Chinese civil aircraft to South Korea compelled the Chinese to send an official delegation to Seoul to negotiate the return of the plane, crew, and passengers. The Interparliamentary Union meeting scheduled for Seoul in September 1983, the Asian Games in 1986, and the Olympics in 1988 will test Chinese willingness to refrain from attending important international events to accommodate Kim Il-sung.

The approach of 1997, the year the British lease on the New Territories expires, is forcing China to decide the future of Hong Kong. The Chinese inserted in their new constitution a provision for special administrative districts, intended to apply to Hong Kong and Taiwan, which permits such areas to maintain political and economic systems differing from those in the rest of China. The Chinese and British governments, which agree on the importance of preserving Hong Kong's prosperity, began negotiations on the timing and modalities of the PRC's "recovery of sovereignty" over Hong Kong. Chinese officials indicated that the territory will be governed by the people of Hong Kong, but the selection of the new administration and the source of its authority remain to be determined.

Analysts of the Hong Kong problem generally agree that the prosperity of Hong Kong depends on the confidence that businessmen have in its future. Confidence, in turn, depends on maintaining three critical underpinnings: (1) a freely convertible currency, (2) a basically unchanged legal system, and (3) an administration that keeps taxes low and interferes little in economic life.

Chinese leaders recognize the economic importance of Hong Kong to China since it produces 30–40 percent of China's foreign exchange earnings. They clearly want to preserve its economic dynamism under Chinese sovereignty. But whether they can tolerate the laissez-faire administration that has fostered Hong Kong's dynamism will be a severe test. The decline in the value of the Hong Kong dollar in 1983 suggests some lack of confidence among Hong Kong investors that the PRC can pass the test.

The Third World

Chinese foreign policy since mid-1981, in addition to tempering expectations concerning relations with the United States and seeking a lowering of tensions with the Soviet Union, placed greater stress on China's relations with the Third World. The increased emphasis is largely rhetorical, based on a feeling that China and other Third World countries have suffered in common from domination by imperialists and suffer unfair treatment by advanced industrial nations today. Despite the rhetorical inclusion of China in the Third World, most Chinese do not equate China with other large Third World countries such as Brazil or India. They see China as unique in size, population, and historical importance. Compared with China, the superpowers are latecomers on the international scene. China did not join the nonaligned group of nations or other bodies that claim to represent Third World views. Despite Chinese calls for increased cooperation among Third World countries, its economic aid to developing countries and the training of Third World students in China have declined. China competes with other developing countries for a share of the funds available from international financial institutions.

China's principal foreign policy concerns are security and economic development. Third World countries can make little positive contributions to China's needs in either area. Security depends primarily on China's relations with the United States and the Soviet Union, and hopes for economic development rest principally on relations with Japan, the United States, and Western Europe. China's substantive relations with Third World countries, as contrasted with rhetoric, were concentrated mainly in areas close to China and based on a hardheaded evaluation of Chinese national interests. Thus the Chinese opposed Soviet action in Afghanistan, maintained their close relationship with Pakistan, and sought improvement in relations with India, Nepal, and Burma.

The Chinese are deeply concerned about the situation in Southeast Asia, where they regard the Vietnamese occupation of Kampuchea and the Soviet alliance with Vietnam as a long-term threat to China's security. They have given matériel and diplomatic support to the Pol Pot forces, as the strongest Kampuchean group continuing armed opposition to Vietnam, and more recently supported the coalition government headed by Prince Norodom Sihanouk. China shifted from opposing ASEAN, as a tool of the United States, to cooperating with ASEAN states in pressing for the withdrawal of Vietnamese forces from Kampuchea.

The "lesson" administered to the Vietnamese by the Chinese attack in 1979 proved less successful than Chinese leaders expected. It revealed serious shortcomings in Chinese military operations. It failed to weaken Vietnamese resolve to maintain a grip on Kampuchea and appears to have strengthened, rather than weakened, the ties between Hanoi and Moscow. The Vietnamese, with Soviet aid, have so strengthened their defenses north of Hanoi that a second Chinese attempt to bring them in line by an attack across the border is unlikely.

China's cooperation with the Thais in opposing Vietnamese occupation of Kampuchea included termination of Chinese support to the communist insurgency in Thailand. Loss of Chinese support and of sanctuaries in Kampuchea and Laos, combined with improvement in the Thai government's counterinsurgency policies, resulted in a sharp decline in the size and effectiveness of the insurgency. Elsewhere, however, the refusal of Chinese leaders to renounce categorically moral support for communist insurgents remains an obstacle to further improvement of relations with ASEAN countries, particularly Indonesia, Malaysia, and Singapore.

The Indonesian government has been unwilling to resume diplomatic relations with Beijing, suspended in 1965, and Singapore has never established diplomatic relations with the PRC.

Implications for the United States

Chinese concerns with security and economic development will favor U.S. efforts to maintain closer and more cooperative relations with China than the Soviet Union can. The advantages to the United States of such a relationship will—

1. Eliminate the need to deploy U.S. forces in the Western Pacific to counter the possible use of Chinese forces against U.S. interests.
2. Diminish the risk of divisive differences with Japan over China policy.
3. Reduce the chances for Sino-Soviet cooperation against U.S. interests.
4. Improve prospects for further constructive Chinese participation in the economic life of the rapidly developing Pacific Basin community.
5. Increase the economic and political cost to the PRC of resorting to force against Taiwan.

6. Keep open the prospect for China to become an increasingly important trading partner for the United States as its grows.

Some lessening of tension between Moscow and Beijing probably will occur, but the Soviets are unlikely to make the concessions to the Chinese needed to draw Beijing closer to Moscow than it is to Washington. Americans need not become nervous every time the Chinese and Soviets sit down to work out differences. Negotiations are likely to be prolonged and difficult.

Differences between Washington and Beijing over their respective policies toward third countries are inevitable, given the differences between Chinese and U.S. national interests and views of the world. Fortunately, in regard to those problems most threatening to Chinese security—Afghanistan, Indochina, and the Soviet military buildup in the Western Pacific—U.S. and PRC policies coincide closely. Only in more distant areas, such as the Middle East and South Africa where the Chinese have little direct interest and relatively little influence, do U.S. and Chinese policies diverge sharply. Consequently the United States and China can adopt parallel policies in those places where such policies can have the greatest effect.

Differences between Washington and Beijing over bilateral issues are also inevitable, and these will increase in number and complexity as relations between the two countries expand. Just as in U.S. relations with other countries, these will have to be dealt with one by one in ways that minimize the damage they do to the overall relationship. The Chinese habit of attributing the emergence of such practical problems to a lack of "sincerity" or "friendship" on the part of the United States is not helpful and may diminish as Chinese diplomacy becomes sophisticated. Exaggeration of differences over ordinary problems often betrays a lack of Chinese understanding of the complexities of the U.S. political system and, on the U.S. side, a lack of appreciation of Chinese political sensitivities.

Differences over Taiwan will be the most intractable problem in U.S.-PRC relations. Chinese leaders find it difficult to admit, even to themselves, that the main obstacle to reunification is not U.S. policy toward Taiwan, but the conviction of the great majority of people of Taiwan that the status quo is preferable to submitting to Beijing's control. The sensitivity of Chinese leaders on this issue and its effectiveness as a weapon in domestic political struggles in China stand in the way of a lasting understanding with the United States, for Taiwan is a politically sensitive issue in the United States also.

Consequently, the dispute will cloud U.S.-PRC relations. The advantages to China of maintaining a fairly close relationship with the United States probably will prevent disagreement over Taiwan from causing relations to deteriorate severely, but that cannot be ruled out. Chinese leaders demonstrated in breaking with the Soviet Union, at a time when they felt a serious threat from the United States, that considerations of national pride can cause great short-term damage to other important national interests.

Notes

1. *Beijing Review*, December 20, 1982, pp. 17–18.
2. *Hong Qi,* March 1983; *FBIS Daily Report–China,* March 17, 1983, pp. K-2–7.
3. *Beijing Review*, September 13, 1983, pp. 30–31.
4. Ibid., p. 32.
5. Ibid., p. 29.
6. Ibid., p. 20.
7. *New York Times*, May 12, 1983.
8. *Beijing Review*, September 13, 1982, p. 30.

Chairmen, Contributors, and Discussants

Henry S. Albinski, Director, Australian Studies Center, Pennsylvania State University, University Park, Pennsylvania

Desmond Ball, Strategic and Defense Studies Center, Australian National University, Canberra, Australia

Gavin Boyd, Specialist in Pacific Community Affairs, St. Mary's College, Halifax, Nova Scotia, Canada

Claude A. Buss, Professor, U.S. Naval Postgraduate School, Monterey, California, Professor Emeritus, Department of History, Stanford University; Visiting Scholar, The Hoover Institution, Stanford University, Stanford, California

Ralph H. Clough, U.S. Foreign Service Officer (ret.), former member, Policy Planning Staff, U.S. Department of State

James Gregor, Professor of Political Science, University of California, Berkeley, California

Han Sung-Joo, Director, Asiatic Research Center, Korea University, Seoul, Korea

Robert J. Hanks, Rear Admiral, U.S. Navy (ret.), former commander, U.S. Middle East Force; member, Institute for Foreign Policy Analysis, Washington, D.C.

Obaid ul Haq, Political Science Department, National University of Singapore

Thomas Hayward, Admiral, U.S. Navy (ret.), former Chief of Naval Operations; member, Pacific Forum, Honolulu, Hawaii

Harold Hinton, Sino-Soviet Institute, George Washington University, Washington, D.C.

B. R. Inman, Admiral, U.S. Navy (ret.); President, Microelectronics and Computer Technology Corporation, Austin, Texas

Chandran Jeshurun, Professor of Political Science, University of Malaya, Kuala Lumpur, Malaysia

U. Alexis Johnson, former U.S. Ambassador to Japan and Thailand; member, The Atlantic Council of the United States, Washington, D.C.

Stephen Jurika, U.S. Naval Postgraduate School, Monterey, California

Birabhongse Kasemsri, Ambassador of Thailand to the United Nations, New York, New York

Richard Kennaway, Political Science Department, University of Canterbury, Christchurch, New Zealand

Kim Kyung Won, Ambassador of the Republic of Korea to the United Nations, New York, New York

Tun-Hwa Ko, Vice Admiral, Navy of the Republic of China (ret.), former Vice-minister of Defense; Professor of Management Sciences, Tan Tung University, Taipei, Republic of China

Koo Youngnok, Department of Political Science, Seoul National University, Seoul, Korea

Shirley W. Y. Kuo, Deputy Governor, Central Bank of China, Taipei, Republic of China

Norman Levin, Specialist on Korean Affairs, The Rand Corporation, Santa Monica, California

Lie Tek Tjeng, National Institute for Cultural Research; member, Board of Specialists, National Defense Institute, Jakarta, Indonesia

R. L. J. Long, Admiral, U.S. Navy (ret.), former commander in chief, Pacific

Salvador P. Lopez, former Ambassador of the Philippines to the United States; former President, University of the Philippines, Quezon City, Philippines

Yoichi Masuzoe, Specialist in European Relations, Political Science Department, Tokyo University, Tokyo, Japan

John Melhuish, Consul General of Australia, San Francisco

T. B. Millar, Head, Strategic and Defence Studies Center, Australian National University, Canberra, Australia

Ramon H. Myers, Curator, East Asian Collection, The Hoover Institution, Stanford University, Stanford, California

Edward Olsen, U.S. Naval Postgraduate School, Monterey, California

Sukhumband Paribatra, Institute of Strategic Studies, Chulalongkorn University, Bangkok, Thailand

Guy Pauker, Specialist in Southeast Asian Affairs, The Rand Corporation, Santa Monica, California

Douglas Pike, Indochina Studies Project, Institute of East Asian Studies, University of California, Berkeley, California

Jonathan D. Pollack, China Specialist, The Rand Corporation, Santa Monica, California

G. J. Price, former Australian High Commissioner to Singapore; Deputy Chief of Mission, Embassy of Australia, Washington, D.C.

Sean Randolph, Policy Planning Staff, U.S. Department of State, Washington, D.C.

Naotoshi Sakonjo, Admiral, Japanese Imperial Navy (ret.); member, Research Institute for Peace and Security, Tokyo, Japan

Rodger Swearingen, Specialist in Northeast Asian Affairs, Department of International Relations, University of Southern California, Los Angeles, California

Yasuo Takeyama, Counselor, Board of Editorials, *Nihon Keizai Shimbun* (Economic Journal of Japan), Tokyo, Japan

Tadae Takubo, Editorial Writer, International Affairs, Jiji Press, Tokyo, Japan

Edward Teller, Senior Research Fellow, The Hoover Institution, Stanford University, Stanford, California

Frank Trager, National Strategy Information Center, New York; U.S. Naval Postgraduate School, Monterey, California

Lloyd R. Vasey, Rear Admiral, U.S. Navy (ret.); member, Pacific Forum, Honolulu, Hawaii

Yung Wei, Adjunct Professor, Political Science Department, National Taiwan University, Taipei, Taiwan; Chairman, Research, Development, and Evaluation Commission, Executive Yuan, Taipei, Taiwan

Albert Wohlstetter, Senior Fellow, The Hoover Institution, Stanford University, Stanford, California

Charles Wolf, President, The Rand Corporation, Santa Monica, California

Paul Wolfowitz, Assistant Secretary of State, East Asia and Pacific Affairs, Washington, D.C.

Yuan-li Wu, Consultant, The Hoover Institution, Stanford University, Stanford, California

Index

Afghanistan, 8, 11–12, 20, 30, 63, 121, 136, 174
Alice Springs, 145
Andaman Sea, 124
Anglo-Malayan Defense Agreement, 198
Anti-Americanism in New Zealand, 115
ANZAC, 117, 119–20, 127
ANZUS alliance, 13, 32, 39, 46, 111–16, 120–31, 161
Armacost, Michael, 155
Article 9, Japanese Constitution, 60, 104
Asia Development Bank (ADB), 13, 223
Asian and Pacific Cooperation (ASPAC), 77, 199
Asian Games, 81, 106, 303
Association of Southeast Asian Nations (ASEAN), 13, 14, 16, 32, 102, 175, 223
Australia, 32, 38, 112; anti-nuclear movement in, 128, 136; defense forces, 123; relations with Indonesia, 126, 140; relations with Japan, 142; relations with the United States, 135, 138, 147–48; United States installations in, 114, 123, 138, 144–46

Australian Labor Party (ALP), 113–16, 120–32, 140, 158

Backfire bombers, 4, 6, 12, 28, 56, 61, 105
Badger bombers, 105
Baikal-Amur-Mainline (BAM) Railway, 45, 55, 56
Balance of power in the Pacific, 225
Baldrige, Malcolm, 299
Bali Declaration, 223
Baoshan steel mill, 302
Beetham, Bruce, 161
Bowen Lionel, 125
Bush, Vice-President George, 161
Butterworth, 124

Cain, John, 129
Caldicott, Dr. Helen, 164
Camranh Bay, 6, 38, 266
Carter administration, 3, 35, 49, 73, 87
Carter Doctrine, 37
Troop withdrawal from Korea, 73
China (Peoples Republic of China; PRC), 18, 19, 33, 40; Cultural Revolution, 40, 248; Four Modernizations, 248, 293; relations with

China (continued)
  ANZUS, 121; relations with Japan, 250, 301; relations with Korea, 249, 264, 301; relations with the United States, 249, 252, 259, 278, 289, 297; relations with the USSR, 91–95, 248, 260, 295; relations with Vietnam, 264, 304
China (Republic of China; ROC), 33, 250; and the Pacific Basin, 287; economics, 18, 271, 281–84; military value, 277, 280, 284; national interests and policies, 273–74, 290; relations with the United States, 278, 290, 291–92; reunification with mainland China, 267, 274
Chun Doo-Hwan, 13, 49, 51, 72, 75, 88–89
CIA in Australia, 155
CINCPAC, 36–37
Clark Field, 178, 227
Cockburn Sound, 124, 138, 145
Cocos Island, 125
Collective Defense Treaty, *see under* Southeast Asia
Communism and communists, 47, 64
Comprehensive security, 38, 62, 65, 100
Cooper, Warren, 122
Corpuz, Dr. Onofre D., 222
Credibility gap, 68
Cross-recognition, 82, 89

Darwin, Australia, 152
Defense White Paper, *see under* Japan
Democracy Wall, 299
Deng Xiaoping, 247, 249, 255–56, 289
Diego Garcia, 119, 125, 138

Economic growth in the Pacific Basin, 17, 27, 34, 41
Emergency in Malaysia, 198
Encirclement, 93
European Economic Community (EEC), 47, 223–24

Five-Power Defense Arrangement (FPDA), 113, 125, 138, 140, 143, 199, 208
Fraser, Malcolm, 120
"Free ride" for Japan, 60, 65, 99, 107
French nuclear testing, 127
Fukuda, Prime Minister, 47

Gaiatsu (foreign pressure), 62, 65, 68
Gang of Four, 248, 293

Hanoi Politburo, 184, 189, 236
Hawke, Prime Minister Robert, 114, 120, 123, 156
Hayden, Bill, 122, 149
Hayward, Admiral Thomas, 36, 39
Hegemonism, 92
Ho Chi Minh, 236
Holyoke, Sir Keith, 167
Hong Kong, 250, 267, 301–304
Horn of Africa, 119
Hu Na defections, 298
Hu Yaobang, 296, 302

Indian Ocean, 19, 38, 39, 119
Indochina problem, 175, 180
Indonesia, 176, 191–93, 223
Indo-Pacific region, U.S. interests in, 117
INF (Intermediate Range Nuclear Forces), 103
Insurgency in Malaysia, 202
Integrated Air Defense System (IADS), 113, 125, 138, 203
Irian Jaya, 126
Islamic population in Southeast Asia, 98

Jakarta, *see* Indonesia
Japan: Defense White Paper, 38, 61, 90, 100; economic assistance, 32, 65; economic power, 17, 65; in Southeast Asia, 179, 195, 201; military capability, 67, 104; relations with China (PRC), 47; relations with China (ROC), 47; relations with North Korea, 46; relations with

South Korea, 46, 50, 63, 88; relations with the USSR, 17, 46, 57; Self-Defense Forces, 63, 66, 103, technology, 100
Japanese attitudes, 63–65, 68
Juche, 79

Kampuchea, 14, 33, 126, 139, 176, 180–81, 189, 305
Keyworth, George, 300
Kidd, Douglas, 161
Kim Chong-il, 303
Kim Il-sung, 76, 98, 249, 266, 267, 302–303
Konfrontasi, 198, 231
Koreagate, 87
Korea, North, 18, 28; military buildup, 89; relations with China (PRC), 50; relations with the USSR, 50
Korea, South (ROK), 18, 46, 48; economic and political development, 73–76, 106; human rights in, 87; national interests, 72; national security, 72; relations with nonaligned nations, 81, 91; unification, 73, 76
Korean overseas workers, 78
Kuala Lumpur Declaration, 199
Kurile Islands, 45, 57

Labor Party, *see* Australian Labor Party; *see under* New Zealand
Lange, David, 130, 162
Law of the Sea, 47, 104, 238
Lee Bum Suk, 81
Lee Kuan-Yew, 102, 208–12
Liao, Zhengzhi, 274
Liberal Democratic Party (LDP), 102
Lin Biao, 293
"Look East" policy, 201

Macapagal, Diasdado, 221
Magsaysay, Ramon, 222
Mahatir, Prime Minister Datuk of Malaysia, 47, 103, 201
Malaysia, 18, 34, 176, 197

Manila Pact, 216, 222
Mansfield, Ambassador Mike, 57
Maphilindo, 223
Marcos, President Ferdinand, 47, 102, 141, 218, 223
Mao Zedong, 247
Melbourne, HMAS, 122
Micronesia, 119
Monroe Doctrine for the Pacific, 135
Muldoon, Robert, 120, 123, 125, 160–61
Muslim National Liberation Front (MNLF), 220
MX missile, 136

Nakasone, Prime Minister Yasuhiro, 13, 38, 47, 67, 100–103
National Defense Program Outline (NDPO), 67
National People's Army (NPA), 220
New Zealand, 32, 115; and ANZUS, 162; anti-nuclear movement, 115, 165; defense forces, 123; Labor Party, 160; national interests, 159; national party, 115, 120, 160; Social Credit Party, 130, 160, 163; U.S. installations in, 165; visits of nuclear ships, 160, 162, 165
Nikaido, Susumau, 102
Nixon Doctrine, 175, 199, 208, 227
Nixon-Kissinger breakthrough with Beijing, 261
No confirmation, no denial, 114, 115, 124, 130
No first use, 136
No-war clause, 60
Nonaligned nations, 81
Nonalignment policy, 226
Nonnuclear principles of Japan, 38, 63
North Atlantic Treaty Organization (NATO), 10, 47, 67, 225, 239
North Korea, *see* Korea, North
Northeast Asia security, 13, 45
North West Cape, 114, 145, 148–49, 154–58

Nuclear force in the Pacific, 10, 23
Nuclear-free zones, 115, 127, 160–61
Nuclear freeze, 23
Nurrungar, 114, 145, 150

Offshore oil and gas, 98
Ohira, Prime Minister Masayoshi, 61
Oil crisis, 49, 61, 98
Olympics in Seoul, 81, 106, 249, 303
Overseas Chinese population, 98

Pacific Community, 116, 216
Pacific islands, 132
Pacific NATO, 13; see also North Atlantic Treaty Organization
Pacific summit, 77
Pancasila philosophy, 192
Pan-Pacific community, 99
Papua New Guinea, 113, 126, 141
Park, Chunghee, 73, 87
PAVN, see under Vietnam
Penghu Islands, 271
Peoples Republic of China, see China (Peoples Republic of China)
Persian Gulf, 32, 37, 119
Philippines, 98, 178, 218; insurgency in, 220; relations with Japan, 220; relations with socialist states, 220; security interests, 229, 242; special relations with the United States, 221, 222; U.S. bases in, 119, 141, 178, 226–29, 239
Pine Gap, 114, 145, 154–58
Polpot, 176, 180
Port Darwin, 114, 124
Prebble, Richard, 161
Prem Tinsulanond, General and Prime Minister of Thailand, 47, 102
Pyongyang, 91, 93–95, 266, 302

Rajaratnam, S., 207
Rapid Deployment Force, 137
Reagan, President Ronald, 24, 35, 47, 50, 61, 88–89, 99, 237, 262
Reciprocity in U.S.-Japan relations, 108

Republic of Korea (ROK), see Korea, South
Rhee, Syngman, 75, 80
Rhyolite satellites, 153
RIMPAC exercises, 66, 113, 123, 141
Rowling, Bill, 130, 167
Roxas, Manuel, 218

Sabah (North Borneo), 198
Sakhalin, 45, 65
Sakurauchi, Hoshio, 102
Sarawak, 198
Scholes, Gordon, 156
Sea lines of communication, 38, 100, 113, 142, 179
Security concept, 28, 34
Self-Defense Forces, see under Japan
Shultz, George, 29, 86
Siberia and the Soviet Far East, 45, 52–57, 65; commercial complex, 54; military complex, 56; resources, 52
Sihanouk, Prince, 176
SIGINT, Australia, 148
Sinai Multinational Force, 122
Singapore, 14, 176, 107
Sino-Soviet split, 247
Smithfield, 145
South Korea, see Korea, South
South Pacific Forum 119, 161, 167
South Pacific island-states, 41
Southeast Asia: attitudes toward the United States, 174, 210, 233; Collective Defense Treaty, 140; regional defense in, 120; Soviets in, 120, 138, 174, 210
Southeast Pacific: interests of the United States in, 112
Sovietskaya Gavan, 45, 56
Soviet Union: economic strength, 19; hegemonism, 248; in Afghanistan, 11, 12; military capability, 19, 56; national interests in East Asia/Pacific, 45; Pacific Fleet, 138; relations with China, 6; relations with Viet-

nam, 12, 175; strength in the Pacific, 4, 8, 11, 28; use of force, 20, 30
Spratly Islands, 242
SS-20 missiles, 6, 12, 57, 61, 103
Stallings, Richard, 154
Strait of Malacca, 124, 236
Straits of Japan Sea, 103
Strategic deterrents, 24, 39
Subic Bay Naval Base, 38, 178, 227
Suharto, President, 47, 102, 192–93
Sukarno, President, 192–93
Suzuki, Prime Minister Zenko, 67, 302
Swing strategy, 35, 78

Taiwan, *see* China, Republic of China
Taiwan Relations Act, 251, 300
Team Spirit, 86
Texas, USS, 162
Thailand, 18, 119, 140, 173, 174, 193, 223; refugees in, 238
Thanat-Rusk Agreement, 140, 216
Third World, 98, 219, 304
Tibet, 275
Timor, Eastern, 113, 126
Trade in the Pacific Basin, 9, 27
Tun Abdul Razak, 201

Uganda, Commonwealth Military Training Team in, 122
Union of Soviet Socialist Republics (USSR), *see* Soviet Union
United Nations Development Program, 223
United States: bases in Japan, 66; commitments to allies, 49, 88; interests in East Asia/Pacific 30, 32; policy objectives in the Pacific, 29; relations with China, 299; relations with Japan, 13, 31, 48; relations with South Korea, 49, 74; troops in Korea, 49; Soviet relations, 3, 24, 139; strength in the Pacific Basin, 4, 15, 16

Vietnam, 18, 28, 126; internal factors, 184; invasion of Kampuchea, 181; People's Army of (PAVN), 181, 186–88, 189; relations with China, 176, 181; relations with the United States, 176; relations with the USSR, 176, 183
Vladivostok, 6

Waring, Marilyn, 161
Watsonia, Victoria, 124
"Weathervane" diplomacy, 215
West Irian, 192
Weinberger, Caspar W., 62, 156, 262
White Paper, *see under* Japan
Whitlam, Prime Minister Gough, 140, 141, 154
Wolf, Charles, 231
Wrangel, 45

Ye Jianying, 274, 300
Yushin Constitution, 72, 75

Zhang Aiping, 294
Zhao Ziyang, Premier, 262, 294, 302
Zhenbaodao (Manchurian border), 293
ZOPFAN, 177, 193–94, 199, 200, 215, 236